Graph Theoretic Approaches for Analyzing Large-Scale Social Networks

Natarajan Meghanathan
Jackson State University, USA

A volume in the Advances in Wireless
Technologies and Telecommunication (AWTT)
Book Series

Published in the United States of America by
    IGI Global
    Information Science Reference (an imprint of IGI Global)
    701 E. Chocolate Avenue
    Hershey PA, USA 17033
    Tel: 717-533-8845
    Fax: 717-533-8661
    E-mail: cust@igi-global.com
    Web site: http://www.igi-global.com

Library of Congress Cataloging-in-Publication Data

Names: Meghanathan, Natarajan, 1977- editor.
Title: Graph theoretic approaches for analyzing large-scale social networks /
  Natarajan Meghanathan, editor.
Description: Hershey, PA : Information Science Reference, [2018]
Identifiers: LCCN 2017010785| ISBN 9781522528142 (hardcover) | ISBN
  9781522528159 (ebook)
Subjects: LCSH: Social networks. | Sociometry. | Social sciences--Network
  analysis. | Graph theory.
Classification: LCC HM741 .G73 2018 | DDC 302.3--dc23 LC record available at https://lccn.loc.gov/2017010785

This book is published in the IGI Global book series Advances in Wireless Technologies and Telecommunication (AWTT) (ISSN: 2327-3305; eISSN: 2327-3313)

Advances in Wireless Technologies and Telecommunication (AWTT) Book Series

Xiaoge Xu
The University of Nottingham Ningbo China, China

ISSN:2327-3305
EISSN:2327-3313

MISSION

The wireless computing industry is constantly evolving, redesigning the ways in which individuals share information. Wireless technology and telecommunication remain one of the most important technologies in business organizations. The utilization of these technologies has enhanced business efficiency by enabling dynamic resources in all aspects of society.

The **Advances in Wireless Technologies and Telecommunication Book Series** aims to provide researchers and academic communities with quality research on the concepts and developments in the wireless technology fields. Developers, engineers, students, research strategists, and IT managers will find this series useful to gain insight into next generation wireless technologies and telecommunication.

COVERAGE

- Network Management
- Wireless sensor networks
- Virtual Network Operations
- Broadcasting
- Digital Communication
- Mobile Technology
- Global Telecommunications
- Radio Communication
- Grid Communications
- Wireless Technologies

IGI Global is currently accepting manuscripts for publication within this series. To submit a proposal for a volume in this series, please contact our Acquisition Editors at Acquisitions@igi-global.com or visit: http://www.igi-global.com/publish/.

Titles in this Series

For a list of additional titles in this series, please visit: www.igi-global.com/book-series

Routing Protocols and Architectural Solutions for Optimal Wireless Networks and Security
Dharm Singh (Namibia University of Science and Technology, Namibia)
Information Science Reference • ©2017 • 277pp • H/C (ISBN: 9781522523420) • US $205.00

Sliding Mode in Intellectual Control and Communication Emerging Research and Opportunities
Vardan Mkrttchian (HHH University, Australia) and Ekaterina Aleshina (Penza State University, Russia)
Information Science Reference • ©2017 • 128pp • H/C (ISBN: 9781522522928) • US $140.00

Emerging Trends and Applications of the Internet of Things
Petar Kocovic (Union – Nikola Tesla University, Serbia) Reinhold Behringer (Leeds Beckett University, UK) Muthu
Ramachandran (Leeds Beckett University, UK) and Radomir Mihajlovic (New York Institute of Technology, USA)
Information Science Reference • ©2017 • 330pp • H/C (ISBN: 9781522524373) • US $195.00

Resource Allocation in Next-Generation Broadband Wireless Access Networks
Chetna Singhal (Indian Institute of Technology Kharagpur, India) and Swades De (Indian Institute of Technology
Delhi, India)
Information Science Reference • ©2017 • 334pp • H/C (ISBN: 9781522520238) • US $190.00

Multimedia Services and Applications in Mission Critical Communication Systems
Khalid Al-Begain (University of South Wales, UK) and Ashraf Ali (The Hashemite University, Jordan & University
of South Wales, UK)
Information Science Reference • ©2017 • 331pp • H/C (ISBN: 9781522521136) • US $200.00

Big Data Applications in the Telecommunications Industry
Ye Ouyang (Verizon Wirless, USA) and Mantian Hu (Chinese University of Hong Kong, China)
Information Science Reference • ©2017 • 216pp • H/C (ISBN: 9781522517504) • US $145.00

Handbook of Research on Recent Developments in Intelligent Communication Application
Siddhartha Bhattacharyya (RCC Institute of Information Technology, India) Nibaran Das (Jadavpur University,
India) Debotosh Bhattacharjee (Jadavpur University, India) and Anirban Mukherjee (RCC Institute of Information
Technology, India)
Information Science Reference • ©2017 • 671pp • H/C (ISBN: 9781522517856) • US $360.00

701 East Chocolate Avenue, Hershey, PA 17033, USA
Tel: 717-533-8845 x100 • Fax: 717-533-8661
E-Mail: cust@igi-global.com • www.igi-global.com

Table of Contents

Detailed Table of Contents

Chapter 1

Atul Srivastava, YMCA University of Science and Technology, India
Anuradha Pillai, YMCA University of Science and Technology, India
Dimple Juneja Gupta, NIT Kurukshetra, India

Since last more than forty years, social network analysis (SNA) techniques have evolved as one of the successful applications of Internet. Numerous reasons demand better understanding of the structure of social networks, need of their analysis and their impact on future Internet and society. For instance, finding the shared interest and trust could be one of the reasons to study social networks. Moreover, if in future, distributed online social networks are popular and bandwidth intensive, they can have a significant impact on Internet traffic, just as current peer-to-peer content distribution networks do. Regardless of one's stance on these phenomena, a better understanding of the structure of social networks is likely to improve our understanding of the opportunities, limitations and threats associated with these ideas. For instance, gigantic size of online social networks, their dynamic behavior, clustering and privacy policies held by users are some of the major challenges. This chapter presents an engraved review spanning from need of SNA to the implications associated with it.

Chapter 2

Nadeem Akhtar, Aligarh Muslim University, India
Mohd Vasim Ahamad, Aligarh Muslim University, India

A social network can be defined as a complex graph, which is a collection of nodes connected via edges. Nodes represent individual actors or people in the network, whereas edges define relationships among those actors. Most popular social networks are Facebook, Twitter, and Google+. To analyze these social networks, one needs specialized tools for analysis. This chapter presents a comparative study of such tools based on the general graph aspects as well as the social network mining aspects. While considering the general graph aspects, this chapter presents a comparative study of four social network analysis tools—NetworkX, Gephi, Pajek, and IGraph—based on the platform, execution time, graph types, algorithm complexity, input file format, and graph features. On the basis of the social network mining aspects, the chapter provides a comparative study on five specialized tools—Weka, NetMiner 4, RapidMiner, KNIME, and R—with respect to the supported mining tasks, main functionality, acceptable input formats, output formats, and platform used.

Chapter 3

Bapuji Rao, IGIT, India
Sasmita Mishra, IGIT, India
Sarojananda Mishra, IGIT, India

This chapter focuses on methods to study communication in a real world social network using the basic concepts of graph theory. The initial section of this chapter starts with a general introduction consisting of related literature and definitions towards understanding the basic concepts of graph mining and graph theory, defining a telephone graph and use of telephone graph for social contexts. The authors have proposed an algorithm for extracting different network provider's sub-graphs, weak and strong connected sub-graphs and extracting incoming and outgoing calls of subscribers which have direct application for studying the human behavior in telephone network. The authors have considered two examples. The authors have implemented the proposed algorithm in C++ programming language and obtained satisfactory results. Finally, the authors have included the snapshots of the output in the chapter to enhance the interest of the readers.

Chapter 4

Alessandro Di Stefano, University of Catania, Italy
Marialisa Scatà, University of Catania, Italy
Aurelio La Corte, University of Catania, Italy
Evelina Giacchi, University of Catania, Italy

Complexity and dynamics characterize a social network and its processes. Social network analysis and graph theory could be used to describe and explore the connectedness among the different entities. Network dynamics further increases the complexity, as each entity with its personal knowledge, cognitive and reasoning capabilities, thinks, decides and acts in a social network, characterized by the heterogeneity of nodes and ties among them. Social network analysis becomes critical to the decision-making process, where a network node will consider both its personal knowledge and the influences received from its neighbors. Network dynamics and the node's context-awareness affect the relationships among criteria, modifying their ranking in a multiple criteria decision-making process, and hence the decision itself. Thus, the main aim has been to model the decision-making process within a social network, considering both context-awareness and network dynamics. Moreover, we have introduced a process of knowledge-transfer, where the criteria are represented by the knowledge-related values.

Chapter 5

Juan-Francisco Martínez-Cerdá, Universitat Oberta de Catalunya (UOC), Spain
Joan Torrent-Sellens, Universitat Oberta de Catalunya (UOC), Spain

This chapter explores how graph analysis techniques are able to complement and speed up the process of learning analytics and probability theory. It uses a sample of 2,353 e-learners from six European countries (France, Germany, Greece, Poland, Portugal, and Spain), who were enrolled in their first year of open online courses offered by HarvardX and MITX. After controlling the variables for socio-demographics and online content interactions, the research reveals two main results relating student-content interactions and online behavior. First, a multiple binary logistic regression model tests that students who explore online chapters are more likely to be certified. Second, the authors propose an algorithm to generate an undirected bipartite network based on tabular data of student-content interactions (2,392 nodes, 25,883 edges, a visual representation based on modularity, degree and ForceAtlas2 layout); the graph shows a clear relationship between interactions with online chapters and chances of getting certified.

With the advent of online social media, it is possible to collect large information and extract information. One of the powerful roles that networks play is to bridge gap between the local and the global perspectives. For example, social network analysis could be used to offer explanations for how simple processes at the level of individual nodes and links can have a global effect. Social networks like Twitter, Facebook, LinkedIn are very large in size with millions of vertices and billions of edges. To collect meaningful information from these densely connected graphs and huge volume of data, it is important to find proper topology of the network as well as conduct analysis based on different network parameters. The main objective of this work is to study the network parameters commonly used to explain social structures. We extract data from the three real-time Facebook accounts using the Netvizz application, analyze and evaluate their network parameters on some widely recognized graph topology using Gephi, a free and open source software.

#### Chapter 7

In this chapter, the authors apply context specific methods to formalize communicational parameters for different profile groups in a social network platform, taking Facebook as an example. Information is posted to or shared with distinct user groups. The context specific approach is used to describe informational content of exchanged data and to formalize privacy settings in a social graph. Communicational and informational parameters are specified with direction and communicational content in a context specific model. Relations are defined to model communicational and informational interactions as well as environmental factors taking influence on the profile groups. The textual representation of this approach is introduced to describe models in a text-based form.

#### Chapter 8

Complex network analysis comprises a popular set of tools for the analysis of online social networks. Among these techniques, k-shell decomposition of a network is a technique that has been used for centrality analysis, for communities' discovery, for the detection of influential spreaders, and so on. The huge volume of input graphs and the environments where the algorithm needs to run, i.e., large data centers, makes none of the existing algorithms appropriate for the decomposition of graphs into shells. In this article, we develop for a distributed algorithm based on MapReduce for the k-shell decomposition of a graph. We furthermore, provide an implementation and assessment of the algorithm using real social network datasets. We analyze the tradeoffs and speedup of the proposed algorithm and conclude for its virtues and shortcomings.

Ahmad Askarian, University of Texas at Dallas, USA
Rupei Xu, University of Texas at Dallas, USA
Andras Farago, University of Texas at Dallas, USA

The rapidly emerging area of Social Network Analysis is typically based on graph models. They include directed/undirected graphs, as well as a multitude of random graph representations that reflect the inherent randomness of social networks. A large number of parameters and metrics are derived from these graphs. Overall, this gives rise to two fundamental research/development directions: (1) advancements in models and algorithms, and (2) implementing the algorithms for huge real-life systems. The model and algorithm development part deals with finding the right graph models for various applications, along with algorithms to treat the associated tasks, as well as computing the appropriate parameters and metrics. In this chapter we would like to focus on the second area: on implementing the algorithms for very large graphs. The approach is based on the Spark framework and the GraphX API which runs on top of the Hadoop distributed file system.

Sovan Samanta, Tamralipta Mahavidyalaya, India
Madhumangal Pal, Vidyasagar University, India

Social network is a topic of current research. Relations are broken and new relations are increased. This chapter will discuss the scope or predictions of new links in social networks. Here different approaches for link predictions are described. Among them friend recommendation model is latest. There are some other methods like common neighborhood method which is also analyzed here. The comparison among them to predict links in social networks is described. The significance of this research work is to find strong dense networks in future.

Michele A. Brandão, Universidade Federal de Minas Gerais, Brazil
Matheus A. Diniz, Universidade Federal de Minas Gerais, Brazil
Guilherme A. de Sousa, Universidade Federal de Minas Gerais, Brazil
Mirella M. Moro, Universidade Federal de Minas Gerais, Brazil

Studies have analyzed social networks considering a plethora of metrics for different goals, from improving e-learning to recommend people and things. Here, we focus on large-scale social networks defined by researchers and their common published articles, which form co-authorship social networks. Then, we introduce CNARe, an online tool that analyzes the networks and present recommendations of collaborations based on three different algorithms (Affin, CORALS and MVCWalker). Through visualizations and social networks metrics, CNARe also allows to investigate how the recommendations affect the co-authorship social networks, how researchers' networks are in a central and eagle-eye context, and how the strength of ties behaves in large co-authorship social networks. Furthermore, users can upload their own network in CNARe and make their own recommendation and social network analysis.

    S Rao Chintalapudi, Jawaharlal Nehru Technological University, Kakinada (JNTU-K),
        India
    M. H. M. Krishna Prasad, Jawaharlal Nehru Technological University, Kakinada (JNTU-K),
        India

Community Structure is one of the most important properties of social networks. Detecting such structures is a challenging problem in the area of social network analysis. Community is a collection of nodes with dense connections than with the rest of the network. It is similar to clustering problem in which intra cluster edge density is more than the inter cluster edge density. Community detection algorithms are of two categories, one is disjoint community detection, in which a node can be a member of only one community at most, and the other is overlapping community detection, in which a node can be a member of more than one community. This chapter reviews the state-of-the-art disjoint and overlapping community detection algorithms. Also, the measures needed to evaluate a disjoint and overlapping community detection algorithms are discussed in detail.

    Alexander Troussov, The Russian Presidential Academy of National Economy and Public
        Administration, Russia
    Sergey Maruev, The Russian Presidential Academy of National Economy and Public
        Administration, Russia
    Sergey Vinogradov, The Russian Presidential Academy of National Economy and Public
        Administration, Russia
    Mikhail Zhizhin, Colorado University of Boulder, USA

Techno-social systems generate data, which are rather different, than data, traditionally studied in social network analysis and other fields. In massive social networks agents simultaneously participate in several contexts, in different communities. Network models of many real data from techno-social systems reflect various dimensionalities and rationales of actor's actions and interactions. The data are inherently multidimensional, where "everything is deeply intertwingled". The multidimensional nature of Big Data and the emergence of typical network characteristics in Big Data, makes it reasonable to address the challenges of structure detection in network models, including a) development of novel methods for local overlapping clustering with outliers, b) with near linear performance, c) preferably combined with the computation of the structural importance of nodes. In this chapter the spreading connectivity based clustering method is introduced. The viability of the approach and its advantages are demonstrated on the data from the largest European social network VK.

#### Chapter 14

In this chapter, scalable and parallelized method for cluster analysis based on random walks is presented. The aim of the algorithm introduced in this chapter is to detect dense sub graphs (clusters) and sparse sub graphs (bridges) which are responsible for information spreading among found clusters. The algorithm is sensitive to the uncertainty involved in assignment of vertices. It distinguishes groups of nodes that form sparse clusters. These groups are mostly located in places crucial for information spreading so one can control signal propagation between separated dense sub graphs by using algorithm provided in this work. Authors have also proposed new coefficient which measures quality of given clustering with respect to information spread control between clusters. Measures presented in this paper can be used for determining quality of whole partitioning or a single bridge.

#### Chapter 15

Human motions determine spatial social contacts that influence the way information spreads in a population. With the Eternal-Return model, we simulate an artificial world populated by heterogeneous individuals who differ in their mobility. This mobility model is synthetic but it represents regular patterns and it integrates the principles of periodicity, circular trajectory and variable amplitude of real patterns. We use a multi-agent framework for simulation and we endow agents with simple rules on how to move around the space and how to establish proximity-contacts. We distinguish different kinds of mobile agents, from sedentary ones to travelers. To summarize the dynamics induced by mobility over time, we define the mobility-based "social proximity network" as the network of all distinct contacts between agents. Properties such as the emergence of a giant component are given insight in the process of information spreading. We have conducted simulations to understand which density threshold allows percolation on the network when the mobility is constant and when it is varying.

#### Chapter 16

The Online Social Networks (OSN) have a positive evolution due to the diversity of social media and the increase in the number of users. The revenue of the social media organizations is generated from the analysis of users' profiles and behaviors, knowing that surfers maintain several accounts on different OSNs. To satisfy its users, the social media organizations have initiated projects for ensuring interoperability to allow for users creating other accounts on other OSN using an initial account, and sharing content from one media to others. Believing that the future generations of Internet will be based on the semantic web technologies, multiple academic and industrial projects have emerged with the objective of modeling semantically the OSNs to ensure interoperability or data aggregation and analysis. In this chapter, we present related works and argue the necessity of a unified semantic model (USM) for OSNs; we introduce a kernel of a USM using standard social ontologies to support the principal social media and it can be extended to support other future social media.

Chapter 17

Leila Weitzel, Universidade Federal Fluminense, Brazil
Paulo Quaresma, Universidade de Evora, Brazil
Jose Palazzo Moreira de Oliveira, Universidade Federal do Rio Grande do Sul, Brazil
Danilo Artigas, Universidade Federal Fluminense, Brazil

The Internet is becoming increasingly an important source of information for people who are seeking healthcare information. Users do so without professional guidance and may lack sufficient knowledge and training to evaluate the validity and quality of health web content. This is particularly problematic in the era of Web 2.0. Hence, the main goal of this research is to propose an approach to infer user reputation based on social interactions. Reputation is a social evaluation towards a person or a group of people. The results show that our rank methodology and the network topology succeeded in achieving user reputation. The results also show that centrality measures associated with the weighted ties approach suitably controls suitably the ranking of nodes.

Preface

Social Network Analysis is a rapidly emerging area within the discipline of Data Science and is of immense research interest for both theory and practice. Social Network Analysis is typically conducted by modeling the social network as a directed or undirected graph of nodes and edges. With the phenomenal growth of social networks as well as the Internet and web, it is imperative that we need algorithms to analyze such large-scale networks modeled as graphs and extract useful information (like communities in the networks, information diffusion, critical nodes for network robustness, etc.). Social Network Analysis involves the analysis and visualization of large-scale complex real-world network graphs and the development of efficient algorithms to study networks comprising hundreds and thousands of nodes.

Social Network Analysis falls within the realm of "Big Data Computing" where the Big Data is the large-scale graphs that model complex real-world social networks. The overall objective of the book is to bring together the recent research advances in the field of graph theory for analyzing large-scale social networks. The currently available books on social network analysis mostly focus on applying traditional graph theoretic algorithms and techniques for social network analysis. The graph theory algorithms discussed in these books are not scalable enough for analyzing social networks involving several thousands of users as well as not effectively designed to handle the various Vs of Big Data (volume, variety and velocity) emanating from the current generation of social networks. The book brings together the research advances in state-of-the-art graph theory algorithms and techniques that have contributed to the effective analysis of social networks, especially those networks that generate significant amount of data and involve several hundreds and thousands of users.

The book includes chapters presenting research advances in graph theory-based algorithms and solution approaches for analyzing large-scale social networks. The book presents the applications of the theoretical algorithms and graph models to analyze real-world large-scale social networks and the data emanating from them as well as characterize the topology and behavior of these networks. The chapters explore the use of advanced graph theoretic approaches for paradigms like centrality metrics, community detection, anomaly detection, diffusion, behavior and identity detection, link prediction, etc. with respect to the analysis of large-scale social networks.

The book will serve as an ideal example to illustrate the practical applications of theoretical research. The chapters collected for the book present how graph theory research can be conducted in conjunction with research in social network analysis and demonstrate the potential benefits of research efforts in analyzing large-scale graphs for the Big Data community. We expect the analytical approaches discussed in these chapters to be of potential use for integration with the current generation of social networks as well as with the open source tools that are available for analyzing social networks. We anticipate the capability of these tools to analyze large-scale social networks to be significantly improved with the incorporation of the algorithms and methodologies proposed in our chapters to analyze network graphs comprising of several hundreds and thousands of users.

With respect to the target audience, we anticipate our book to serve as a good source of reference for both students and faculty pursuing research in social network analysis. As a majority of the books in social network analysis are textbook-oriented and focus on using only the traditional graph theoretic measures for analyzing social networks, the research-oriented chapters in our book will serve as a good source for students and faculty to identify open research problems and the state-of-the-art graph theory-based solution techniques that have been introduced to solve these problems. We are very confident that the book will motivate graduate students to explore open research problems in graph theory that if solved would lead to further advances in social network analysis, especially in the context of analyzing large-scale social networks and the data emanating from these networks. In this context, we expect the book to serve as a recommended book for graduate-level courses in the Network Science and Data Science areas as it could potentially aid the graduate students to identify research problems that they could work on for their theses and dissertations.

A high-level overview of the 17 chapters in this book are as follows. Chapter 1 presents a detailed review of social networks and their analysis with respect to the size, dynamic behavior of users, clustering and privacy policies, threats, etc. Chapters 2-5 focus on extracting information from social networks using graph mining techniques. Chapters 6-7 focus on identifying the parameters that could explain the social structures and profile groups observed in Facebook user accounts. Chapters 8-9 focus on distributed implementations (based on MapReduce and Spark) of graph-theoretic algorithms for analyzing large-scale social networks. Chapters 10-11 focus on link prediction and visualization for social networks using different state-of-the-art algorithms. Chapters 12-14 focus on community detection (both disjoint and overlapping communities) in social networks in the form of an exhaustive survey as well as novel proposals of scalable and parallelizable methods. Chapter 15 presents a human mobility model with diverse movement patterns and uses it to simulate information percolation in a social proximity network and study the emergence of several characteristic properties for diffusion. Chapter 16 presents a unified semantic model to ensure interoperability and data aggregation among user profiles created in different online social networks. Finally, Chapter 17 presents an approach to infer user reputation based on social interactions and applies this approach to rank websites presenting healthcare information. We now briefly describe the contributions of each of the chapters.

The structure of a social network needs to be thoroughly understood in order to comprehend the dynamics of the network and analyze its impact on the society. In Chapter 1, the authors Atul Srivastava, Anuradha Pillai and Dimple Juneja Gupta present a detailed review of the structural aspects of social networks, their size, dynamic behavior, clustering, privacy policies, and etc. The chapter discusses the opportunities, limitations and threats associated with social networks. The chapter also examines the impact of the structure of distributed online social networks on the Internet traffic.

Software tools are very critical to the analysis of large-scale social networks. It is almost impossible to find a single software tool that could comprehensively analyze social networks. In Chapter 2, the authors Nadeem Akhtar and Mohd Vasim Ahamad present a suite of tools that exist in the social network community and categorizes their use with respect to general graph theoretic aspects and social network mining aspects. The tools considered with respect to the general graph theoretic aspects are NetworkX,

Gephi, Pajek and IGraph, and these tools are compared with respect to factors such as: platform, execution time, graph types, algorithm complexity and input file format. The tools considered with respect to social network mining aspects are: Weka, NetMiner 4, RapidMiner, KNIME and R, and these tools are compared with respect to factors such as: supported mining tasks, main functionality, acceptable input formats, output formats and platform used.

Graph mining techniques are critical to extracting hidden information in social networks. In Chapter 3, the authors Bapuji Rao, Sasmita Mishra and Saroja Nanda Mishra present a graph mining algorithm that could be used to extract information about the behavior of subscribers of a telephone network based on the sub graphs modeling the incoming and outgoing calls. The sub graphs could be strong or weakly connected and the algorithm has been observed to provide satisfactory results in both cases. The implementation of the algorithm has been done in C++.

The decision-making process of users in a social network is affected by the network dynamics (like the heterogeneity and ties) as well as the influence of the users among their peers in the network. In Chapter 4, the authors Alessandro Di Stefano, Marialisa Scatà, Aurelio La Corte and Evelina Giacchi model the decision-making process of users in a social network with respect to network dynamics and context-awareness, and analyze their impact on the ranking of the various criteria behind the process. The criteria are represented as knowledge-related values and decision-making is modeled as a process of knowledge transfer.

A bipartite graph is a graph with two partitions of vertices such that all the edges in the graph connect the vertices in the two partitions and no edge exists between vertices within the same partition. In Chapter 5, the authors Juan-Francisco Martínez-Cerdá and Joan Torrent-Sellens present a case study for using graph theory analytics to correlate the likelihood of students to get certified in a technical subject vs. their online browsing interactions. In this perspective, the authors also propose an algorithm to recode tabular data of student-content interactions to an undirected bipartite network graph of e-learners and the online course materials (as vertices) and the interactions of students with these materials (as edges). The authors conduct a multiple binary logistic regression analysis to claim that students who referred to online course materials are more likely to be certified.

Real-time social network graphs (like those based on Facebook, Twitter, etc) are so huge that it becomes almost impossible to analyze them in their entirety. One strategy that is widely used in social network analysis is to analyze the network in a local perspective (at the node level and edge level) and infer informative conclusions at the global level. In such cases, it becomes imperative to identify the appropriate local characteristics and the parameters to determine the same. In Chapter 6, the authors Paramita Dey and Krishnendu Dutta explore the appropriate parameters that would be needed to analyze large Facebook networks of users. In this perspective, the authors use Gephi to explore the network parameters that could be employed to explain social structures observed in three real-time Facebook accounts.

The profiles of user groups posted in social networks could have communicational and informational parameters that might be common. In Chapter 7, the authors Johannes Schick, Martin Kuboschek and Wolfram-Manfred Lippe apply context-specific methods to formalize the communicational and informational parameters for different profile groups in a social network platform (Facebook is used as an example). The authors develop relational models that also take into consideration the environmental factors that influence on the profile groups. The context-specific modeling approach facilitates to formalize privacy settings in a social graph. The models developed in this chapter are represented in textual form.

K-shell decomposition has been a widely used technique in complex network analysis for computation of node centrality, detection of communities, identification of influential spreaders and etc. However, with large social network graphs, the existing algorithms for K-shell decomposition are not scalable and cannot be run in a centralized fashion. In Chapter 8, the authors Katerina Pechlivanidou, Dimitrios Katsaros and Leandros Tassiulas propose a MapReduce-based distributed algorithm for the K-shell decomposition of large social network graphs. The authors discuss in detail the implementation of the algorithm as well as analyze its performance on real social network datasets. The potential tradeoffs and speedup possible are also explored.

Chapter 9 is also on the same lines of Chapter 8, but explores an alternative platform: the Spark framework and the GraphX API that run on top of the Hadoop distributed file system, to implement the graph theoretic algorithms for analyzing large-scale social networks. The authors Ahmad Askarian, Rupei Xu and Andras Farago demonstrate the use of the implementation to derive a large number of parameters and metrics for both directed and undirected graphs, including random graph representations that reflect the inherent randomness of social networks.

Social networks are prone to creation and deletion of links. In Chapter 10, the authors Sovan Samanta and Madhumangal Pal present different approaches for link prediction in social networks and focus more on the latest friend recommendation and common neighborhood models for social networks. The authors present a comparative study of the two models for link prediction in social networks and explore their potential to detect the evolution of large dense networks.

Network visualization is one of the key aspects of social network analysis. It becomes very useful to compare a social network as it is vs. its possibly evolved version in the future, as a result of the addition of new links and deletion of certain existing links. In Chapter 11, the authors Matheus A. Diniz, Guilherme A. de Sousa, Michele A. Brandão and Mirella M. Moro present the development of a new tool (called CNARe) that could take a social network as input (demonstrated with the use of co-authorship networks) and present visualizations of the predicted network along with the recommendations. Application of CNAREe for co-authorship networks could be useful to predict potential collaborations among researchers in a subject area. CNARe uses three different algorithms (Affin, CORALS and MVCWalker) to recommend new links.

Community detection is a classical problem in social network analysis. A community is a sub set of the nodes in a network such that the density of the edges between any two vertices within the community (intra cluster density) is significantly larger than the density of the edges to vertices outside the community (inter cluster density). Algorithms for community detection could be of two types: those that detect overlapping communities (one or more vertices are part of more than one community) and disjoint communities (a vertex is part of only one community). In Chapter 12, the authors S Rao Chintalapudi and M. H. M. Krishna Prasad present an exhaustive survey of algorithms for detecting disjoint and overlapping communities in social networks as well as discuss measures to evaluate the performance of these algorithms.

Techno-social systems generate data (typically Big Data) that is inherently multi-dimensional and different from data that is traditionally processed using classical techniques for social network analysis. The multi-dimensional Big Data generated from techno-social systems contains inherent information about the structural characteristics of the network (from which the data emanated). In Chapter 13, the authors Alexander Troussov, Sergey Maruev, Sergey Vinogradov and Mikhail Zhizhin motivate the need for methods that could analyze such multi-dimensional Big Data to detect overlapping communities of vertices, identify vertices that are outliers as well as rank the vertices in the order of their structural importance, all preferably done in near linear time. In this pursuit, the authors propose one such method called "the spreading connectivity based method" that could be used for cluster detection in the multi-dimensional Big Data emanating from techno-social systems. The authors demonstrate the viability of the method by applying it on the data collected from VK, the largest European social network.

Dense Clusters (larger sub graph of vertices) in a social network are typically separated by sparse clusters (could be a single bridge node or a smaller sub graph of vertices) that could act as a controlling hub for information flow across the network. Chapter 14 proposes a scalable and parallelized method for detecting such sparse clusters based on the approach of random walks. The authors Michal Wojtasiewicz and Mieczysław Kłopotek also propose new measures that could be used to evaluate the quality of a given partitioning of social networks with respect to the information spread control between the clusters.

Mobility among the users in a social network influences the way information spreads among the population (and within a community of nodes) in the network. There is a need to develop synthetic mobility models that could be used to simulate information spread in a social network and study the dynamics of the network. In Chapter 15, the authors Martine Collard, Philippe Collard and Erick Stattner develop one such synthetic mobility model (called the Eternal-Return model) that could be used to simulate a variety of movement patterns among the agents in a social network. With time, the social network could get transformed to a mobility-based "social proximity network" wherein the contacts between agents start controlling the spread of information. The authors conduct detailed simulations to study the density threshold values that would be necessary to control percolation in the network at different levels of node mobility.

The number of social media platforms and the features they offer have become so diverse that users typically maintain an account in more than one social media platform. For example, it is very common to see a user maintaining a Facebook account (or a Twitter account) for casual networking in addition to maintaining a LinkedIn account for professional networking. In such cases, it becomes imperative to facilitate users to share contents (like images) posted in one account to other accounts as well as to setup profiles with some common features across the different social media accounts. There is a need to develop semantic web technologies that could capture the semantics in the different social media accounts of a user and ensure their interoperability as well as data aggregation. In Chapter 16, the authors Asmae El Kassiri and Fatima-Zahra Belouadha introduce a kernel for a unified semantic model that has a standard social ontology for a particular social media as its base and could be easily extended using ontologies of other social media.

People often use the Internet and social media to seek healthcare information and most of the times adopt them without proper professional guidance. Thus, there is a need to evaluate the validity and quality of healthcare information posted in social media before they are considered for adoption. In Chapter 17, the authors Leila Weitzel, Paulo Quaresma, Jose Palazzo Moreira de Oliveira and Danilo Artigas propose a reputation-based approach to rank the methodologies and the nodes (websites and social media that post healthcare information) and demonstrate its successful use.

With the proliferation of social networks, we need a book that specifically focuses on discussing the recent advances in graph theory research targeted for analyzing the next generation of large-scale social networks and the magnitude of data emanating from them. With a diverse set of chapters (as outlined above) discussing state-of-the-art research in this subject area, we are confident that our book will be a one-stop reference for both beginners and professionals in the area of social network analysis and will be a good guiding material for further research in academics as well as for implementing the graph theory algorithms, models and analytical measures for practical applications and commercial/real-time software involving large-scale social networks. To the best of our knowledge, we have not come across such a research-oriented compilation of chapters focusing on the latest advances in social network analysis that are tightly integrated with the latest advances in graph theory research.

Natarajan Meghanathan
Jackson State University, USA

Chapter 1

A Walk Through Social Network Analysis:
Opportunities, Limitations, and Threats

Atul Srivastava
YMCA University of Science and Technology, India

Anuradha Pillai
YMCA University of Science and Technology, India

Dimple Juneja Gupta
NIT Kurukshetra, India

ABSTRACT

Since last more than forty years, social network analysis (SNA) techniques have evolved as one of the successful applications of Internet. Numerous reasons demand better understanding of the structure of social networks, need of their analysis and their impact on future Internet and society. For instance, finding the shared interest and trust could be one of the reasons to study social networks. Moreover, if in future, distributed online social networks are popular and bandwidth intensive, they can have a significant impact on Internet traffic, just as current peer-to-peer content distribution networks do. Regardless of one's stance on these phenomena, a better understanding of the structure of social networks is likely to improve our understanding of the opportunities, limitations and threats associated with these ideas. For instance, gigantic size of online social networks, their dynamic behavior, clustering and privacy policies held by users are some of the major challenges. This chapter presents an engraved review spanning from need of SNA to the implications associated with it.

DOI: 10.4018/978-1-5225-2814-2.ch001

1. INTRODUCTION

Social Network Analysis (SNA) analyses the structural properties of individuals or groups of individuals in a network. These measurements not only depict perspectives of the interconnections and relationships amongst various individuals but also consider the effect of these interconnections on each other as well as on the group of interconnected individuals.

The term online social network more commonly known as social network deals with the interconnections amongst socially active individuals hereon referred to as actors. In fact, social network offers a platform to people for sharing knowledge, thoughts or opinions and more often to maintain societal relationship.

As shown in Figure 1, analytically, these can be observed as large graphs in which the users are represented as nodes and relationships between nodes are depicted as edges between them. The edge may or may not be directed depending on the structure of the social network. And also an edge between two nodes depicts that the connected nodes have already shared some information.

Figure 1. A graphical representation of social network

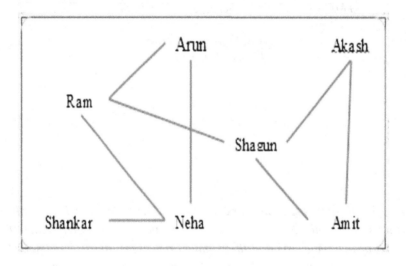

Table 1. Adjacency matrix representation of social network

Actors/ Users	Actors/Users						
	Ram	*Arun*	*Akash*	*Shankar*	*Neha*	*Shagun*	*Amit*
Ram	--	1	0	0	1	1	0
Arun	1	--	0	0	1	0	0
Akash	0	0	--	0	0	1	1
Shankar	0	0	0	--	1	0	0
Neha	1	1	0	1	--	0	0
Shagun	1	0	1	0	0	--	1
Amit	0	0	1	0	0	1	--

As an alternative representation, adjacency matrix delineated in Table 1 also represents Figure 1.

Further, a social network may contain only homogeneous ties or relationship or all heterogeneous ties or both and each tie is possessed with different weights. Homogeneous ties means that all connections among actors in the network have similar characteristics. Heterogeneous ties in contrast have different characteristics for example some ties may be unidirectional, or degree of intensity of the relationship between actors may differ etc. A network with multiple relations is called multi-relational network.

As depicted in Figure 2, a real social network can be combination of four variants i.e. homogeneous nodes connected through undirected associations, homogeneous nodes with both directed and undirected edges, heterogeneous types and weights of associations and heterogeneous types and weights of nodes.

2. ORIGIN OF ONLINE SOCIAL NETWORKS (OSNS)

Stupendous growth of information technology transformed social networks to Online Social Networks (OSNs) (Boyd et. al., 2007) while a social network analysis examines the structure of social relationships in a group to uncover the informative connections between people. In a consulting setting, these relationships are often based on communication, awareness, trust, and decision-making from the first OSN site SixDegrees.com (Boyd et. al., 2007) emerging in 1997 to the current largest OSN site FaceBook (facebook.com), OSNs have been emerging, developing and changing exponentially. Figure 3 represents chronological order of inception of OSNs.

Figure 2. Examples of different types of social networks: a) a social network with homogeneous nodes and undirected associations. b) a social network with homogeneous nodes connected through directed and undirected associations. c) a social network with heterogeneous types and weights of associations. d) a social network with heterogeneous nodes in terms of types and weights.

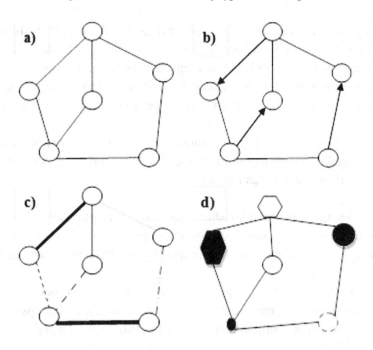

Figure 3. Chronological inceptions of major OSNs

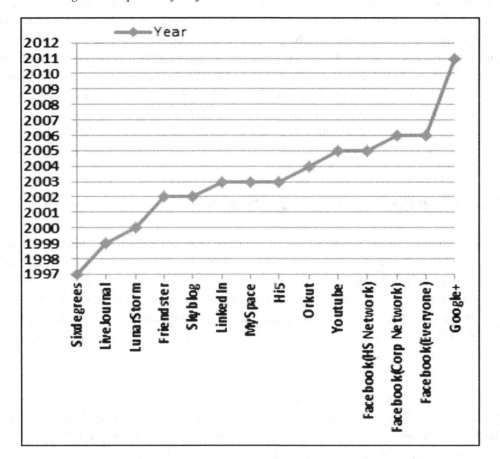

Social networking sites are defined as web-based services that allow individuals to not only construct a public or semi-public profile within a bounded system but also, to articulate list of other users with whom they share a connection, view and traverse their list of connections and also those made by others within the system. The nature and nomenclature of these connections may vary from site to site. Online social networking sites are usually run by individual corporations such as Google and Yahoo!, and are accessible via the Web.

Basically, SNA includes understanding the contents contained in the network and also uncovers the process of digging up embedded structural information from social networks. Efforts are ongoing to define SNA and few of them are listed as follows:

1. The mapping and measuring of relationships and flows between people (Krebs, 2006),
2. The technique focusing on uncovered patterns of people's interaction (Freeman, 2002),
3. A set of methods for the investigation of relational aspects of social structures (Scott, 1992).

In general, an online social network comprises of three components namely users, links and groups. Here, users are the individuals who must register with a site, possibly under a pseudonym. Despite the fact that some sites allow browsing of public data without explicit sign-up and users may volunteer information about them. For instance, personal information and already established links or relationships with other users, place of residence or interests which are added to the user's profile. While few OSNs such as Flicker (flickr.com) and LiveJournal (livejournal.com) allow registered users to establish links without consent from the target, few others like Facebook (facebook.com), Orkut (orkut.com), LinkedIn (linkedin.com) etc. require consent from both the creator and the target before a link is established between these users.

In fact, users establish these links for one of several reasons– such as the connected nodes can be either real-world acquaintances, online acquaintances, or business contacts; common interests; content being contributed by one another, just to list a few. Some users even see the acquisition of a number of links as a goal in itself (Jamali et. al., 2006). Such links in social networks can serve the purpose of both hyperlinks and bookmarks in the Web.

Since the connections established between the respective profiles are visible to foreign visitors, users are able to explore the social network by following user-to-user links, browsing the profile information and contributed content of their own as well as any other visitor. Certain sites, such as LinkedIn (linkedin.com), only allow a user to browse other user accounts within her neighborhood (i.e. a user can only view other users that are within two hops in the social network); other sites, including the ones we aim to analyze, allow users to view any other user account in the system.

Further, most of the sites enable users to create and join groups that are of similar interests, wherein common messages and content can be posted and uploaded respectively. These groups can be classified as moderate and unrestricted where former allows modifications and by the group moderator only while later allows any member to join and post messages and content. As is already mentioned in literature (Carrinfton et. al., 2005, Freeman, 2002, Krebs, 2006, Scott, 1992, Wasserman et. al., 1994) that social networks have now emerged as a domain to represent, identify and measure correlations between any kind of entities, such as words, web pages, people, organizations, animals, cells, computers and other information or knowledge.

Social network analysis is usually carried out on the network of actors involved in any social activity or interaction where actors are defined as active individual members of the network having connections amongst them and primarily execute in two phases, data collection (Nooy et. al., 2005, Ye et. al., 2010) and data analysis (Saroop et. al., 2011, Xio et. al., 2012).

First step of SNA can be stating the parameters and scope of analysis. Parameters may include type of network to be analyzed, various characteristics of social network graph that are desirable, time frame for the analysis, quality parameters etc.

Next step of SNA is data gathering according to the parameters defined in first step. Data gathering is mainly of two types – elicitation and registration (Nooy et. al., 2005). Elicitation simply deals with questionnaire/survey while registration deals with extraction of information from registered entities/ information. Through fast development of computer technologies and universal computer applications of computers, automated data acquisitions are formed in most if not all fields. There are many large databases that maintain records like MEDLINE, the database that covers published papers on the bio-medical research and had about two million records from 1995 to 1999 (Newman, 2001).

There are numerous reasons that justify the need of analysis, understanding the structure of OSN, and also studying the impact of OSN on future internet. For instance, finding the shared interest and trust could be one of the reasons to study a social network. It is trivial fact that adjacent users in a social network tend to trust each other and may have common interests. Users browse neighboring regions of their social network because they are likely to find content that is of interest to them.

Moreover, if future distributed online social networks are popular and bandwidth-intensive, they can have a significant impact on Internet traffic, just as current peer-to-peer content distribution networks do. Understanding the structure of online social networks is not only critical to understanding the robustness and security of distributed online social networks, but also to understanding their impact on the future Internet. In the light of above mentioned facts, studying the structure of online social networks would definitely improve the understanding of online campaigning and viral marketing. Regardless of one's stance on these phenomena, a better understanding of the structure of social networks is likely to improve our understanding of the opportunities, limitations, and threats associated with these ideas.

Based on the above reasons, researchers have been putting efforts to understand the structure and types of social network. Many important studies can be carried out by understanding structure of a network. Next section presents a thorough study of literature reflecting the efforts, parameters required for SNA and its promising benefits.

3. RELATED WORK

Combating terrorism is one of the fields where SNA techniques have important and successful applications. Terrorist organizations have special structures on recruitment, evolution, and radical ideas diffusion (Ressler, 2006). SNA tools can be used to identify these unique organization structures and provide critical information for terrorist detection and terrorism prediction. Now a day, SNA techniques are finding applications in organizational management also. Also, by applying SNA to mapping of co-authors and to mapping of related research paper keywords a team of diverse individuals with similar interests and aptitude can be generated (Cheathan et. al., 2006).

Authors (Almansoori et. al., 2011) have applied SNA and data mining techniques successfully in medical referral process. Social networks of general practitioners and specialists are analyzed from time to time to discover the diseases which are more prominent than others so that precautionary measures can be taken well in advance.

A prompt application of SNA for clustering the web using query graph is being described in (Weiduo et. al., 2010). Each item of search log contains two parts, search terms and returning URL. If the similarity between two websites is beyond the threshold limit as depicted by the nodes in the graph, a graph clique partition method is used to find clusters. In addition, in order to achieve website supervision, website clustering can detect spam websites, pornographic websites and political sensitive websites. SNA can be integrated to other popular fields such as WWW, blogosphere, semantic web (Ding et. al., 2003, Golbeck et. al., 2003).

It is a well-known fact that the web pages are hyper linked to other web pages and further to leverage the existence of hyperlinks, web is modeled as graph where web pages represent the vertices and subsequent hyperlinks form the edges. Therefore, web can be treated as a perfect example of social network and to add to this analysis, PageRank algorithms (Brin et. al.,1998) used by Google search engine and HITS (Klinburg, 1998) can be seen as applications of SNA.

Now a day's blogs are also contributing towards social media where a blog is typically a web-site that consists of dated entries in reverse chronological order written and maintained by a user (blogger) using a specialized tool. Since a blog entry can have hyperlinks to Web pages or other blog entries, the information structure of blogs and links (sometimes called the blogspace) can be seen as a network of multiple communities. On a similar pattern, there exists weblogs which are subsets of web and hence can also be treated as social network. The only difference between blogs and weblogs is the structural difference in terms of entering comments and entry to other links.

Researchers (Deconta et. al., 2003, Swartz et. al., 2001) have been putting revolutionary efforts towards making the web meaningful, understandable, and machine-processable, whether it is based in an intranet, extranet, or internet. This is called the semantic web and primary objective is to bring a transition towards a knowledge-centric viewpoint of everything. The semantic web and social network model support each another. On one hand, the semantic web enables online and explicitly represents social information, while on the other hand social networks especially trust networks (Ding et. al., 2003, Golbeck et. al., 2003) provide a new paradigm for knowledge management in which users outsource knowledge and beliefs via their social networks.

Other major areas where SNA techniques are successfully applied with promising outcomes are emergency information management (Kang et. al., 2011), and disaster management (Zelenkauskaite et. al., 2012). An SNA researcher Krebs (Krebs, 2006) listed a number of recent successful applications of SNA such as:-

- Examine a network of farm animals to analyze how disease spreads from one cow to another.
- Discover emergent communities of interest amongst faculty at various universities.
- Revealing cross-border knowledge flows based on research publications to list a few.

Although there exists several applications of social network and already the strong need of analysis of the same has been highlighted but the work mentioned in (Ye et. al., 2010) emphasizes on issues such as efficiency, sensitivity and bias associated with data collection process for SNA where, efficiency defines the efficiency of crawler in discovering the nodes/links, sensitivity reflects the effect of OSN and protected users on crawlers and finally bias is concerned with skewing of graphs.

Xio et. al. (Xio et. al., 2012) and Swaroop and his co-authors (Saroop et. al., 2011) proposed an architectural design and implementation of crawler for Facebook and Twitter respectively. In the former case, a multithreaded crawler using Java is designed based on interaction simulation and the analysis results could conclude few assertions such as enhanced awareness of privacy provisions among users etc. whereas the later focuses on the dynamic behavior of OSNs and biasing. Different approaches for sampling large network are compared from biasing point of view and a fast crawler is designed to handle dynamism.

An engraved look at the given literature highlights the fact that the social networks are able to make their space in the era of internet and now researchers and allied communities have started demanding for the critical analysis of these online social media so as to better design the architecture, improve efficiency, sensitivity and biasing as well. In this regard, various attributes of social networks are being explored and are presented in the next section.

4. ATTRIBUTES OF SOCIAL NETWORKS FOR SNA

Based upon the literature dwelled upon, it is found that SNA is primarily based on several attributes some of which are defined as characteristics of graphs and some as distribution of information and behavior of actors. A few considerable components around which SNA revolves are mentioned in following subsections:

4.1 Degree

Degree of a node is the number of edges connecting this node with other nodes if graph is undirected. Whereas if graph is directed then a node has in-degree defined as number of incoming edges and out degree defined as number of outgoing edges. Social network researchers have always been concerned with the degree of node. The distribution of node degree in a network follows the power law. More precisely

$$P_k \propto K^{-\alpha} \tag{1}$$

P_k is the probability that a node has a degree k, and α is a constant and usually α is a value between 1.6 and 3.0 (Newman, 2003).

4.2 Geodesic Distance and Diameter (Hanneman et. al., 2005)

To define more complex properties of an individual's position and complete structure of a network a particular definition of distance between actors can be used. This quantity is the geodesic distance. For both directed and undirected graph, the geodesic distance is the number of edges in the shortest possible walk from one actor to another. The geodesic distance is widely used in network analysis. There may be more than one connection between two actors in a network. But if we consider relation between two actors to participate in opportunities and constraints, it may be the case that all connections do not count at all.

To see how big a network is in one sense that is, how many hops are necessary to reach from one side of a network to another side of the network, the diameter is useful. The diameter of a network on the other hand is the largest geodesic distance in the(connected) network. The diameter is also a useful quantity for specifying an upper bound on the lengths of connections that we study.

4.3 Cliques and Subgroups (Hanneman et. al., 2005)

To understand that how the network is likely to behave, it is necessary to partition the actors into cliques or "sub-groups". It can be a very important aspect of social structure. The general definition of a clique is: a clique is simply a sub-graph in which all nodes are more closely tied to each other than they are to actors who are not part of the sub-graph. If the sub-graph is complete-graph (there exists every possible tie among nodes) then it is called maximal clique.

The strict restriction on maximal clique (fully connected sub-graph) may be too strong for many purposes. One relaxation to this definition can be if the restriction is put on the distance at which each node will be connected to every other node of the clique. This distance is restricted to be one in case of maximal clique and can be greater than one to achieve relaxation in definition. Such sub-structure is called N-clique, where N stands for the length of the path allowed to make a connection to all other members.

In some cases it is possible for members of N-clique have the connection path containing actors which are not, themselves, part of the clique. To avoid such possibilities another restriction is suggested that forces all connection paths to contain only members of the clique. This approach is the N-clan approach.

Another relaxation in strict definition of maximal clique can be k-plex. This approach says that a node can be member of a clique of size n if it has one length connections with n-k members of the clique.

The above relaxation has a more relaxed alternative as k-core approach that says a node can be member of a clique of any size if it has direct ties with k members of the clique. By varying the value of k (that is, how many members of the group do you have to be connected to), different pictures can emerge. K-cores can be (and usually are) more inclusive than k-plexes. And, as k becomes smaller, group sizes will increase.

4.4 Maximum Flow

Reachability of an actor to another depends on the number of actors in neighborhood that lead to the target. If an actor A has to send a message to another actor B and there is only one actor C to whom A can send message then A has a weak connectivity with B even if C has many ways to reach B. on the other hand if A can send message (destined to B) to four intermediate actors then connection between A and B is stronger. This flow shows that the strength of a tie between two actors depends on the weakest link in the chain of connections.

4.5 Centrality

Centrality is a measure that quantifies the influence of an actor in the network. It is normally assumed that central people have more influence than people who are less central in the network. As shown in Figure 4, node X is the most central node in the network (Kate et. al., 2005).

Many approaches have been identified to define centrality. Three of which are most relevant –degree, closeness and betweenness centrality.

a. **Degree Centrality:** It is most common centrality measure in which centrality of a node depends on the number of nodes attached to it directly. For a network with g nodes, the degree centrality of node n_i is defined as following:

$$C_d\left(n_i\right) = d\left(n_i\right) \qquad (2)$$

Figure 4. Most central node in the network

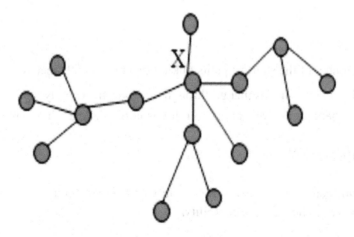

The degree of a node, denoted by d(n_i) is the number of nodes adjacent to it. Apparently, a node's degree centrality is a count ranging from 0 to g–1.

Degree centrality reflects true centrality of a node. The only disadvantage is it cannot differentiate among nodes on the line network.

In order to compare degree centrality of nodes in different networks degree centrality is normalized as shown in equation 3. The degree centrality of node n_i after normalization is:

$$C_D\left(n_i\right) = d\left(n_i\right) / \left(g-1\right) \tag{3}$$

b.   *Closeness Centrality:* Degree centrality takes into account only the immediate ties a node has but there may be a possibility that this most central node is not close to rest of the nodes. Closeness centrality overcomes this shortcoming by considering the sum of the geodesic distances between a given node and the rest. For the network with g nodes, the closeness centrality of node n_i is defined as following,

$$C_c\left(n_i\right) = \left[\sum_{j-1}^{g} d\left(n_i - n_j\right)\right]^{-1} \tag{4}$$

Where, $d\left(n_i - n_j\right)$ is the number of edges in the geodesic linking n_i and n_j. Closeness centrality is normalized as shown in equation 5.

$$C_C\left(n_i\right) = \left(g-1\right) C_c\left(n_i\right) \tag{5}$$

c.   *Betweenness Centrality*: Two nodes which are not adjacent may also influence each other significantly through other nodes in the network. Betweenness centrality highlights those nodes that fall in the connecting path of many nodes. For a network with g nodes, the betweenness centrality for node n_i is defined as the sum of the shortest paths that go through node n_i, over the sum of all the shortest paths of all pairs of nodes:

$$C_b\left(x\right) = \sum_{j<k} g_{jk}\left(n_i\right) / g_{jk} \tag{6}$$

Here, g_{jk} is the number of the shortest paths linking two nodes in the network. $g_{jk}\left(n_i\right)$ is the number of shortest path linking two nodes that go through the node n_i. Clearly, maximum number of such paths is (g-1)(g-2)/2. Therefore betweenness centrality is normalized as shown in equation 7:

$$C_B = C_b / \left[\left(g-1\right)\left(g-2\right)/2\right] \tag{7}$$

Figure 5 clearly differentiates betweenness centrality and degree centrality. X has highest betweenness centrality and Y has highest degree centrality.

Figure 5. Comparison between degree centrality and betweenness centrality measures

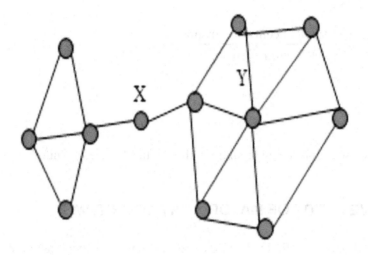

4.6 Power

Power is a fundamental property of social structure even if there is a dispute over its formal definition and analysis and its consequences. Table 2 summarizes some of the main approaches that social network analysts have developed to study power, and the closely related concept of centrality.

4.7 Small World Effect (Newman, 2003, Watts et. al., 1998)

Small World Effect describes that network size does not have any effect on length of ties among nodes. In other words, the distance between any pair of nodes is much smaller than the size of the network.

4.8 Clustering Coefficient (Newman, 2003, Watts et. al., 1998)

A triplet is an ordered set of three vertices, (i, v, j), where v is considered the focal point and there are undirected edges <i, v> and <v, j>. An open triplet is defined as three vertices in which only the required two are connected. A closed triplet is defined as three vertices in which there are three edges. A triangle is made up of three closed triplets, one for each vertex of the triangle.

Table 2. Comparing three aspects of power in Sociograms

Power Aspect Name	Definition	Influence
Degree	Number of ties for an actor	Having more opportunities and alternatives
Closeness	Length of paths to other actors	Direct bargaining and exchange with other actors
Betweenness	Lying between each other pairs of actors	Brokering contacts among actors to isolate them or prevent connections

The local clustering coefficient of vertex v is

$$C_v = \frac{\text{number of closed triplets centered around v}}{\text{number of triplets centered around v}}$$

$$= \frac{T_v}{d_v(d_v - 1)} \tag{8}$$

Where T_v is the closed triplet count around v and d_v is the degree of v (number of adjacent vertices).

5. COMPARATIVE STUDY OF MAJOR SNA ALGORITHMS

The main objective of SNA is to find what is most appealing in the social network. This might be any individual actor (central) in the network or a circumscribed area in the network (cluster). Therefore most of the SNA tasks focus on centrality measures and clustering of network.

Centrality is measurement of how central a node is in the network. Section 4.5 elaborates centrality in detail. Degree centrality is most basic centrality measurement. The algorithm to calculate degree centrality is scalable linearly with number of neighbors of the node and incurs time complexity of O(n). Eigen vector centrality takes wider part of the network and thereby gives a better prediction of influence. It scales almost linear with the number of nodes, n and edges, m with the time complexity O(n+m).

Betweenness centrality is one of the most used centrality methods. The global betweenness centrality algorithm has poor scalability and incurs time complexity of O(n*m).

A group of more closely connected nodes in a network is often called clusters. There are two different ways to define clusters–definition clusters, one node can belong to more than one cluster (cliques), and hierarchal clusters in which each node can belong to any one of the clusters (community). Cliques are more elaborately defined in section 5.3. All maximum cliques can be calculated with Bron-Kerbosch Algorithm (Cazal et. al., 2008). The time complexity is linear with the number of clusters but it is not scalable as the number of clusters increases with the size of network. There a number of approximation algorithms with varying tradeoff between performance and quality of the analysis. Most of them are based on greedy algorithm incurring the time complexity approximately o(n). Some are described by Protasi (Battitti et. al., 2001) and Du et al. (Du et. al., 1991).

Community structure is based in hierarchal clustering that divides the network into small parts whether in top-down or bottom-up fashion. The betweenness algorithm needs to be executed several times and hence results in poor scalability (the time complexity is approximately O(n3)).

Table 3 presents a comparison between original algorithms and approximation algorithms.

Table 3. Comparison between Original algorithms and approximation algorithms

	Scalability	Time Complexity
Global Betweenness Centrality Algorithm	Not Scalable	O(n*m) O(n⁴)
Ego Network Betweenness Centrality Algorithm	Scalable	O(n)
Born-Kerbosch Clique Algorithm	Not Scalable	O(#Cliques)
Greedy k-plex Algorithm	Scalable	O(n)

6. UNFOLDED CHALLENGES

6.1 Size

SNA has been applied in a broad range of research fields. Due to the wide usage of computerized and rapid developments of networked information sharing techniques, many types of large social networks have emerged in a wide range of research fields which play critical role in studying structural properties.

There are many large social networks which have emerged from various fields. These include networks of acquaintance/communication (Campbell, 2004), Live Journal (livejournal.com), MySpace (myspace. com), Facebook (facebook.com), phone calls (Aiello et. al., 2000), collaboration (Barabasi et. al., 2002, Newman, 2001), sexual contact (Liljeros et. al., 2001), paper citation (Redner, 1998), World Wide Web (www) pages network (Adamic, 1999, Broder et. al., 2002), linguistic network (Cancho et. al., 2001) etc. The stupendous size of social networks implies following challenges:

1. **Long Processing Time:** An obvious characteristic of large network is the huge network size as the largest OSN site Facebook has had a total of 680 million monthly active users by the end of the December 2012 (newsroom.fb.com/key-facts). The size of the friendship/acquaintance network based on the LiveJournal database is more than 10 million. Moreover these networks keep expanding. As network size increases the time for analysing network grows rapidly, which is usually not linear. Although computer power has been growing fast, handling large network will take a huge amount of time even if we use the fastest single processor available. However in many applications time is vital.

2. **Large Computation Resource Requirement:** Processing large social networks will require a great amount of computational resources, such as memories in computers. Every social network analysis package runs on a single computer making it bottlenecked both by processor speed and memory size. A 32 bit processor cannot address more than 232 bytes of memory limiting the total system memory to approximately 4GB. Computing the shortest paths for all pairs of actors requires n2 memory where n is the number of actors. If we allow 4 bytes per actor then the maximum number of actors allowable in an all in memory serial SNA is $\sqrt{2^{32}}\Big/4 \approx 16{,}000$ actors. Thus, we can see that it is infeasible to employ a single processor to perform analysis on large social networks.

6.2 Graph Dynamism

Almost all networks are dynamic communities in friendship/acquaintance networks. They keep evolving as people join new groups and/or quit old ones. There are always new papers or collaborative work inserted in citation or co-authorship network. Graph dynamism does not seem troublesome if the size of network is small as analyzing small networks takes small time and changes occurring during this time either have little effect or changed can be analyzed again. However dynamism is vital for large network analysis process.

Processing time for analyzing large social network is longer as already discussed and therefore outcomes of the analysis may not be valid anymore as the whole network might have changed during the time analysis was undergoing.

6.3 Diverse Representation of Social Networks

Social networks are generally combination of different or similar kind of actors connected through different kind of links or same kind of links with different weights as discussed in the introduction. For example, graph representation of Facebook has undirected edges because friendship on face is both directional i.e. if X is friend of Y then Y is also friend of X. But in case of Twitter the edges are directed because associations (follow) on Twitter are not bidirectional i.e. 'X follows Y' does not necessarily imply 'Y also follows X'. Diverse representation of social networks restricts SNA solutions to become universally applicable to all networks.

6.4 Biasing

Large social networks are infeasible to crawl completely. Most of the approaches rely on the statistical properties of sample, smaller in size, as representative of complete network. Many sampling algorithms suffer from biasing (Leskovee et. al., 2006) i.e. most of the algorithms select nodes with the higher degree first. Biasing affects resemblance of sample to the actual network considerably. Few sampling algorithms have arrangements to avoid biasing but additional cost is incurred in the form of large storage space requirement, maintaining extra information about out degree of nodes and use of external authentication tokens (Gjoka et. al., 2010).

7. CONCLUSION

Social Network Analysis has always been popular to give analytical inferences about the society which have diverse areas of successful applications. Development of computer technology played a catalytic role to make social networking (OSN) as part of every human being's daily routine. And it took little time to encounter very large social networks which are continuously growing rapidly. Social network analysis methods provide some useful tools for addressing many aspects of large social networks.

At the analysis level social networks are seen as graph having nodes representing actors and edges as links between them. Therefore structural and statistical properties of graphs can be directly used to draw useful inferences as the outcome of the analysis. Attempting to analyze the entire graph is tempting because more data usually leads to better analysis. As online social networks grow in size exponentially, the practicality of complete coverage demises.

Another barrier is dynamic behavior of most of the social networks (mostly OSNs). Nodes may join or leave the network quickly or there may be a behavioral change in their association links. How these changes are reflected on the sample collected for analysis is a challenge.

REFERENCES

Adamic, L. A. (1999). The Small World Web. *Proceedings of the Third European Conference, 443.*

Aiello, W., Chung, F., & Lu, L. (2000). A Random Graph Model for Massive Graphs. *Proceedings of the 32nd ACM Symposium on the Theory of Computing*, 171. doi:10.1145/335305.335326

Almansoori, W., Zarour, O., Jarada, T. N., Karampales, P., Rokne, J., & Alhajj, R. (2011). Applications of Social Network Construction and Analysis in the Medical Referral Process. *Proceedings of IEEE Ninth International Conference on Dependable, Autonomic and Secure Computing (DASC)*, 816-823. doi:10.1109/DASC.2011.140

Barabasi, A. L., Jeong, H., Neda, Z., Ravasz, E., Schubert, A., & Vicsek, T. (2002). Evolution of the Social Network of Scientific Collaborations. *Physica A, 331*(3-4), 590–614. doi:10.1016/S0378-4371(02)00736-7

Battiti, R., & Protasi, M. (2001). Reactive Local Search for the Maximum Clique Problem. *Algorithmica, 29*(4), 610–637. doi:10.1007/s004530010074

Boyd, D. M., & Ellison, N. B. (2007, October). Social Network Sites: Definition, History, and Scholarship. *J. Comp.- Mediated Comm., 13*(1), 210–230. doi:10.1111/j.1083-6101.2007.00393.x

Brin, S., & Page, L. (1998). The anatomy of a large-scale hypertextual web search engine. *Proceedings of the 7th World-Wide-Web Conference (WWW7).* doi:10.1016/S0169-7552(98)00110-X

Broder, A., Kumar, R., Maghoul, F., Raghavan, P., Rajagopalan, S., Stata, R., & Wiener, J. et al. (2002). Graph Structure in the Web. *Computer Networks, 33*(1-6), 309–320. doi:10.1016/S1389-1286(00)00083-9

Campbell, A. P. (2004). Using LiveJournal for Authentic Communication in EFL Classes. The Internet TESL Journal, 5(9).

Cancho, R. F., & Sole, R. V. (2001). *The Small-World of Human Language.* Santa Fe Institute Working Paper 01-03-016.

Carrington, P. J., Scott, J., & Wasserman, S. (2005). *Models and Methods in Social Network Analysis.* Cambridge University Press. doi:10.1017/CBO9780511811395

Cazals, F., & Karande, C. (2008). *A note on the problem of reporting maximal cliques.* Academic Press.

Cheathan, M., & Cleereman, K. (2006). Application of Social Network Analysis to Collaborative Team Formation. *International Symposium on Collaborative Technologies and Systems*, 306-311. doi:10.1109/CTS.2006.18

Deconta, M. C., Obrst, L. J., & Smith, K. T. (2003). *The Semantic Web: A guide to future of XML, Web Services and Knowledge Management.* Wiley Publishing Inc.

Ding, L., Zhou, L., & Finin, T. (2003). Trust based knowledge outsourcing for semantic web agents. *Proceedings of IEEE/WIC International Conference on Web Intelligence.* doi:10.1109/WI.2003.1241219

Du, D. Z., & Pardalos, P. M. (1991). *The Maximum Clique Problem. In Handbook of Combinatorial Optimization: Supplement* (Vol. A, pp. 1–74). Springer.

Freeman, L. C. (2002). *The Study of Social Networks.* Available: http://www.insna.org/INSNA/na_inf.html

Gjoka, M., Kurant, M., Butts, C. T., & Markopoulou, A. (2010). A walk in Facebook: Uniform sampling of users in online social networks. *Proceedings - IEEE INFOCOM.*

Golbeck, L., Parsia, B., & Hendler, J. (2003). Trust network on the semantic web. Proceedings of Co-operative Intelligent Agents. doi:10.1007/978-3-540-45217-1_18

Hanneman, R., & Riddle, M. (2005). *Introduction to Social Network Methods.* Available: http://www.faculty.ucr.edu/~hanneman/nettext/

Jamali, M., & Abolhassani, H. (2006). Different Aspects of Social Network Analysis. *IEEE/WIC/ACM International Conference on Web Intelligence,* 66-72.

Kate, E., & Inga, C. (2005). *Inside Social Network Analysis.* IBM Technical Report.

Klienburg. (1998). Authoritative sources in a hyperlinked environment. *Proceedings of Ninth Annual ACM-SIAM Symposium on Discrete Algorithms.*

Krebs, V. (2006). *How to do Social Network Analysis.* Available: http://www.orgnet.com/sna.html

Leskovee, J., & Faloutsos, C. (2006). Sampling from Large Graphs. *KDD'06 Proceedings of the 12th ACM SIGKDD International Conference on Knowledge Discovery & Datamining,* 631-636.

Liljeros, F., Edling, C. R., Amaral, L A N., Stanley, H. E., & Aberg, Y. (2001). The Web of Human Sexual Contacts. *Nature, 411*(6840), 907–908. doi:10.1038/35082140 PMID:11418846

Newman, M. E. J. (2003). The Structure and Function of Complex Networks. *SIAM Review, 45*(2), 167–256. doi:10.1137/S003614450342480

Newman, M. E. J. (2001). The Structure of Scientific Collaboration Networks. *Proceedings of the National Academy of Sciences of the United States of America, 98,* 404.

Nooy, W., Mrvar, A., & Batagelj, V. (2005). *Exploratory Social Network Analysis with Pajek.* Cambridge University Press. doi:10.1017/CBO9780511806452

Redner, S. (1998). How Popular is Your Paper? An Empirical Study of the Citation Distribution. *The European Physical Journal B, 4*(2), 131–134. doi:10.1007/s100510050359

Ressler, S. (2006). Social Network Analysis as an Approach to Combat Terrorism: Past, Present, and Future Research. *Homeland Security Affairs, 2*(2).

Saroop, A., & Karnik, A. (2011). Crawlers for social networks & structural analysis of Twitter. *Proceedings of IEEE 5th International Conference on Internet Multimedia Systems Architecture and Application (IMSAA)*, 1-8. doi:10.1109/IMSAA.2011.6156368

Scott, J. (1992). *Social Network Analysis*. Newbury Park, CA: Sage.

Swartz, A., & Hedler, J. (2001). The Semantic Web: A network of content for the digital city. *Proceedings of Second Annual Digital Cities Workshop*.

Wang, W., Wu, B., & Zhang, Z. (2010). Website clustering from query graph using social network analysis. *Proceedings of IEEE International Conference on Emergency Management and Management Sciences (ICEMMS)*, 439-442.

Wasserman, S., & Faust, K. (1994). *Social Network Analysis, Methods and Applications*. Cambridge University Press. doi:10.1017/CBO9780511815478

Watts, D. J., & Strogatz, S. H. (1998). Collective Dynamics of 'Small-World Networks. *Nature, 393*(6684), 440–442. doi:10.1038/30918 PMID:9623998

Wei, , Wen, & Lin. (2011). Research on emergency information management based on the social network analysis — A case analysis of panic buying of salt. *Proceedings of International Conference on Management Science and Engineering (ICMSE)*, 1302-1310.

Ye, S., Lang, J., & Wu, F. (2010). Crawling online social graphs. *Proceedings of International Asia-Pacific Web Conference*, 236–242.

Zelenkauskaite, A., Bessis, N., Sotiriadis, S., & Asimakopoulou, E. (2012). Interconnectedness of Complex Systems of Internet of Things through Social Network Analysis for Disaster Management. *Proceedings of 4th International Conference on Intelligent Networking and Collaborative Systems (INCoS)*, 503-508. doi:10.1109/iNCoS.2012.25

Zhefeng, X., Bo, L., Huaping, H., & Tian, Z. (2012). Design and Implementation of Facebook Crawler Based on Interaction Simulation. *Proceedings of IEEE 11th International Conference on Trust, Security and Privacy in Computing and Communications (TrustCom)*, 1109-1112.

Chapter 2
Graph Tools for Social Network Analysis

Nadeem Akhtar
Aligarh Muslim University, India

Mohd Vasim Ahamad
Aligarh Muslim University, India

ABSTRACT

A social network can be defined as a complex graph, which is a collection of nodes connected via edges. Nodes represent individual actors or people in the network, whereas edges define relationships among those actors. Most popular social networks are Facebook, Twitter, and Google+. To analyze these social networks, one needs specialized tools for analysis. This chapter presents a comparative study of such tools based on the general graph aspects as well as the social network mining aspects. While considering the general graph aspects, this chapter presents a comparative study of four social network analysis tools—NetworkX, Gephi, Pajek, and IGraph—based on the platform, execution time, graph types, algorithm complexity, input file format, and graph features. On the basis of the social network mining aspects, the chapter provides a comparative study on five specialized tools—Weka, NetMiner 4, RapidMiner, KNIME, and R—with respect to the supported mining tasks, main functionality, acceptable input formats, output formats, and platform used.

1. INTRODUCTION

In present era, social networks are the fastest growing applications over the web. It has become the main interaction medium among people around the world. A social network can be considered as a graph having nodes and edges, where nodes represents actor or people and edges connect actors in communication (Alan Mislove, 2007). Social networks and the techniques to analyze them existed since decades (Carrington, 2011). In earlier decades, social networks are analyzed to understand the behavior and evolution of human networks (J. Scott., 1994; S. Wasserman, 1994). A social network can be an email network, a telephone network or a collaborative network. But nowadays, most popular and most visited social

DOI: 10.4018/978-1-5225-2814-2.ch002

networks are Facebook, Twitter, LinkedIn, Myspace and Google+ which have acquired huge number of users. Facebook is said to have about 1.71 billion monthly active users, as of second quarter of 2016.

The structure of social networks and their analysis has evolved from graph theory, statistics and sociology. Social network analysis is used in several other fields like information science, business application, communication, economy etc. Since, social network mimics the structure of graphs, analyzing a social network is quite similar to the analysis of a graph. There are a number of tools for graph analysis that are in existence from decades. But they are not able to analyze a social network graph because of its huge size and complex properties. It may contain millions of nodes and edges. Social networks are dynamic i.e. there is continuous evolution and expansion. In a social network, a node or actor usually has several attributes. There can be small and large communities within social networks. Because of the complex structure and very large size of the social networks, old graph analysis tools are not designed to analyze social networks.

In this chapter, we present a comparative study of such tools based on the general graph aspects as well as the social network mining aspect. While considering the general graph aspects, we present the comparative study of some social network analysis tools based on the platform, execution time, Graph types, algorithm complexity, input file format, graph features. Under the social network mining aspect, we are dedicated to provide a comparison study of some specialized tools with respect to the supported mining tasks, main functionality, acceptable input formats, output formats, and platform used.

2. SOCIAL NETWORK ANALYSIS

The internet has revolutionized the sharing of information through number of information sharing systems, including the Web. As of July 2015, number of internet users are 3.17 billion. Out of them, 2.3 billion users are active on social media having an average of 5.54 social media accounts. As of April 2016, Instagram has over 400 million users, and LinkedIn has over 450 million users. Facebook is said to have about 1.71 billion monthly active users, as of second quarter of 2016. These numbers significantly shows how popular social networks are.

Social network analysis (SNA) is the methodical analysis of social networks through the use of network structure and graph theories. Social network analysis views social relationships in terms of network theory, consisting of nodes (representing individual actors within the network) and ties (which represent relationships between the individuals, such as friendship, kinship, organizational position, social relationships, etc.) (Monclar, 2011).

Analysis tasks of social networks includes following:

- Discovering the structure of social network
- Finding various attribute values for the network- Ex. radius, diameter, centrality, betweenness, shortest paths, density etc.
- Finding communities in the social network
- Visualizing the whole or part of the social network

Several works has been done on various social networks to analyze and discover various kinds of relationships and information (N. Akhtar, 2013; Zelenkauskaite, 2012; Li, 2010; Alan E. Mislove, 2009).

2.1 Kinds of Network Analysis

There are two basic kinds of social network analysis, ego network analysis, and complete network analysis. Ego network analysis is concerned with analysis of individual nodes. A network can have as many egos as nodes in the graph. Egos can be persons, organizations or whole society. In ego network analysis, individual behavior and its variation is mined and described. Complete network analysis is concerned with the analysis of all the relationships among a set of nodes. Techniques such as subgroup analysis, equivalence analysis and measures like centrality (closeness, degree, and betweenness) all require complete networks (NextMEDIA, 2010).

2.2 Applications of Social Network Analysis

Following are some applications of social network analysis: (BASNA, 2013; INSNA, 2016)

- Identify new scientific trends becoming commercially viable, e.g. RFID, Genome sequencing, tissue engineering.
- Analyze expert network, Co-authorship networks, cocitation networks, patent networks.
- Measurement of success.
- Ranking of trends, of authors, of companies commercializing trend.
- Analyzing page importance Page Rank (Related to recursive in-degree computation), Authorities/ Hubs.
- Discovering Communities: Finding near-cliques.
- Analyzing Trust: Propagating Trust.
- Using propagated trust to fight spam: In Email, In Web page ranking.

3. SOCIAL NETWORK ANALYSIS TOOLS

Social network analysis tools are used to identify, analyze, visualize or simulate nodes (organizations, or knowledge) and edges (relationship or interaction) from various types of input data including mathematical models of social networks. There are several tools available for analysis of social networks. The International Network for Social Network Analysis (INSNA) maintains a large list of software packages and libraries.

We have selected four analysis tools for comparison namely Gephi, Networkx, IGraph and Pajek. The selection is based on several facts. All four selected software are freely available for use and they can handle large graph size. Network analysis tools are either GUI based or packages/libraries which can be used in a programming language. Gephi and Pajek are GUI based network tools whereas Networkx and IGraph are packages based tools. Following are the brief detail about each of these four tools-

- **Networkx:** Is a Python language software package for the creation, manipulation and the study of structure and functions of the complex networks. With this tool you can load and store networks in standard data formats, can generate many types of random and classic networks, analyze network structure, build network models, draw networks, and much more. Networkx has many features like language data structures for graphs, dIGraphs, and multIGraphs. Nodes can be "anything"

Table 1. General Comparison of Tools

Software	NETWORKX	IGRAPH	GEPHI	PAJEK
Type	Library	Library	Stand Alone	Stand Alone
Platform	Python	Python\R\C Library	Windows	Windows
Computational Time	Fast	Fast	Fast	Medium
No. Of Nodes	1 Million	1 Million	0.15 Million	1 Million

(e.g. text, images), Edges can hold arbitrary data (e.g. weights, time-series), Standard graph algorithms, Network structure and analysis measures etc.

- **Gephi:** Is an interactive visualization and exploration platform for all kinds of networks, dynamic and hierarchical graphs. Runs on Windows, Linux and Mac OS X. Gephi are a tool for people that have to explore and understand graphs. Like Photoshop but for data, the user interacts with the representation; manipulate the structures, shapes and colors to reveal hidden properties.
- **Pajek**: A widely used Software for drawing networks, Pajek also has analytical capabilities, and can be used to compute most centrality measures, identify structural holes, blockmodel, and so on.
- **IGraph:** Is a free software package for creating and manipulating graphs. It includes implementations for classic graph theory problems like minimum spanning trees and network flow, and also implements algorithms like community structure search. The efficient implementation of IGraph allows it to handle graphs with millions of nodes and edges. IGraph can be installed as libraries for C, R, Python and Ruby. Above four tools are compared on the following six criterion- platform, Graph types, algorithm time complexity, graph layout, graph input file format, graph features
- **Dataset for SNA Tools Comparisons:** We have used Slashdot dataset (J. Scott, 1994). It contains 77317 nodes and 982787 edges (Directed). Slashdot is a technology-related news website features user-submitted and evaluated news stories about science and technology related topics.

4. SOCIAL NETWORK SOFTWARE TOOLS COMPARISON

In this section, we have compared the four selected social networking analysis tools on the basis of various criterion. Following sub-sections describes each of the selected criterion and comparison of the tools.

4.1 Comparison Based on Platform

Social network analysis tools Pajek and Gephi are standalone software, Networkx and IGraph are libraries. Pajek/gephi runs on windows platforms and Networkx use python library and IGraph use python/r/c library for social network analysis. Networkx, IGraph or Pajek can handle more than one million nodes and Gephi can handle up to 150000 nodes.

4.2 Comparison Based on Network Types

In social network Analysis there are four types of network Graph (Monclar, 2011).

Table 2. Comparison Based on the Network Types Supported by Tools

Graph Type	NETWORKX	IGRAPH	GEPHI	PAJEK
1-Mode Network	Yes	Yes	Yes	Yes
2-Mode Network	Yes	Yes	Yes	Yes
Multi Relational Network Graph	No	No	No	Yes
Temporarily Network Graph	Yes	No	No	Yes

In a one-mode network, each vertex can be related to each other vertex. In one mode network we have only one set of nodes and ties are connected to these nodes. In a two-mode network, vertices are divided into two sets and vertices can only be related to vertices in the other set.

Two mode network Graph are a particular type of networks with two sets of nodes and ties are only established between nodes belonging to different sets. Techniques for analyzing one-mode networks cannot always be applied to two-mode networks without modification or change of meaning. Special techniques for two-mode networks are very complicated. We can create two one-mode networks from a two-mode network

In Multi relational network there will be multiple kinds of relations between nodes. Nodes may be closely-linked in one relational network, but distant in another.

In temporal networks (dynamic graphs) networks can change over time. The lines and vertices in a temporal network should satisfy the consistency condition: if a line is active in time t then also its end-vertices are active in time t. For one mode or two mode network analysis we can use any of software tools but for multi relational network graph we have only Pajek software tools .for temporarily network graph we have Networkx and Pajek tools.

4.3 Comparison Based on Graph Layout

In social network analysis we have many layout algorithms. IGraph or Pajek have most famous and recent layout algorithms Fruchterman Reingold or Kamanda Kawai. All of them software have circular

Table 3. Comparison Based on Graph Layout Supported by Tools

Layout	NETWORKX	IGRAPH	GEPHI	PAJEK
Circular Layout	Yes	Yes	Yes	Yes
Random Layout	Yes	Yes	Yes	No
Spectral Layout	Yes	No	No	No
Spring Layout	Yes	Yes	Yes	Yes
Graphviz Layout	Yes	No	No	No
Kamanda Kawai	No	Yes	Yes	No
Fruchterman Reingold	No	Yes	Yes	No
Force Atlas Layout	No	No	Yes	No

Table 4. Algorithmic Time Complexities

FEATURES	NETWORKX	IGRAPH	GEPHI	PAJEK
Isomorphism	$O(N^2)$	exp	Na	Na
CORE M M=No. Of Lines	$O(M)$	$O(M)$	$O(M)$	$O(M)$
Cliques	$O(|V|/(Log)2)$	$O(3|V|/3)$	Na	$O(N)$
Shortest Path	$O(|V|.|E|)$	$O(|V|+|E|)$	$O(|V|+|E|)$	$O(|V|+|E|)$
Clustering	$O(V)$	Na	$O(V)$	Na
All Simple Path	$O(|V|+|E|)$	$O(|V|+|E|)$	Na	Na
Closeness Centrality	$O(N.|E|)$	$O(N.|E|)$	Na	Na
Density	$O(N^3)$	$O(1)$	Na	Na
MST	Na	$O(|V|+|E|)$	Na	Na
Cycles	$O((|V|+|E|).C+1)$	Na	Na	Na
PageRank	Na	$O(E)$	$O(E)$	Na
Betweenness	Na	$O(|V|.|E|)$	Na	Na
Eigenvector	Na	$O(|V|+|E|)$	Na	Na

or spring layout. Gephi provide user friendly layout capability for user. Gephi provide capability like Photoshop where users have many additional facilities. Force layout is another famous layout algorithm given by Gephi software. For user friendly visualization we can use Gephi software but it cannot handle large or complex graphs. For large and complex network we can use either Networkx or IGraph. IGraph or Networkx provide support for many other tools for visualization. For small dataset we can use stand-alone software (Gephi, Pajek) because we can handle standalone software easily.

4.4 Comparison Based on Algorithm and Running Time Complexity

For analyzing large graphs, processing time is very critical. We compared the selected four tools on the basis of algorithmic as well as running time complexities of available features.

Table 4 shows the comparison among the four tools on the basis of algorithmic time complexities. To find the time complexities of various algorithms, we first found the algorithm for the feature and then searched for the literature associated with the algorithm. After studying the literature, we found the algorithmic complexity of the feature. We are unable to find the algorithmic complexity for some of the features. These are shown as NA (Not Available) in the Table.

Table 5 shows the comparison among the running time of listed features of graph tools. A computer with normal configuration is used for performing all the experiments. Based on algorithms running time, we can say that IGraph is more useful software compare to other. IGraph provide efficient algorithms for page rank, all types of centrality, density, MST and shortest path. Networkx is comparatively too slow for large graphs.

Table 5. Execution Time for Various Features

SNA FEATURES	NETWORKX	IGRAPH	GEPHI	PAJEK
Load time	54.67 sec	3.707 sec	29 sec	3 sec
Degree centrality	58.57 sec	6.199 sec	4 sec	2 sec
Graph degree	60.87 sec	6.22 sec	4 sec	2 sec
Page rank	120.78 sec	9.81 sec	10 sec	Na
Hits	57.23 sec	15.43 sec	8 sec	Na
Cliques	66.98 sec	9.35 sec	Na	Na
Density	58.94 sec	3.302 sec	4 sec	Na
Modularity	81.4 sec	9 sec	30 sec	6 sec
Network diameter	35 sec	3.51 sec	120 sec	Na
Core	65.84 sec	6.532 sec	Na	1 sec
Cohesion	Na	8.943 sec	Na	Na
Clustering coefficient	3303.99 sec	1800 sec	1200 sec	108 sec
Hub	76.57 sec	5.831 sec	3 sec	Na
Authority	Array is to big	6.783 sec	3 sec	Na

4.5 Comparison Based on Graph Features and Input File Formats

Social network analysis tools has many algorithms for graph features. We compare these tools on the basis of availability of these graph features. We have selected only a few important graph features for comparison due to space problem. Table 6 lists these important graph features and their availability in the four graph mining tools. IGraph, Gephi and Networkx have algorithms for maximum number of features. Pajek lags in supporting several of the main graph features like flow, cohesion, clique and isomorphism.

A graph can be stored in a variety of file formats. Supporting multiple file formats allows flexibility. Table 7 summarizes the various file formats supported by the graph tools. Networkx and IGraph supports almost all the available graph file formats. Pajek supports only .Net and .Dat file formats, besides supporting its own format.

5. SOCIAL NETWORK MINING TOOLS

Recently, social networks are the fastest growing applications over the web. It has become the main interaction medium among people around the world. Easy access of social network sites such as Twitter, Facebook and LinkedIn making them more and more popular. Users are accessing social networks for news updates, trending topics information, collecting opinion of other users on some topics, connecting to a community, etc. The usage list of social networks are endless nowadays, that's why it is generating massive data which are dynamic and sometimes noisy. Due to the dynamic and noisy nature of the huge data coming from social networks, it is almost impossible to analyze it manually. Data mining is a set of techniques for extracting useful information from massive datasets coming from the social media.

Table 6. Various Graph Features Supported by Tools

GRAPH FEATURE	Networkx	Igraph	Gephi	Pajek
Approximation	Yes	No	No	No
Assortivity	Yes	Yes	No	No
Centrality	Yes	Yes	Yes	Yes
Network Diameter	Yes	Yes	Yes	Yes
Clustering	Yes	Yes	Yes	Yes
Flow	Yes	Yes	Yes	No
Communities	Yes	Yes	No	Yes
Cohesion	No	Yes	No	No
Block Modeling	Yes	No	Yes	No
Dendrogam	Yes	Yes	Yes	No
Clique	Yes	Yes	Yes	No
PageRank	Yes	Yes	Yes	Yes
BFS	Yes	Yes	Yes	No
DFS	Yes	Yes	Yes	No
HITS	Yes	Yes	Yes	Yes
Density	Yes	Yes	Yes	Yes
CORE	Yes	Yes	Yes	No
Isomorphism	Yes	Yes	Yes	No
Partition	No	No	Yes	No
Powerlaw	Yes	Yes	No	No
MST	Yes	Yes	Yes	No
BI PARTILE	Yes	Yes	Yes	No
BRIDGE	Yes	Yes	Yes	No
DYAD	Yes	Yes	Yes	No
HITS	Yes	No	No	Yes

The primary objective of data mining is to process huge dataset and extract meaningful, actionable information. Very huge amount of valuable and actionable information is hidden in various social networks. This valuable information can be sentiment analysis data, trust analysis data of actors in the social network, friend recommendation, actor relationship analysis data, etc. This is the primary cause which provides us opportunities to use specialized social network analysis tools to mine the above mentioned information. In social network analysis, text data is heavily involved. It is a challenging task to choose the best social network analysis tool for mining text data. Social networks also have very complex relationship among its actors and hence it is very difficult to find required relationship information such as friend recommendation from the social network.

Under the social network mining aspect, we are dedicated to provide a comparison study of five specialized tools - Weka, NetMiner, RapidMiner, KNIME and R.

Table 7. File Formats Supported By Tools

Input File Format	NETWORKX	IGRAPH	GEPHI	PAJEK
.Net Format	Yes	Yes	Yes	Yes
.Gml	Yes	Yes	Yes	No
.Graphgml	Yes	Yes	Yes	No
Edgeslist(.Txt)	Yes	Yes	No	No
Edgeslist(.Csv)	Yes	Yes	No	No
.Dot	Yes	Yes	Yes	No
.Pajek	No	Yes	No	Yes
.Dat	No	No	No	Yes
Adjacency List	Yes	Yes	No	No
.Gdf	No	No	Yes	No
Graph Db	No	Yes	Yes	No

- **Weka:** Is an open source, free data mining tool consists of machine learning algorithms for different data mining tasks. It is java based data mining tool which supports data pre-processing, classification, regression, clustering, association rules mining, and data visualization. It also includes advanced text mining features.
- **NetMiner:** Is a data mining tool for data analysis and data visualization of large network data. It analyzes the social network data interactively and provides visual representation of that data, also detects patterns and structures of social networks. NetMiner supports different social analysis tasks such as data transformation, network analysis, statistics, data visualization, etc. It is based on the Python programming language and provides following features in support to social network analysis:
  - Network analysis of more than a million of nodes in a network
  - Data visualization and interactive network analysis
  - Provides facilities for data management, etc
- **RapidMiner:** A data mining tool that is based on client-server model with the server offers its services as SaaS. It supports integrated environments for machine learning, data mining, text data mining, predictive & business analytics, recommendations, etc. It supports all steps of the data mining task and applicable in all areas like business, academic researches & training, prototyping & application development.
- **KNIME** (Konstanz Information Miner): Is another open source tool that supports all data mining steps. KNIME is based on the Eclipse platform and it can be easily integrated with Weka tool and R.
- **R:** Is an open source tool for statistical analysis as well as a programming language. The R language is widely used for developing statistical data analysis.

5.1 Comparison Based on Functionality, Supported File Format, Language and Platform

In table 8, comparison among the five social networks mining tools is shown on the basis of functionality, input file supported, output file supported, platform, programming language and database supported, open source and community support.

Table 8 shows that Weka, RapidMiner, KNIME and R are open source and supported by windows, Linux and Mac based operating systems. NetMiner is not an open source software and supported by windows operating system only. All of the above social media mining tools supports .txt and .csv file formats in addition to other formats supported by different tools separately. Each of the above mentioned tool have database support associated with them. Weka, KNIME and R supports MySQL, Postgre SQL & Microsoft SQL whereas other tools only support SQL Server in addition to tool specific database supports. RapidMiner and R tools are best for machine learning, statistical analysis and data visualization,

Table 8. Comparison based on functionality, supported file format, language & platform

	Weka	**NetMiner**	**RapidMiner**	**KNIME**	**R**
Functionality	machine learning, data pre-processing, classification, clustering, and association rule mining	Network Analysis and Visualization	machine learning, Statistical analysis, data mining, predictive analytics.	Enterprise Analytics & Reporting, Business Intelligence, Data mining	machine learning, Statistical analysis and graphics,
Input format supported	textual files (.txt, .csv) .arff, .libsvm, database table, Data from URL	.xls,.xlsx, .csv, .dl(UCINET), .net, .vec, .clu, .per (pajek), .dat(StOCNET), .gml; NMF(proprietary)	textual files (.txt, .csv) .arff, .xrff, Excel/ Spreadsheet (.xls, .xlsx), database table	textual files (.txt, .csv), database table, Data from URL	textual files (.txt, .csv), .xlsx, database table (RODBC), Online Data from Web
Output format	textual files (.txt, .csv) .arff, .libsvm, etc	.xls,.xlsx, .csv, .dl(UCINET), .net(Pajek), .dat(StOCNET), .gml; NMF(proprietary)	textual files (.txt, .csv) .arff, .xrff, Excel/ Spreadsheet (.xls, .xlsx), database table	.csv, .xls, .pmml, .xml, .arff, etc	textual files (.txt, .csv) Excel/ Spreadsheet (.xlsx), etc
Programming Language Support	Java	Python	Java	Java	C, FORTRAN, R
Platform Support	Cross Platform	Windows	Cross Platform	Linux, Windows, OS X	Windows, Linux, Mac
Database Support	MySQL Database, Postgre SQL, MSQL Server, Oracle Database	SQL Server, Oracle Database	Oracle, DB2, MSQL Server	MySQL, SQLite, Postgre SQL, Hive	SQLite, MySQL and Postgre SQL
GUI	YES (Command Line also)	YES	YES	YES	YES (Command Line also)
Community support (no of users)	~200,000 Users	NA	~200,000 Users	~ 15000 Users	~ 2 M Users
Open Source	YES	NO	YES	YES	YES

whereas, NetMiner can be used at its best for network analysis and data visualization. Weka, RapidMiner and R support very large number of users in comparison to NetMiner and KNIME.

5.2 Comparison Based on Different Data Mining Tasks

Table 9, shows comparisons among the above mentioned social networks mining tools on the basis of different data mining tasks.

Data mining over social media can be done by using a number of methods & machine learning algorithms and data mining. Machine learning algorithms for data mining can be categorized into supervised, unsupervised, and semi-supervised machine learning algorithms. Classification is an example of supervised machine learning approach, whereas, clustering is an example of unsupervised machine learning approach. Data mining also includes other approaches for data analysis such as association rule mining, instance based learning, and data visualization. All of the above mentioned tools supports CART and Naïve Bayes classification algorithms under supervised learning approach. In unsupervised machine learning, all of them support k-means clustering, DBSCAN and EM clustering (Except Net-Miner). Weka, RapideMiner and KNIME support FP-Growth algorithm under association rule mining, whereas NetMIner and R support frequent subgraph and Apriori algorithms respectively. To visualize data, all of them support histograms, whereas RapidMiner, KNIME and R also support scatterplots.

6. TEXT MINING IN SOCIAL NETWORKS

A social network can be considered as a graph having nodes and edges, where nodes represents actor or people and edges connect actors in communication. Social networks allow users to communicate with other users in the network having different moral and social values, and different goals for generating information. Social networks can take any form such as, an email network, a telephone network or a

Table 9. Comparison based on data mining tasks

	Weka	NetMiner	RapidMiner	KNIME	R
Classification Algorithms	ID3, C4.5, CART	CART, Multilayer Perceptron, SVMs	ID3, C4.5, CART	ID3, CART	C4.5, CART
Bayesian Networks	Naive Bayes, full bayesian network	Naïve Bayes	Naive Bayes, full bayesian network	Naive Bayes	Naive Bayes
Instance based Learning Algorithms	kNN, LWL	kNN	kNN	kNN	LBR
Clustering	linkage-based, K-Means, EM clustering, DBSCAN, OPTICS	K-Means, GMM	linkage-based, K-Means, EM clustering, DBSCAN	linkage-based, K-Means, Fuzzy c menas, EM clustering, DBSCAN	linkage-based, AGNES, BIRCH, K-Means, EM clustering, DBSCAN
Association Rule Mining Algorithms	FP-Growth, Apriori	Frequent Subgraph	FP-Growth, Apriori	FP-Growth, Apriori	Apriori (arules)
Data visualization Techniques	histograms	NA	histograms scatterplots	histograms scatterplots	histograms scatterplots

collaborative network. But nowadays, Facebook, Twitter and LinkedIn are most popular and most visited social networks, acquiring large number of users. Facebook is said to have about 1.71 billion monthly active users, as of second quarter of 2016. The social network provides a way for communication among different users which enables them to share valuable information.

Text mining in social networks can be considered as the process of extracting the high-quality information from text generated from social network interactions. From past few years, text mining in social networks has gained high popularity because users are sharing textual data in abundance. Textual data, generated in social networks, can be characterized by its unstructured nature. Text mining is basically the analysis of data to produce previously unknown pattern (Hearst, 1999). Generally, text mining consists of different tasks such as text pre-processing, text categorization, text clustering, concept/feature extraction, etc. Applications of text mining in social networks include Topic Modeling, Sentiment & Opinion Analysis, Recommendations, Summarization of text documents, etc.

6.1 Topic Modeling

In social networks, the amount of the text information generated every day is far away from currently available processing capacity. Topic modeling provides insights analytics in order to understand huge repository of unstructured text documents. Topic modelling employs different techniques to extract hidden topics behind textual documents shared as a part of social network communications (Youngchul Cha, 2012). Topic Modeling is used as text mining approach and can be used extracting the latent topics from a collection of text documents generated in social networks. If a document is given about a particular topic, one would expect particular words to appear in the document more or less frequently such as "lion" and "roar" will appear more often in documents about lions.

6.2 Sentiment Analysis and Opinion Mining

Sentiment analysis, sometimes also referred as opinion mining, is the collection of natural language processing and text mining approaches, to analyze the textual information from social networks. The basic aim of sentiment analysis is to determine the attitude of a user in social network towards a topic or emotional reaction to a document, interaction, or event.

6.3 Recommendations in Social Networks

Recommender system is a subclass of information retrieval and filtering system that recommends the "rating" or "preference" that a user would give to a particular topic, item or text document (Francesco Ricci, 2011). Recommendation in social networks is based on the fact that users who connected in a social network have greater possibility to share the similar interests, and can be easily influenced by the friends in that network (Pritam Gundecha, 2012). Recommender systems have become increasingly popular in a variety of areas such as research articles, search queries, social tags and recommender systems for experts, (H. Chen, 2015) & Twitter pages (Pankaj Gupta, 2013).

6.4 Automatic Text Summarization

Automatic summarization (which is a part of machine learning and text data mining) is the process of reducing a text document to create a summary automatically, that consists of the most important points of the input text document. The idea behind automatic text summarization is to extract a representative summary of the data, which contains the information of the entire set of documents.

Table 10 shows that, RapidMiner provides Edda (Extensions for Binominal Text Classification for Topic Modeling. The text analysis extension in RapdMiner AYLIEN extracts insight from textual data such as news articles, social comments, tweets and reviews. RecSys framework is used as recommendation extension in RapidMiner for recommendations, which consists of item rating prediction and item ranking recommendation.

In R, topicmodels and TraMineR packages are used to perform topic modeling over text documents. "topicmodels" package provides an interface to LDA (Latent Dirichlet Allocation) algorithm and Correlated Topics Models (CTM) for topic modeling. TraMineR is an R package for text data mining, which describes and visualizes the sequence data. The "sentiment" package is the most general package for sentiment analysis with machine learning in R. RTextTools is an R package for automatic text classification by using the classification algorithms: svm, slda, boosting, bagging, random forests, glmnet, decision trees, neural networks and maximum entropy. The "recomederlab" R package provides an interface to test and develop recommender algorithms. The "genericSummary" package selects sentences from a text that best describe its topic. Package 'lexRankr' is used for automatic summarization of text data.

7. CONCLUSION

In this chapter, we have compared and summarized four network analysis tools Networkx, Pajek, Gephi and IGraph on the basis of their general graph features. We also compared and summarized five social network mining tools Weka, NetMiner, RapidMiner, KNIME and R on the basis of their general functionality, data mining and text mining tasks. In the following paragraphs, we summed up our conclusions:

Stand-alone software is very useful for graph Visualization (up to a maximum of few thousands of nodes), data format conversion. IGraph is fastest tools that provide most of graph features and handle large and complex network. Libraries (Networkx or IGraph) are more useful for tasks involving millions of nodes and for operations such as the union and the difference between sets of nodes or for the clustering. Stand-alone software are easy to use and easy to learn so for beginner Pajek and Gephi is suitable software. For complex dataset and research purpose we can use Networkx and IGraph software.

Table 10. Comparison based on text mining tasks

	Topic Modeling	Sentiment Analysis & Opinion Mining	Recommendations	Text Summarization
RapidMiner	Edda - Extensions for Binominal Text Classification	AYLIEN – Text Analysis Extension	RecSys (RapidMiner Recommender Extension)	--
R	topicmodels, tm, TraMineR	twitterR, tm, sentimentR, RTextTools	recommenderlab, tm	genericSummary, tm, lexRankr

For one mode or two mode network analysis we can use any of software tools but for multi-relational network graph, we have only Pajek software tools. For temporarily network graph we have Networkx and Pajek tools. All of the software can handle .Net file format. But mostly data are present in .txt format. We can easily understand or handle .txt format or many websites provides data set in .txt format so we can use IGraph or Networkx software tools. We have many file format conversion software they can convert .txt file format into .Net file format but these software can handle only small size file. So for large size data set we use IGraph or Networkx software tools.

IGraph provides mostly graph features and it also handle large and complex network. All of them software can compute centrality, clustering coefficient, network diameter, page rank, density. But if we want to compute some specific feature we choose different software. If we want to compute Cohesion, we can Use Networkx or IGraph tools. If we want to compute Bridge and dyad, we can use Networkx, IGraph and Pajek software tools. Gephi does not provide the facilities for dyad or bridge computation. IGraph and Pajek are faster software Tools compare to others. But Pajek does not provide all graph features. So if we want to analyse all graph features we can use IGraph software. IGraph gives fastest result to almost all graph features. Load time is minimum for Pajek software. Execution time for centrality, page rank, graph degree and cliques is minimum in IGraph software. So based on execution time IGraph is better software.

The primary objective of data mining is to process large amount of data and extract meaningful, actionable information. In social network analysis, text data is heavily involved. It is a challenging task to choose the best social network analysis tool for mining text data. Social networks also have very complex relationship among its actors and hence it is very difficult to find required relationship information such as friend recommendation from the social network. There are huge number of Social Network Mining tools available which can be used to mine social network data to extract meaningful information. Every tool has its own pros and cons. Among all tools, Weka, NetMIner 4, RapidMiner, KNIME and R are most of the desired characteristics for a fully-functional DM platform and therefore their use can be recommended for most of the DM tasks.

Weka, RapidMiner, KNIME and R are open source and supported by windows, Linux and Mac based operating systems. NetMiner is not an open source software and supported by windows operating system only. All of the above social media mining tools supports .txt and .csv file formats in addition to other formats supported by different tools separately. Each of the above mentioned tool have database support associated with them. Weka, KNIME and R supports MySQL, Postgre SQL & Microsoft SQL whereas other tools only support SQL Server in addition to tool specific database supports. RapidMiner and R tools are best for machine learning, statistical analysis and data visualization, whereas, NetMiner can be used at its best for network analysis and data visualization. Weka, RapidMiner and R support very large number of users in comparison to NetMiner and KNIME.

Weka, RapidMiner, NetMiner, KNIME and R supports CART and Naïve Bayes classification algorithms under supervised learning approach. In unsupervised machine learning, all of them support k-means clustering, DBSCAN and EM clustering (Except NetMiner). Weka, RapideMiner and KNIME support FP-Growth algorithm under association rule mining, whereas NetMIner and R support Frequent subgraph and Apriori algorithms respectively. To visualize data, all of them support histograms, whereas RapidMiner, KNIME and R also support scatterplots.

Text mining in social networks, can be considered as the process of extracting the high-quality information from text generated from social network interactions, having applications in social networks include Topic Modeling, Sentiment & Opinion Analysis, Recommendations, Summarization of text documents, etc. RapidMiner provides Edda (Extensions for Binominal Text Classification for Topic Modeling, AYLIEN extension for text analysis and RecSys framework is used as recommendation extension. In R, topicmodels and TraMineR packages are used to perform topic modeling over text documents. TraMineR is an R package for mining, describing and visualizing sequences of states or events, and more generally discrete sequence data. The "sentiment" package is the most general package for sentiment analysis with machine learning in R. RTextTools is a machine learning package for automatic text classification. The "recomederlab" R package used for providing recommendations. The "genericSummary" and 'lexRankr' packages are used for automatic summarization of text data.

REFERENCES

Akhtar, Javed, & Sengar. (2013). Analysis of High Degree Nodes in a Social Network. *International Journal of Electronics, Communication and Computer Engineering, 4*(3).

Akhtar, N., Javed, H., & Sengar, G. (2013). Analysis of Facebook Social Network. *IEEE International Conference on Computational Intelligence and Computer Networks (CICN)*.

Automatic Summarization. (n.d.). In *Wikipedia*. Retrieved from https://en.wikipedia.org/wiki/Automatic_summarization

Business Application of Social Network Analysis (BASNA). (2013). Retrieved from www.basna.in

Carrington, P. J., & Scott, J. (2011). Introduction. In *The Sage Handbook of Social Network Analysis*. SAGE. Retrieved from http://www.facebook.com/notes/facebook/500millionstories/409753352130

Cha, Y., & Cho, J. (2012). Social-Network Analysis Using Topic Models. *SIGIR'12*. doi:10.1145/2348283.2348360

Chen, Ororbia II, & Giles. (2015). *ExpertSeer: a Keyphrase Based Expert Recommender for Digital Libraries*. arXiv preprint.

Combe, D., Largeron, C., Egyed-Zsigmond, E., & Géry, M. (2010). A comparative study of social network analysis tools. *International Workshop on Web Intelligence and Virtual Enterprises, 2*.

Gephi. (n.d.). Retrieved from https://gephi.org

Gundecha, P., & Liu, H. (2012). *Mining Social Media: A Brief Introduction. In Tutorials in Operations Research*. INFORMS.

Gupta, Goel, Lin, Sharma, Wang, & Zadeh. (n.d.). WTF: The who-to-follow system at Twitter. *Proceedings of the 22nd international conference on World Wide Web*.

Hearst, M. A. (1999). Untangling text data mining. *Proc. of 37th ACL*, 3- 10.

Huisman & van duijn. (2011). *Software for social network analysis*. 2004 Graph and Network Analysis Dr. Derek Greene Clique Research Cluster. University College Dublin.

IGraph. (n.d.). Retrieved from IGraph.sourceforge.net

International Network of Social Network Analysis (INSNA). (n.d.). Retrieved from www.insna.org

J. Scott. (1994). *Social Network Analysis: A handbook*. Newbury Park, CA: Sage Publications.

Li, J., Chen, Y., & Lin, Y. (2010). Research on traffic layout based on social network analysis. *Education Technology and Computer (ICETC), 2010 2nd International Conference on*. IEEE.

Measurement and Analysis of Online Social Networks by Alan Mislove. (2007). Max Planck Institute for Software Systems.

Monclar, R. S. (2011). Using social networks analysis for collaboration and team formation identification. *Computer Supported Cooperative Work in Design (CSCWD), 2011 15th International Conference on*. IEEE. doi:10.1109/CSCWD.2011.5960128

NetMiner. (n.d.). Retrieved from http://www.netminer.com/

Networkx. (n.d.). Retrieved from http://Networkx.lanl.gov/index.html

Pajek. (n.d.). Retrieved from vlado.fmf.uni-lj.si/pub/networks/pajek

Ricci, F., Rokach, L., & Shapira, B. (2011). *Introduction. In Recommender Systems Handbook* (pp. 1–35). Springer.

Sentiment Analysis. (n.d.). In *Wikipedia*. Retrieved from https://en.wikipedia.org/wiki/Sentiment_analysis

Stavrianou, Andritsos, & Nicoloyannis. (2007). Overview and Semantic Issues of Text Mining. *SIGMOD Record, 36*(3).

Topic Model. (n.d.). In *Wikipedia*. Retrieved from https://en.wikipedia.org/wiki/Topic_model

Wasserman, S., & Faust, K. (1994). *Social Network Analysis*. Cambridge University Press. doi:10.1017/CBO9780511815478

Zelenkauskaite, A. (2012). Interconnectedness of complex systems of internet of things through social network analysis for disaster management. *Intelligent Networking and Collaborative Systems (INCoS), 2012 4th International Conference on*. IEEE. doi:10.1109/iNCoS.2012.25

Chapter 3
An Approach to Mining Information From Telephone Graph Using Graph Mining Techniques

Bapuji Rao
IGIT, India

Sasmita Mishra
IGIT, India

Sarojananda Mishra
IGIT, India

ABSTRACT

This chapter focuses on methods to study communication in a real world social network using the basic concepts of graph theory. The initial section of this chapter starts with a general introduction consisting of related literature and definitions towards understanding the basic concepts of graph mining and graph theory, defining a telephone graph and use of telephone graph for social contexts. The authors have proposed an algorithm for extracting different network provider's sub-graphs, weak and strong connected sub-graphs and extracting incoming and outgoing calls of subscribers which have direct application for studying the human behavior in telephone network. The authors have considered two examples. The authors have implemented the proposed algorithm in C++ programming language and obtained satisfactory results. Finally, the authors have included the snapshots of the output in the chapter to enhance the interest of the readers.

1. INTRODUCTION

Social networks show strong community relationships. So a group of people interact with each other whether inside a community group or outside the group. To measure the community relationships, one

DOI: 10.4018/978-1-5225-2814-2.ch003

related concept is transitivity. For example, friends of a friend are likely to be friends. Transitivity factor can be measured using Clustering coefficient, the probability of connections between neighboring nodes or vertices (Cook et. al., 2007).

Due to such property of strong community effect, the actors or the social entities in a network form a group which is closely connected. These groups are known as communities, clusters, cohesive subgroups or modules in different ways. The authors have observed that individuals interact more frequently within a group. To detect similar groups in a social network known as same community detection (Girvan et. al., 2002; Rao et. al., 2014-ICHPCA) remains a major problem in social network analysis. To find out such type of communities make helping for solving other related tasks of social network analysis. Several works in terms of definitions and approaches are available in the area of community detection. There is an assumption of non randomness or locality. This condition is the hardest to formalize, but highly important in relationships to form a cluster. Let entities (say E_1, E_2 and E_3) E_1 is related to both E_2 and E_3. Then there is a higher probability than average that E_2 and E_3 are related.

Social networks are generally modeled as graphs, which sometimes we refer as a social graph where entities are the nodes or vertices, and an edge or arc connects two nodes if they are related. Social graphs are undirected or directed depending on the kind of relationships. There are many examples of social networks other than "friends" networks. Some of the examples are Telephone Networks, Email Networks, Authors Networks, Research Paper Networks, Collaboration Networks of Authors and Papers, Collaboration Networks of Teachers, Students, and Text Books (Girvan et. al., 2002). This paper works on these properties in details and proposes a new algorithm for telephone network using graph mining techniques.

2. MODELING TELEPHONE NETWORK

The authors have observed that some of the real life social network examples include Telephone Networks, Email Networks, Authors Networks, Research Paper Networks, Collaboration Networks of Authors and Papers, Collaboration Networks of Teachers, Students, and Text Books (Girvan et. al., 2002). Such type of interactive and dynamic social network can easily be represented graphically using node and edge relationships. The authors have used matrix to represent Telephone Network in the computer's memory. So as one can analyze on it by using graph mining techniques to get the desired and efficient knowledge easily and faster. The telephone networks representation and analysis has been explained in detail.

The nodes of the telephone network represent subscriber phone numbers, which are real world individuals. There is an edge between two nodes if a call has been made between those phones in some fixed period of time, such as last month, or for the last six months. The edges could be weighted by the number of calls made between these phones during the period. Communities in a telephone network will form from groups of people that communicate frequently: groups of friends, members of a club, or people working in the same organization. So as one can acquire the knowledge by extracting a particular service provider's sub-graph, strong-connector sub-graph, weak-connector sub-graph, finding number of incoming calls and outgoing calls of a particular user for a particular period of time from a large telephone network.

The telephone network can be represented as a graph (Rao et. al., 2014; Rao et. al., 2014-ICCIC; Rao et. al., 2014-ICHPCA; Rao et. al., 2015-ICRTC; Rao et. al., 2015-ICACNI) having nodes and these nodes are connected with a directed edge which shows calls have been made from a particular subscriber node to the pointed subscriber node. The edges are labeled by the number of calls made between these

*Figure 1. Weighted Telephone Graph **G** having 20 Vertices of Service Providers **A**, **B**, and **C***

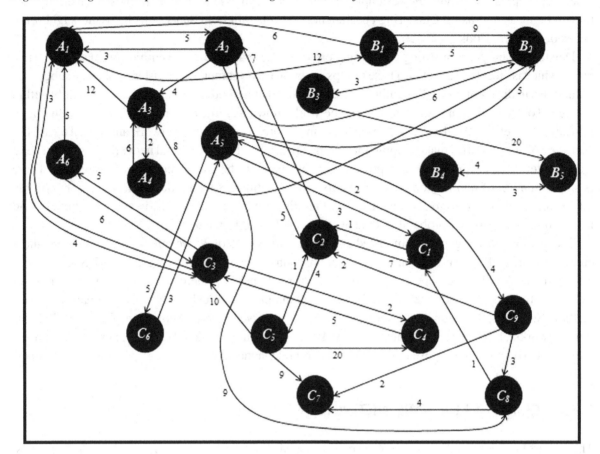

subscribers during the period. So as it can be represented as a weighted directed graph or weighted digraph which is depicted in "Figure 1". Its adjacency matrix mainly consists of zeros and non-zeros. The indication of non-zero is the weight where the total calls made from a subscriber to the particular subscriber node and the indication of zero means no calls have been made during a particular period of time. Hence the authors have represented the Telephone Graph as Weighted Directed Graph or Digraph.

The authors have proposed a telephone graph G (Kuramochi et. al., 2001; Rao et. al., 2015-ICRTC; Rao et. al., 2015- ICACNI) having twenty numbers of subscribers A_1, A_2, A_3, A_4, A_5, A_6, B_1, B_2, B_3, B_4, B_5, C_1, C_2, C_3, C_4, C_5, C_6, C_7, C_8, and C_9 from service providers A, B, and C depicted in "Figure 1". Its weighted adjacency matrix which is considered as the second dataset for the proposed algorithm which only consists of zeros and non-zeros as weights (i.e. number of calls made between the subscribers during a particular period of time) depicted in "Figure 9".

From the telephone graph depicted in "Figure 1", one can extract the following knowledge: extraction of weak connected sub-graph, extraction of strong connected sub-graph, and extraction of different service provider's sub-graph.

A weak connection or weak edge, where a communication is occurred in between two subscribers in one direction only is considered as weak communicators. From "Figure 1" participation of all twenty subscriber nodes depicted in "Figure 2". A strong connection or strong edge, where a communication is

Figure 2. Weak-Connected Telephone Graph of Figure 1

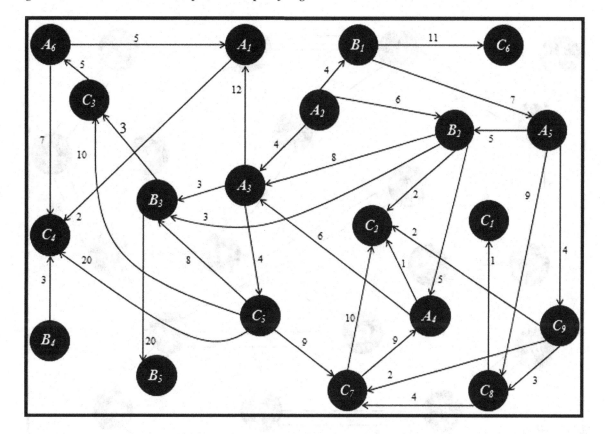

occurred in between two subscribers in both directions and considered as strong communicators. From "Figure 1" participation of nineteen subscriber nodes excluding C_9 subscriber node, depicted in "Figure 3". Three service providers sub-graph can be extracted since the service providers are A, B, and C respectively. The service providers A, B, and C's sub-graphs are depicted from "Figure 4" to "Figure 6" respectively.

One more important knowledge can be extracted from the telephone graph i.e. degree of a subscriber (phone number) which is the total number of incoming (in-degree) calls and outgoing (out-degree) calls for a particular period of time and depicted in "Figure 17". In this figure the last column **OG** is referred as total outgoing calls of all the subscribers. The outgoing calls of all the subscribers are 16, 23, 39, 10, 9, 8, 19, 7, 24, 21, ..., 11, 0, 8, 6, 12, 3, 11, 17, 19, and 24 respectively. Similarly the last row **IC** is referred as total incoming calls of all the subscribers. The incoming calls of all the subscribers are 0, 27, 11, 8, 14, 21, 6, 21, 17, 23,......, 25, 11, 10, 16, 8, 16, 26, 13, 6, and 15 respectively.

In service provider A's sub-graph, the subscriber node A_5 has no relations with remaining five subscriber nodes $\{A_1, A_2, A_3, A_4, A_6\}$. In service provider B's sub-graph, all the five subscriber nodes are related among themselves. Where as in service provider C's sub-graph, the subscriber nodes $\{C_1, C_2, C_3, C_4, C_5, C_7, C_8, C_9\}$ are related among themselves excluding the subscriber node C_6.

Figure 3. Strong-Connected Telephone Graph of Figure 1

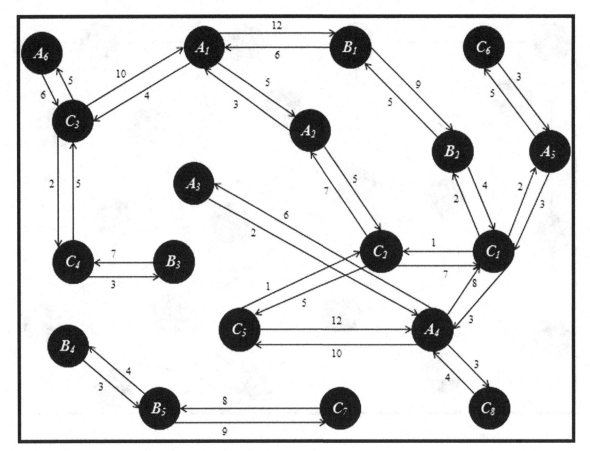

3. PROPOSED ALGORITHM

The authors have proposed an algorithm for mining weak and strong connected sub-graphs, different network provider's sub-graphs, as well as number of incoming and outgoing calls of every subscriber from a weighted telephone graph.

3.1 Algorithm for Mining Knowledge from Weighted Telephone Graph

```
Algorithm Mining_Weighted_Telephone_Graph()
Algorithm Convention (Horowitz et. al., 2008; Lipschutz, 2004)
// Global Declarations
serdata.txt: Text file contains total number of service providers, service
provider code, number of subscribers, and subscriber codes.
wtdata.txt: Text file contains number of calls among the subscribers as edge
data.
n: To assign number of service providers.
SPA[n][2]: To hold service provider code and number of subscribers of order
nX2.
```

Figure 4. Service Provider A's Sub-Graph

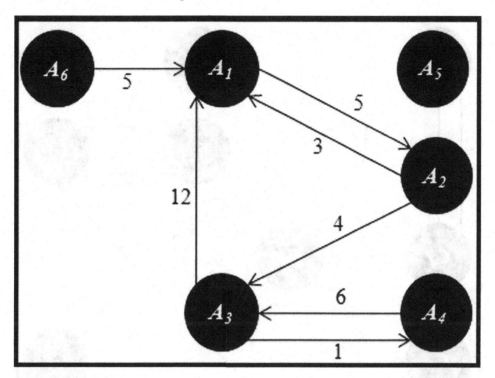

Figure 5. Service Provider B's Sub-Graph

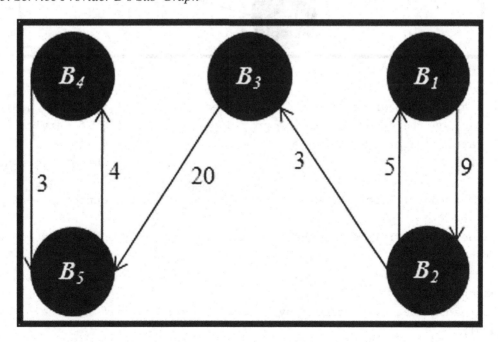

Figure 6. Service Provider C's Sub-Graph

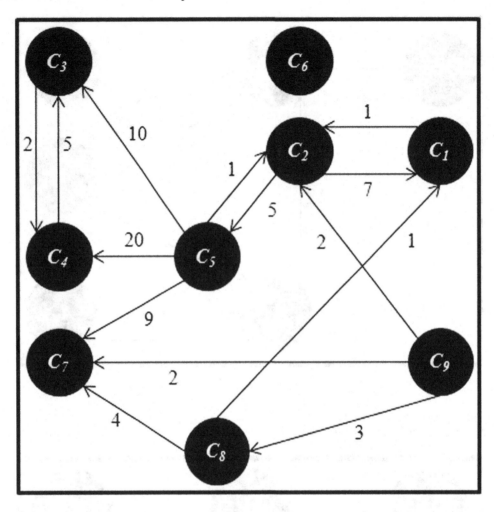

```
Order: To assign the order of weighted adjacency matrix of telephone graph.
Size: To assign the order of service provider for displaying of service pro-
vider adjacency matrix.
wmatrix[Order][Order]: To store the adjacency matrix of weighted telephone
graph.
weak[Order][Order]: To store the adjacency matrix of weak connected telephone
graph.
strong[Order][Order]: To store the adjacency matrix of strong connected tele-
phone graph.
{
    Order:=0;
    // to read number of service providers from 'serdata.txt' file
    read(n);
    for i:=1to n do
```

```
    {
        // to read service provider code from 'serdata.txt' file
            read (SPA[i][1]);
        // to read number of subscribers from 'serdata.txt' file
            read (SPA[i][2]);
            Order:= Order + SPA[i][2];
    }
Weight_Matrix_Creation(wmatrix, Order);
size:=0;
file_name:= "Sub";
for i:=1 to m do
{
    file_name:= file_name + SPA[i][1] + ".txt" ;
    size:= size + SPA[i][2];
    Write_Subscriber_Matrix(wmatrix, size, file_name);
    file_name:= "Sub";
}
Weak_Connected_Matrix(wmatrix, Order);
Strong_Connected_Matrix(wmatrix, Order);
// to write Weak Connected Adjacency Matrix
Write_Matrix(weak, Order, file_name);
// to write Strong Connected Adjacency Matrix
Write_Matrix(strong, Order, file_name);
// to count total number of Outgoing and Incoming Calls
Outgoing_Incoming_Counting(wmatrix, Order);
// to write Weighted Telephone Adjacency Matrix with Outgoing and Incoming
Calls
Write_Matrix(wmatrix, Order, file_name);
}
```

3.2 Procedure for Weight Matrix Creation

```
Procedure Weight_Matrix_Creation(mat, Order)
mat[Order][Order]:To store the weighted adjacency matrix.
{
    // to open file "wtdata.txt" for reading purpose
    open("wtdata.txt");
    for i:=1 to Order do
    {
      for j:=1 to Order do
      {
        // to read edges from the file "wtdata.txt" which only contains 0s &
non-zeros (weights)
        read(mat[i][j]);
```

```
      }
    }
      close("wtdata.txt");
}
```

3.3 Procedure for Write Matrix

```
Procedure Write_Matrix(mat, Order, file_name)
mat[Order][Order]: To store the weighted adjacency matrix.
file_name: It holds the name of data file for creation.
outdeg[Order], indeg[Order]: Global arrays hold the outgoing and incoming
calls.
{
   // to open file file_name for writing purpose
   open (file_name);
   for i:=1 to Order do
   {
       for j:=1 to Order do
       {
          // to write in the file file_name
          write(mat[i][j]);
       }
       if (file_name = "matrix.txt")
       then
       {
          // to write outgoing calls in the file
          write(outdeg[i]);
       }
   }
       for i:=1 to Order do
       {
          // to write incoming calls in the file
          write(indeg[i]);
       }
   close(file_name);
}
```

3.4 Procedure for Counting Outgoing and Incoming Calls

```
Procedure Outgoing_Incoming_Counting(mat, Order)
mat[Order][Order]:To store the weighted adjacency matrix.
// Global Declarations
outdeg[Order]: To assign total outgoing calls.
```

```
indeg[Order]: To assign total incoming calls.
{
    for i:=1 to Order do
    {
      outdeg[i]:=0;   indeg[i]:=0;
      for j:=1 to Order do
      {
        if (mat[i][j] ≠ 0) then outdeg[i]:= outdeg[i] + mat[i][j];
        if (mat[j][i] ≠ 0) then indeg[i]:= indeg[i] + mat[j][i];
      }
    }
}
```

3.5 Procedure for Writing of Subscriber Matrices

```
Procedure Write_Subscriber_Matrix(mat, size, file_name)
mat[Order][Order]:To store the weighted adjacency matrix.
file_name: To store the name of subscriber data file for creation.
{
    // to open file file_name for writing purpose
    open(file_name);
    x:= 0; // x is a static kind
    count:= x;
    for i:=count to size do
    {
        for j:=count to size do
        {
          // to write in the file file_name
          write(mat[i][j]);
        }
          x:=x+1;
    }
      x:=x-1;
      close(file_name);
}
```

3.6 Procedure for Creation of Weak Connected Matrix

```
Procedure Weak_Connected_Matrix(mat, Order)
mat[Order][Order]: To store the weighted adjacency matrix.
{
    for i:=1 to Order do
    {
```

```
    for j:=1 to Order do
    {
        // to select weak connected subscriber and assign in weak[ ][ ]
        if (mat[i][j] ≠ 0 AND mat[j][i] ≠ 0) then continue;
          else if (mat[j][i] ≠ 0) then continue;
            else if (mat[i][j] ≠ 0) then weak[i][j]:=mat[i][j];
    }
    }
}
```

3.7 Procedure for Creation of Strong Connected Matrix

```
Procedure Strong_Connected_Matrix(mat, Order)
mat[Order][Order]: To store the weighted adjacency matrix.
{
    for i:=1 to Order do
    {
        for j:=1 to Order do
        { // to select strong connected subscriber and assign in strong[ ][ ]
            if (mat[i][j] ≠ 0 AND mat[j][i] ≠ 0) then
            {
              strong[i][j]:=mat[i][j];
              strong[j][i]:=mat[j][i];
            }
        }
    }
}
```

The proposed algorithm has six procedures. First it reads the 1st dataset file '*serdata.txt*' which contains total number of service providers, service provider code, number of subscribers, and subscriber codes. The total number of service providers data is assigned to 'n'. The service provider code is assigned to the matrix SPA[][1] and the total number of subscribers is assigned to the matrix SPA[][2]. Now the order of weighted adjacency matrix is calculated by using SPA[][2] and is assigned to 'Order'. By using 'Order' the initial form of wmatrix[Order][Order], weak[Order][Order], and strong[Order][Order] are created.

The procedure Weight_Matrix_Creation(wmatrix, Order) reads the 2nd dataset file '*wtdata.txt*' which contains number of calls among the subscribers as edge data i.e. non-zeros(number of calls between the subscribers), and make these data assigned to the matrix wmatrix[Order][Order].

The procedure Write_Subscriber_Matrix(wmatrix, size, file_name) for formation of 'n' service providers adjacency matrices and writes in the corresponding text files as results.

The procedures Weak_Connected_Matrix(wmatrix,Order) and Strong_Connected_Matrix(wmatrix, Order) for creation of weak and strong adjacency matrices, and is assigned to the matrices weak[Order][Order] and strong[Order][Order].

The procedure Outgoing_Incoming_Counting(wmatrix, Order) for counting of outgoing and incoming calls and make it assigned to the arrays outdeg[Order] and indeg[Order] respectively. Its result is depicted in "Figure 17" of example in experiment.

Finally the procedure Write_Matrix() is called for three times i.e. Write_Matrix(weak, Order, File_Name), Write_Matrix(strong, Order, File_Name), and Write_Matrix(wmatrix, Order, File_Name) for writing the weak adjacency matrix, strong adjacency matrix, and weighted outgoing and incoming adjacency matrix in the corresponding text files as results. For experimental result, the example telephone graph depicted in "Figure 7" has five service providers namely A, B, C, D, and E respectively. The weak and strong adjacency matrices are written in two text files and depicted in "Figure 10" and "Figure 11" respectively. Similarly five number of text files are created for five service providers successfully and are depicted from "Figure 12" to "Figure 16".

4. EXPERIMENTAL RESULTS

The authors have evaluated the performance of the proposed algorithm with one example which has been explained below. The algorithm was written in C++ and compiled with TurboC++ and run on Intel Core I5-3230M CPU +2.60 GHz Laptop with 4GB memory running MS-Windows 7.

4.1 Example

The Weighted Telephone Graph G with **127** vertices and each vertex is considered as subscriber from the service providers A, B, C, D, and E which is depicted in "Figure 7". The service provider A, D, and E have 24 subscribers each, service provider B has 32 subscribers, and service provider C has 23 subscribers respectively.

To implement this graph as example, the authors have created two datasets namely "Tel_Sub2.Txt" and "Weight2.Txt". The 1st dataset "Tel_Sub2.Txt" which contains 'Number of Service Providers ', 'Service Providers Code', 'Number of Subscribers', and 'Subscriber Codes' and depicted in "Figure 8". Similarly the 2nd dataset "Weight2.Txt" which contains all the one twenty seven subscribers' edge data and depicted in "Figure 9" since the Telephone Graph is considered as the weighted one which is depicted in "Figure 7".

4.2 Result

Upon inputting 1st and 2nd dataset "Tel_Sub2.Txt" and "Weight2.Txt" in place of 'serdata.txt' and 'wtdata.txt' to the algorithm, the total number of service providers data is 5 and assigned to 'n'. The service provider codes i.e. {1, 2, 3, 4, 5} is assigned to the matrix SPA[][1] and the total number of subscribers i.e. {24, 32, 23, 24, 24} is assigned to the matrix SPA[][2]. Now the order of weighted adjacency matrix is calculated by using SPA[][2] as 127 and assigned to 'Order'. By using 'Order' the initial form of wmatrix[Order][Order], weak[Order][Order], and strong[Order][Order] are created.

The procedure Weight_Matrix_Creation(wmatrix, Order) reads the 2nd dataset file 'wtdata.txt' which contains number of calls among the subscribers as edge data and assigned to the matrix wmatrix[Order][Or-

*Figure 7. Weighted Telephone Graph **G** having 127 Vertices of Service Providers **A**, **B**, **C**, **D**, and **E***

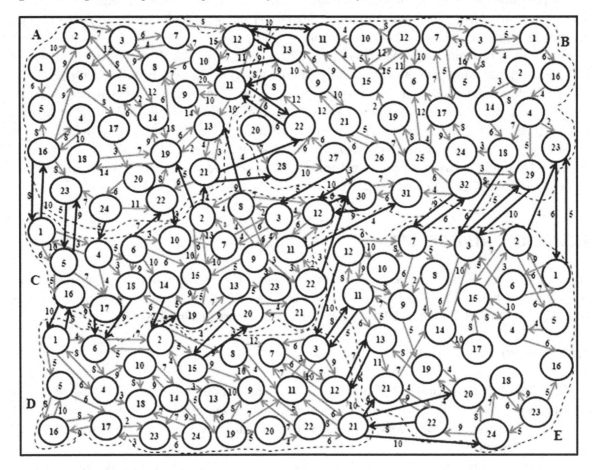

Figure 8. Tel_Sub2.Txt

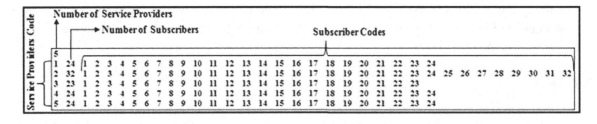

der]. The procedures Weak_Connected_Matrix(wmatrix, Order) and Strong_Connected_Matrix(wmatrix, Order) are called for creation of weak[Order][Order] and strong[Order][Order] matrices which hold the adjacency matrices of weak and strong sub-graphs. By calling procedure for weak sub-graph as Write_Matrix(weak, Order, "weak.txt") and for strong sub-graph as Write_Matrix(weak, Order, "strong.txt") which successfully writes the weak and strong adjacency matrices in the respective text files "weak.txt" and "strong.txt" respectively and depicted in "Figure 10" and "Figure 11".

Figure 9. Weight2.Txt

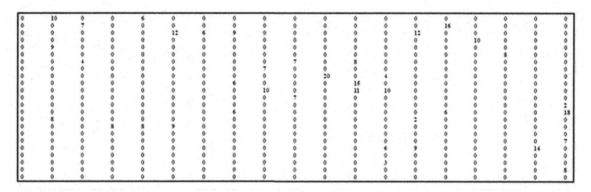

Figure 10. Weak Connected Adjacency Matrix

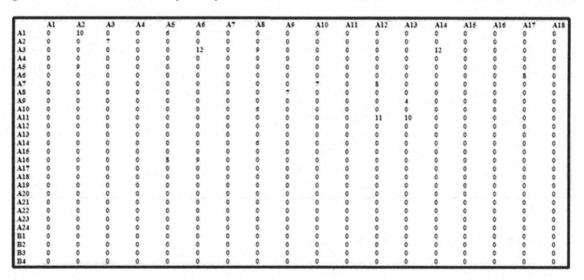

Figure 11. Strong Connected Adjacency Matrix

Figure 12. Service Provider A's Adjacency Matrix

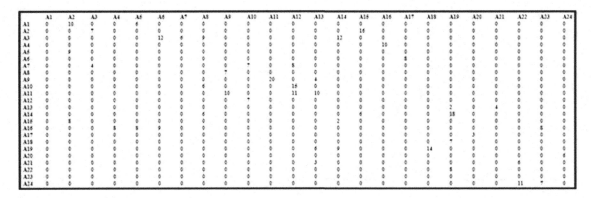

Figure 13. Service Provider B's Adjacency Matrix

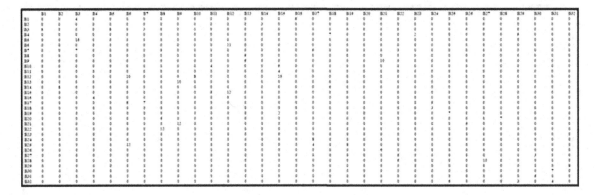

Figure 14.Service Provider C's Adjacency Matrix

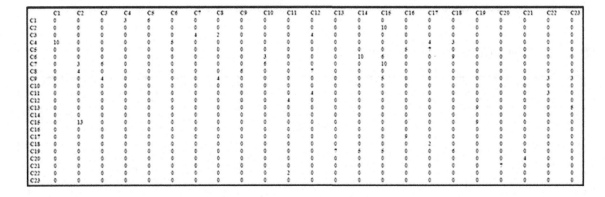

By calling Write_Subscriber_Matrix(wmatrix, size, file_name) 'n' times which writes five service providers adjacency matrices in five text files namely SubA.txt, SubB.txt, SubC.txt, SubD.txt, and SubE. txt successfully, and are depicted from "Figure 12" to "Figure 16" respectively.

Figure 15. Service Provider D's Adjacency Matrix

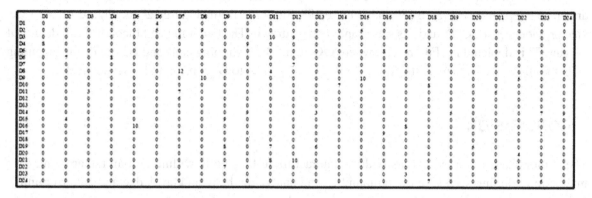

Figure 16. Service Provider E's Adjacency Matrix

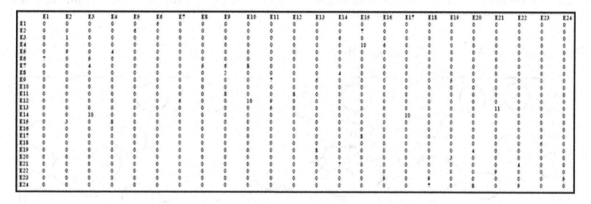

Figure 17. Adjacency Matrix of Outgoing-Incoming Call Details

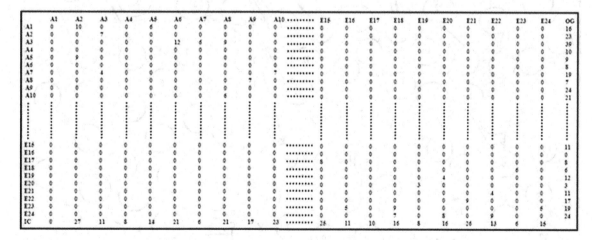

From "Figure 10" and "Figure 11", the weak-connected and strong-connected sub-graphs can be drawn and depicted in "Figure 18" and "Figure 19". Similarly from "Figure 12" to "Figure 16", the service providers A, B, C, D, and E's sub-graphs can be drawn. The Outgoing and Incoming call details of "Figure 7" is depicted in "Figure 17", where **OG** stands for Outgoing calls and **IC** stands for Incoming calls for all the subscribers A_1 to A_{24}, B_1 to B_{32}, C_1 to C_{23}, D_1 to D_{24}, and E_1 to E_{24} respectively.

5. CONCLUSION

The authors have observed that individuals interact more frequently within a group rather than group interaction. Finding such type of communities and analyzing, helps in knowledge and pattern mining. This chapter has focused on methods to study a real world social network communications using the basic concepts of graph theory. Two examples from telephone network have been considered. The authors have proposed an algorithm for extraction of different network provider's sub-graph, weak and

Figure 18. Weak-Connected Telephone Graph of Figure 7

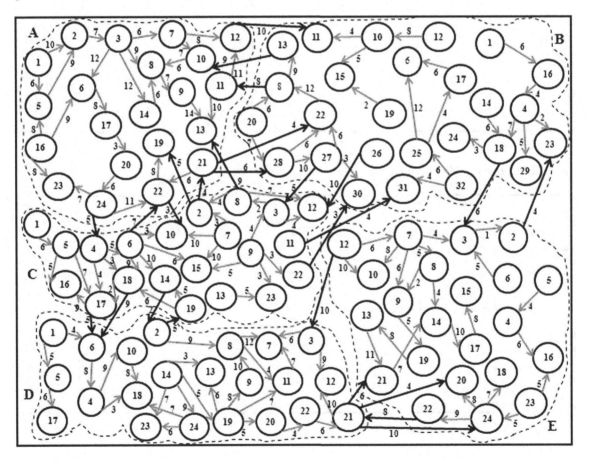

Figure 19. Strong-Connected Telephone Graph of Figure 7

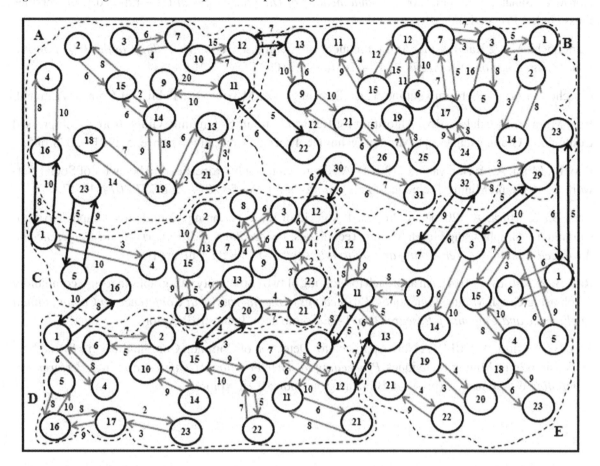

strong connected sub-graph as well as the outgoing and incoming calls for a particular period which has direct application for studying the human behaviour in telephone network. The authors have verified one example for the proposed algorithm and implemented in C++ programming language. The obtained results have been satisfactory.

REFERENCES

Cook, D. J., & Holder, L. B. (2007). *Mining Graph Data, Electrical Engineering and Computer Science, Washington State University*. Pullman, WA: John Wiley & Sons, Inc.

Girvan, M., & Newman, M. E. J. (2002). Community structure in social and bi-ological networks. *Proceedings of the National Academy of Sciences of the United States of America, 99*(12), 7821–7826. doi:10.1073/pnas.122653799 PMID:12060727

Horowitz, Sahani, & Mehta. (2008). *Fundamentals of Data Structures in C++* (2nd ed.). Universities Press (India) Private Limited.

Kuramochi, M., & Karypis, G. (2001). Frequent subgraph discovery. *Proceedings of the 2001 International Conference on Data Mining*, 313–320. doi:10.1109/ICDM.2001.989534

Lipschutz, S. (2004). Schaum's outline of Data Structures. Tata McGraw-Hill Publishing Company Limited.

Rao, Mitra, & Mondal. (2015). Algorithm for Retrieval of Sub-Community Graph from a Compressed Community Graph using Graph Mining Technique. Procedia Computer Science, 57(2015), 678-685.

Rao, B., Mitra, A., & Narayana, U. (2014). An approach to study properties and behavior of Social Network using Graph Mining Techniques. *Proceedings of DIGNATE 2014:ETEECT 2014*, 13-17.

Rao, B., & Mitra, A. (2015). A Proposed Algorithm for Partitioning Community Graph into Sub-Community Graphs using Graph Mining Techniques. *Proceedings of 3rd International Conference on Advanced Computing, Networking and Informatics* (pp. 3-15). KIIT University.

Rao, B., & Mitra, A. (2014). An approach to Merging of two community sub-graphs to form a community graph using Graph Mining Techniques. *Proceedings of the International Conference on Computational Intelligence and Computing Research* (pp. 1-7). Coimbatore, India: IEEEXplore.

Rao, B., & Mitra, A. (2014). A New Approach for Detection of Common Communities in a Social Network using Graph Mining Techniques. *Proceedings of the International Conference on High Performance Computing & Application* (pp. 1-6). Bhubaneswar, India: IEEEXplore.

Chapter 4
A Dynamic and Context-Aware Social Network Approach for Multiple Criteria Decision Making Through a Graph-Based Knowledge Learning

Alessandro Di Stefano
University of Catania, Italy

Aurelio La Corte
University of Catania, Italy

Marialisa Scatà
University of Catania, Italy

Evelina Giacchi
University of Catania, Italy

ABSTRACT

Complexity and dynamics characterize a social network and its processes. Social network analysis and graph theory could be used to describe and explore the connectedness among the different entities. Network dynamics further increases the complexity, as each entity with its personal knowledge, cognitive and reasoning capabilities, thinks, decides and acts in a social network, characterized by the heterogeneity of nodes and ties among them. Social network analysis becomes critical to the decision-making process, where a network node will consider both its personal knowledge and the influences received from its neighbors. Network dynamics and the node's context-awareness affect the relationships among criteria, modifying their ranking in a multiple criteria decision-making process, and hence the decision itself. Thus, the main aim has been to model the decision-making process within a social network, considering both context-awareness and network dynamics. Moreover, we have introduced a process of knowledge-transfer, where the criteria are represented by the knowledge-related values.

DOI: 10.4018/978-1-5225-2814-2.ch004

1. INTRODUCTION

One of the most important challenges of future ICT is to develop innovative methodologies, tools and algorithms to extract knowledge from several and heterogeneous sources, linked to multiple types of data. The Big Data revolution allows to look at many perspectives of single or correlated aspects, and it raises the issue of unifying these heterogenous resources. The challenge is to combine relevant information in the most efficient way and obtain a mining process, leading to a comprehensive understanding and a real knowledge extraction. The extraction of knowledge is strictly related to the value it can generate in a network, other than its rate of growth. A key aspect in this future ICT approach is based on adopting a bio-inspired approach applied to social networks, making nodes increasingly more smart and human, by introducing cognitive modules and making them able to decide and make inferences using context-aware strategies according to the specific context. Nodes are part of a complex social network, whose dynamics, influences and contagion processes affect the decision process of the single nodes and communites they belong to. The ubiquitous and dynamic nature of the network requires smart entities, which can decide using context-aware strategies according to the specific context (Scatà et. al., 2014).

To better analyze, in a deeper way, each process in a social network, there is a need to mine knowledge from variours sources, studying the phenomena occuring within a social network. Each process is characterized by a number of entities, which gives a contribute in order to establish the entire path that forms the whole system. Each entity, interacting through its relationships in the social network, is inevitably influenced in its opinion and actions as a consequence (Asavathiratham et. al. 2001; Grabisch & Rusinowska 2010; Barjis et. al., 2011; Pachidi et. al., 2014). As reported in (López-Pintado, 2008), *"individual decisions are often influenced by the decisions of other individuals"*. Without considering any interaction, nodes easily rank criteria in terms of importance following an individual cognitive model (Korhonen & Wallenius 1997). Therefore, each individual cannot be considered as an isolated entity, since the behavior of each entity is the result of the interactions between its preferences and the dynamic nature of relationships within the social network, impacting every individual's decision, inserting it in a complex and dynamic social perspective (Pentland 2014). Social phenomena are characterized by the influence, which is related to every process inside the network, such as innovation diffusion, cultural events, and each flow which involves entities. As a consequence of the influence exercised by the nodes in the network, the preferences of each node could change during the decision-making process bringing to different decisions over time.

As highlighted by a vast literature, social networking plays a key role in the decision-making process (Kempe et. al., 2015; Anagnostopoulos et. al., 2015). Some works have focused on the importance of influence inside social networks. In (kempe et. al., 2015), the authors have faced the issue of influence maximization in viral marketing aplications. Recently, in (Anagnostopoulos et. al., 2015), it has been presented a model for the diffusion of competing alternatives in a social network, where nodes decide among different alternatives.

Social network analysis (SNA) is intended to deepen the nature of nodes and ties, the actions and interactions between them and all the features and behaviors emerging from the combination of both aspects. Nodes interact and influence each other and, most importantly, these interactions are not only among connected neighbors, but analyzing the network structure and the dynamics, it emerges how the influence runs through the ties connecting nodes, with regards to several phenomena at a population scale, such as diseases, smoking, happiness, etc. (Christakis & Fowler, 2013). Then, network thinking is central in the analysis of contagion processes (Vespignani et. al., 2009). SNA methodologies allow to describe and study the relationships among individuals and how theses interconnections can drive the processes and phenomena inside the network. Thus, SNA is a key analytical tool for analyzing the dynamics and diffusion of social behaviors, allowing a better understanding and unveiling the operation of highly connected systems and entities, which form a complex social structure (Aggarwal, 2011). In terms of network theory, a social network is composed by different parts, including entities (actors, values, sentiments, ideas, etc.), represented by nodes, relationships among them, referred as edges, links, ties or connections, and aggregations, referred as dyads, triads, and clusters (Cioffi-Revilla, 2014; Bottazzi et. al., 2007). The resulting structures are complex graphs connecting social contacts. Graph theory allows describing the relationships between nodes, using metrics, such as centrality measures (betweenness, degree, closeness, eigenvector, etc.), clustering coefficients and community detection algorithms, etc. (Fortunato, 2010; Wasserman & Faust, 1994).

In terms of decision-making modeling, the relationships among nodes and the structural properties of the network may affect the node's decisions also more than the individual's features, if considered isolated. Some works have highlighted the importance of other social mechanisms, constituted by social selection or homophily and influence (McPherson et. al. 2001; Di Stefano et. al. 2015; Scatà et. al., 2016). Homophily is the phenomenon for which "birds of a feather flock together" and it derives from the principle that "similarity breeds connection" or, in other words, humans tend to associate to and cooperate with someone else who has similar characteristics (Di Stefano et. al. 2015; Scatà et. al., 2016). Instead, influence is the tendency for characteristics and behaviors to spread through social ties such that friends increasingly resemble one another over time, and this influence may affect the choices (Lewis et. al. 2012). In (Cacioppo et. al., 2009; Christakis & Fowler, 2007) an empirical analysis using social network data has demonstrated how the social influence plays an important role in the spread or contagion of some behaviors and psychological states. The social contagion process is able to amplify the spread of information in a social network, and this is the reason why understanding the mechanics of social contagion is crucial to predict how far it will spread and with what intensity. Therefore, SNA is functional to the decision-making process, as it allows to discover social patterns, behaviors, and structural properties which influence the strategies and the decisions of the single node, as a connected entity, and of the clusters it belongs to. In this context, decision-making process plays a central role, because the network node, as a result of each change of the network, ranging from its structure to its security, has to take decisions that will affect current and future network processes. In a social context, where a node, the decision maker (DM), is not alone, a decision will be the output of the system that will consider not only the personal capabilities of the node, but also the influences from its neighboring nodes. These influences will alter the stimulus perception in a way that can be positive or negative, leading to a knowledge and a context-awareness that can be close to or far from reality. The decision's criteria will be affected by these dynamics, modifying its relations, both in terms of type and importance, according to time, decision's context and awareness. The decision-maker, both a human and a network node, makes choices among a set of alternatives, considered in different contexts and conditions. Thus, a decision is the result of a choice of alternatives based on a set of criteria to achieve one or more objectives. In a decision-making process, the set of criteria plays a central and important role, allowing to evaluate and comparing potential actions according to a well-defined perspective and this evaluation has to consider all the influences, effects and attributes linked to the considered point of view. The set of criteria can be composed of one element (mono-criterion) or more (multiple-criteria). In this chapter a multiple criteria decision-making model is proposed since the monocriterion analysis is limited, and in most of cases, unreal and in contrast with the paradigm of the decision process itself, that is the comparison of different perspectives, emphasizing the advantages and drawbacks of each single alternative. For this reason, Multiple Criteria Decision Analysis (MCDA) has gained a central role in the decision theory, thanks to its versatility to solve, rank, sort and choice problems. Due to the heterogeneous and different perspectives of a social context and to the large amount of information, the decision becomes dynamic, time- and context-dependent, following the evolution and the adaptation process of the node and the network itself (Giacchi et. al., 2014).

The main aim of the proposed model is to apply analytical tools provided by the social network analysis to multiple criteria decision-making processes, helping to better understand and to correctly model the decision making process within a social network (Giacchi et. al., 2014). The node's context-awareness, together with the time and the decision's context, plays a central role in the decision-making process, modifying the position, in a scale of importance and centrality, of a criterion with respect to each other, leading to a particular choice.

For the development of each decision making process the context in which the decision is taken has a key role. In this sense, decisions depend not only on the preferences of the decision maker, but also on the context in which the decision making process takes place and, more specifically, on the context-awareness of the individual. In particular, if the same decision making process is considered in two different contexts, the decisions of two processes could not be the same even if the processes are equivalent. This explains why many scientists have addressed their attention to the importance of the context in each process and to give a suitable definition. So, among the multitude definitions of context, for the description of the presented model, it is used the one given in (Abowd et al. 1999), where context is defined as *"any information that can be used to characterise the situation of an entity"*.

In addition to the context, another fundamental feature that has to be considered for the development of a decision making process is represented by the social influence mechanism. Several works focus their attention on the effects that the social network as well as other individuals to which the decision maker is connected, has on the development of individual processes (Hoede & Baker, 1982; Rusinowska & de Swart, 2006; Grabisch and Rusinowska, 2010). Due to the role and the importance of the context and the mechanism of social influence in each process, a context-aware multiple criteria decision making model is proposed, in order to analyze how the decision taken by a node within a social network varies dynamically.

In the era of innovation and technology advance and in line with future ICT, information and knowledge play a key role in any process regarding each aspect of the social development. The main aim for all the countries is to become "knowledge-based societies" in continuous development, thanks to the limitless knowledge growth which generate an incommensurable value. Furthermore, the evolution of ICT generates no boundaries on when, where and how knowledge has to be transferred among individuals.

Knowledge has a key role in a social network and it can be shared, transferred and exchanged (Graham et. al., 2006; Luo et. Al., 2015). Knowledge sharing corresponds to the provision of information, a know-how of a task among individuals inside and outside a community (Cummings, 2004). Knowledge transfer includes two phases: the sharing of knowledge from a source and its acquisition from a recipient. Knowledge exchange involves both knowledge sharing, by which a source provides knowledge, and knowledge seeking, where a receiver searches for knowledge from sources (Wang & Noe, 2010). Various works have analyzed the processes related to the knowledge in a network by using different views (Lambiotte & Panzarasa, 2009; Tasselli, 2015; Hatak & Roessl, 2015). By considering the concept of knowledge, nodes can decide individually with whom transfer it. Using a context-aware decision making perspective and considering each single node as a decision maker that has to decide in a particular context whether accept the transfer or not, it is interesting to understand how and why certain mechanisms and behavioral patterns arise.

In section 5 of the chapter, it is proposed and modeled a process of knowledge transfer using a context-aware decision making perspective (Giacchi et. al., 2014) in which, the acceptance or rejection of knowledge from one of its neighbors is performed by a node evaluating some criteria, i.e. knowledge distance and confidence, dynamically updated at each time step on the basis of the quality of the knowledge transferred (see Section 5). If the knowledge transfer is realized and the receiver node accepts the transfer, it will perform a control mechanism, resulting in a knowledge learning process.

The chapter is organized as it follows. The next section gives a brief overview of the multiple criteria decision analysis, social network analysis and graph theory. Section 3 reviews the concept of context-awareness in social networks. Then, section 4 constitutes the core part of the chapter, where the model, the role of context-awareness in the MCDM model, the dynamic criteria interaction and the decision-making model are explained. Section 5 includes the concept of knowledge transfer and the graph-based knowledge learning. Finally, section 6 includes conclusions and future works.

2. MULTIPLE CRITERIA DECISION ANALYSIS, SOCIAL NETWORK ANALYSIS AND GRAPH THEORY

2.1 Multiple Criteria Decision Analysis (MCDA)

The decision-making process has been subject of study of a lot of disciplines, from psychology to mathematics, in order to have a model that would serve to represent the individual or group decision-making process. The decision-maker, both a human or a network node, makes choices among a set of alternatives, considered in different contexts and conditions. As defined in (Wang & Ruhe, 2007), a decision d is the result of a choice of an alternative aj belonging to a set of n alternatives $A = \{a_1, a_2, ..., a_n\}$, based on a set of k criteria $C = \{c_1, c_2, ..., c_k\}$ to achieve one or more objectives. Mathematically, it can be represented as follows:

$$d = f(A, C) = f : A x C \rightarrow A$$

So, in the process, the set C of criteria plays a central and important role, because *"a criterion is a tool constructed for evaluating and comparing potential actions according to a point of view which must be well-defined. This evaluation must take into account, for each action a, all the pertinent effects or attributes linked to the point of view considered. It is denoted by c(a) and called the performance of a according to this criterion"* (Roy, 2005). The set C can be composed of one element (mono-criterion) or more (multiple-criteria). But the mono-criterion analysis is limited, and in most of cases, unreal and in contrast with the paradigm of the decision process itself, which regards the comparison of different perspectives, that can emphasize the pros and the cons of each single alternative (Greco et. al., 2005).

Instead, Multiple Criteria Decision Analysis (MCDA) has gained a central role in the decision sciences, thanks to its versatility to solve, rank, sort and choice problems (Greco et. al., 2005). Due to the heterogeneous and different perspectives present in a social context and to the large amount of information, the decision becomes dynamic, time- and context- dependent, following the evolution and the adaptation process of the node and the network itself.

To better represent a real decision making problem, the decision maker evaluates each alternative according to a set of two or more criteria. A criterion *c* is defined as *"a tool constructed for evaluating and comparing potential actions according to a point of view which must be (as far as it is possible) well-defined"*. The main function of each criterion is to stress the advantages or drawbacks of each alternative among which the decision maker has to take a decision. So, considering only one decision criterion cannot be helpful for the decision maker and cannot represent the intrinsic paradigm of the decision making process itself. This explains why for our model we decide to consider and use the analytical tools of Multiple Criteria Decision Making (MCDM). To give a more rigorous definition, in a MCDM problem (Figueira et al. 2005) a set of alternatives $A = \{a_1, a_2, ..., a_m\}$ composed of m elements is evaluated on the basis of a set of n criteria $C = \{c_1, c_2, ..., c_n\}$ that has to be exhaustive (all the criteria necessary to the evaluation of the alternatives have to be considered), cohesive (if alternative a is at least as good as b for all except that for one criterion c_h and a is better than b for c_h, then alternative a should be preferred to b) and non-redundant (the elimination of one criterion from the set C makes it not exhaustive and cohesive).

Using the analytical tools of MCDM it is possible to solve three decision problems:

1. Choice: the decision maker has to choose among the alternatives one or more elements which represent for it the best ones;
2. Ranking: the decision maker orders all the alternatives from the best to the worst;
3. Sorting: the decision maker initially defines a set of classes preferentially ordered. Each alternative is assigned to one or more contiguous classes.

Considering the evaluation of alternatives, the only relation that it is possible to extract is the dominance one. The dominance, in case of several criteria, cannot be helpful for the decision itself, because it does not provide a satisfactory accuracy in the problem handling. Infact, comparing two alternatives a and b, a could be preferred to b considering a subset of criteria. On the contrary, b could be preferred to a if the rest of criteria is taken into account. This is why it becomes necessary to aggregate the evaluation of the alternatives. In MCDM there are three main ways to aggregate the evaluation (Keeney & Raiffa, 1993; Brans & Vincke, 1985; Figueira et. al., 2013).

Specific parameters such as weights of criteria, marginal value functions and threshold are used for aggregation in the first two ways listed before. Such parameters can be obtained in a direct o in an indirect way. In the former case, the DM can directly recognize a value to be assigned to each parameter. In the latter case, the DM points out some preferences on reference alternatives. In such a way, the parameters close to the selected preferences can be elicited. The indirect technique is the most used method in practice (Jacquet-Lagrèze & Siskos, 2001). In addition to the indirect methods, also called Compatible Model, the Robust Ordinal Regression (ROR) builds a necessary and possible preference relation (*a* is at least as good as *b* for all or for at least one compatible model) with the preferences provided by the DM.

2.2 Social Network Analysis and Graph Theory

As said in Section 1, SNA is a key methodology to analyze the relationships among individuals, the dynamics of processes and phenomena inside the network. SNA produces a different perspective, where the relational ties among actors within the network are more important than the attributes of actors.

The study of social networks, primarily designed on the basis of the interactions between the different actors, is also a social influence analysis, as different interacting actors often influence one another in terms of their behavior. SNA means a study of network in terms of structure, links, relationships, and for this aim of understanding networks, graph theory helps to develop a language for talking about the typical structural features of networks (Easley & Kleinberg, 2010). SNA is functional to the decision-making process, as it allows to discover social patterns, behaviors, and structural properties which influence the strategies and the decisions of the single node, as a connected entity, and of the clusters it belongs to.

To apply the complex systems approach and discovering social patterns, behaviors and properties influencing and eventually improving the decision making process is useful to introduce as background overview of graph theory. As defined in (Easley & Kleinberg, 2010) a graph is a way of specifying relationships among a collection of elements. It consists of a set of nodes, in pairs connected by links, in general called edges. To investigate about complex systems, first it requires to know how components of a graph interact with each other. Two nodes are neighbors if they are connected by an edge. Typically, nodes of a graph are drawn using a little circle, whereas an edge with a line connecting each pair of nodes. In some settings, an edge coud be represented with a simmetric relationship or an asymmetric reletionship, which representation conceived by the type of the graph: directed or undirected. A network represented by the graph theory, the number of nodes, or N, represents the number of components in the system. N is the size of the network, while L the number of links, representing the total number of interactions between the nodes. Links are rarely labeled, as they can be identified through the nodes they connect. Graphs, appearing in many scientific domains, are useful for the network structures, since they serve as mathematical models, to represent how things are either phisically or logically linked to one another. In particular, for the aim of this work, it is taken into account a broad class of graph structure, that is the social networks, in which nodes are people or groups of people, and the edges represent some social interaction. Graph theory is a systematic and logical approach that can be used to model various systems and can be employed for evaluation of the structural properties of the networks to the aim of analyze the impact on decisions. This theory provide concepts, such as paths, cycles and components, as showed in (Axelrod, 2015), that are useful to understanding the interconnections whitin the network structures. Graph theory, formulates models of knowledge of network structures, in environments where people's decisions affect each other's outcomes. As underlined in (Walker, 2013), the graph theory is able to take potential for a huge of applications, because it provides explicit representation of spatial phenomena such as connectivity to reflect the impact of the decisions within a spatial social context. For this reason, a social network is modeled as a graph $G (V, E)$, where V represents a set of users and the edge set $E = \{(x,y) \mid x,y \in V\}$ represents relationship among them.

3. CONTEXT-AWARENESS IN SOCIAL NETWORKS

As stated in Section 1, one of the main features that influences the development of a decision making process is represented by the context. Several attempts to formalize a general definition of context have been made. Starting from the one given in (Schilit et al., 1994) where context depends on the location, nearby person, host or objects and their evolution over time, there is not yet a general and unique context definition, even if a lot of definition are present in the scientific literature (Brown et al., 1997; Liu et al., 2011; Ahn & Kim, 2006). Most of researchers accept the definition given in (Abowd et al., 1999) where context is defined as *"any information that can be used to characterise the situation of an entity. An entity is a person, place or object that is considered relevant to the interaction between a user and an application, including the user and applications themselves"*. As a consequence, other two definitions can be given: context-aware and context-awareness. A system is context-aware *"if it uses context to provide relevant information and/or services to the user, where relevancy depends on the users's task"*. Whereas context-awareness is defined as the ability of mobile user's application to recognize and respond to a change or changes of the environment in which they are in (Schilit & Theimer, 1994). Furthermore,depending on the way of reacting to the changing conditions of the environment, context-awareness can be classified in two different classes: active and passive context-awareness. In the first case the system modifies its behaviour according to the changing environment; on the contrary, in the second case it is the user that decides, after the system has communicated the chang of the conditions.

A context-aware application can be implemented in several fields like healthcare and well-being, transportation and location, social networking and environmental monitoring, thanks to the integration of context ubiquitous sensing and geographic information systems (GIS) (Gui et. al., 2011). Considering the work presented in (Guermah et. al. 2013), a context-aware application is used for e-health, monitoring different patients with different diseases in order to guarantee and adequate level of assistance. In order to accelerate the assistance process, it is important that the system can extract all the useful information to adapt its behaviour to the new system's conditions. A social networking context-aware application is represented by SAMOA (Socially Aware and Mobile Architecture), where all the users are grouped according to the context visibility (place and profile visibility).

4. A DYNAMIC AND CONTEXT-AWARE DECISION MODEL USING A SOCIAL NETWORK APPROACH

4.1 Context-Awareness

As defined in (Cioffi-Revilla, 2014), a network N consists of a finite set N of entities, called nodes or vertices, denoted by $\{n_1, n_2,..., n_g\}$ and a set of relations L, called links, $\{l_1, l_2,..., l_j\}$ defined on the set of nodes. Considering a node n_1 in a social network a set of relations for n_1 can be defined, characterized by an intensity, an importance and influence level and uniqueness within the network. When n_1 is subject to a stimulus, its perception can vary and may be influenced not only by its personal capabilities but also by what it receives from the rest of the network. These causes influence the actions of the node and can be represented in the process as a noise, which intensity is different depending on the level of influence. This noise alters, in a positive or negative way, the stimulus perception as described by the Weber-Fechner Law (Dehaene, 2003). So, it is possible to distinguish two types of noise:

- **"Constructive" Noise:** It contains and conveys information, and it exercises a positive influence on the node behavior and actions. This can be defined as a Positive Awareness.
- **"Destructive" Noise:** It influences in a negative way because it conveys only disorder. The stimulus perception is altered and not enriched of information. This can be defined as a Negative Awareness.

So for a network N, in addition to the adjacency matrix A_{ij}, it is possible to define a new network matrix, the Awareness Matrix, $AW_{i\to j}^{K}$, that represents the awareness that each single node perceives from all the rest of the network to which it is connected. As the expression suggests, the awareness matrix is defined for elements of the space of decision's context $K = \{K_1, K_2, ..., K_N\}$. Each element $aw_{i\to j}^{K}$ of the matrix $AW_{i\to j}^{K}$ is characterized by a magnitude, a $sign(\pm)$, and in a graph it is represented by an arrow with a versus. Each element is not symmetric, so the awareness that the i-th node has on the j-th node is different from the awareness that the j-th has on the i-th node ($aw_{i\to j}^{K} \neq aw_{i\leftarrow j}^{K}$).

In order to evaluate the awareness on the node i from the other nodes j in a decision-making process of the node i, given a particular decisional context K_k, it must taken into account both the similarity measure (homophily), which takes into account metrics to evaluate bio-inspired features of each node and in terms of genotype-phenotype, and also the centrality measures of the connected nodes to the node i, with regards to the context K_k, so which nodes are best connected to others or have most influence. It is important to note that a node j could be central in a particular decisional context K_k, but not in another one (K_q), so the influence on the node i from the node j could be negligible considering different decisional contexts.

The awareness from node i to j, given the decisional context K_k, depends on various parameters: the similarity between i and j, the centrality of the node i in the context K_k, and the centrality of the node i in its community. Severe centrality measures have been proposed over the time to quantify the importance and so the influence produced by a node in a social network. These measures are based on two different conceptual ideas and therefore it is possible to distinguish two classes of centrality measures (Latora & Marchiori, 2007). In the first class the centrality of a node in a network is related to how is it near to the other nodes (degree and closeness centralities). The second class of centrality measures is based on the idea that central nodes stand between others on the path of communication, these centrality measures include betweenness, eigenvector and Katz centralities. The information centrality (Latora & Marchiori, 2007), which is a combination of the two ideas of centrality discussed above, takes into account the efficient propagation of information over the network, so it is the ability of the network to respond to the deactivation of the node. Centralization is the process by which the activities of an organization, particularly those regarding planning decision-making, become concentrated within a particular location and/or group. Another important aspect is the centrality in the clusters, in fact one may notice that in each community, there are usually some members (or leaders) who play a key role in that community and have the greatest structural importance in a network, therefore these leader nodes are better able to influence the nodes in the cluster even if their centrality could change according to the decisional context.

To weight awareness, the idea is to consider the different centrality measures and apply a new metric, starting from MCA (Multiple Centrality Assessment) (Porta et. al., 2008) moving from spatial networks and the metric computation of distances in the urban planning to influence networks, using the different centrality measures, creating an influence map for decision-making.

A central problem for social influence is to understand the interplay between similarity and social ties (Crandall et. al., 2008). Homophily is one of the most fundamental characteristics of social networks (McPherson et. al. 2001; Di Stefano et. al. 2015; Scatà et. al., 2016). This suggests that an actor in the social network tends to be similar to their connected neighbors or "friends". The phenomenon of homophily can originate from many different mechanisms: (a) social influence: this indicates that people tend to follow the behaviors of their friends. The social influence effect leads people to adopt behaviors exhibited by their neighbors. (b) Selection: this indicates that people tend to create relationships with other people who are already similar to them; (c) confounding variables: other unknown variables exist, which may cause friends to behave similarly with one another. These three factors are often interweaved in real social networks, and the overall effect is to provide a strong support for the homophily phenomenon. Social influence refers to the behavioral change of individuals affected by others in a network. Social influence is an intuitive and well-accepted phenomenon in social networks (Easley & Kleinberg, 2010).

It is also important to stress the importance of the variable time t when analyzing and modeling the stimulus perception and the influence of the network (Norwich, 1993). Time cannot be supposed to be a constant variable, because the stimuli perception is deeply linked with the time instant in which it is considered.

4.2 Dynamic Criteria Interaction

In a multiple criteria decision-making process, the criteria have not always the same priority and they are not independent each other (Yu et. al., 2013). So in this case, if a criterion c_1 has a priority that is higher than the criterion c_2, an alternative will not be chosen until the decision maker will not have a minimal level of satisfaction to c_1, and in particular it is not sufficient to have only a gain in criteria c_2 (Yager, 2004).

Especially in a social network, where a node receives influences by its neighborhood, the criteria relations and dominance are subjected to change dynamically following the network evolution.

As for the representation of human belief systems in (Cioffi-Revilla, 2014), the criteria can be represented as a network, in which each node is a decision's criterion of the cognitive system and each edge represents a cognitive association among the criteria. Dynamically, they are all connected, weakly or strongly, depending on these three important dimensions: Time (T), decision's context (K) and Awareness (AW).

In Figure 1 it is represented an example considering a set $C = \{c_1, c_2, c_3, c_4, c_5, c_6\}$ of six decision's criteria, which relations vary along the three axis. To give an example, considering the criterion c_1, in the first block it is connected only with c_2 and c_3, instead in the second one it is connected with c_4, c_5, and c_6, loosing all the connections with c_2 and c_3. The evaluation of alternatives in a decision-making process, at a given time instant t_1, will depend on the level of awareness and on the decision's context that will determine which criterion prevails among the others. The explanation is that the social network evolves along the temporal dimensions, modifying its structure, adding new nodes and cutting off others, and functionality. So, the way to perform each process and, in this case, a decision-making process, depends on when it takes place, because the priority and the dominance of a criterion over all the others and their ties can vary substantially.

The personal social relationships determine the awareness of a node in the network and, in conjunction with the decision's context considered, modify the criteria relations and dominance. For example, considering a context K_1 at a time t_1, where most of the network nodes consider more important a criterion c_1 rather than all the other, this affects the single node way to perceive the world, to decide and to act, leading it, probably, to conform to the other, through processes of adaptation (Cioffi-Revilla, 2014) and social contagion (Christakis & Fowler, 2007). Instead in a context K_2 and at a time t_2, the criterion c_4 may have most importance and acquires a greater level of importance in the network. All these three dimensions depend on each other and affect the personal perception of the world, creating images from which each individual extracts data regarding the real world (Cioffi-Revilla, 2014) and the problem considered.

Figure 1. Criteria relationships with time, decision's context and awareness

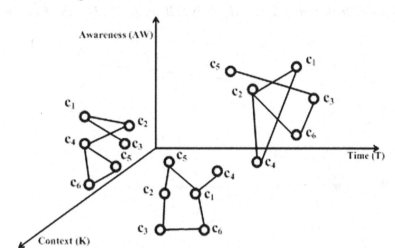

4.3 Decision-Making Model

Each decisional process is strictly connected to the elements of the space K of the decision's context in which it is considered. An element $K_1 \in K$ may have contexts closer or more distant, through which influences can spatially propagate. For example, it is possible to consider a network portion N_1, as reported in Figure 2, composed by a set $N = \{A, B, C, D, E, F\}$ of six nodes. For each node of the network all the metrics that characterize itself are defined, such as centrality, betweenness, degree, etc.. All of these also contribute to define the role of the node within the network. At a network level, the adjacency matrix for N_1 is the following:

$$A_{ij} = \begin{bmatrix} - & 1 & 0 & 1 & 1 & 1 \\ 1 & - & 1 & 1 & 1 & 0 \\ 0 & 1 & - & 1 & 0 & 1 \\ 1 & 1 & 1 & - & 1 & 0 \\ 1 & 1 & 0 & 1 & - & 1 \\ 1 & 0 & 1 & 0 & 1 & - \end{bmatrix}$$

But, considering the space K, it is possible to introduce a greater level of accuracy, diversifying each relationship among all the nodes, according to the element $K_k \in K$, in order to understand how and why certain decisions have been taken.

In Figure 3, the same 6 nodes are considered in four different situation: K_1, K_2, K_3, that are contexts belonging to space K and the fourth in which they do not belong to any context of the space K. The dashed line represents a negative awareness, instead the continuous line represents a positive awareness. The different dimensions of the node represent its centrality C_i^K depending on the context (Giacchi et. al., 2014).

Figure 2. Example of network with N = 6 nodes. The two different colors represent the levels of similarity among the network nodes. In this case, A is similar only to B, instead C, D, E anf F are similar each other

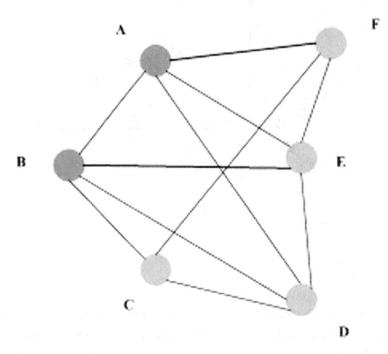

Figure 3. Network Representation in terms of awareness

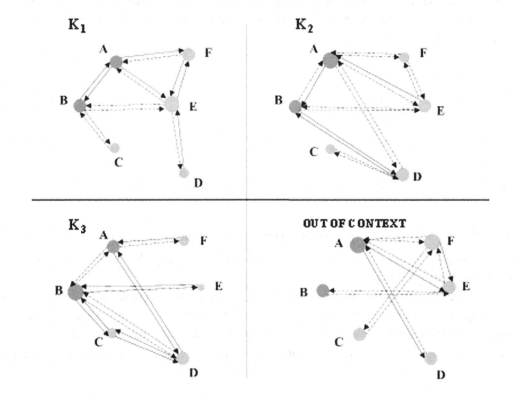

So each context varies the network structure and its relations, giving a significant contribute to the modification of the network, the node parameters and measures, changing how the decision-making process performs and then the decision itself. For more than one context, e.g. K_1, K_2 and K_3, the awareness matrix can be defined, but here, for simplicity, only the awareness matrix for the context K_1 is defined as follows:

$$
AW^{K_1}_{ij} =
\begin{bmatrix}
- & +aw^{K_1}_{A \to B} & 0 & 0 & +aw^{K_1}_{A \to E} & +aw^{K_1}_{A \to F} \\
+aw^{K_1}_{B \to A} & - & -aw^{K_1}_{B \to C} & 0 & -aw^{K_1}_{B \to E} & 0 \\
0 & -aw^{K_1}_{C \to B} & - & 0 & 0 & 0 \\
0 & 0 & 0 & - & +aw^{K_1}_{D \to E} & 0 \\
-aw^{K_1}_{E \to A} & -aw^{K_1}_{E \to B} & 0 & -aw^{K_1}_{E \to D} & - & +aw^{K_1}_{E \to F} \\
-aw^{K_1}_{F \to A} & 0 & 0 & 0 & +aw^{K_1}_{F \to E} & -
\end{bmatrix}
$$

For each element $K_k \in K$, the block diagram in Figure 4 represents how the decision-making process takes place, according to what expressed in the previous paragraphs.

For each block, the following are the functionalities:

- **Stimuli Perception + Noise:** It is the block that gives as output the data regarding the problem. These data can represent a true or a distort image of reality and of the problem, depending on the influences received from the social network.
- **Information Processing:** Considering a layered architecture, from the incoming data, information, which has a central role to understand the process, is extracted in order to create knowledge and a greater awareness about the problem considered.
- **Inference:** This block is composed by context-awareness and the evaluation of alternatives. Having the knowledge about the problem and the real world, the node becomes aware of the context. The node acquires the ability to adapt according to the location, the collection of neighboring nodes, hosts and accessible devices, as well as to changes to such things over the time. So the node will be able to define where it is, with whom it is and what resources it has (Schilit et. al., 1994). So, at this time, defined a space of context $K = \{K_1, K_2,...., K_k\}$ for a network N composed by a set $N = \{n_1, n_2, ..., n_n\}$ of nodes and a set $L = \{l_1, l_2,....,l_l\}$ of relationships, it is possible to define a function $\phi^K_i(t)$, which represents the decision's state of the node at a time t:

$$
\varphi^K_i(t) = \varphi^K_i(0) + A_{ij} \cdot \sum_{j=1}^{N-1} \left| AW^K_{ij} \right|
$$

where $\phi^K_i(0)$ represents the initial condition, A_{ij} is the adjacency matrix of N, AW^K_{ij} is the awareness matrix. The state of the node at a time t will vary the criteria relations and positions in a scale of dominance, influencing the decision. It is important to highlight that the state of the node cannot be the real representation of the problem.

Figure 4. Dynamic Context-Aware Multiple Criteria Decision-Making Process

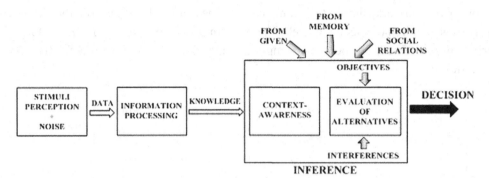

After that, defined the objectives and become aware of its state, the node can evaluate the alternatives, taking into account the possible interferences during the inference process. There are two types of inference, as defined in (Gigerenzer & Goldstein, 1996; Di Stefano et. al., 2013):

- **Inference From Given**: Decisions are taken considering data and information extracted from a calculation or data extracted from an experiment.
- **Inference From Memory:** Decisions are taken considering declared knowledge, studies, memory and history.
- At this time, another kind of inference is added, as it follows:
- **Inference From Social Relationships:** Decisions are not only a consequence of the history and/ or information acquired by nodes, but they are related to "cue values" deriving also from the social influence produced by the social relationships and the dynamical and structural properties of the network, such as similarity and centrality measures, which characterize the awareness of a node in the network.

5. KNOWLEDGE TRANSFER AND THE GRAPH-BASED KNOWLEDGE LEARNING

In this section, by taking into account the importance of knowledge in a social network, the knoweldge transfer process is modeled, including also a graph-based knowledge learning process. As for the decision making process, two of the main features of the processes that involve knowledge are complexity, which characterizes the definition of knowledge itself, and dynamism, caused by the continuous change of knowledge characteristics. Both these features are also related to the property of the environment itself in which the processes are considered. Knowledge is defined as *"a fluid mix of framed experience, values, contextual information, and expert insight that provides a framework for evaluating and incorporating new experiences and information"* (Davenport & Prusak, 1998). Hence, in addition to complexity and dynamism, the third feature that characterizes a process involving knowledge is its context-dependance consequence, as for the other two features, of the environment in which each process takes place. Using a decision-making perspective, a process of knowledge transfer can be considered as an individual decision making process (Luo et. al., 2015), where each node is involved in a process of knowledge transfer and, in particular, it has to decide to accept or not knowledge incoming from its neighboring nodes, which represent the set of alternatives. In this case the decision to accept or not the knowledge offered from another node in the network is based on two criteria, e.g. knowledge distance and confidence, and, as well as a decision making process, each alternative has an evaluation on each of the them. The evaluation of each alternative changes dynamically at each time instant, due to the modification of some paramenters characterising the network. In particular, the importance of the context is represented by the variation of the weights and of the knowledge level and, as a consequence, of all the other measures that depend on them, giving a characterization of the network at a specific time instant. Among the different contexts where every network node thinks, acts and decides there is a correlation, that it is observable representing each context as a plane of the space. Taking one context as a reference plane, the nearest two planes are more similar they are, on the contrary they are less similar. In this way, the measures that characterize the network in each context will dynamically vary depending on the considered context.

Using this new perspective and the analytical tools provided by MCDM, the process of knowledge transfer becomes more selective, allowing each node to decide on the basis of updated information of its neighborhood.

For the description of the model, the following notation will be used: $N = \{n_1, ..., n_i, ..., n_m\}$, a finite set of nodes; $K = \{K_1, ..., K_k, ..., K_p\}$, a finite set of contexts; $v_{i,1}^{K_k}(t) = \left\{v_{i,1}^{K_k}(t), ..., v_{i,l}^{K_k}(t), ... v_{i,q}^{K_k}(t)\right\}$ is the knowledge vector of the node ni with respect to the q categories and the context K_k at time t; $A_{ij}^{K_k} = \left\{a_{ij}^{K_k}\right\}$ is the adjacency matrix representing the network in the context K_k, where each element, $a_{ij}^{K_k} = \{0,1\}$, identifies if the link between nodes n_i and n_j is present or not; $N_i^{K_k} = \left\{n_j \in N : a_{ij}^{K_k} = 1\right\}$ is the set of nodes linked to node n_i in the context K_k and represents the set of alternatives for node n_i.

One of roles of the context is to characterize and differentiate the strength of each node's connection and the structure of the network itself. In order to do so, it is introduced a vector of weights $w_i^{K_k}$, where each element

$w_{i,j}^{K_k}$, represents the strength of the relation between node n_i and node n_j in the context K_k. $w_{i,j}^{K_k}$ can be different from $w_{j,i}^{K_k}$. As said before and differently from the previous models, the decision whether to accept or not the knowledge offered from another node in the network is based on two criteria, i. e. knowledge distance and confidence. Each alternative $n_j \in N_i^{K_k}$ is evaluated based on each of the two criteria. The first is the distance, defined as follows:

$$d_{ij,l}^{K_k}(t) = v_{j,l}^{K_k}(t) - v_{i,l}^{K_k}(t)$$

It corresponds to the amount of knowledge that node n_i could receive from node n_j in the category l within the considered context. The knowledge distance can be considered the expression of the knowledge heterogeneity of the two nodes involved in the process. If there is a high knowledge gap between two network nodes (high heterogeneity), node n_i could have no gain from the knowledge received from node n_j (Luo et. al., 2015). The second criterion is represented by the confidence, defined as follows:

$$c_{ij,l}^{K_k}(t) = \frac{w_{i,j}^{K_k}(t) + J_{i,j}^{K_k}(t)}{2}$$

where $c_{ij,l}^{K_k}\left(t\right)$ is the confidence that the node n_i has in node n_j in the context K_k, and $w_{i,j}^{K_k}\left(t\right)$ is the weight that node n_i gives to the link with node n_j. $J_{i,j}^{K_k}$ is the Jaccard similarity, i. e. an expression of the concept of homophily (Di Stefano et al., 2015; McPherson et. al. 2001; Scatà et. al., 2016), calculated as the ratio of the common neighbors of the nodes n_i and n_j to the number of nodes that are neighbors of at least one between n_i and n_j. The greater is the confidence that n_i has in n_j, the more susceptible node n_i is to learn from node n_j (Pentland, 2014). In order to ensure that the knowledge transfer process to take place, the evaluation of alternative n_j belonging to the set $N_i^{K_k}$ in each of the two decision criteria has to satisfy, at the same time, the two constraints, for which the knowledge distance must be under a knowledge distance threshold d and the confidence has must be over a confidence threshold c. Among the set of nodes satisfying at the same time both the two constraints related to the two criteria, node n_i for each knowledge category will accept knowledge from the one that can give it the greatest amount of knowledge. The knowledge level of node n_i in the category l in the context K_k will become:

$$v_{i,l}^{K_k}\left(t+1\right)=v_{i,l}^{K_k}\left(t\right)+max_{n_j\in N_i^{K_k}}\left(\left(\gamma_{ij,l}^{K_k}\left(\gamma_{j,l}^{K_k}\left(t\right)-\gamma_{i,l}^{K_k}\left(t\right)\right)\right)\right)$$

where $v_{i,l}^{K_k}\left(t\right)$ (or $v_{j,l}^{K_k}\left(t\right)$) represents the knowledge level of node n_i (or n_j) in category l in the context K_k at time t; $\gamma_{ij,l}^{K_k}$ represents the absorptive capacity of node n_i with respect to the knowledge received from node n_j in the category l. In this model, it is assumed that the value of $\gamma_{ij,l}^{K_k}$ is strictly related to the risk attitude of node n_i and its value is a function of the knowledge distance, that is: $\gamma_{ij,l}^{K_k}\left(t\right)=\dfrac{1}{exp^{d_{ij,l}^{K_k}}\left(t\right)}$.

According to this formulation, the values that $\gamma_{ij,l}^{K_k}\left(t\right)$ can assume are included in the set $\left[\dfrac{1}{exp^d};1\right]$. In such a way if the values are closer to $\dfrac{1}{exp^d}$, it means that node n_i is more risk averse and then it assimilates less knowledge, than a node with a value close to 1 which assimilates more knowledge. After that, node n_i will control the received knowledge before learning it, that is the evaluation of its quality on the basis of three criteria (Bukowitz & Williams, 2000):

- *Accessibility*, defined as the capability for the receiver node to easily access to the whole knowledge that it has received;
- *Guidance*, defined as the knowledge property to be divided into topics or domain in order to avoid an information overload;
- *Completeness*, defined as the knowledge property to contain all the information requested by the receiver node

If the evaluation of the received knowledge exceeds the quality threshold in at least two of the three criteria, node n_i will learn and assimilate knowledge at all. Furthermore, it will increase the weight and then the confidence in node n_j. On the contrary, node n_i will learn only the 20% of the received knowledge and its confidence in node n_j will decrease.

6. CONCLUSION AND FUTURE WORKS

Nowadays social networks have rapidly grown in popularity, size and complexity, allowing network nodes to create new connections and relationships. Information can be considered the core part of the network, from which creating knowledge, allowing individuals to acquire more and more context-awareness. In this way, all the processes, especially the decision-making ones, have become more complex, due to the continuous and dynamic changes to which each node of the network is subjected. Thus, the research of a conjunction point among the mathematical model of multiple criteria decision analysis and the social network analysis can be considered as the first step to build a tool useful for the analysis of network dynamics, also to predict individual or community behavior and decisions, varying the initial conditions and the structure of the network. To perform the different processes, each node has to take into account not only its personal knowledge but also the influences perceived from its surroundings. Considering this scenario, each decision will be the result of a complex and dynamical process, affecting the present and the future status of the node. Consequently, given a set of alternatives and a set of criteria within social network, the definition of decision provided in (Wang & Ruhe, 2007) has to be extended including the influence that a node can have on the preferences of the other nodes in the network. In this context, it is important to distinguish between positive and negative influences. For this reason, before making its decisions, the node has to become aware of what it has nearby and what resources it has. A crucial part of the decision process is therefore the context-awareness, that allows a node to make an aware cognitive decision on the basis of the available information. Furthermore, in the presented model it has been taken into account a particular scheme of the decision's criteria that, as a result of the interaction among nodes in the network, can assume different priorities depending on three dimensions: time, context and awareness (Giacchi et. al., 2014).

The paradigm, presented in this chapter, has its core idea in taking into account the dynamics and context-awareness. In fact, the model dynamic is represented by the variation of decision's criteria relationships due to the changes of the awareness matrix which, in turn, varies based on the bio-inspired features and structure of the node and of the network. The analysis of the data, information and knowledge diffusion patterns could be helpful to predict and study phenomena and node's behavior within the network itself. Furthermore, by considering the context as a variable that affects the network structure and the knowledge held by the single node, it adds further complexity and dynamism to a process that already has these features. Thus, one of the aims of the presented model has been to understand why a node, part of a network and considered as a decision maker, decides whether to accept or not knowledge from its neighboring nodes that represent the set of alternatives. The decision is based on the evaluation of each alternative based on two decision criteria, the knowledge distance and the confidence. In such a way, the structure of the network and, in particular, the typology of the node's connections, both depending on the context, affect the node's decision. This process is also characterized by a mechanism of confidence increasing and decreasing, that occurs after the evaluation of the quality of the knowledge received at each time instant and which adds dynamism to the model. In this sense, the presented model is a first attempt to investigate how the introduction of a context-aware decision making perspective in the processes involving knowledge may vary its diffusion's pattern.

Future works will be focused to build a more complex and comprehensive analytical model and simulate the proposed decision-making process model in different types of network. The target is to predict and study the phenomena and behavioral patterns within the social network. Furthermore, the idea may be to analyze the process involving knowledge with the introduction of other decision criteria, considering different contexts and adding or removing links in the network. In such a way different decision making scenarios and their impact on the knowledge diffusion will be taken into account.

REFERENCES

Abowd, G. D., Dey, A. K., Brown, P. J., Davies, N., Smith, M., & Steggles, P. (1999, September). Towards a better understanding of context and context-awareness. In *International Symposium on Handheld and Ubiquitous Computing* (pp. 304-307). Springer Berlin Heidelberg. doi:10.1007/3-540-48157-5_29

Aggarwal, C. C. (2011). An introduction to social network data analytics. In Social network data analytics (pp. 1-15). Springer US. doi:10.1007/978-1-4419-8462-3_1

Ahn, S., & Kim, D. (2006, February). Proactive context-aware sensor networks. In *European Workshop on Wireless Sensor Networks* (pp. 38-53). Springer Berlin Heidelberg.

Anagnostopoulos, A., Becchetti, L., Bordino, I., Leonardi, S., Mele, I., & Sankowski, P. (2015). Stochastic query covering for fast approximate document retrieval. *ACM Transactions on Information Systems*, *33*(3), 11. doi:10.1145/2699671

Asavathiratham, C., Roy, S., Lesieutre, B., & Verghese, G. (2001). The influence model. *IEEE Control Systems*, *21*(6), 52–64. doi:10.1109/37.969135

Axelrod, R. (Ed.). (2015). *Structure of decision: The cognitive maps of political elites*. Princeton university press.

Barjis, J., Gupta, A., & Sharda, R. (2011). Knowledge work and communication challenges in networked enterprises. *Information Systems Frontiers*, *13*(5), 615–619. doi:10.1007/s10796-010-9240-6

Bottazzi, D., Montanari, R., & Toninelli, A. (2007). Context-aware middleware for anytime, anywhere social networks. *IEEE Intelligent Systems*, *22*(5), 23–32. doi:10.1109/MIS.2007.4338491

Brans, J., & Vincke, P. (1985). A preference ranking organisation method: The PROMETHEE method for MCDM. *Management Science*, *31*(6), 647–656. doi:10.1287/mnsc.31.6.647

Brown, P. J., Bovey, J. D., & Chen, X. (1997). Context-awareness applications: From the laboratory to the marketplace. *IEEE Pers. Commun.*, *4*(5), 58–64. doi:10.1109/98.626984

Bukowitz, W. R., & Williams, R. L. (2000). *The knowledge management fieldbook*. Financial Times/ Prentice Hall.

Cacioppo, J. T., Fowler, J. H., & Christakis, N. A. (2009). Alone in the crowd: The structure and spread of loneliness in a large social network. *Journal of Personality and Social Psychology*, *97*(6), 977–991. doi:10.1037/a0016076 PMID:19968414

Christakis, N. A., & Fowler, J. H. (2007). The spread of obesity in a large social network over 32 years. *The New England Journal of Medicine, 357*(4), 370–379. doi:10.1056/NEJMsa066082 PMID:17652652

Christakis, N. A., & Fowler, J. H. (2013). Social contagion theory: Examining dynamic social networks and human behavior. *Statistics in Medicine, 32*(4), 556–577. doi:10.1002/sim.5408 PMID:22711416

Cioffi-Revilla, C. (2014). Computation and Social Science. In *Introduction to Computational Social Science* (pp. 23–66). Springer London. doi:10.1007/978-1-4471-5661-1_2

Crandall, D., Cosley, D., Huttenlocher, D., Kleinberg, J., & Suri, S. (2008, August). Feedback effects between similarity and social influence in online communities. In *Proceedings of the 14th ACM SIGKDD international conference on Knowledge discovery and data mining* (pp. 160-168). ACM. doi:10.1145/1401890.1401914

Cummings, J. N. (2004). Work groups, structural diversity, and knowledge sharing in a global organization. *Management Science, 50*(3), 352–364. doi:10.1287/mnsc.1030.0134

Dehaene, S. (2003). The neural basis of the Weber–Fechner law: A logarithmic mental number line. *Trends in Cognitive Sciences, 7*(4), 145–147. doi:10.1016/S1364-6613(03)00055-X PMID:12691758

Di Stefano, A., La Corte, A., Leotta, M., Lió, P., & Scatá, M. (2013). It measures like me: An IoTs algorithm in WSNs based on heuristics behavior and clustering methods. *Ad Hoc Networks, 11*(8), 2637–2647. doi:10.1016/j.adhoc.2013.04.011

Di Stefano, A., Scatà, M., La Corte, A., Liò, P., Catania, E., Guardo, E., & Pagano, S. (2015). Quantifying the role of homophily in human cooperation using multiplex evolutionary game theory. *PLoS ONE, 10*(10), e0140646. doi:10.1371/journal.pone.0140646 PMID:26496351

Easley, D., & Kleinberg, J. (2010). *Networks, crowds, and markets: Reasoning about a highly connected world*. Cambridge University Press. doi:10.1017/CBO9780511761942

Figueira, J. R., Greco, S., Roy, B., & Słowiński, R. (2013). An overview of ELECTRE methods and their recent extensions. *Journal of Multi-Criteria Decision Analysis, 20*(1-2), 61–85. doi:10.1002/mcda.1482

Fortunato, S. (2010). Community detection in graphs. *Physics Reports, 486*(3), 75–174. doi:10.1016/j.physrep.2009.11.002

Giacchi, E., Di Stefano, A., La Corte, A., & Scatà, M. (2014, November). A dynamic context-aware multiple criteria decision making model in social networks. In *Information Society (i-Society), 2014 International Conference on* (pp. 157-162). IEEE. doi:10.1109/i-Society.2014.7009032

Gigerenzer, G., & Goldstein, D. G. (1996). Reasoning the fast and frugal way: Models of bounded rationality. *Psychological Review, 103*(4), 650–669. doi:10.1037/0033-295X.103.4.650 PMID:8888650

Grabisch, M., & Rusinowska, A. (2010). A model of influence in a social network. *Theory and Decision, 69*(1), 69–96. doi:10.1007/s11238-008-9109-z

Graham, I. D., Logan, J., Harrison, M. B., Straus, S. E., Tetroe, J., Caswell, W., & Robinson, N. (2006). Lost in knowledge translation: Time for a map? *The Journal of Continuing Education in the Health Professions, 26*(1), 13–24. doi:10.1002/chp.47 PMID:16557505

Greco, S., Figueira, J., & Ehrgott, M. (2005). *Multiple criteria decision analysis*. Springer's International Series.

Guermah, H., Fissaa, T., Hafiddi, H., Nassar, M., & Kriouile, A. (2013, May). Context modeling and reasoning for building context aware services. In *Computer Systems and Applications (AICCSA), 2013 ACS International Conference on* (pp. 1-7). IEEE. doi:10.1109/AICCSA.2013.6616439

Gui, N., De Florio, V., Sun, H., & Blondia, C. (2011). Toward architecture-based context-aware deployment and adaptation. *Journal of Systems and Software*, *84*(2), 185–197. doi:10.1016/j.jss.2010.09.017

Hatak, I. R., & Roessl, D. (2015). Relational Competence-Based Knowledge Transfer Within Intrafamily Succession An Experimental Study. *Family Business Review*, *28*(1), 10–25. doi:10.1177/0894486513480386

Hoede, C., & Bakker, R. R. (1982). A theory of decisional power. *The Journal of Mathematical Sociology*, *8*(2), 309–322. doi:10.1080/0022250X.1982.9989927

Jacquet-Lagreze, E., & Siskos, Y. (2001). Preference disaggregation: 20 years of MCDA experience. *European Journal of Operational Research*, *130*(2), 233–245. doi:10.1016/S0377-2217(00)00035-7

Keeney, R. L., & Raiffa, H. (1993). *Decisions with multiple objectives: preferences and value trade-offs*. Cambridge University Press. doi:10.1017/CBO9781139174084

Kempe, D., Kleinberg, J., & Tardos, É. (2003, August). Maximizing the spread of influence through a social network. In *Proceedings of the ninth ACM SIGKDD international conference on Knowledge discovery and data mining* (pp. 137-146). ACM. doi:10.1145/956750.956769

Korhonen, P., & Wallenius, J. (1997). Behavioral issues in MCDM: Neglected research questions. In *Multicriteria analysis* (pp. 412–422). Springer Berlin Heidelberg. doi:10.1007/978-3-642-60667-0_39

Lambiotte, R., & Panzarasa, P. (2009). Communities, knowledge creation, and information diffusion. *Journal of Informetrics*, *3*(3), 180–190. doi:10.1016/j.joi.2009.03.007

Latora, V., & Marchiori, M. (2007). A measure of centrality based on network efficiency. *New Journal of Physics*, *9*(6), 188. doi:10.1088/1367-2630/9/6/188

Lewis, K., Gonzalez, M., & Kaufman, J. (2012). Social selection and peer influence in an online social network. *Proceedings of the National Academy of Sciences of the United States of America*, *109*(1), 68–72. doi:10.1073/pnas.1109739109 PMID:22184242

Liu, W., Li, X., & Huang, D. (2011, June). A survey on context awareness. In *Computer Science and Service System (CSSS), 2011 International Conference on* (pp. 144-147). IEEE.

López-Pintado, D. (2008). Diffusion in complex social networks. *Games and Economic Behavior*, *62*(2), 573–590. doi:10.1016/j.geb.2007.08.001

Luo, S., Du, Y., Liu, P., Xuan, Z., & Wang, Y. (2015). A study on coevolutionary dynamics of knowledge diffusion and social network structure. *Expert Systems with Applications*, *42*(7), 3619–3633. doi:10.1016/j.eswa.2014.12.038

Norwich, K. H. (1993). *Information, sensation, and perception*. San Diego, CA: Academic Press.

Pachidi, S., Spruit, M., & Van De Weerd, I. (2014). Understanding users behavior with software operation data mining. *Computers in Human Behavior, 30*, 583–594. doi:10.1016/j.chb.2013.07.049

Pentland, A. (2014). *Social physics: How good ideas spread-the lessons from a new science*. Penguin.

Porta, S., Crucitti, P., & Latora, V. (2008). Multiple centrality assessment in Parma: a network analysis of paths and open spaces. *Urban Design International, 13*(1), 41-50.

Roy, B. (2005). Paradigms and challenges. In *Multiple criteria decision analysis: state of the art surveys* (pp. 3–24). Springer New York. doi:10.1007/0-387-23081-5_1

Roy, B. (2013). *Multicriteria methodology for decision aiding* (Vol. 12). Springer Science & Business Media.

Rusinowska, A., & de Swart, H. (2006). Generalizing and modifying the Hoede-Bakker index. In *Theory and Applications of Relational Structures as Knowledge Instruments II* (pp. 60–88). Springer Berlin Heidelberg. doi:10.1007/11964810_4

Scatà, M., Di Stefano, A., Giacchi, E., La Corte, A., & Liò, P. (2014, August). The bio-inspired and social evolution of node and data in a multilayer network. In *Data Communication Networking (DCNET), 2014 5th International Conference on* (pp. 1-6). SCITEPRESS. doi:10.5220/0005119600410046

Scatà, M., Di Stefano, A., La Corte, A., Liò, P., Catania, E., Guardo, E., & Pagano, S. (2016). Combining evolutionary game theory and network theory to analyze human cooperation patterns. *Chaos, Solitons, and Fractals, 91*, 17–24. doi:10.1016/j.chaos.2016.04.018

Schilit, B., Adams, N., & Want, R. (1994, December). Context-aware computing applications. In *Mobile Computing Systems and Applications, 1994. WMCSA 1994. First Workshop on* (pp. 85-90). IEEE. doi:10.1109/WMCSA.1994.16

Schilit, B. N., & Theimer, M. M. (1994). Disseminating active map information to mobile hosts. *IEEE Network, 8*(5), 22–32. doi:10.1109/65.313011

Tasselli, S. (2015). Social networks and inter-professional knowledge transfer: The case of healthcare professionals. *Organization Studies*.

Vespignani, A. (2009). Predicting the behavior of techno-social systems. *Science, 325*(5939), 425–428. doi:10.1126/science.1171990 PMID:19628859

Walker, R., Arima, E., Messina, J., Soares-Filho, B., Perz, S., Vergara, D., & Castro, W. et al. (2013). Modeling spatial decisions with graph theory: Logging roads and forest fragmentation in the Brazilian Amazon. *Ecological Applications, 23*(1), 239–254. doi:10.1890/11-1800.1 PMID:23495649

Wang, S., & Noe, R. A. (2010). Knowledge sharing: A review and directions for future research. *Human Resource Management Review, 20*(2), 115–131. doi:10.1016/j.hrmr.2009.10.001

Wang, Y., & Ruhe, G. (2007). The Cognitive Process of Decision Making. *International Journal of Cognitive Informatics and Natural Intelligence, 1*(2), 73–85. doi:10.4018/jcini.2007040105

Wasserman, S., & Faust, K. (1994). *Social network analysis: Methods and applications* (Vol. 8). Cambridge university press. doi:10.1017/CBO9780511815478

Yager, R. R. (2004). Modeling prioritized multicriteria decision making. *IEEE Transactions on Systems, Man, and Cybernetics. Part B, Cybernetics*, *34*(6), 2396–2404. doi:10.1109/TSMCB.2004.837348 PMID:15619938

Yu, X., Xu, Z., & Liu, S. (2013). Prioritized multi-criteria decision making based on preference relations. *Computers & Industrial Engineering*, *66*(1), 104–115. doi:10.1016/j.cie.2013.06.007

Chapter 5
Undirected Bipartite Networks as an Alternative Methodology to Probabilistic Exploration:
Online Interaction and Academic Attainment in MOOC

Juan-Francisco Martínez-Cerdá
Universitat Oberta de Catalunya (UOC), Spain

Joan Torrent-Sellens
Universitat Oberta de Catalunya (UOC), Spain

ABSTRACT

This chapter explores how graph analysis techniques are able to complement and speed up the process of learning analytics and probability theory. It uses a sample of 2,353 e-learners from six European countries (France, Germany, Greece, Poland, Portugal, and Spain), who were enrolled in their first year of open online courses offered by HarvardX and MITX. After controlling the variables for socio-demographics and online content interactions, the research reveals two main results relating student-content interactions and online behavior. First, a multiple binary logistic regression model tests that students who explore online chapters are more likely to be certified. Second, the authors propose an algorithm to generate an undirected bipartite network based on tabular data of student-content interactions (2,392 nodes, 25,883 edges, a visual representation based on modularity, degree and ForceAtlas2 layout); the graph shows a clear relationship between interactions with online chapters and chances of getting certified.

DOI: 10.4018/978-1-5225-2814-2.ch005

1. INTRODUCTION

During the last decades, the increase in the computer-based calculation capabilities and advances in data sciences (i.e. the integration of data sciences into educational environments), have enabled the development of research oriented to educational environments, especially through two approaches well described by Siemens and Baker (2012): i) educational data mining (EDM), aimed at statistical data analysis about students, settings, and automated findings; and ii) learning analytics (LA), oriented to understand the complexity of learning contexts by using mixed methodology for data analysis. In fact, the origin of EDM and the use of data mining in educational context comes from 1995 (Romero & Ventura, 2007; Baker & Yacef, 2009). Thus, LA has tried to produce knowledge about the whole learning ecosystem by analysing the huge number of interactions that exist between students, instructors, and content. In this way, many technologies and solutions have been used, such as business intelligence, web analytics, academic analytics, and action analytics (Elias, 2011). Recent research on using LA beyond traditional school environments have been conducted, such as in workplaces (Laat & Schreurs, 2013) and connecting EDM, LA, big data, and Massive Open Online Courses (MOOC) (Nisar, Fard, & Miller, 2013; Calvet Liñán & Juan Pérez, 2015).

On the other hand, since late last century international organizations have been drafting proposals aimed at the use of online education systems as tools for the qualification of workers through lifelong learning (Delors et al., 1996; Aceto, Borotis, Devine, & Fischer, 2014). This has led to a large increase in: i) use of new pedagogies and related technologies in open online courses, such as HarvardX and MITx (Anderson & McGreal, 2012), which have facilitated mobile and ubiquitous learning (Kinshuk, Hui-Wen, Sampson, & Chen, 2013); and ii) a wealth of educational data that have to be analysed according to several ethical principles (Ferguson, 2012; Slade & Prinsloo, 2013).

Therefore, LA should continue developing new interesting solutions on this scientific field. In this issue, note that new graph analysis techniques are being very useful for assessing of our daily scientific work (Brandes, Kenis, & Raab, 2006). These new approaches should go beyond the interesting proposals that have combined quantitative and qualitative methodologies in LA (Fournier, Kop, & Sitlia, 2011), and they should analyse behavior of online students and relationships between interaction with online resources and academic attainment in the context of MOOC. In this way, LA should be complemented with graph analytics methodologies, which have been useful for visualization MOOC data (Coffrin, Corrin, de Barba, & Kennedy, 2014), new frameworks (Satish et al., 2014), and interactive data repository for visualization (Rossi & Ahmed, 2015). Moreover, these new approaches and methodologies should be tested with traditional statistical techniques, helping to understand whether standard statistics could take advantage of them.

2. THEORETICAL CONTEXT AND HYPOTHESES

This chapter is developed within a context associated with three theoretical fields. First, we find adults developing their skills and knowledge through online education methodologies, which is an action related to the human capital theory developed by Theodore W. Schultz (1961) and Gary S. Becker (1993) in the sixties. This theory has to do with the huge significance of skills, education, and training existing in workers, as key factors for productivity of companies and countries in the knowledge economy. Moreover, people want to increase their employability according to theory of discrimination by Kenneth J. Arrow (1971), who proposed that companies select those workers who have developed more their human capital. During the last decades a trend that points to an increasing use of lifelong e-learning is observed, within the context of globalization, open educational resources (OER), and seamless learning (Varis & Puukko, 2010).

Second, this research is framed within the activity theory, collecting ideas by Lev S. Vygotski that were formalized mainly by Alexei N. Leontiev (1978). His approach is related to the analysis of all activities carried out by humans under a systemic view that takes into account subjects, objects, actions, and operations (Leontiev, 1974; Nardi, 1996). It has theoretical implications on issues related to online behavior and learning interactions between learners, instructors, and content (Moore, 1989), with recent developments aimed to activity systems (Engeström, 1987) and online education (Wagner, 1997). Specifically, for instance, it has been proved that student-content interaction is a key factor in second language acquisition theories (Krashen, 1982, 1985; Ariza & Hancock, 2003; Moore & Kearsley, 2011). From this perspective, the analysis of activities through EDM and LA has provided results in the field of skills developed by constructionist (Berland, Baker, & Blikstein, 2014) and connectivist learning approaches in open online courses (Kop, 2011). These outcomes have also been linked to skills acquired by students in technology enhanced learning platforms (Mazzola & Mazza, 2011), eAssessment of skills useful in 21st Century (Redecker, Punie, & Ferrari, 2012), interests of teachers (Dyckhoff, Zielke, Bultmann, Chatti, & Schroeder, 2012), and the use of data mining techniques for students skills assessment (Sao Pedro, Baker, & Gobert, 2013).

Finally, the third theoretical approach is related to graph theory, which has been analysing structures and relations between objects since Leonhard Euler drafted a paper in 1736. There has been an explosion of applications of graph theory to complex problems related to social sciences in recent years (Boccaletti, Latora, Moreno, Chávez, & Hwang, 2006; Jiang, Ferreira, & González, 2012), and going beyond of data mining on content interaction in e-learning (Pahl, 2004). Specifically, online learning has been analyzed under the parameters of network analysis (Jones, 2004; Jacobson & Wilensky, 2006), and because its usefulness and versatility, seminal research has been developed on using graph analytics with tabular data (Liu, Navathe, & Stasko, 2011, 2014) and survey data (Martínez-Cerdá & Torrent-Sellens, 2015), which proposes that graph theory can be a tool for studying sociotechnical systems related to online education (Upadhyaya & Mallik, 2013).

Therefore, it is relevant to test whether graph analysis can be useful for analysing behavior of online students, specifically, interactions between e-learners and online content on MOOC contexts. This situation will be tested by comparing results between traditional statistics and graph analysis. Thus, the two hypotheses are defined, which will be proved below by using multivariate regression analysis and network analysis in a case study related to students from six European non-English-speaking countries enrolled in open online courses:

H1: There is a linear, positive and statistically significant relationship between online content interactions (independent variable) and to earn a certificate (dependent variable).

H2: There is a graph with a visual representation based on modularity, degree, and ForceAtlas2 layout that shows the strong visual proximity between these two variables: content interactions and to be certified.

3. METHODOLOGY

3.1 HarvardX and MITx Dataset

Data Collection

We used public microdata from the first year of open online courses at the edX platform by HarvardX and MITx (Ho et al., 2014). The HarvardX-MITx Person-Course dataset AY2013 had data about 13 online courses from the Fall of 2013 to the Summer of 2014. This dataset had data at the level of one row per-person, per-course, which generated 641,138 rows and 20 columns (variables) with de-identified information both administrative and user-provided data (one of them related to random ID number).

Participants

Our analysis had to do with students from six non-English speaking European countries (France, Germany, Greece, Poland, Portugal, and Spain), who were enrolled on edX. According to our objectives of analysis, our own dataset was obtained by eliminating many cases from the original microdata that were not useful for us: other countries, missing values (NA), blank values, inconsistent records, and gender=other. After this process, we obtained a dataset DS1 with valid data for 2,353 rows (per-person, per-course) according to Table 1 ($\chi^2(55)=695.227$, $r_\phi=0.544$, $p=0.000$ in both), which shows that most students per course were from Spain ($N=821$), Poland ($N=517$), and Germany ($N=489$), and were enrolled in "Introduction to Computer Science and Programming" ($N=961$ in 2012-2013).

Table 1. Students distribution per country and online course (N=2,353)

Course	Country						Total
	France	Germany	Greece	Poland	Portugal	Spain	
Health in Numbers: Quantitative Methods in Clinical & Public Health Research (Fall 2012)	26	43	10	7	25	131	242
Human Health and Global Environmental Change (Summer 2013)	15	57	22	7	6	42	149
The Challenges of Global Poverty (Spring 2013)	64	90	6	3	2	53	218
Elements of Structures Spring (Summer 2013)	2	3	1	11	3	25	45
Introduction to Solid State Chemistry (Fall 2012)	3	17	0	7	0	52	79
Introduction to Solid State Chemistry (Spring 2013)	0	3	1	2	1	8	15
Circuits and Electronics (Fall 2012)	10	34	9	84	8	61	206
Circuits and Electronics (Spring 2013)	4	18	9	49	10	30	120
Introduction to Computer Science and Programming (Fall 2012)	42	94	48	67	47	202	500
Introduction to Computer Science and Programming (Spring 2013)	23	73	28	214	28	95	461
Introduction to Biology – The Secret of Life (Spring 2013)	11	25	5	22	8	28	99
Electricity and Magnetism (Spring 2013)	13	32	24	44	12	94	219
Total	213	489	163	517	150	821	2,353

3.2 Measures

Socio-Demographics and Individual-Level Information

Students were grouped according to their country and highest level of education successfully completed (Less than Secondary, Secondary, Bachelor's, Master's, and Doctorate). Additionally, students provided information about if they had earned a certificate from the edX platform, its courseware, and basic demographic information such as gender and age.

Online Interactions

Data about e-learners' interactions were analyzed according to their online course. Specifically, information about several variables related to online interactions in the courseware over the time were used: number of chapters with which the student interacted, access at least half of the chapters (explored), number of video play events, number of unique days student interacted, and number of interactions (from tracking logs). According to that, we used 11 columns (variables) from the original dataset.

3.3 Data Analysis

Recoding

Several variables were calculated and recoded for our analysis with a multiple binary logistic regression model, where the dependent variable was to earn a certificate, which was dichotomous per definition. Regarding independent variables, several dichotomous and ordinal variables classified data according to mean values of corresponding variables: people in two age groups (29 and under, and 30 and over), number of interations (1,753 and under, 1,754 and over), number of unique days student interacted (15 and under, 16 and over), number of video play events (211 and under, 212 and over), and number of chapters with which the student interacted (5 and under, 6 and over). The *Chi-square test of independence* showed that all these groups were statistically independent with respect to the dependent variable ($\chi^2=3.953$, $p=0.047$ in age groups, and $\chi^2=1,114.835$, $\chi^2=1,119.545$, $\chi^2=808.135$, $\chi^2=1,038.122$, $p=0.000$ in other groups, respectively). Other independent variables were recoded according to their own definition: gender (nominal), education level (ordinal), course (nominal), country (nominal), and chapters explored (dichotomous). In this sense, the *Chi-square test of independence* proved that these groups were statistically independent to the dependent variable ($\chi^2=6.941$ and $p=0.008$, $\chi^2=13.033$ and $p=0.011$, $\chi^2=79.857$ and $p=0.000$, $\chi^2=14.355$ and $p=0.014$, and $\chi^2=1,459.536$ and $p=0.000$, respectively).

Statistical Methods

Using the software *IBM SPSS Statistics Version 22* to prove our two hypotheses, we began with descriptive, means (M), standard deviations (SD), and initial bivariate relationships of our data. Specifically, in bivariate correlations, several appropriated significance tests were used: Spearman's rho (r_s) between ordinal variables and phi (r_ϕ) between dichotomous and pairs formed by dichotomous and ordinal variables. Table 3 reports the coefficients of these tests. A multiple binary logistic regression was analyzed to determine the relationship between earning a certificate (dependent variable) and every independent variables, and testing and controlling effects among variables. Table 4 shows regression coefficients (*B*), standard errors (*SE*), Wald tests of significance (*Wald*), odds ratios (*Exp(B)*), and the confidence interval for odds ratios (*95% CI*). The odds ratios helped to determine the relative importance of significant independent variables, and *Omnibus χ^2*, *Hosmer and Lemeshow Test (Sig.)*, *Cox & Snell R^2*, and *Nagelkerke R^2* established the significance and the overall fit of the multiple regression, useful for knowing the level of explanation of the model. The *Box-Tidwell's test* was not necessary because out dataset has not any continuous variable.

3.4 Algorithm for Graph Analysis

From our dataset DS1, we worked with its 2,353 rows (per-person, per-course), with one column for data related to random ID number, and eleven columns for other information (1 dependent variable + 10 independent variables): to be certified (dependent), and gender, education level, name of online course, name of country, chapters explored, age group, group of number of interactions, group of number of unique days student interacted, group of number of video play events, and group of number of chapter with which the student interacted. Thus, we transformed these tabular data into a new dataset DS2 ready to be analyzed as an undirected bipartite graph as described in the following algorithm, based on differences about social network data exposed by Hanneman and Riddle (2005): (1) we copied from dataset DS1 the column with variable related to random ID number, and we pasted it in the new dataset DS2 as its first column (which was called "source"); (2) we copied from DS1 a column related to any variable, and we pasted it in DS2 as its second column (which was called "target"); (3) we copied from DS1 the column with variable related to random ID number, and we added these data to existing data in column 1 (=source) in DS2; (4) we copied from DS1 another column related to any variable not previously selected in (2), and we added these data to existing data in column 2 (=target) in DS2; (5) we repeated (3) and (4) until all the 11 variables considered in (4) had been copied and pasted into dataset DS2; and (6) we added a new column in DS2 (which was called "type") with the same value for all its rows (="undirected").

Through to these steps, we transformed our original dataset DS1 into a new dataset DS2 that could be interpreted as an undirected bipartite network. Table 2 shows the process followed during this transformation.

We analyzed the generated network from the DS2 dataset (Figure 1) with *Gephi*, an opensource software tool for visualizing, exploring, and manipulating networks (Bastian, Heymann, & Jacomy, 2009). Specifically, we only used two network metrics: (1) *degree* (the sum of edges for a node) for the size of nodes; and (2) *modularity* (community detection, or sub-networks) for the colour of nodes (Blondel, Guillaume, Lambiotte, & Lefebvre, 2008; Lambiotte, Delvenne, & Barahona, 2009). We used *ForceAtlas2* as layout for network visualization (Jacomy, Venturini, Heymann, & Bastian, 2014).

4. RESULTS

4.1 Descriptive and Bivariate Analysis

Table 3 shows the differences between the means and correlations in sociodemographic and content interactions variables. First, it was observed that less than one-fifth of students earned a certificate,

Table 2. Original tabular dataset into a dataset ready for a bipartite network

Original tabular dataset DS1				Dataset DS2 = Edges from rows of Dataset DS1 Ready for a bipartite network		
Random ID number (Source)	Variable_1 (Target 1)	...	Variable_11 (Target 11)	Source node	Target node	Type of network
ID_1	Answer_ID_1__Variable_1	...	Answer_ID_1__Variable_11	ID_1	Answer_ID_1__Variable_1	Undirected
ID_2	Answer_ID_2__Variable_1	...	Answer_ID_2__Variable_11	ID_2	Answer_ID_2__Variable_1	Undirected
...	...	...	...	...	...	Undirected
ID_2,353	Answer_ID_2,353__Variable_1	...	Answer_ID_2,353__Variable_11	ID_2,353	Answer_ID_2,353__Variable_1	Undirected
				ID_1	...	...
				ID_2	...	...
				...	...	...
				ID_2,353	...	...
				ID_1	Answer_ID_1__Variable_11	Undirected
				ID_2	Answer_ID_2__Variable_11	Undirected
				...	...	Undirected
				ID_2,353	Answer_ID_2,353__Variable_11	Undirected

most were men, had a degree, and were 30 years old or less: 16% (M=0.16, SD=0.36), 80% (M=0.80, SD=0.40), M=2.21 (SD=0.86), and M=0.46 (SD=0.50), respectively. Regarding content interactions, the sample showed that almost a quarter of students explored the content (explored), i.e., accessed at least half of the chapters (M=0.23, SD=0.42). Moreover, the means of number of interactions (events), number of unique days student interacted (days), number of video play events (play videos), and number of chapters with which the student interacted (chapters) had similar values: M=0.25 (SD=0.44), M=0.26 (SD=0.44), M=0.22 (SD=0.41), and M=0.29 (SD=0.46). The *mode* of course is 8 (="Introduction to Computer Science and Programming (Fall 2012)") and the *mode* of country is 5 (=Spain).

Regarding relationships between variables, very positive correlations between earning a certificate and various variables related to content interactions were detected: explored, events, days, play videos, and chapters (r_ϕ=0.79, r_ϕ=0.69, r_ϕ=0.69, r_ϕ=0.59, r_ϕ=0.66, respectively, and p=0.000 in all cases). In this way, there were also very positive and significant correlations among all content interactions variables, between: (1) explored and events, days, play videos, and chapters (r_ϕ=0.81, r_ϕ=0.81, r_ϕ=0.68, r_ϕ=0.84, respectively, and p=0.000 in all cases); (2) events and days, play videos, and chapters (r_S=0.86, r_S=0.77, r_S=0.83, respectively, and p=0.000 in all cases); (3) days and play videos, and chapters (r_S=0.75, r_S=0.80, respectively, and p=0.000 in both); and (4) play videos and chapters (r_S=0.69, p=0.000). Regarding control variables, it was found that the more age the more educational level (r_S=0.59, p=0.000), and that women had higher education level (r_ϕ=-0.11, p=0.000).

Figure 1. Original tabular dataset into a dataset ready for a bipartite network

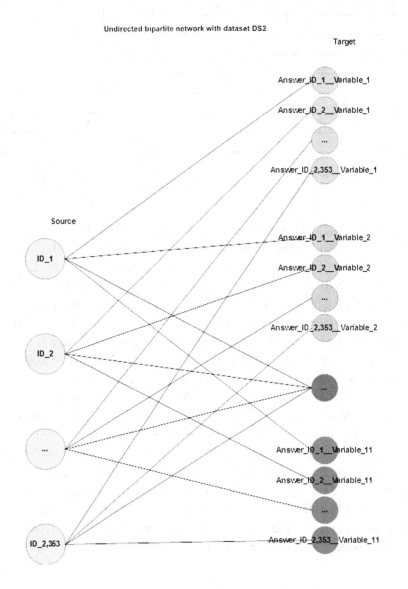

Table 3. Means, standard deviations and correlations (N=2,353)

	M	SD	(1)	(2)	(3)	(4)	(5)	(6)	(7)	(8)	(9)
Certified (1)	0.16	0.36	-								
Gender (2)	0.80	0.40	-0.05**	-							
Education (3)	2.21	0.86	0.05*	-0.11***	-						
Explored (4)	0.23	0.42	0.79***	-0.04*	0.04	-					
Age (5)	0.46	0.50	0.04*	-0.02	0.59***	0.05*	-				
Events (6)	0.25	0.44	0.69***	-0.05*	0.01	0.81***	0.02	-			
Days (7)	0.26	0.44	0.69***	-0.03	0.01	0.81***	0.04*	0.86***	-		
Play videos (8)	0.22	0.41	0.59***	-0.04*	0.04	0.68***	0.07**	0.77***	0.75***	-	
Chapters (9)	0.29	0.46	0.66***	-0.02	0.01	0.84***	0.03	0.83***	0.80***	0.69***	-

$* p < 0.05; ** p < 0.01; *** p = 0.000$

Certified (1)={0=No, 1=Yes}
Gender (2)={0=Female, 1=Male}
Education (3)={0=Less than Secondary, 1=Secondary, 2=Bachelor's, 3=Master's, 4=Doctorate}
Explored (4)={0=No, 1=Yes}
Age (5)={0=*Mean* and under, 1 = *Mean* + 1 and over [*Mean*=29.7]}
Events (6)={0=*Mean* and under, 1 = *Mean* + 1 and over [*Mean*=1,753.2]}
Days (7)={0=*Mean* and under, 1 = *Mean* + 1 and over [*Mean*=15.2]}
Play videos (8)={0=*Mean* and under, 1 = *Mean* + 1 and over [*Mean*=212.0]}
Chapters (9)={0=*Mean* and under, 1 = *Mean* + 1 and over [*Mean*=5.5]}

4.2 Multivariate Analysis

In order to observe bivariate relationships and the weight of the contribution relative to the explanatory variables, Table 4 shows a multiple binary logistic regression related to edX education activities carried out between Fall 2012 and Summer 2013 in six non-English speaking European countries: France, Germany, Greece, Poland, Portugal, and Spain. Globally, and taking into account the size of the sample obtained, the adjustment obtained for the proposed model had valid values: i) *Omnibus* χ^2(27) of 1,444.272 (*p*=0.000); and ii) the inferential goodness-of-fit obtained by the *Hosmer–Lemeshow test* yielded a χ^2(8) of 1.737, and was insignificant (*p*=0.988), suggesting that the model was fit to the data well. Moreover, the *Cox and Snell's* (0.459) and *Nagelkerke's* (0.790) R^2 indices had good measurements of goodness-of-fit, too, helping to know the proportion of the variation in the dependent variable explained by the predictors in the models.

Thus, to earn a edX certificate by students from six non-English speaking European countries was statistically higher among people who explored online content (*Exp(B)*=103.545, *p*=0.000, and compared to the reference group of people who did not explored online content). We must emphasize the importance of this variable because odds ratio of other significant variables were very low: *Exp(B)*=13.764 in Master's (*p*<0.05), compared to the reference group of education level lower than Secondary); *Exp(B)*=7.610 in course called "The Challenges of Global Poverty (Spring 2013)" (*p*=0.000), compared to the reference group of "Health in Numbers: Quantitative Methods in Clinical & Public Health Research (Fall 2012)"); *Exp(B)*=5.510 in course called "Introduction to Solid State Chemistry (Fall 2012)" (*p*<0.05), compared to the reference group of "Health in Numbers: Quantitative Methods in Clinical & Public Health Research (Fall 2012)"); *Exp(B)*=5.313 in number of unique days student interacted 16 and over (*p*<0.01), compared to the reference group of days 15 and under); and *Exp(B)*=3.755 in course called "Human Health and Global Environmental Change (Summer 2013)" (*p*<0.05), compared to the reference group of "Health in Numbers: Quantitative Methods in Clinical & Public Health Research (Fall 2012)").

Table 4. Multiple binary logistic regression (dependent variable=certified)

Independent variables	B	SE	Wald	Exp(B)	95% CI
Intercept	-11.163	1.653	45.586***	0.000	-
Gender Female Male	- 0.032	- 0.288	- 0.012	- 1.033	- [0.588, 1.814]
Age 29 and under 30 and over	- -0.402	- 0.276	- 2.125	- 0.669	- [0.390, 1.149]
Education Less than Secondary Secondary Bachelor's Master's Doctorate	- 2.082 2.084 2.622 2.381	- 1.170 1.184 1.196 1.421	7.521 3.166 3.101 4.808* 2.805	- 8.017 8.037 13.764 10.812	- [0.809, 79.405] [0.790, 81.746] [1.321, 143.420] [0.667, 175.291]
Course					
Health in Numbers: Quantitative Methods in Clinical & Public Health Research (Fall 2012)	-	-	30.138**	-	-
Human Health and Global Environmental Change (Summer 2013)	1.323	0.665	3.959*	3.755	[1.020, 13.820]
The Challenges of Global Poverty (Spring 2013)	2.029	0.521	15.181***	7.610	[2.742, 21.120]
Elements of Structures Spring (Summer 2013)	0.060	0.627	0.009	1.061	[0.311, 3.627]
Introduction to Solid State Chemistry (Fall 2012)	1.707	0.664	6.596*	5.510	[1.498, 20.265]
Introduction to Solid State Chemistry (Spring 2013)	2.349	2.769	0.720	10.480	[0.046, 2,383.914]
Circuits and Electronics (Fall 2012)	0.056	0.441	0.016	1.058	[0.446, 2.509]
Circuits and Electronics (Spring 2013)	1.084	0.654	2.744	2.957	[0.820, 10.664]
Introduction to Computer Science and Programming (Fall 2012)	0.214	0.374	0.328	1.239	[0.595, 2.582]
Introduction to Computer Science and Programming (Spring 2013)	0.277	0.420	0.436	1.319	[0.580, 3.002]
Introduction to Biology – The Secret of Life (Spring 2013)	0.736	0.567	1.686	2.088	[0.687, 6.345]
Electricity and Magnetism (Spring 2013)	-0.362	0.464	0.608	0.696	[0.281, 1.729]
Country France Germany Greece Poland Portugal Spain	- 0.953 0.112 0.692 0.590 0.359	- 0.513 0.595 0.501 0.671 0.456	6.029 3.458 0.035 1.904 0.772 0.619	- 2.594 1.118 1.997 1.803 1.432	- [0.950, 7.085] [0.349, 3.588] [0.748, 5.333] [0.484, 6.717] [0.586, 3.499]
Explored (access at least half of the chapters) No Yes	- 4.640	- 0.746	- 38.638***	- 103.545	- [23.974, 447.220]

continued on following page

Table 4. Continued

Independent variables	B	SE	Wald	Exp(B)	95% CI
Interactions					
Number of events					
1,753 and under	-	-	-	-	-
1,754 and over	0.609	0.432	1.988	1.838	[0.789, 4.285]
Number of days					
15 and under	-	-	-	-	-
16 and over	1.670	0.493	11.453**	5.313	[2.020, 13.975]
Number of play videos					
211 and under	-	-	-	-	-
212 and over	0.263	0.256	1.059	1.301	[0.788, 2.149]
Number of chapters					
5 and under	-	-	-	-	-
6 and over	1.983	1.271	2.434	7.267	[0.602, 87.777]
Model summary					
Cox & Snell R^2	0.459				
Nagelkerke R^2	0.790				
Hosmer & Lemeshow χ^2 (df)	1.737 (8)				
Hosmer & Lemeshow Test (Sig.)	0.988				
Omnibus χ^2 (df)	1,444.272 (27)				
Omnibus χ^2 (Sig.)	0.000				
Sample size	2,353				

* $p<0.05$; ** $p<0.01$; *** $p=0.000$

4.3 Network Analysis

The calculation of *modularity* was 0.133 (*randomize*=on, *use edge weights*=off, and *resolution*=1.0), with four classes with different frequencies for our 2,392 nodes and 25,883 edges: modularity class "0"=49.75%, modularity class "1"=8.40%, modularity class "2"=22.24%, and modularity class "3"=19.61%. Figure 2 shows this situation.

Bipartite graph (Figure 3) allows to detect various characteristics of the network variables analyzed. First, the spatial distribution of variables located on the upper side of the graph, which are related to online content interactions: to earn a certificate (certified), to explore the online content (explored), and the number of events, days, video play events, and chapters greater than their corresponding means (nevents≥1,754, ndays_act≥16, nplay_video≥212, nchapters≥6). It was also noted that these variables have the same purple colour because they belong to the same communality (modularity class "3"). Note that these relationships are very related to bivariate analysis showed in Table 3. Specifically, note the proximity between the three more important variables -certified, explored, and number of days-, like the regression analysis obtained in Table 4.

Secondly, there are nodes at the bottom of the graph that represent an opposite situation to those at the top (non-certified, non-explored, nevents<1,754, ndays_act<16, nplay_video<212, nchapters<6). They have a blue colour because they belong to a different communality (modularity class "0"). Their sizes are bigger because they have more edges. In addition, other nodes in blue colour can also be observed, mainly related to the following variables: age≥30, education level="Master's", gender="Woman", country="Germany", and course="Introduction to Computer Science and Programming (Fall 2012)".

Third, different nodes located at the central-right area of the figure are highlighted. They are related to variables that forms a community of orange colour nodes that is different from the previous two ones

Figure 2. Size distribution of modularity classes

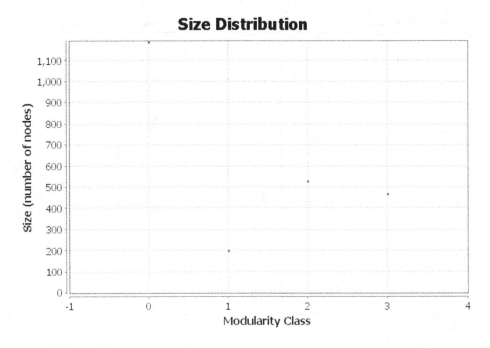

(modularity class "2"). In this case, nodes with both large (gender="Man", age<30) and small (education level="Secondary", and country="Poland") size are observed. Finally, the nodes belonging to the last detected communality at the central area of the figure, which are represented in green colour (modularity class "1"). Also smaller, mainly they relate to the following variables: country="Spain", education level="Bachelor's", and course="Introduction to Computer Science and Programming (Spring 2013)". In addition, different clouds of nodes corresponding to other variables considered in the dataset are observed.

5. DISCUSSION

5.1 Overview of Key Findings

Taking into account that e-learning and lifelong learning are being used increasingly, this chapter has researched on learning analytics through an approach based on graph analysis of content interactions developed on MOOC platforms. It has used public microdata from HarvardX and MITx, with European non-English-speaking countries enrolled, and controlling for socio-demographics and students' behavior variables. Thus, the research reveals two main outcomes: i) online content interactions are factors to provide an adequate explanation to earn a certificate; and ii) by using an algorithm for transforming our tabular data into an undirected bipartite network, graph analytics helps to find similar results to traditional statistics, especifically, to multiple binary logistic regression model.

On the one hand, the bivariate analysis finds that the more online content interactions (content explored, and frequency of access, days, videos and chapters consulted) the more certified students. These facts are especially relevant in the multivariable analyses, which proves that influence of content interactions

Figure 3. Graph visualization with network of variables

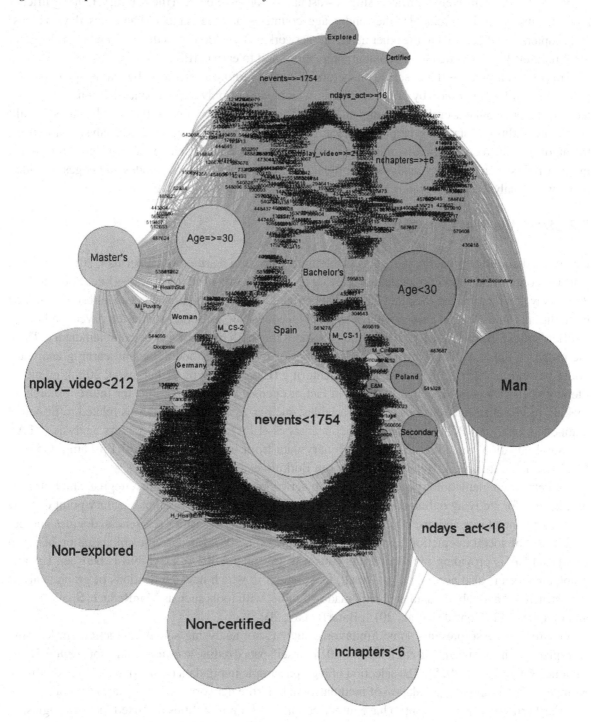

For a more accurate representation of this figure, please see the electronic version.

has to do almost exclusively with accessing at least half of the chapters. On the contrary, non-significant relationships in variables related to the gender, age, countries, and the number of accesses, days, videos, and chapters, are detected. On the other hand, our network analysis confirms this by showing a clear and great relationships existing among content interactions and to earn certificates variables.

This research suggests that research on factors influence earning a certificate by online open learning platforms can be performed by graph analytics, which can not only supplement traditional statistical techniques, but can be useful for learning analytics. The findings also suggest that graph analysis could accelerate traditional statistics, helping to select the key variables for multivariable analysis. Moreover, the algorithm for recoding tabular data into variables network could open new uses of graph analytics in other fields such as survey analysis. Finally, the use of metrics related to nodes and edges provided by network analysis could add new approaches and results to learning analytics, too.

5.2 Strengths and Limitations

Outcomes demonstrate that the more access the more success in learning (Zimmerman, 2012), and that learning content and support material are relevant to acquire better academic results (Lee, Yoon, & Lee, 2009; Inayat, Amin, Inayat, & Salim, 2013). This research offers a comparison between results obtained by traditional statistics and graph analytics applied on education, like other studies on psychopathology (Höfler, Brückl, Bittner, & Lieb, 2007), and concludes that both methods can be complementary. Thus, the proposed approach is oriented toward new lines of research methodologies in learning analytics, going beyond measuring of processes of e-mentoring (Liu, Macintyre, & Ferguson, 2012), or media literacy skills (Dawson & Siemens, 2014). In fact, it opens a way on directions for future research by seeking to visualize relationships among variables, such as psychometric analysis related to principal component analysis (PCA), exploratory factor analysis (EFA), confirmatory factors analysis (CFA), structural equation modelling (SEM), and binary data from traditional statistics (Epskamp, Cramer, Waldorp, Schmittmann, & Borsboom, 2012; van Borkulo et al., 2014).

The proposed methodology uses metrics from network analytics (community, degree, and ForceAtlas2 layout) for studying online content interactions. It offers a new and complementary point of view of learner-content interactions, which has into account centrality measures (closeness, degrees and betweenness) of social interactions among students (Dawson, 2008). Because the collaboration between EDM and LA is providing excellent fruits (Baker & Inventado, 2014), a symbiosis between LA and graph analytics is also necessary. Above all, in a context in which new applications of graph analysis to unstructured and tabular data are being made possible, with tools such as MapReduce, Spark, Dryad and GraphX API (Gonzalez et al., 2014; Batarfi et al., 2015).

Our research also presents some limitations, such as not analysing social interactions in learning workplaces (Virtanen, Tynjälä, & Eteläpelto, 2014) or self-paced online learning (Anderson, Upton, Dron, Malone, & Poelhuber, 2015). The selection of a graph sample in big data (Ahmed, Duffield, Neville, & Kompella, 2014) and the calculation of modularity in bipartite networks (Barber, 2007) are constraints, too. Furthermore, it is important to have into account the real possibilities of mixed methodologies, as already discussed in using quantitative and qualitative indicators in LA to support students (Persico, Pozzi, & Sarti, 2010).

6. CONCLUSION

Problems arising from the existence of a huge amounts of educational data, such as their usage and management, exist since the last quarter of the twentieth century, as seen since the late 70s in research related with the world of open education in UK (McIntosh, 1979). The advances made in recent decades in the world of ICT and telecommunications have caused that these problems have been accentuated even more. This has created new areas of research linking knowledge fields on education, statistics, and computer science, such as educational data mining and learning analytics. They have important future challenges related to their relations with learning sciences, large datasets, needs of students, and valid ethical codes that propose how to manage the use of massive data and privacy aspects. The research proposes the use of graph analysis techniques for developing learning analytics, demonstrating that they are valid in a case study related to students from six European non-English-speaking countries who were enrolled in online courses conducted in HarvardX and MITx. Controlling for socio-demographics and online content interactions characteristics, and proposing an algorithm for recoding tabular data into undirected bipartite networks, findings prove the effects of online content interactions and their influence in earning certificates, and suggest that graph analytics and learning analytics via traditional statistics can work in perfect harmony.

ACKNOWLEDGMENT

Juan-Francisco Martínez-Cerdá would like to acknowledge the support of a doctoral grant from the Universitat Oberta de Catalunya (UOC). The authors would like to thank Dr. Julià Minguillón for his initial advices related to graph and network analysis. They would like to thank Isuru Balasooriya for his help in the English revision of the manuscript.

REFERENCES

Aceto, S., Borotis, S., Devine, J., & Fischer, T. (2014). *Mapping and Analysing Prospective Technologies for Learning* (P. Kampylis & Y. Punie, Eds.). Seville, Spain: Joint Research Centre, Institute for Prospective Technological Studies.

Ahmed, N. K., Duffield, N., Neville, J., & Kompella, R. (2014). Graph Sample and Hold: A Framework for Big-graph Analytics. In *Proceedings of the 20th ACM SIGKDD International Conference on Knowledge Discovery and Data Mining* (pp. 1446–1455). New York, NY: ACM. doi:10.1145/2623330.2623757

Anderson, T., & McGreal, R. (2012). Disruptive Pedagogies and Technologies in Universities. *Journal of Educational Technology & Society*, 15(4), 380–389.

Anderson, T., Upton, L., Dron, J., Malone, J., & Poelhuber, B. (2015). Social Interaction in Self-paced Distance Education. *Open Praxis*, 7(1), 7–23. doi:10.5944/openpraxis.7.1.164

Ariza, E. N., & Hancock, S. (2003). Second Language Acquisition Theories as a Framework for Creating Distance Learning Courses. *The International Review of Research in Open and Distributed Learning*, 4(2). doi:10.19173/irrodl.v4i2.142

Arrow, K. J. (1971). *The theory of discrimination* (Working Paper No. No. 30A). Princeton, NJ: Princeton University.

Baker, R. S., & Inventado, P. S. (2014). Educational Data Mining and Learning Analytics. In J. A. Larusson & B. White (Eds.), *Learning Analytics: from research to practice* (pp. 61–75). New York: Springer New York. doi:10.1007/978-1-4614-3305-7_4

Baker, R. S. J. D., & Yacef, K. (2009). The State of Educational Data Mining in 2009: A Review and Future Visions. *Journal of Educational Data Mining, 1*(1), 3–17.

Barber, M. J. (2007). Modularity and community detection in bipartite networks. *Physical Review E: Statistical, Nonlinear, and Soft Matter Physics, 76*(6), 11. doi:10.1103/PhysRevE.76.066102 PMID:18233893

Bastian, M., Heymann, S., & Jacomy, M. (2009). Gephi: An Open Source Software for Exploring and Manipulating Networks. In *Third International AAAI Conference on Weblogs and Social Media* (p. 9). San José, CA: The AAAI Press.

Batarfi, O., Shawi, R. E., Fayoumi, A. G., Nouri, R., Beheshti, S.-M.-R., Barnawi, A., & Sakr, S. (2015). Large scale graph processing systems: Survey and an experimental evaluation. *Cluster Computing, 18*(3), 1189–1213. doi:10.1007/s10586-015-0472-6

Becker, G.-S. (1993). *Human capital: a theoretical and empirical analysis, with special reference to education* (3rd ed.). New York: National Bureau of Economic Research: Distributed by Columbia University Press. doi:10.7208/chicago/9780226041223.001.0001

Berland, M., Baker, R. S., & Blikstein, P. (2014). Educational Data Mining and Learning Analytics: Applications to Constructionist Research. *Technology. Knowledge and Learning, 19*(1–2), 205–220. doi:10.1007/s10758-014-9223-7

Blondel, V. D., Guillaume, J.-L., Lambiotte, R., & Lefebvre, E. (2008). Fast unfolding of communities in large networks. *Journal of Statistical Mechanics, 2008*(10), P10008. doi:10.1088/1742-5468/2008/10/P10008

Boccaletti, S., Latora, V., Moreno, Y., Chávez, M., & Hwang, D.-U. (2006). Complex networks: Structure and dynamics. *Physics Reports, 424*(4–5), 175–308. doi:10.1016/j.physrep.2005.10.009

Brandes, U., Kenis, P., & Raab, J. (2006). Explanation through network visualization. *Methodology: European Journal of Research Methods for the Behavioral and Social Sciences, 2*(1), 16–23. doi:10.1027/1614-2241.2.1.16

Calvet Liñán, L., & Juan Pérez, Á. A. (2015). Educational Data Mining and Learning Analytics: Differences, similarities, and time evolution. *RUSC Universities and Knowledge Society Journal, 12*(3), 98. doi:10.7238/rusc.v12i3.2515

Coffrin, C., Corrin, L., de Barba, P., & Kennedy, G. (2014). Visualizing Patterns of Student Engagement and Performance in MOOCs. In *Proceedings of the Fourth International Conference on Learning Analytics And Knowledge* (pp. 83–92). New York, NY: ACM. doi:10.1145/2567574.2567586

Dawson, S. (2008). A Study of the Relationship between Student Social Networks and Sense of Community. *Journal of Educational Technology & Society, 11*(3), 224–238.

Dawson, S., & Siemens, G. (2014). Analytics to literacies: The development of a learning analytics framework for multiliteracies assessment. *International Review of Research in Open and Distance Learning*, *15*(4). doi:10.19173/irrodl.v15i4.1878

de Laat, M., & Schreurs, B. (2013). Visualizing Informal Professional Development Networks Building a Case for Learning Analytics in the Workplace. *The American Behavioral Scientist*, *57*(10), 1421–1438. doi:10.1177/0002764213479364

Delors, J., Mufti, I. A., Amagi, I., Carneiro, R., Chung, F., & Geremek, B. (1996). International Commission on Education for the Twenty-First Century. Learning, the treasure within: Report to UNESCO of the International Commission on Education for the Twenty-first Century. Paris: UNESCO.

Dyckhoff, A. L., Zielke, D., Bültmann, M., Chatti, M. A., & Schroeder, U. (2012). Design and Implementation of a Learning Analytics Toolkit for Teachers. *Journal of Educational Technology & Society*, *15*(3), 58–76.

Elias, T. (2011). *Learning Analytics: The Definitions, the Processes, and the Potential*. Retrieved from http://learninganalytics.net/LearningAnalyticsDefinitionsProcessesPotential.pdf

Engeström, Y. (1987). *Learning by Expanding: An Activity-theoretical Approach to Developmental Research*. Helsinki: Orienta-Konsultit.

Epskamp, S., Cramer, A. O. J., Waldorp, L. J., Schmittmann, V. D., & Borsboom, D. (2012). qgraph: Network visualizations of relationships in psychometric data. *Journal of Statistical Software*, *48*(4), 1–18. doi:10.18637/jss.v048.i04

Ferguson, R. (2012). Learning Analytics: Drivers, Developments and Challenges. *International Journal of Technology Enhanced Learning*, *4*(5/6), 304–317. doi:10.1504/IJTEL.2012.051816

Fournier, H., Kop, R., & Sitlia, H. (2011). The Value of Learning Analytics to Networked Learning on a Personal Learning Environment. In *Proceedings of the 1st International Conference on Learning Analytics and Knowledge* (pp. 104–109). New York, NY: ACM. doi:10.1145/2090116.2090131

Gonzalez, J. E., Xin, R. S., Dave, A., Crankshaw, D., Franklin, M. J., & Stoica, I. (2014). GraphX: Graph Processing in a Distributed Dataflow Framework. In *Proceedings of the 11th USENIX Symposium on Operating Systems Design and Implementation* (pp. 599–613). Broomfield, CO: USENIX.

Hanneman, R. A., & Riddle, M. (2005). *Introduction to social network methods*. Riverside, CA: University of California.

Ho, A. D., Reich, J., Nesterko, S. O., Seaton, D. T., Mullaney, T., Waldo, J., & Chuang, I. (2014). *HarvardX and MITx: The First Year of Open Online Courses, Fall 2012-Summer 2013 (SSRN Scholarly Paper No. No. 1)*. Rochester, NY: Social Science Research Network. doi:10.2139/ssrn.2381263

Höfler, M., Brückl, T., Bittner, A., & Lieb, R. (2007). Visualizing multivariate dependencies with association chain graphs. *Methodology: European Journal of Research Methods for the Behavioral and Social Sciences*, *3*(1), 24–34. doi:10.1027/1614-2241.3.1.24

Inayat, I., Amin, R., Inayat, Z., & Salim, S. S. (2013). Effects of Collaborative Web Based Vocational Education and Training (VET) on Learning Outcomes. *Computers & Education*, *68*, 153–166. doi:10.1016/j.compedu.2013.04.027

Jacobson, M. J., & Wilensky, U. (2006). Complex Systems in Education: Scientific and Educational Importance and Implications for the Learning Sciences. *Journal of the Learning Sciences*, *15*(1), 11–34. doi:10.1207/s15327809jls1501_4

Jacomy, M., Venturini, T., Heymann, S., & Bastian, M. (2014). ForceAtlas2, a Continuous Graph Layout Algorithm for Handy Network Visualization Designed for the Gephi Software. *PLoS ONE*, *9*(6), e98679. doi:10.1371/journal.pone.0098679 PMID:24914678

Jiang, S., Ferreira, J., & González, M. C. (2012). Clustering daily patterns of human activities in the city. *Data Mining and Knowledge Discovery*, *25*(3), 478–510. doi:10.1007/s10618-012-0264-z

Jones, C. (2004). Networks and learning: Communities, practices and the metaphor of networks. *Research in Learning Technology*, *12*(1). doi:10.3402/rlt.v12i1.11227

Kinshuk, Hui-Wen, H., Sampson, D., & Chen, N.-S. (2013). Trends in Educational Technology through the Lens of the Highly Cited Articles Published in the Journal of Educational Technology and Society. *Journal of Educational Technology & Society*, *16*(2), 3–20.

Kop, R. (2011). The challenges to connectivist learning on open online networks: Learning experiences during a massive open online course. *The International Review of Research in Open and Distributed Learning*, *12*(3), 19–38. doi:10.19173/irrodl.v12i3.882

Krashen, S. D. (1982). *Principles and practice in second language acquisition*. Oxford, UK: Pergamon.

Krashen, S. D. (1985). *The input hypothesis: issues and implications*. London: Longman.

Lambiotte, R., Delvenne, J.-C., & Barahona, M. (2009). *Laplacian dynamics and multiscale modular structure in networks*. arXiv:0812.1770

Lee, B.-C., Yoon, J.-O., & Lee, I. (2009). Learners acceptance of e-learning in South Korea: Theories and results. *Computers & Education*, *53*(4), 1320–1329. doi:10.1016/j.compedu.2009.06.014

Leontiev, A. N. (1974). The Problem of Activity in Psychology. *Social Psychology*, *13*(2), 4–33. doi:10.2753/RPO1061-040513024

Leontiev, A. N. (1978). *Activity, consciousness, and personality*. Englewood Cliffs, NJ: Prentice-Hall.

Liu, H., Macintyre, R., & Ferguson, R. (2012). Exploring Qualitative Analytics for e-Mentoring Relationships Building in an Online Social Learning Environment. In *Proceedings of the 2Nd International Conference on Learning Analytics and Knowledge* (pp. 179–183). New York, NY: ACM. doi:10.1145/2330601.2330646

Liu, Z., Navathe, S. B., & Stasko, J. T. (2011). Network-based Visual Analysis of Tabular Data. In *Visual Analytics Science and Technology (VAST), 2011 IEEE Conference on* (pp. 41–50). Providence, RI: IEEE. doi:10.1109/VAST.2011.6102440

Liu, Z., Navathe, S. B., & Stasko, J. T. (2014). Ploceus: Modeling, visualizing, and analyzing tabular data as networks. *Information Visualization, 13*(1), 59–89. doi:10.1177/1473871613488591

Martínez-Cerdá, J.-F., & Torrent-Sellens, J. (2015). Graph analysis to survey data: A first approximation. *International Journal of Complex Systems in Science, 5*(1), 29–36.

Mazzola, L., & Mazza, R. (2011). Visualizing learner models through data aggregation: a test case. *Proceedings of the red-conference, rethinking education in the knowledge society,* 372–380.

McIntosh, N. E. (1979). Barriers to implementing research in higher education. *Studies in Higher Education, 4*(1), 77–86. doi:10.1080/03075077912331377121

Moore, M. G. (1989). Editorial: Three types of interaction. *American Journal of Distance Education, 3*(2), 1–7. doi:10.1080/08923648909526659

Moore, M. G., & Kearsley, G. (2011). *Distance education: A systems view of online learning.* Belmont, CA: Wadsworth Cengage Learning.

Nardi, B. A. (1996). Studying context: A comparison of activity theory, situated action models and distributed cognition. In B. A. Nardi (Ed.), *Context and consciousness: Activity theory and human-computer interaction* (pp. 69–102). Cambridge, MA: MIT Press.

Nisar, M. U., Fard, A., & Miller, J. A. (2013). Techniques for Graph Analytics on Big Data. In *2013 IEEE International Congress on Big Data* (pp. 255–262). Santa Clara, CA: IEEE. doi:10.1109/BigData.Congress.2013.78

Pahl, C. (2004). Data Mining Technology for the Evaluation of Learning Content Interaction. *International Journal on E-Learning, 3*(4), 47–55.

Persico, D., Pozzi, F., & Sarti, L. (2010). Monitoring collaborative activities in computer supported collaborative learning. *Distance Education, 31*(1), 5–22. doi:10.1080/01587911003724603

Redecker, C., Punie, Y., & Ferrari, A. (2012). eAssessment for 21st Century Learning and Skills. In A. Ravenscroft, S. Lindstaedt, C. D. Kloos, & D. Hernández-Leo (Eds.), 21st Century Learning for 21st Century Skills (pp. 292–305). Saarbrücken, Germany: Springer Berlin Heidelberg.

Romero, C., & Ventura, S. (2007). Educational data mining: A survey from 1995 to 2005. *Expert Systems with Applications, 33*(1), 135–146. doi:10.1016/j.eswa.2006.04.005

Rossi, R., & Ahmed, N. (2015). The Network Data Repository with Interactive Graph Analytics and Visualization. In *AAAI 2015 Proceeding* (pp. 4292–4293). Austin, TX: The AAAI Press.

Sao Pedro, M. A., Baker, R. S. J. D., & Gobert, J. D. (2013). What Different Kinds of Stratification Can Reveal About the Generalizability of Data-mined Skill Assessment Models. In *Proceedings of the Third International Conference on Learning Analytics and Knowledge* (pp. 190–194). New York, NY: ACM. doi:10.1145/2460296.2460334

Satish, N., Sundaram, N., Patwary, M. M. A., Seo, J., Park, J., & Hassaan, M. A., … Dubey, P. (2014). Navigating the Maze of Graph Analytics Frameworks Using Massive Graph Datasets. In *Proceedings of the 2014 ACM SIGMOD International Conference on Management of Data* (pp. 979–990). New York, NY: ACM. doi:10.1145/2588555.2610518

Schultz, T.-W. (1961). Investment in Human Capital. *The American Economic Review, 51*(1), 1–17.

Siemens, G., & Baker, R. S. J. d. (2012). Learning Analytics and Educational Data Mining: Towards Communication and Collaboration. In *Proceedings of the 2Nd International Conference on Learning Analytics and Knowledge* (pp. 252–254). New York, NY: ACM. doi:10.1145/2330601.2330661

Slade, S., & Prinsloo, P. (2013). Learning Analytics Ethical Issues and Dilemmas. *The American Behavioral Scientist, 57*(10), 1510–1529. doi:10.1177/0002764213479366

Upadhyaya, K. T., & Mallik, D. (2013). E-Learning as a Socio-Technical System: An Insight into Factors Influencing its Effectiveness. *Business Perspectives & Research, 2*(1), 1–12. doi:10.1177/2278533720130101

van Borkulo, C. D., Borsboom, D., Epskamp, S., Blanken, T. F., Boschloo, L., Schoevers, R. A., & Waldorp, L. J. (2014). A new method for constructing networks from binary data. *Scientific Reports, 4,* 10. doi:10.1038/srep05918 PMID:25082149

Varis, T., & Puukko, M. (Eds.). (2010). *Challenges of Global eLearning.* Tampere: Tampere University, Research Centre for Vocational Education.

Virtanen, A., Tynjälä, P., & Eteläpelto, A. (2014). Factors promoting vocational students learning at work: Study on student experiences. *Journal of Education and Work, 27*(1), 43–70. doi:10.1080/1363 9080.2012.718748

Wagner, E. D. (1997). Interactivity: From Agents to Outcomes. *New Directions for Teaching and Learning, 1997*(71), 19–26. doi:10.1002/tl.7103

Zimmerman, T. D. (2012). Exploring learner to content interaction as a success factor in online courses. *The International Review of Research in Open and Distributed Learning, 13*(4), 152–165. doi:10.19173/irrodl.v13i4.1302

Chapter 6
Social Network Analysis of Different Parameters Derived From Real-Time Facebook Profiles

Paramita Dey
Government College of Engineering and Ceramic Technology, Spain

Krishnendu Dutta
Government College of Engineering and Ceramic Technology, Spain

ABSTRACT

With the advent of online social media, it is possible to collect large information and extract information. One of the powerful roles that networks play is to bridge gap between the local and the global perspectives. For example, social network analysis could be used to offer explanations for how simple processes at the level of individual nodes and links can have a global effect. Social networks like Twitter, Facebook, LinkedIn are very large in size with millions of vertices and billions of edges. To collect meaningful information from these densely connected graphs and huge volume of data, it is important to find proper topology of the network as well as conduct analysis based on different network parameters. The main objective of this work is to study the network parameters commonly used to explain social structures. We extract data from the three real-time Facebook accounts using the Netvizz application, analyze and evaluate their network parameters on some widely recognized graph topology using Gephi, a free and open source software.

1. INTRODUCTION

In the last few years, we have witnessed an explosive growth of online social networks (OSNs) that have attracted most attention from all over the world [Benevenuto et.al, 2009]. Facebook, a social network service, has attracted over 1.86 billion monthly active users as on December, 2016 (source: facebook.com). This huge user base of these OSNs provides an open platform for social network analysis includ-

DOI: 10.4018/978-1-5225-2814-2.ch006

ing user behavior measurements, social interaction characterization and information propagation studies. However, the huge size of social network, represent in the form of graphs, hinders researchers for better understanding of data properties. Due to the huge datasets of these OSN, analysis of the same requires well-equipped computer clusters, as well as large time and computation overhead. So, it would be beneficial for us, if we extract the useful network parameters of these graphs and use it for further characterization. Every user in social network possesses a user profile which contains basic information like name, date of birth etc. as well as complex information like group formation, educational or professional information, area of interest etc. It becomes abstract of real world, where users interact, keep in touch and exchange data.

The main objective of this paper is to study the dynamics of different parameters involved in social network analytics. We have considered three realtime facebook profiles. Some selected network parameters are derived from these profiles for analysis. A comparative analysis is also presented here. Filtering approaches are used to reduce the data set without effecting basic properties especially node degree distribution (NDD) and clustering coefficient (CC).

A brief overview on related research work is depicted in section 2. Different social network parameters relevant to this paper are briefly discussed in Section 3. In Section 4 two open source software tools, Netvizz and Gephi are discussed which are used respectively to extract and analyze the data. Results derived from real time facebook accounts are presented in Section 5 and a comparative analysis is done in perspective of social networking. In Section 6, concluding remarks are made based on the analysis along with future scope of this work in this area.

2. RELATED RESEARCH WORK

With the rise of online networking communities like whatsapp, viber, Skype and Orkut along with the popularization of the notions of "six degrees of separation" and the Kevin Bacon game, the concept of a social network becomes popular [Albert R. and Barabasi, A.L., 2002]. Significant works have been done by psychologists and sociologists in 1950's [Scott J, 1988], [Wilson, R .E. et al., 2012] which are found from histological survey of Wasserman and Faust's book. Due to huge calculation and data collection requirements, people generally preferred small network at that time. The study of Internet platforms via data extraction has seen rapid growth over the last two decades and in recent time the concept of big data analysis takes significant role. For researchers from the humanities and social sciences, the possibility to analyze the expressions and behavioral traces from very large numbers of individuals or groups using these platforms can provide valuable insights into the arrays of meaning and practice that emerge and manifest themselves online [Bonato A, 2005], [Perer, S., 2006]. Though online social network analysis simulates only virtual space, supposed to be distinct from real life, the Internet can be considered as "a source of data about society and culture".

3. SOCIAL NETWORK PARAMETERS

Social network analysis (SNA) is the mapping and measuring of relationships and flows between people, groups, organizations and other connected knowledge entities. The nodes in such networks are the people or group while the links show relationships or flows between the nodes. SNA provides both a visual and a mathematical analysis of human relationships. In a social network, a node represents a social entity, typically a person, an organization, or any other relevant unit. An edge stands for a specific relationship between its incident nodes. In contrast to other areas in social sciences in which it is important to understand what characterizes social entities (e.g., by considering their attributes), social network analysis concentrates on the structure of relationships and tries to explain social phenomena from those structures. For example, in social network, two nodes are connected if they regularly talk to each other, or interact by some means.

Some useful network parameters are discussed in this section.

3.1 Diameter and Radius

Two of the most commonly observed parameters of a graph in this field are its radius and diameter. The diameter of a connected graph G, denoted by $diam(G)$, is the maximum distance between two vertices [Rodriguez J.A. and Yebra J.L.A., 1999]. The eccentricity of a vertex is the maximum distance from it to any other vertex [Wayne,G. and Ortrud R. O., 2011]. The minimum eccentricity among all vertices of G is defined as the radius and denoted by $rad(G)$. Obviously, the diameter is the maximum eccentricity among all vertices. For a weighted undirected graph $G: rad(G) \leq diam(G) \leq 2rad(G)$. The upperbound follows from the triangle inequality. The radius and diameter can be easily computed for simple graphs. In SNA, diameter denotes the connectivity that can be between two furthest nodes. For a well-connected and dense network, the diameter will be large while radius is sufficiently small.

3.2 Centrality Measures

In graph theory and network analysis, centrality refers to indicator to identify the most important vertices within a network. Similarly, in a social network, it is used to identify the most influential person(s) in that network. Different centrality measures are briefly discussed in sequel.

- **Degree Centrality:** Degree centrality indicate the nodes that have maximum in-degree and out-degree connections i.e., the number of direct connections. The larger the number of neighbors for a node, the higher the degree centrality of the node.
- **Betweenness Centrality:** Betweenness centrality denotes the nodes that have many direct connections in the network. This node occur maximum within all possible shortest paths in the network. It plays a 'broker' /powerful role in the network. But the disadvantage is that this node is a single point of failure. A node with high betweenness centrality has great influence in the network.
- **Closeness Centrality:** The nodes that have fewer connections, yet the pattern of their direct and indirect connectivity allow them to access all the nodes in the network more quickly than anyone else. They have the shortest paths with all other nodes in the network. The closeness centrality of a node is defined as the inverse of the sum of shortest path distances from that node to every other nodes in the network. These nodes are in excellent position to monitor the information flow in the network and thereby have the best visibility into what is happening in the network.

Individual network centralities provide insight into the individual's location in the network [Freeman L.C, 1978/1979]. The relationship between the centralities of all nodes can reveal much about the overall network structure. A very centralized network is dominated by one or few nodes with high centrality. If these nodes are removed or damaged, the network quickly fragments into disconnected sub-networks. A highly central node can becomes a single point of failure. A network centralized around a well-connected hub can fail abruptly if that hub is disabled or removed. Hubs are nodes with high degree and betweeness centrality. On the other hand, a less centralized network has no single points of failure. It is resilient in the face of many intentional attacks or random failures in a way many nodes or links can fail while the remaining nodes are still connected over other network paths. Networks of low centralization fail gracefully.

3.3 Community Detection

Community detection is the problem of identifying community structure in social network analysis. Community structure is denoted as the grouping of nodes in the network such that the grouping demonstrates property of high coupling and low cohesion, i.e., the number of edges within a group are maximized and the number of edges amongst the groups are minimized. Detecting community structure in a graph is a well studied problem in social network analysis. Communities, also called clusters or modules, are groups of vertices which probably share common properties and/or play similar roles within the graph. In Figure 1 a schematic example of a graph with communities is shown.

Figure 1. Community detection and clustering

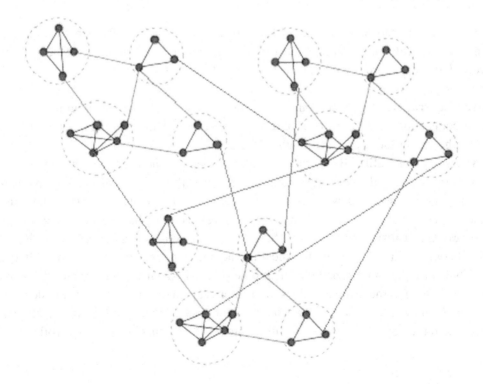

Identifying modules and their boundaries allows for a classification of vertices, according to their structural position in the modules. So, vertices with a central position in their clusters, i.e., sharing a large number of edges with the other group partners, may have an important function of control and stability within the group; vertices lying at the boundaries between modules play an important role of mediation and lead the relationships and exchanges between different communities.

In social studies, four types of criteria were identified for community detection, namely complete mutuality, reach ability, vertex degree and the comparison of internal versus external cohesion. The corresponding communities are mostly maximal sub graphs, which cannot be enlarged with the addition of new vertices and edges without losing the property which defines them. Generally, social communities can be defined in a very strict sense as subgroups whose members are all friends to each other (complete mutuality). In graph theoretic terms, this corresponds to a clique, i.e., a subset whose vertices are all adjacent to each other. In social network analysis, a clique is a maximal complete sub graph. Communities can also be identified by fitness measure, expressing to which extent a sub graph satisfies a given property related to its cohesion [Ronald S. B., 1987]. The larger fitness signifies the more definite community.

3.4 Clustering Coefficient

Clustering Coefficient (CC)[Freeman L.C, 1978/1979] is a measure of the degree to which nodes in a graph tend to cluster together. The local clustering coefficient for node u in undirected graphs is given by:

$$C_u = \begin{cases} \dfrac{2|E_{v,w}|}{k_u(k_u-1)} & if\, k_u > 1 \\ 0 & otherwise \end{cases}$$

Where $E_{v,w}$ is the set of edges among neighbours of u. The average clustering coefficient is the network average clusteringcoefficient (NACC) of all nodes in the graphs:

$$\bar{C} = \frac{1}{n}\sum_{n=1}^{n} C_i$$

Where n is the total number of nodes in the graphs.

Another approach for finding clustering coefficients [Latapy, M., 2008], main-memory triangle computations for very large (sparse(power-law)) graphs is used. The clustering coefficient of avertex v (of degree at least 2) is the probability that any two randomly chosen neighbors of v are linked together. It is computed by dividing the number of triangles containing v by the number of possible edges between its neighbors i.e., $\binom{d(v)}{2}$ if $d(v)$ denotes the number of neighbors of v. One may then define the clustering coefficient of the whole graph as the average of these value for all the vertices (of degree at least 2).

3.5 Node Degree Distribution

On directed graphs, there are two types of degree for a vertex v :the in-degree, i.e., the number of edges into v and the out-degree, i. e., the number of edges going out from v. The analogue of degree on a weighted graph is the strength, i.e., the sum of the weights of the edges adjacent to the vertex. Node degree distribution (NDD) is one of the most important properties of a graph [Wang T. et al, 2011]. Generally, node degree represents the number of users with whom one user interacts within that social networking site. It is a very useful metric to study the user behavior.

The rank of a graph G is defined as $r\left(G\right) = n - c$, where n is the number of vertices on G and c is the number of connected component. Rank is usually used to estimate the importance of a node in a network. It mainly counts the number and quality of links to a node. The underlying assumption is that more important nodes are likely to receive more links from other nodes. In social network analysis, the node with maximum rank is considered as seed or leader node of the network [Kleinberg J, 1998].

3.6 Average Path Length

The average path length is defined as average distance of a graph $G = \left(V, E\right)$ of order n. It is denoted by the expected distance between a randomly chosen pair of distinct vertices; i.e.,

$$\mu\left(G\right) = \frac{1}{\binom{n}{2}} \sum_{u,v \subset V} d\left(u, v\right)$$

The study of the average distance began with the Chemist Wiener, who noticed that the melting point of certain hydrocarbons is proportional to the sum of all distances between unordered pairs of vertices of the corresponding graph. This sum is now called the Wiener number or Wiener index of the graph and is denoted by $\sigma\left(G\right)$. (Note that $\sigma\left(G\right) = \binom{n}{2}\mu\left(G\right)$). The average distance of agraph has been used for comparing the compactness of graph. Doyle and Graver were the first to define it as a graph parameter.

Average path length signifies how well the members of the graphs are connected in a social network. Another important aspect of average path length is that, it helps to remove edges when we filter the data. We can measure the effect of an edge e's removal from G by considering either the difference or the ratio. In both the cases the best edge is one whose removal minimizes the quantity in question, and the worst edge is one that maximizes the quantity. These questions which are of importance in network design are. how badly failure of an edge would made impact the network, or how much would the network suffer if we omitted a particular link to save costs.

4. GRAPH VISUALIZATION SOFTWARES

Netvizz [Rieder B., 2013] and Gephi [Bastian M. et al., 2009] are used for data extraction and graph analysis. Both tools are free and open source. These tools are briefly discussed in the following subsections.

4.1 Netvizz

Netvizz is a tool that extracts data from different sections of the facebook platform (personal profile, groups, pages) for research purposes. File outputs can be stored in text or svg format and can be easily analyzed in standard software. The data can be extracted in different network based on the following information.

- **Personal Network:** Extracts user's friends and the friendship connections between them.
- **Personal Like Network:** Creates a network that combinesuser's friends and the objects they liked in a bipartite graph.
- **Group Data:** Creates networks and tabular files for both friendships and interactions in groups.
- **Page Like Network:** Creates a network of pages connected through the likes between them.
- **Page Data:** Creates networks and tabular files for useractivity around posts on pages.

This application allows a facebook user to create gdf files(a simple text format that specifies an undirected graph) from the friendships relations of personal network or the group of which the user is a member. These files then can be analyzed or visualized using graph visualization software.

4.2 Gephi

Gephi is open source software for graph and network analysis. It is a tool for people that have to explore and understand graphs. In Gephi, users can interact with the representation; manipulate the structures, shapes and colors to reveal hidden properties. The goal is to help data analysts to make hypothesis, intuitively discover patterns, and isolate structure singularities or faults during data analysis. This is a software for exploratory data analysis, a paradigm appearance in the visual analytic field of research. Gephi can be used for many graph analysis purposes. Some application areas are listed below.

- **Exploratory Data Analysis:** Intuition-oriented analysis by networks manipulations in real time.
- **Link Analysis:** Revealing the underlying structures of associations between objects, in particular in scale-free networks.
- **Social Network Analysis:** Easy creation of social data connectors to map community organizations and small-world networks.
- **Biological Network Analysis:** Representing patterns of biological data.
- **Poster Creation:** Scientific work promotion with hi-quality printable maps.

Gephi is a fast graph visualization engine to speed-up understanding and pattern discovery in large graphs. Gephi uses a 3D render engine to display large networks in real-time and to speed up the exploration. Modules can import, visualize, spatialize, filter, manipulate and export different networks. Networks can be explored in an interactive way with the visualization module; it can also be exported as a SVG or PDF file. Gephi uses ad-hoc OpenGL engine; which pushes the envelope on how interactive and efficient network exploration it would be. It can analyze Networks up to 50,000 nodes and 1,000,000 edges and can iterate through visualization using dynamic filtering and has a rich tools for meaningful graph manipulation. For Layout Designing, the layout palette allows user to change layout settings while running, and thus increases user feedback and experience. The approaches are based on force-based and multi-level algorithms. Statistics and metrics framework offer the most common metrics for social network analysis (SNA) and scale-free networks. It can measure betweenness, closeness, diameter, clustering coefficient, average shortest path, PageRank, HITS, community detection (modularity), random generators etc. Gephi is an ideal platform for leading innovation about dynamic network analysis (DNA). Dynamic structures, such as social networks can be filtered with the time-line component. It import temporal graph with the GEXF file format, generate graph streaming ready, create cartography, use ranking or partition of data to make meaningful network representation. It customizes colors, size or labels for better network representation. The vectorial preview module lets user to put the final touch and care about aesthetics, before exporting in SVG or PDF. It is also used for clustering, explore multi-level graphs by facilitating exploration and edition of large networks, hierarchically structured graphs, e.g., social communities, biochemical pathways or network traffic graphs. For Dynamic filtering, Gephi filters the network to select nodes and/or edges based on the network structure of data.

5. ANALYSIS AND COMPARATIVE STUDY

For the analysis purposes three Facebook profile was used to extract the data using Netvizz. These three profiles are three disjoint data sets as they are not in the friend list of each other. From the perspective of social network, it is informative to study their interactions within the network and find the implication of these results [Wilson, R .E. et al, 2012]. A partial view of data table of profile is shown in Figure 2.

After importing the data tables from Netvizz, it forms initial network where each node represents each person and each edge represents the communication between them. Initially it looks like a hairball. Though from these networks, no information can be derived but an initial idea can be made. From the following profiles, it can be seen that the first profile consists of small number of edges which signifies the users within these group shares less communication within them. A comparative view of these three initial networks is given in Figure 3.

Networks are formed using Forced Atlas. Force Atlas 2 [Jacomy M, 2010]integrate different techniques such as Barnes Hut simulation, degree-dependent repulsive force, local and global adaptive temperatures. The algorithm consider that nodes repulse to each other and the edges attract together. It is a continuous force directed layout. According to Fruchterman-Reingold model [Fruchterman T. M. Jand Reingold E. M., 1991], continuous network modeling was done depending on distributing the vertices evenly in the frame, making edge lengths uniform and reflect inherent symmetry. These two networks of profile 2 are shown in Figure 4.

As discussed earlier, maximum eccentricity implies diameter while minimum implies radius. From eccentricity distribution and betwenness centrality distribution, radius, diameter, average path lengths, number of shortest paths can be calculated. In Figure 5, eccentricity distribution and betweenness distributions of profile 2 are shown.

Figure 2. Partial Data table derived from facebook using netvizz and Gephi

Id	Label	... sex	locale	agerank
515828435	Vineet Bhatli	male	en_US	234
524088802	Lokesh Kaushal	male	en_US	233
567839072	Prerit Gupta	male	en_US	231
575094967	Avi Biswas	male	en_US	230
582834098	Ashish Garg	male	en_US	229
596396962	Vikash Jha	male	en_US	228
597213244	Bandana Kaur	female	en_US	227
597589223	Naveen Sharma	male	en_US	226
597806319	Preet Mohinder Singh	male	en_US	225
597927593	Neeraj Sharma	male	en_US	224
598483277	Sunny Lather	male	en_US	223
604943838	Indrajit Das	male	en_US	222
613199048	Ayesha Hazra	female	en_US	221
624458386	Saujanya Das	male	en_US	220
628122703	Aniruddha Sen	male	en_GB	219
629252904	Supriyo Sengupta	male	en_US	218
638385109	Pankaj Mittal	male	en_GB	217
641102918	Raveesh Srinivas	male	en_US	216
641292694	Abhishek Sabharwal	male	en_US	215
659451218	Sunandan Lahiry	male	en_US	214

Figure 3. Initial network formation

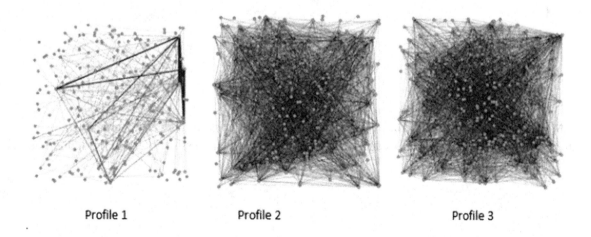

Profile 1   Profile 2   Profile 3

Figure 4. Network formation using force atlas 2 and Frutcherman Reingold respectively

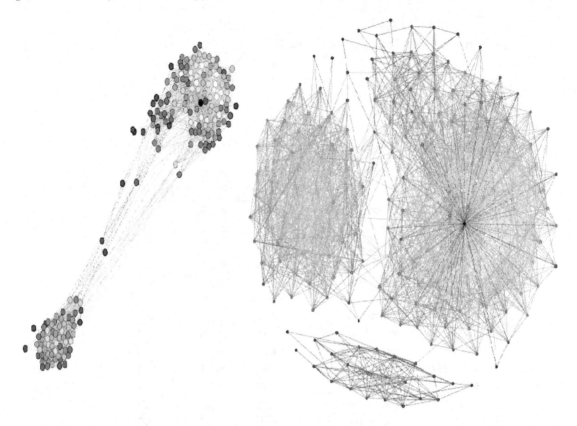

Figure 5. (a) Eccentricity Distribution, (b) Betweenness Centrality Distribution

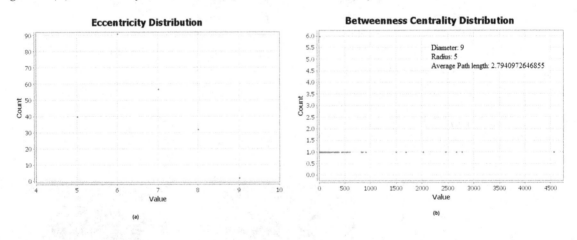

As discussed in earlier section, NDD plays an important role for network characterization. NDD can be improved by reducing nodes and edges. This is the basic process of filtering. In Figure 6 degree distributions are shown.

Figure 6. Degree distribution with modularity class

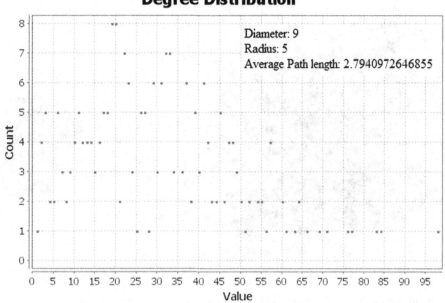

Clustering coefficient(CC) defines the centers of different communities.One have to be made sure whatever may be the change of network, clustering centers should not be changed. It is the measure of centrality.

In centrality distribution, we measure the shortest path between two nodes. In social networking terms, it defines how fast the information can be spread. The distribution is shown in Figure 7. In figure 7(a) Closeness centrality distribution is shown .In Figure 7(b) Eigen vector centrality distribution of profile 2 is shown. It is a measure of the influence of a node in a network. It assigns relative scores to all nodes in the network based on the concept that connections to high-scoring nodes contribute more to the score of the node in question than equal connections to low-scoring nodes. It is evident that, besides some small number of nodes, it centralized most of the nodes. The distributions are taken after 100 iterations.

Figure 7. (a) Closeness centrality distribution, (b) Eigen vector centrality distribution

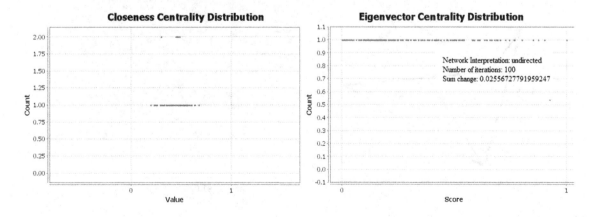

Figure 8. Community distribution with modularity class

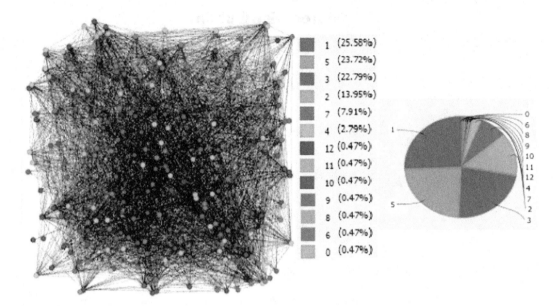

For a more accurate representation of this figure, please see the electronic version.

Community distribution denotes different communities where maximum interaction takes place. In Figure 8, community distribution over modularity classes are shown. A pie chart corresponds to percentage of different communities is also shown in this figure. Basically, it reflects different clusters.

Another distribution that reflects rank of the profiles and the percentages of male-female is shown in Figure 9. As all three profile of our case study belongs to male user, it shows a less percentages of female

Figure 9. (a) Community distribution with most connected edges and (b) male female percentage distribution

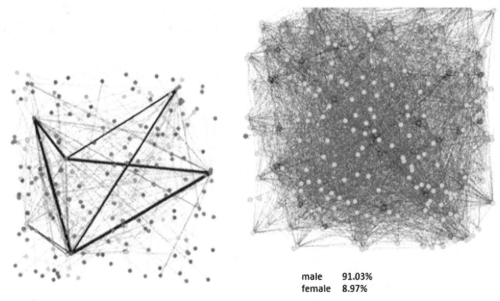

male   91.03%
female   8.97%

For a more accurate representation of this figure, please see the electronic version.

Table 1. Comparative study of network parameters

Matrices	Profile 1	Profile 2	Profile 3
No. of nodes	259	215	234
No. of edges	357	3114	3310
Diameter	6	7	9
Radius	1	0.1	0.1
Average path lengths	3.492	2.538	2.794
Number of communities	21	17	13
Density	0.012	0.135	0.121
Average weighted degree	3.202	28.967	28.291
Average clustering coefficient	0	0.561	0.592
Average path length (after clustering)	3.492	2.538	2.794
Number of shortest path (after clustering)	47326	43056	49062

community (refer to Figure 9.b).Rank signifies the number of connections of each node. The nodes with maximum ranks can form the most significant network. In Figure 9.a, the darker edges represent the most connected edges of the graph. We can also filter the data based on that criterion.

Summarize all these properties derived from above distributions, it is shown in the Table 1. Though numbers of nodes in all three profiles is almost same but in the first profile number of edges are significantly less. It signifies the cohesion between all the nodes are relatively less. It is also reflects in density parameters which is only 1% compare to 13% and 12% of other two profiles. Diameter of profile 3 is maximum refers that any two nodes of that profile attached through a distant communication. So, profile 3 plays a powerful role in the network. Average clustering coefficient in profile 2 and profile 3 is around 0.5 whereas for profile 1, it is less than 0.01, which signifies clusters are less connected compare to other two profiles.

CONCLUSION AND FUTURE SCOPE

In social network analysis, people deal with relational data of the user. In this context, network visualization extracts key features of the network. The main objective of this work is to understand the basic features of the social network, extract and analyzed the important parameters that characterized the social network. As open source tools are used and external module can be added to them, these data can be further characterized. Extracted information can be used for designing graph sampling and game theory based network design.

REFERENCES

Albert, R., & Barabasi, A. L. (2002). Statistical mechanics of complex networks. *Reviews of Modern Physics*, *74*(1), 47–97. doi:10.1103/RevModPhys.74.47

Bastian, M., Heymann, S., & Jacomy, M. (2009). *Gephi: An Open Source Software for Exploring and Manipulating Networks.* Association for the Advancement of Artificial Intelligence.

Benevenuto, F., Rodrigues, F., & Cha, M. (2009). Characterizing User Behavior in Online Social Networks. *Proc. of ACM IMC.* doi:10.1145/1644893.1644900

Bonato, A. (2005). A survey of models of the web graph,Combinatorial and algorithmic aspects of networking. *Lecture Notes in Computer Science, 3405,* 159-172.

Freeman, L. C. (1978). Centrality in social networks: Conceptual clarification. *Social Networks, 1*(3), 215–239. doi:10.1016/0378-8733(78)90021-7

Fruchterman, T. M. J., & Reingold, E. M. (1991). Graph drawing by force-directed placement. *Software, Practice & Experience, 21*(11), 1129–1164. doi:10.1002/spe.4380211102

Jacomy, M., Heymann, S., Venturini, T., & Bastian, M. (2010). ForceAtlas2, A Continuous Graph Layout Algorithm for Handy Network Visualization. *PLoS ONE, 9*(6). PMID:24914678

Kleinberg, J. (1998). Authoritative sources in a hyperlinked environment. *Proc. 9th ACM-SIAM Symposium on Discrete Algorithms.*

Latapy, M. (2008). Main-memory triangle computations for verylarge(sparse (power-law)) graphs. *Theoretical Computer Science, 407*(1-3), 458–473. doi:10.1016/j.tcs.2008.07.017

Perer, S. (2006). Balancing systematic and flexible exploration of social networks.Visualization and Computer Graphics. *IEEE Transactions, 12*(5), 693–700.

Rieder, B. (2013). *Studying Facebook via Data Extraction: The Netvizz Application. In WebSci'13* (pp. 2–4). Paris, France: ACM. doi:10.1145/2464464.2464475

Rodriguez, J. A., & Yebra, J. L. A. (1999). Bounding the diameter and the mean distance of a graph from its eigenvalues: Laplacian versus adjacency matrix methods. *Discrete Mathematics, 196*(1-3), 267–275. doi:10.1016/S0012-365X(98)00206-4

Ronald, S. B. (1987). Social contagion and innovation: Cohesion versus structural equivalence. *American Journal of Sociology, 92*(6), 1287–1335. doi:10.1086/228667

Scott, J. (1988). Social Network Analysis. *Sociology, 22*(1), 109–127. doi:10.1177/0038038588022001007

Wang, T. Chen, Y., Zhang, Xu, T., Jin, L., Hui, P., … Li, x. (2011). Understanding Graph Sampling Algorithms for Social Network Analysis, *Simplex'11. IEEE ICDCS,* 123-128.

Wayne, G., & Ortrud, R. O. (2011). *Distance in Graphs, structural Analysis of Complex Networks.* Springer.

Wilson, R. E., Gosling, S. D., & Graham, L. T. (2012). A Review of Facebook Research in the Social Sciences Perspectives. *Psychological Science, 7*(3), 203–220.

Chapter 7
Context Specific Modeling of Communicational and Informational Content in Facebook

Johannes Schick
University of Münster, Germany

Martin Kuboschek
Informationstechnikzentrum Bund, Germany

Wolfram Manfred Lippe
University of Münster, Germany

ABSTRACT

In this chapter, the authors apply context specific methods to formalize communicational parameters for different profile groups in a social network platform, taking Facebook as an example. Information is posted to or shared with distinct user groups. The context specific approach is used to describe informational content of exchanged data and to formalize privacy settings in a social graph. Communicational and informational parameters are specified with direction and communicational content in a context specific model. Relations are defined to model communicational and informational interactions as well as environmental factors taking influence on the profile groups. The textual representation of this approach is introduced to describe models in a text-based form.

INTRODUCTION

Communication is the most essential factor in social networks and conduces the exchange of information. Social networks like Facebook (Debatin, Lovejoy, Horn, & Huges, 2009) connect people and promote the transfer of information along a network of personal relations. The use of privacy settings while using social networks differs strongly with gender, age or personal experiences. The modeling and formaliza-

DOI: 10.4018/978-1-5225-2814-2.ch007

tion of information (Shlaer & Mellor, 1988) which is presented to other users, simplifies the handling of data and gives an overview of published and forwarded information.

The context specific approach allows the formalized description of information in interdependence with behavior and rules (Linnert, 1975) and the focus on sociometric data and communicational flows (Roger & Agarwala-Rogers, 1976). Communicators are defined as entities (Chen, 1976; Schick, Kuboschek, & Lippe, 2014). They have relations between each other, which can be specified in an arbitrary level of detail. Information, which is transmitted between communicators, is formalized in Context-domains. Informational content between environmental factors and communicators is specified with Informationdomains.

A case study of this approach is presented in this chapter. Informational content is formalized for the presentation of user data with the context specific approach using the example of Facebook. Like other social networks, Facebook controls the publication of information to different user groups with privacy settings. Information is shared or posted to distinct user groups (Ibrahim, Blandford, & Bianchi-Berthouze, 2012). These relations between the communicators are figured as a social graph (Fong, Anwar, & Zhao, 2009) in a context specific model.

The outline of the chapter is as follows. The authors give some background information about the modeling of data in social networks. A basic overview of the context specific approach (Schick, Kuboschek, & Lippe, 2014) with the model components is given. After that, the privacy components of Facebook are described with focus on privacy groups. This leads to the case study, which gives a detailed example of the usage of the modeling language and the textual representation. The authors conclude with some recommendations and the focus on future work.

BACKGROUND

The modeling of social structures has a long tradition in the social science (Freeman, 2004). With the spread of the internet, the formalization of social structures has new significance for the specification of social interactions and data mining. The large amount of distributed data has to be structured and stored. In addition, the modeling of exchanged information between communicators is an interesting aspect. Communicational content provides information about behavior and gains a fast possibility to get and analyze data (Russell 2014). Therefore, the structuring and formalization of these data is an important aspect for further processing.

Social networks are social structures. Vertices can be modeled as individuals and the links between them can be represented as e.g. friendship (Han, Kamber, & Pei, 2012). Modeling languages like Entity-Relationship Modeling (Chen, 1976) have a very intuitive view on the real world, but cannot cover the aim to model high distributed data and data flows in social structures. Graph-based databases have their main focus on the nodes in a graph and the relations between them (Foster, Ghani, Jarmin, Kreuter, & Lane, 2016). Each system of communicators is embedded in an environment. Environmental factors take influence on communicators and their behavior.

MODEL COMPONENTS

The context specific approach consists of different component types. A model is represented graph-based or in form of the textual representation. The graph-based (Scott, 2013; Hage & Harary, 1983) form is denoted as graphical representation. The textual representation is a text-based form of a model (Lippe, 2009; Watt, 1990). Both forms are isomorphic and completely represent a model with its components. A social network is a set of relations (Kadushin 2012). Basic components are entities. They are sender or receiver (Shannon, 1948) of information.

Definition (Entity): An entity $e \in \mathcal{E}$ is a distinctly identified and impartible unit relating to the modeling context.

Entities represent single communicators, groups of communicators or organizational unites (Schick, Kuboschek, & Lippe, 2014) with behavioral properties. Modeling the communication behavior, rule-bases are assigned to entities. Rule-bases consist of IF-THEN rules (Lippe, 2006; Holland, 2006). IF-THEN rules are a generalized form of decision rules. A rule has a premise in the IF part and a conclusion in the THEN part. A premise consists of a statement. It is the assumption and is followed by the implication with the conclusion. The conclusion is also a statement. This makes it possible to describe conditions and events.

Relations between entities are called Contextdomains. Contextdomains specify the communication between communicators. Contextdomains are uni- or bidirectional, depending on the communication flow between communicators.

Definition (Contextdomain): Let $\mathcal{E}$ be a set of entities, $\mathcal{B}$ a set of identifiers and $\nabla = \{$unidirectional, bidirectional$\}$. A Contextdomain $\mathcal{D}$ is a tuple $\mathcal{D} = (e_1, e_2, b, \delta)$ with $e_1, e_2 \in \mathcal{E}$, $b \in \mathcal{B}$ and $\delta \in \nabla$.

These relations formalize the task of a communicational domain. During the modeling process of a Contextdomain, the involved communication mediums are described in an extended Contextdomain. The communicational structure between entities is a multi-relational network (Lin, 1975; Wassermann & Faust, 1994) and is represented graph-based with the Communicationgraph.

Definition (Communicationgraph): A Communicationgraph is a tuple $K = (\mathcal{E}, S\mathcal{D})$. The nodes are a finite set $\mathcal{E}$ of entities and the edges are a finite set $S\mathcal{D}$ of Contextdomains. An entity can have a finite amount of uni- or bidirectional Contextdomains to other entities, so that a weighted multigraph will be created.

In general, communicators with very close relations or strong social dependencies are encapsulated in a subsystem. Entities and Contextdomains can be aggregated to subsystems.

Definition (Subsystem): Let K be a Communicationgraph with the entities $e_1, ..., e_n \in \mathcal{E}$. A subsystem $\mathcal{C}$ is a subgraph of K.

Subsystems are illustrated in an implicit or an explicit form. A subsystem in implicit form hides the internal structure and makes a model in graphical representation more readable. An explicit subsystem shows the internal structure with communicators and relations. A system of communicators is delimited and parameterized by environmental factors (Luhmann, 1987). Environmental factors are always specified at the top level of a model.

Definition (Environmental factor): An environmental factor $u \in \mathcal{U}$ is an impartible element of the environment.

They take influence on a system of communicators and do not cause a direct communication flow between them. Relations between environmental factors and entities are called Informationdomains.

Definition (Informationdomain): Let $\mathcal{U}$ be a set of environmental factors, $\mathcal{E}$ a set of entities and L a set of identifiers. An Informationdomain is a tuple $\mathcal{W} = (u, e, l)$ with $u \in \mathcal{U}$, $e \in \mathcal{E}$ and $l \in L$.

Informationdomains are unidirectional relations from environmental factors to entities. A Communicationgraph with environmental factors is called extended Communicationgraph.

Definition (Extended Communicationgraph): Let $\mathcal{E}$ be a set of entities, $\mathcal{U}$ a set of environmental factors, $S\mathcal{D}$ a set of Contextdomains and $S\mathcal{W}$ a set of Informationdomains. An extended Communicationgraph is a tuple $K^* = (\mathcal{E}, \mathcal{U}, S\mathcal{D}, S\mathcal{W})$ regarding the following constraints:
1. An entity has a finite number of Contextdomains.
2. An environment factor has a finite number of Informationdomains.

Thereby a weighted multigraph is created.

In the following, an extended Communicationgraph simplified is called Communicationgraph.

Contexttrees provide to define the communicational and informational content of Context- and Informationdomains. The root node will be specified with the communicators and the environmental factors of the Context- or Informationdomain.

Definition (Contexttree): A Contexttree is a rooted tree $\mathcal{T} = (P, S)$ with the following characteristics:
1. P is a set of parameters and represents the nodes in the tree.
2. S is a set of edges.

The leafs represent the detailed parameters of the relations.

Relations between communicators and environmental factors are aggregated in Contexttables. They depict Contextdomains with the same direction between two entities or Informationdomains between an environmental factor and an entity. Contextscenarios illustrate interactions of different communicators and environmental factors for an issue. Contextscenarios are subgraphs of a Communicationgraph, resulting in a structural and graph-based view.

Definition (Contextscenario): Let K^* be an extended Communicationgraph. A Contextscenario is a subgraph $K^+ \subset K^*$. The nodes and edges of a Contextscenario refer to a specific issue.

Temporal sequences (Keller, Nüttgens, & Scheer, 1992; Prior, 1957) are modeled using process diagrams.

Definition (Process): A process is a tuple $\mathcal{F} = (\mathcal{E}, S\mathcal{D})$. $\mathcal{E}$ is a set of entities and $S\mathcal{D}$ a set of Contextdomains with the following characteristics
1. Entities are chained in flow direction with uni- and bidirectional Contextdomains.
2. Branches in this chained flow are only possible with consistent bidirectional Contextdomains.

The main path of a process has a higher precedence than the branches. Therefore, the end state is in the main path of a process. Tasks are illustrated with the main focus on the temporal order of Contextdomains. As a result, the sequence of information flows between the entities is modeled in process diagrams.

A common way to create a model is to identify the entities and the environmental factors of the Communicationgraph. After that, the relations between these components can be appointed. Entities with strong organizational or social dependencies are aggregated with their Contextdomains in subsystems. Contexttrees can be specified for each relation. The components of the Communicationgraph are the basic elements for the modeling of processes and Contextscenarios. Processes use the defined Contextdomains and Contextscenarios the Context- and Informationdomains of a Communicationgraph. This method is reflected in the structural composition of the textual representation and can be adapted for each model.

Figure 1. Communicationgraph of the model

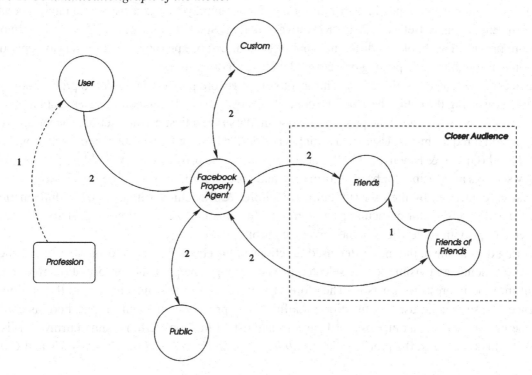

Table 1. Context- and Informationdomains of the Communicationgraph

Communicator	Communicator	Direction	Name	Mediums
User	Facebook Property Agent	unidirectional	Editing Parameters	Facebook
User	Facebook Property Agent	unidirectional	Editing Posts	Facebook
Facebook Property Agent	Public	bidirectional	Public Information	Facebook
Facebook Property Agent	Friends	bidirectional	Personal Information	Facebook
Facebook Property Agent	Custom	bidirectional	Released Information	Facebook
Facebook Property Agent	Friends of Friends	bidirectional	Profile Information	Facebook
Facebook Property Agent	Public	bidirectional	Public Posts	Facebook
Facebook Property Agent	Friends	bidirectional	Private Posts	Facebook
Facebook Property Agent	Custom	bidirectional	Constraint Posts	Facebook
Facebook Property Agent	Friends of Friends	bidirectional	Extended Posts	Facebook
Friends of Friends	Friends	bidirectional	Mutual Friendship	Facebook
Environmental Factor	**Communicator**	**-**	**Name**	**-**
Profession	User	-	Job Concerns	-

PROFILE GROUPS AND PRIVACY SETTUNGS IN FACEBOOK

Social networks are made of ties (Waters & Ackerman, 2011; Granovetter, 1973) between users. Along these ties, users share informational content or send informations to single recipients and recipient groups. But not every information is intended to all users, not even to every "friend". The most important aspect for users to use privacy mechanisms is the unwanted view of posted or shared content (Qi & Edgar-Nevill, 2011). Users often want to hide information for e.g. future employers, supervisors and family members (Johnson, Engelman, & Bellovin, 2012; Krasnova, Günther, Spiekermann, & Koroleva, 2009). In order to ensure privacy, Facebook has different capabilities to transpose privacy. The user has to apply these functions thoroughly while posting or sharing data to/with other users.

Each user owns a personal account. The account is password protected in order to prevent other persons from misusing the data. Therefore, he controls his own data. He can edit or delete data in his own scope. Another way to control the privacy of personal data is to adjust privacy settings according to the user's personal requirements. Users in a social network (Acquisti & Gross, 2005) are usually organized graph-based (Girvan & Newman, 2002). Facebook transcripts privacy e.g. by building profile groups. Privacy settings are feasible for basic information and posts. The disclosure of nearly all basic information can be controlled by the user (Ibrahim, Blandford, & Bianchi-Berthouze, 2012). Information is provided and published for particular profile groups. Information can be shared or posted, after editing the user groups with some clicks in the privacy control.

Posting data is one of the most often used functions in Facebook. Posted information is published in the user's timeline and visible for the selected privacy group. The published information gives a good insight into the interests of a person. Therefore, it is important to post information to the appropriate audience. A user should use this function mindfully. The privacy component in Facebook is continuously being evolved with a range of profile groups and lists (Liu, Gummadi, Krishnamurthy, & Mislove 2011). In this case study, the profile groups *Public, Friends, Friends of Friends, Only Me* and *Custom* are used. *Public* means that data can be viewed by everybody. *Friends* are confirmed by the user as trustful people, though the common meaning of the term "friend" often exceeds the quality of the user's relationship with members of his *Friends* profile group. *Friends of Friends* are *Friends* of confirmed *Friends*. *Only me* is the user himself. Custom settings can be used to provide data for specific users or exclude particular users from accessing posted or shared data.

Facebook has a feature to check different views on posted or shared data to help users to make sure, that posts and shared information reach the intended audience. With this function, the user has the possibility to adapt the visibility of his Facebook content to particular profile groups.

CASE STUDY

The privacy groups mentioned above are used in this case study. Starting point is the specification of the Communicationgraph. The defined components are used to model Contextscenarios and processes.

Overview of the Textual Representation

A model in the textual representation depicts a graphical model. The language is created in a block-based manner. A program in textual representation starts with the declaration of the model. The beginning and the end of this block is indicated with curly brackets as the other blocks in the language. A model consists of the following parts:

- Graph specification
- Process
- Contextscenarios

The graph specification contains the Communicationgraph. Processes and Contextscenarios are arranged sequentially after the graph specification and are on the same block level as the Communicationgraph.

Entities, subsystems and environmental factors with rule-bases and relations are specified with the corresponding Contexttrees in the Communicationgraph. Subsystems are realized as nested structures (Watt, 1990) in the graph specification. The block level indicates the position of a model component in the graphical representation. Processes and Contextscenarios use the identifiers of relations, which are modeled in the Communicationgraph. The subsequent sections illustrate the specification of a model with the components and the used syntax for the textual representation.

Model and Communicationgraph

The model of the case study contains entities for different communicators. *User* is a real person. *Public, Friends, Friends of Friends* and *Custom* are groups of Facebook users. The *Facebook Property Agent* is a technical entity in this model and applies the privacy settings of a *User* to his communication flows. The complete Communicationgraph is illustrated in Figure 1. The textual representation for the initialization of the entities, the environmental factor and the subsystem with basic model and Communicationgraph specifications is:

```
Model Informational Views Facebook {
    Communicationgraph Facebook Property Interaction {
        Entity    Facebook Property Agent, User, Public,
                  Custom, Friends, Friends of Friends;
        Environ   Profession;
        Subsystem Closer Audience;
    };
};
```

The communication parameters are defined with Contextdomains. The use of Contextdomains is exemplified for the Contextdomain Editing Parameters between the *User* and the *Facebook Property Agent*. The Contextdomain contains the parameters of the *About data* in Facebook:

- Contact Information
- Basic Information
- Current City and Hometown

The *About data* is accessed from a *User* by his Facebook site. He can edit the settings for the parameters to share. *Contact Information* contains private information, e.g. address and mobile phone numbers. Gender, birthday etc. are summarized in *Basic Information*. Location based data is arranged under the node *Current City and Hometown*. The Contexttree in textual representation consists of nodes and child nodes, whereas the name of nodes in the same depth of a Contexttree must be unique. The informational

Figure 2. Contexttree for the Contextdomain Editing Parameters

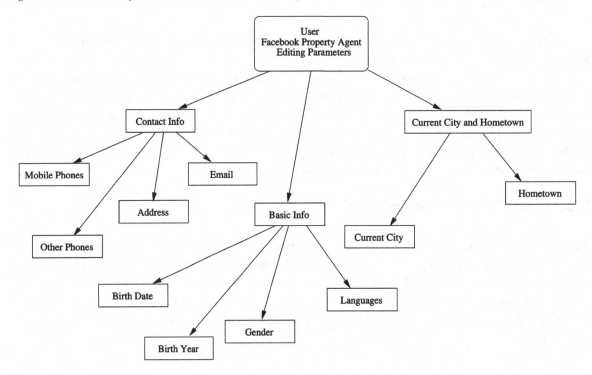

content of a domain is categorized and modeled by splitting up the parameters from general to particular. Exchanged information between communicators is structured with a Contexttree.

Child nodes are discernible with the bracketing of parameters. The Contexttree of the Contextdomain Editing Parameters is depicted in graphical representation (see Figure 2). The textual representation of the Contextdomain and the Contexttree is:

```
User and Facebook Property Agent communicate unidirectional about Editing Pa-
rameters with Facebook {
    Contexttree with Parameters {
        Contact Info (Mobile Phones, Other Phones,
        Address, Email),
        Basic Info (Birth Date, Birth Year, Gender,
        Languages),
        Current City and Hometown (Current City,
        Hometown);
    };
};
```

Posts are much more frequently than changing the privacy settings for personal data. Furthermore, posts give a very personal view of a *User*.

The posting of data is specified with the Contextdomain Editing Posts. The other user groups have bidirectional Contextdomains to receive and view the postings. The *Facebook Property Agent* is publishing the user data. Audience specific views are generated with the privacy settings of the *User*. These settings can be depicted with IF-THEN rules. The rule-base of the *Facebook Property Agent* is:

```
Rulebase for Facebook Property Agent {
    Rule if (Basic Info edited) then (Share to Public);
    Rule if (Contact Info edited) then (Share to Friends);
    Rule if (Current City and Hometown edited) then (Share to Custom);
    Rule if (Post to Public) then (Publish to Public);
    Rule if (Post to Friends) then (Publish to Friends);
    Rule if (Post to Friends of Friends) then (Publish to Friends of Friends);
    Rule if (Post to Custom) then (Publish to Custom);
};
```

Environmental factors take influence on a system of communicators. They are always modeled on the top level of a Communicationgraph and cannot specified inside a subsystem. The *User* configures the settings to publish data for his profile groups. Factors which take influence on his behavior will affect the values of the privacy policy. The profession of a *User* is a decisive reason for publishing data to different profile groups with the aim to protect privacy against his employer (Waters & Ackerman, 2011; Stutzman & Kramer-Duffield, 2010) and a person in charge. It is specified with the Informationdomain Job concerns. Informational parameters which express the restrictive aspects are mentioned in this Informationdomain.

```
User gets information from Profession about Job concerns {
   Contexttree with Parameters {
   Employer (Company name, Person in charge);
   };
};
```

The parameters of an Informationdomain are also depicted in Contexttrees. The syntax for the modeling of Contexttrees is equivalent to Contexttrees in Contextdomains.

Ties diverge to particular social groups (Stutzman & Kramer-Duffield, 2010; Xiang, Neville, & Rogati 2010). *User* have stronger ties to *Friends* than to *Public*. By displaying this correlation, data shared to *Friends* are personal and must not published to unwanted persons. Therefore, the *User* shares Contact Info only to *Friends*. Information that is published to *Public* can also be seen from *Friends*. The Contextdomain Personal Information with Contexttree in textual representation is:

```
Facebook Property Agent and Friends communicate bidirectional about Personal
Information with Facebook {
   Contexttree with Parameters {
      Contact Info (Mobile Phones, Other Phones,
      Address, Email),
      Basic Info (Birth Date, Birth Year, Gender,
      Languages);
   };
};
```

In case of our example, the representation of information is depicted in dependency of the settings for a *User*. The *Facebook Property Agent* provides the publishing of the configured data. The shared data is modeled in Contextdomains between the *Facebook Property Agent* and the specific privacy groups. Shared data for *Public* is only basic information about the *User*. Information about the *Current City and Hometown* is shared only for *Custom* users. Further information is not shared for *Friends of Friends*, so they see only the *Basic Info* of the *User*.

These mentioned aspects, are much more pronounced for posts. Posts contain personal information. They give an impression of the private interests and the surroundings of a person. In particular, misplaced posts in Facebook can be e.g. a decision-making reason for a prospective employee to employ or dismiss a person. To control this data, a thoroughly use of the privacy settings is important. The rules for posting this data are defined in the rule-base of the *Facebook Property Agent*.

The functionalities of subsystems are described in the following section. The Contextdomain between *Friends* and *Friends of Friends* is called Mutual Friendship. They have a strong tie and are agglomerated to a subsystem. The graphical representation has an implicit and an explicit form to depict subsystems. An implicit subsystem is a generalized form of a subsystem. It is illustrated as a rectangle. The internal structure of a subsystem is depicted in the explicit form (see Figure 1). Subsystems can contain other subsystems. The textual representation for a subsystem in implicit form is modeled with the declaration of the subsystem. The explicit form consists of a declaration and an additional specification with the entities inside the subsystem and the corresponding Contextdomain as follows:

Figure 3. The Communicationgraph with an implicit subsystem

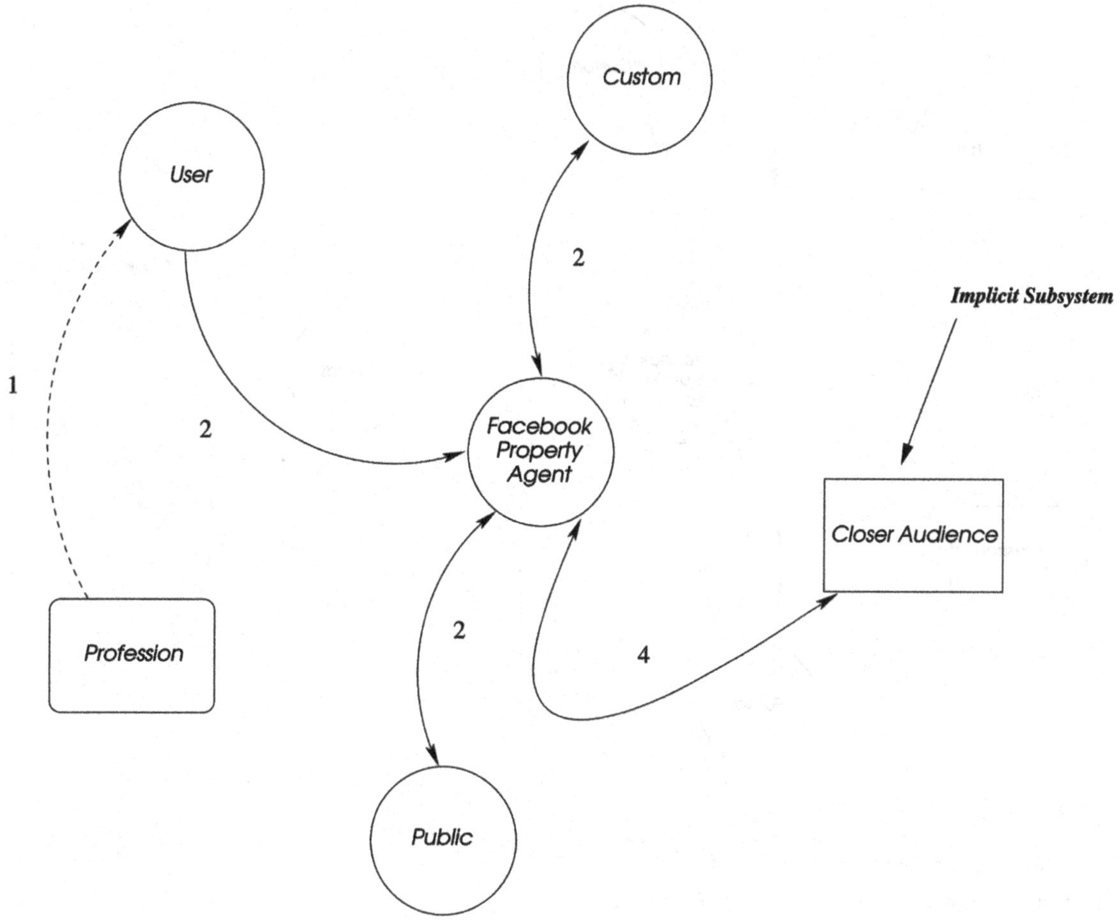

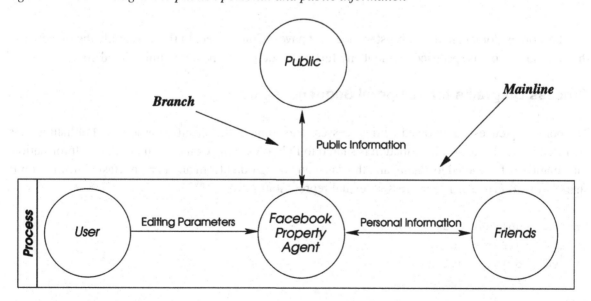

Figure 4. Process diagram to publish personal and public information

Figure 5. Contextscenario for sharing data to profile groups

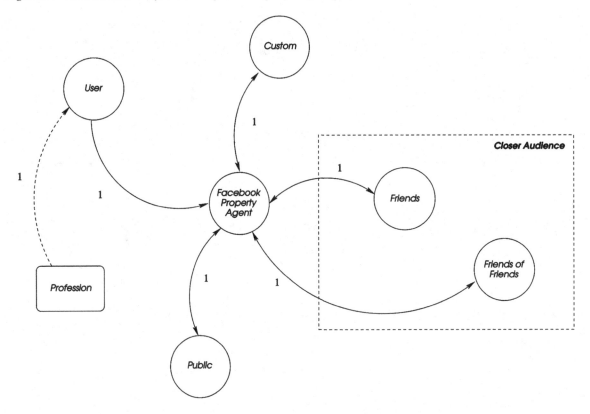

```
Subsystem Constraint User Group {
    Entity Friends, Friends of Friends;
    Friends of Friends and Friends communicate bidirectional about Mutual
    Friendship with Facebook;
};
```

The Contextdomain in this subsystem does not have a Contexttree. In this case, only the tie between the communicators is specified, without any further modeling of the communicational content.

Process Diagrams for Temporal Sequences

Temporal sequences are modeled with processes. The name of the specified process is Publishing data for Friends (see Figure 4). Information is shared to Public with the Contextdomain Public Information. Information is forwarded to *Public* and the data can be regarded from any person. Basic information is shared only to *Friends*. The process in textual representation is:

```
Process Publishing data for Friends {
    Editing Parameters,
    (Public Information),
    Personal Information;
};
```

The listed Contextdomains are ordered sequentially from left to right in the graphical representation. Contextdomains in brackets are branches in a process diagram.

Modeling Contextscenarios

Particular issues of a Communicationgraph are specified with Contextscenarios. A Contextscenario is a subgraph of the Communicationgraph and describes the interrelations between entities and environmental factors. Only for an issue relevant relations are used in a Contextscenario. The Contextscenario Sharing data is depicted in Figure 5. It gives an overview for edited and published information with the conforming environmental factor. Context- and Informationdomains are separately handled in the textual representation. The Contextscenario Sharing data is specified with:

```
Contextscenario for Sharing Data {
    Contextdomains for communication {
        Editing Parameters,
        Personal Information,
        Released Information,
        Profile Information,
        Public Information;
    };
    Informationdomains for depiction {
        Job concerns;
    };
};
```

The shared information with the influencing Informationdomain is modeled in this Contextscenario. The relevant relations and can be reference to the specific Contexttrees with their communicational and informational parameters. Specific entities, subsystems and environmental factors with their relations are depicted in a Contextscenario, resulting in a structural view on an issue.

CONCLUSION

In this cases study, the authors use context specific methods to specify informational content in a social network platform, taking Facebook as an example. The context specific approach gives a general view on shared data and on the rules, which are responsible for the publication of data. Shared and posted information to particular privacy groups are described formally in a graphical and a textual representation. Information is modeled as parameters in Contexttrees and the flow direction of information is specified with the corresponding Contextdomains. These information can be used e.g. for performing real time analytics on the exchanged data.

Temporal sequences are described with processes. These diagrams are based on specified entities and Contextdomains of the Communicationgraph. Specific issues are depicted in Contextscenarios. Contextscenarios give a better overview of relations, which are corresponding to each other. Functional dependencies are emphasized with this diagram type.

The main focus is on the description of social compositions in a structural view. Relations between user groups are formalized and dependencies are modeled with a view on specific tasks. The environment with influence on the communication behavior is represented within a model. An interesting aspect for future research is the specification of direct interdependencies between environmental factors and the behavior of entities with their conducted activities and to extend the language for these issues. These aspects can be important to create metadata for e.g. real-time analytics of exchanged data. The approach gives further application areas to enhance social network analysis with the description of communicational parameters and the interdependencies to their environment. The classification of exchanged data can be approved with this modelling language.

This approach formalizes the interaction between communication partners in social media structures. It provides a graph-based overview of the communicational relations. Based upon this approach, it is possible to implement software modules, which perform an analysis of the posted textual content using appropriate algorithms and heuristics.

REFERENCES

Acquisti, A., & Gross, R. (2005). Information Revelation and Privacy in Online Social Networks. *Proceedings of the 2005 ACM workshop on Privacy in the electronic society (WPES)*.

Chen, P. (1976). The Entity-Relationship Model - Toward a Unified View of Data. *ACM Transactions on Database Systems*, *1*(1), 9–36. doi:10.1145/320434.320440

Debatin, B., Lovejoy, J. P., Horn, A.-K., & Hughes, B. N. (2009). Facebook and Online Privacy: Attitudes, Behaviors, and Unintended Consequences. *Journal of Computer-Mediated Communication*, *15*(1), 83–108. doi:10.1111/j.1083-6101.2009.01494.x

Fong, P. W. L., Anwar, M., & Zhao, Z. (2009). A Privacy Preservation Model for Facebook-Style Social Network Systems. *Proceedings of the 14th European Symposium on Research in Computer Security (ESORICS)*. doi:10.1007/978-3-642-04444-1_19

Foster, I., Ghani, R., Jarmin, R. S., Kreuter, F., & Lane, J. (2016). *Big Data and Social Science. A Practical Guide to Methods and Tools*. Boca Raton, FL: CRC Press.

Freeman, L. C. (2004). *The Development of Social Network Analysis. A Study in the Sociology of Science*. Vancouver: Empirical Press.

Girvan, M., & Newman, M. E. J. (2002). Community structure in social and biological networks. *Proceedings of the National Academy of Sciences of the United States of America*, *99*(12). doi:10.1073/pnas.122653799

Granovetter, M. S. (1973). The Strength of Weak Ties. *American Journal of Sociology*, *78*(6), 1360–1380. doi:10.1086/225469

Hage, P., & Harary, F. (1983). *Structural Models in Anthropology*. Cambridge, UK: Cambridge University Press.

Han, J., Kamber, M., & Pei, J. (2012). *Data Mining. Concepts and Techniques*. Amsterdam: Morgan Kaufmann.

Holland, J. H. (2006). Studying Complex Adaptive Systems. *Journal of Systems Science and Complexity*, *19*(1), 1–8. doi:10.1007/s11424-006-0001-z

Ibrahim, S. Z., Blandford, A., & Bianchi-Berthouze, N. (2012). Privacy Settings on Facebook: Their Roles and Importance. *Proceedings of the 2012 IEEE International Conference on Green Computing and Communications (GreenCom)*. doi:10.1109/GreenCom.2012.67

Johnson, M., Engelman, S., & Bellovin, S. M. (2012). Facebook and Privacy: It's Complicated. *Proceedings of the Eighth Symposium on Usable Privacy and Security (SOUPS)*. doi:10.1145/2335356.2335369

Kadushin, C. (2012). *Understanding Social Networks. Theories, Concepts and Findings*. Oxford, UK: Oxford University Press.

Keller, G., Nüttgens, M., & Scheer, A. W. (1992). Semantische Prozeßmodellierung auf der Grundlage "Ereignisgesteuerter Prozeßketten (EPK)". Institute of Business Informatics, University of Saarland.

Krasnova, H., Günther, O., Spiekermann, S., & Koroleva, K. (2009). Privacy concerns and identity in online social networks. *Identity in the Information Society*, *2*(1), 39–63. doi:10.1007/s12394-009-0019-1

Lin, N. (1975). Analysis of Communication Relations. In G. J. Hanneman & W. J. McElwen (Eds.), *Communication and Behavior*. Reading, MA: Addison-Wesley.

Linnert, P. (1975). Handbuch Organisation. Gernsbach: Deutscher Betriebswirte-Verlag GmbH.

Lippe, W.-M. (2006). *Softcomputing mit Neuronalen Netzen, Fuzzy-Logic und Evolutionären Algorithmen*. Berlin: Springer-Verlag.

Lippe, W.-M. (2009). *Funktionale und Applikative Programmierung*. Berlin: Springer-Verlag.

Liu, Y., Gummadi, K. P., Krishnamurthy, B., & Mislove, A. (2011). Analyzing Facebook Privacy Settings: User Expectations vs. Reality. *Proceedings of the 2011 ACM SIGCOMM conference on Internet measurement conference*. doi:10.1145/2068816.2068823

Luhmann, N. (1987). *Soziale Systeme. Grundriß einer allgemeinen Theorie*. Frankfurt: Suhrkamp Verlag.

Prior, A. N. (1957). *Time and Modality*. Oxford, UK: Oxford University Press.

Qi, M., & Edgar-Nevill, D. (2011). Social networking searching and privacy issues. *Information Security Technical Report*, *16*(2), 74–78.

Roger, E. M., & Agarwala-Rogers, R. (1976). *Communication in Organizations*. New York: The Free Press.

Russell, M. A. (2014). *Mining the Social Web. Data Mining Facebook, Twitter, Linkedin, Google+, Github,and more*. Sebastopol, CA: O'Reilly Media Inc.

Schick, J., Kuboschek, M., & Lippe, W. M. (2014). Context Specific Entity based Modeling of Organizational Structures. *Proceedings of the 2014 IEEE International Conference on Behavioral, Economic, Socio-Cultural Computing (BESC 2014)*. doi:10.1109/BESC.2014.7059513

Scott, J. (2013). *Social Network Analysis*. London: SAGE Publications Ltd.

Shannon, C. E. (1948). A Mathematical Theory of Communication. *The Bell System Technical Journal*, *27*(3), 379–423. doi:10.1002/j.1538-7305.1948.tb01338.x

Shlaer, S., & Mellor, S. J. (1988). *Object-oriented Systems Analysis. Modeling the World in Data*. Englewood Cliffs, NJ: Prentice Hall PTR.

Stutzman, F., & Kramer-Duffield, J. (2010). Friends Only: Examining a Privacy-Enhancing Behavior in Facebook. *Proceedings of the SIGCHI Conference on Human Factors in Computing Systems*. doi:10.1145/1753326.1753559

Wassermann, S., & Faust, K. (1994). *Social Network Analysis. Methods and Applications*. Cambridge, UK: Cambridge University Press. doi:10.1017/CBO9780511815478

Waters, S., & Ackerman, J. (2011). Exploring Privacy Management on Facebook: Motivations and Perceived Consequences of Voluntary Disclosure. *Journal of Computer-Mediated Communication*, *17*(1), 101–115. doi:10.1111/j.1083-6101.2011.01559.x

Watt, D. A. (1990). Programming Language Concepts and Paradigms. Hertfordshire, UK: Prentice Hall International (UK) Ltd.

Xiang, R., Neville, J., & Rogati, M. (2010). Modeling Relationship Strength in Online Social Networks. *Proceedings of the 19th International Conference on World Wide Web*. doi:10.1145/1772690.1772790

Chapter 8
Hadoop–Based Distributed K–Shell Decomposition for Social Networks

Katerina Pechlivanidou
University of Thessaly, Greece

Dimitrios Katsaros
University of Thessaly, Greece

Leandros Tassiulas
Yale University, USA

ABSTRACT

Complex network analysis comprises a popular set of tools for the analysis of online social networks. Among these techniques, k-shell decomposition of a network is a technique that has been used for centrality analysis, for communities' discovery, for the detection of influential spreaders, and so on. The huge volume of input graphs and the environments where the algorithm needs to run, i.e., large data centers, makes none of the existing algorithms appropriate for the decomposition of graphs into shells. In this article, we develop for a distributed algorithm based on MapReduce for the k-shell decomposition of a graph. We furthermore, provide an implementation and assessment of the algorithm using real social network datasets. We analyze the tradeoffs and speedup of the proposed algorithm and conclude for its virtues and shortcomings.

1. INTRODUCTION

The enormous progress in information technology and the seamless connectivity combined with the high availability of data sources but also some great improvements in hardware have created an ideal background for developing Online Social Networks (OSNs). Facebook, Twitter and LinkedIn are only some examples of modern online social networks that handle today huge amount of information, in means of both storing and processing. The data mostly describe pairwise interactions and are thus constructing networks.

DOI: 10.4018/978-1-5225-2814-2.ch008

Since their first appearance in data science, particular emphasis has been given to the analysis and mining of the above networks since they can offer both operational information and business intelligence to the OSN owner. Social Network Analysis, as it is known academically, uses a set of tools coupled with graph theory principles to study OSN's pattern and underlying structures. Due to its importance, it has found a large variety of applications that include methods for centrality discovery of the nodes of a network, estimation of its robustness and finding the hierarchy core structure.

The latter concept is known as the *k*-core or *k*-shell decomposition of a graph (Seideman, 1983) and is particularly appealing as it highlights its underlying core structure and reveals the central nodes even in really complex scenarios. The process of retrieving the *k*-cores of a graph is a highly iterative procedure including node and edge pruning rounds. More specifically, if from a given graph we remove recursively all nodes and the incident lines with them of degree less that *k*, then the remaining graph is called a *k*-core. The procedure is fairly simple; yet the *k*-core decomposition has been used in social network analysis as a centrality measure for various purposes like the discovery of communities (Aksu et al., 2013), for detection of influential spreaders (Basaras et al., 2013) and analysis of the Internet structures (Carmi et al., 2007).

The great scientific interest in the *k*-shell decomposition has resulted a set of algorithms for its computation in diverse computational environments and for different types of networks. For example, there are versions of the algorithm for weighted (Garas et al., 2012) and unweighted graphs, for static or nearly static networks that are slowly acquired in a streaming fashion (Sariyuce et al., 2013). There are also versions of the *k*-shell decomposition method suitable to run on a single machine, either by exploiting its main memory (Batagelj & Zaversnik, 2002) or by running on a secondary storage (Cheng et al., 2011), or on a cluster of machines (Montesor et al., 2012). Of all the above categories of networks, the static graphs or those whose topology is slightly changing over time compared to the time required to analyze it, are encountered in most of the modern online social networks. We therefore focus on static and unweighted networks in our proposed *k*-shell decomposition method.

1.1 Motivation and Contributions

Nowadays modern online social networks handle a huge amount of information, describing social interactions as sets of dyadic ties. They usually comprise of millions of nodes and several millions of edges attached to them. However, the already existing centralized solutions for calculating the *k*-core rely on a single machine's main memory or on a single storage which is inadequate since it does not meet the requirements of such large datasets. Even the distributed solutions proposed for the *k*-shell extraction on small clusters (Miorandi & de Pellegrini, 2010; Montesor et al., 2012) are insufficient, since the process is highly sequential requiring more computational resources.

Motivated by the insufficiency of the already existing solutions to deal with the *k*-shell decomposition of online social networks when their size is extremely large over a huge cluster, we designed a MapReduce-based distributed *k*-shell decomposition algorithm, namely the MR-SD algorithm (MapReduce Shell Decomposition), for large online social networks. Modern OSNs are maintained by service providers like Google or Facebook that operate large datacenters and are hosting clusters of thousands of machines that are programmed by a high performance middleware of MapReduce type (Dean & Ghemawat, 2004). Therefore, a solution based on the MapReduce paradigm is now more than ever necessary. MapReduce-based clusters consist in principle of a master node and several slave nodes. Together they are running a filtering, a sorting and a summary procedure, also known as the MapReduce job. In order to support the MapReduce programming model, we adopted Hadoop, a middleware that allows massive scalability, from a single machine to thousands of computational resources. The individual components of a Hadoop cluster offer both storage and computational power, and the cluster is capable to detect failures delivering also high availability.

Having in mind the above, we designed, for the first time in the literature, a distributed k-shell algorithm that is based on MapReduce and runs on a Hadoop cluster. Our approach is therefore an appealing, tailored solution for the computation of the k-shells of modern social networks since they are very large-sized, but also static and unweighted.

In summary, this chapter makes the following contributions:

- It develops a distributed algorithm, namely the MR-SD (MapReduce Shell Decomposition) algorithm for the computation of k-shells of a very large network.
- It presents for the first time in the literature a distributed algorithm based on the MapReduce programming model and is therefore an ideal solution for datacenter environments.
- The chapter also assesses the performance of the proposed algorithm in an experimental way using real-world datasets. Finally, it analyzes the tradeoffs in its operation.

The rest of the chapter is organized as follows: In Section 2 we describe in details the related work that has already been done in the area of k-shell decomposition for diverse environment settings and for different kinds of networks. In Section 3, we address the challenges that appear in designing the parallel and distributed version of our algorithmic approach. We also provide any necessary background knowledge about the k-shell decomposition and the programming model of MapReduce. In the same section, the MRSD algorithm is described extensively and its workflow is analyzed to give the necessary insights into our study. Section 4 addresses the performance and evaluation of our approach; it is assessed in an experimental way with real networks. Finally, section 5 concludes our work. Throughout the chapter, we use the terms k-shell and k-core as well as link and edge interchangeably, as they are referring to the same thing.

2. RELATED WORK AND MOTIVATION

Since its initial introduction in (Dean & Ghemawat, 2004), the Map-Reduce framework and its implementation in Hadoop have been used in many areas related to huge data processing. MapReduce's most successful application area is Information retrieval, but it has also been used for bioinformatics, data mining and databases. The data management community has contributed fundamental ideas in the improvement and the extension of MapReduce.

One particularly interesting and significant topic in SNA is that of discovering the most "central" or most "influential" nodes in a social network. Apart from the classic centrality measures (degree, closeness, shortest-path betweenness), the notion of k-shell has attracted the attention of "data/network" scientists. It was first proposed in (Seidman, 1983) and found wide application in areas such as Internet topology modeling (Carmi et al., 2007), detection of influential spreaders (Basaras et al., 2013), discovery of communities (Aksu et al., 2013), graph mining (Shin et al., 2016) etc; it has also been generalized for temporal networks (Wu et al., 2015), for uncertain graphs (Bonchi et al., 2014), for weighted graphs (Eidsaa & Almaas, 2013).

In a straightforward implementation of the k-core decomposition algorithm, we need to perform recursive deletions of all vertices and edges incident with them, but efficient versions of the basic algorithm do exist for various settings.

There are two categories of algorithms depending on whether the graph is dynamic (slowly or fast changing) or static (known in advance and not changing). The literature on k-shell decomposition for dynamic graphs includes algorithms that are able to handle only slowly changing graphs when they fit entirely in main memory (Miorandi & de Pellegrini, 2010), for processing in small clusters with the type of distributed algorithms described in (Montesor et al., 2012) and for graphs whose topology is acquired in a streaming mode (Sariyuce et al., 2013) or in incremental manner (Sariyuce et al., 2016). For static networks, when the entire graph can be stored in main memory, the core decomposition of a graph can be done in time O(num_of_edges) due to (Batagelj & Zaversnik, 2002). For larger graphs that have to be stored in secondary storage the techniques described in (Cheng et al., 2011; Wen et al., 2016) can be used. Moving on to progressively larger networks that cannot fit into a single machine, the exploitation of a very small cluster for the k-shell decomposition of a network can be done as in (Montesor et al., 2012).

Clearly, none of the aforementioned solutions is appropriate for the type of infrastructure operated by modern Internet companies such as Google, Yahoo, LinkedIn, Facebook and Twitter. These Internet giants are operating huge data centers with clusters comprised of several thousand low-cost machines. These clusters are usually programmed by MapReduce-type frameworks.

3. THE PROPOSED DISTRIBUTED ALGORITHM

This section discusses our proposed algorithmic approach for the k-shell decomposition of large networks and the necessary background that is studied in this chapter. We discuss the MapReduce programming model along with Hadoop that "hosts" this technique. In each case we illustrate all aspects with examples.

3.1 Background

3.1.1 Definition of the k-Shell Decomposition

In recent years numerous attempts to reveal the underlying structure of networks were undertaken. To this end the k-shell decomposition of a graph is a very appealing one, since it highlights the topological structure of hubs in a network. However, calculating the k-coreness of a graph is a highly iterative procedure. It includes pruning rounds both for nodes and for their incident edges until each node is assigned a single number: its core assignment.

The initial step of the algorithm involves removing all nodes that are of degree one (1) along with their edge. These nodes are considered to have *1*-coreness and are indexed as k=1. After the first pruning round, the remaining graph may include now other nodes that are also of degree 1. These nodes are also considered to have k=1 and are therefore pruned. This process is repeated until no other nodes with degree 1 exist in the remaining network. Once achieved, the next round includes pruning all nodes that have degree 2 to include them in the *2*-core. Similarly, the next rounds involve iterative deletions of the nodes along with their edges with i or fever connections to index them as k=i. The final goal is to assign a core assignment to each node in the network.

Figure 1. k-shells of an example network

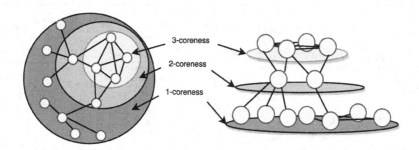

It is worth mentioning that a node is said to have *k*-coreness if it belongs to the *k*-core but not to the $(k+1)$-core; a *k*-shell on the other hand consists of all nodes that have *k*-coreness. However, we use them interchangeably although their definition is different.

3.1.2 Hadoop and MapReduce

Hadoop is an open source software library, in fact a middleware, that is designed for distributed and parallel storing and processing of very large datasets over a cluster of commodity machines. A Hadoop cluster is able to scale up from a single machine to thousands of computing devices. Each individual component of the cluster offers both storage and computational power to the system and is created with the assumption that the hardware failures are common and that the framework will handle them. This automatically means that instead of relying on the hardware layer to deliver high-availability Hadoop handles all failures at the application layer.

In order to process large datasets across a Hadoop cluster the MapReduce paradigm is adopted. MapReduce is the "center-piece" of Hadoop. It is a programming model that is related with generating and processing large datasets with a parallel and distributed algorithm over a cluster of machines. The cluster usually consists of a master node and several slave nodes. A MapReduce job, follows the principles of the functional programming including two different parts/methods: a filtering and sorting procedure,

Figure 2. The MapReduce paradigm

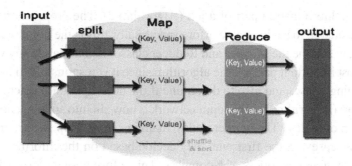

Figure 3. The flow of MR-SD

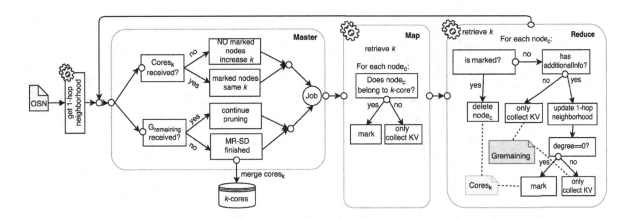

namely the Map() method, and a summary operation named Reduce(). The entire job maintains the parallel and distributed tasks, by marshalling the distributed machines and managing the data exchange between the master and slaves.

3.2 The MR-SD Algorithm

Now that the necessary background on k-shell decomposition and Hadoop clusters is provided, we present the details of our algorithmic proposal. The main aim of the MR-SD algorithm that we describe in detail in this section is to construct the k-cores for a given large input network graph. It is running on the slave nodes and is the actual pruning part of the decomposition. Algorithm 2, on the other hand, is the driver routine that is running on the server side and Algorithm 1 is an auxiliary one.

Our distributed and parallel algorithm consists of chained Map-Reduce pairs that manage to retrieve gradually and recursively all the k-cores of a large input graph. The Hadoop cluster we created for the purposes of this work includes one master node and some slave nodes; both kind of the aforementioned nodes are denoted in this chapter as node$_c$ and nodes of an input graph are referenced as node$_N$. The main concept of MR-SD is that each node$_c$ is in charge of pruning the network and only some are combining the intermediate outcomes of the MapReduce-based k-core decomposition.

Based on the above idea, we consider two computational parts of the algorithm:

Part 1: The progress and termination part of a job (Algorithm 2). The preparation of the MapReduce job should be considered to be done here. More specifically, this is the point where we set the input and output paths, we define the Mapper and Reducer classes and initialize any variables. However, this is one the most important parts of the algorithm since it is responsible to increase the coreness between the pruning phases and also to determine if the decomposition reached its end.

Part 2: The pruning part (Algorithm 3). The input network is now slit into smaller chunks and distributed over the collection of nodes$_c$. The worker nodes$_c$ maintain some Map tasks, some Reduce tasks or even both in some cases. In the first one, they decide based on the information they are handed out if a node of the input network is of k-coreness. This information is forwarded to the Reducers

Figure 4. Algorithm 1 (left) and Algorithm 2 (right)

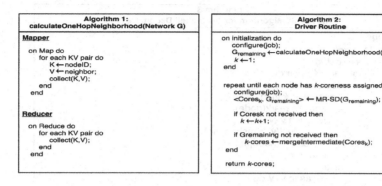

without any significant additional cost. The latter apply the changes to the network according to the information of the Mappers.

Below, we formalize the algorithm in pseudo-code and describe our approach. An important observation, to understand the idea behind the MR-SD algorithm, is that each node$_c$ can only process a part of the actual input network graph and that the k-coreness (the k value here on) must be announced to all parts of the Hadoop cluster efficiently.

Each round of MapReduce of the MR-SD algorithm includes updating the k value and also checking if k-shell decomposition has finished. For this matter, the master node handles a bunch of critical variables of the algorithm:

- k – the k-coreness assignment of the nodes$_N$ currently examined; it is an integer.
- G_{in} – the actual, large input network graph of the user. It is the initial graph of the algorithm containing all the nodes$_N$ and their links.
- $G_{remaining}$ – represents the remaining network after a pruning is performed to the input graph.
- $Cores_k$ – is the current k-shell. It includes all nodes that construct the k-shell.

The master node of the cluster is throughout the whole k-shell decomposition responsible for updating the k value and also for its dissemination. In the first step, the master sets k to 1, initiates a MapReduce job and announces the coreness to all nodes$_c$. As mentioned above, the network is fragmented into independent chunks and those are forwarded to the nodes$_c$ to perform a Map task. During this part each node$_N$ is considered to be an output Key (K) and each neighbor a single Value (V) when forming the Key-Value (KV) pairs. These pairs are then forwarded to the Receiver nodes$_c$, that group the Values and considers the collection as the 1-hop neighborhood of the Key (node$_N$).

The initial step of the algorithm is to find out the one-hop neighborhood for each node appearing in the input network. However, in order to begin a Map task, the slave node has to find out the k-value; it is guaranteed that the k value that each node$_c$ retrieves is always up-to-date since the master node is the only node responsible for increasing the k value and only at the end of a job. Now each slave counts the 1-hop neighbors of each node saved in the V by the previous round, i.e. the degree. The question that each node of the network now needs to answer would be "Is the degree of the node$_N$ less or equal than k?". If so, the particular node$_N$ is marked by the slave in order to be pruned from the remaining graph

Figure 5. The MR-SD Algorithm

```
Algorithm 3:
The MR-SD algorithm for the k-shell Decomposition

Mapper
  on Map do
      k ← get(k);
      for each KV pair do
          degree ← ||V||;
          if degree ≤ k then
              node ← mark(node);
              for each v ϵV do
                  collect(v, attachedInfo);
                  collect(node,k);
              end
          else
              for each v ϵV do
                  V ← V + v;
                  collect(K,V);
              end
          end
      end
  end


Reducer
  on Reduce do
      k ← get(k);
      for each KV pair do
          if attachedInfo received then
              for each attachedInfo do
                  oneHopNeighborhood ←{V} - attachedInfo;
              end

          degree ← ||V||;
          if degree == 0 then
              mark(node);
              Cores_k ← collect(K, k);
          else
              V ← oneHopNeighborhood;
              G_remaining ← collect(K,V);
          end
      end
  end
```

by the Reducer and collected to the *k*-shell. Also, some additional information is attached (referring to the attachedInfo variable of MR-SD) to all nodes included in its 1-hop neighborhood that indicates that the Reducer should exclude the current node from their neighborhood. Should the coreness exceed the *k* threshold, then the $node_N$ is collected as the Key along with its one hop neighbors which are considered as the Value.

The next step includes the Reduce phase where each slave that undertakes a Reduce task retrieves the *k* value and also receives a bunch of KV pairs. The KV pairs represent the nodes of the input graph coupled with their 1-hop neighbors. The algorithm continues now with one of the three possible scenarios that follow:

Scenario 1: Node K was not marked previously by the Mapper.
Scenario 2: Node K was marked previously by the Mapper.
Scenario 3: Node K carries additional information with it.

As described above, when a node of the network is marked by the Mapper this indicates that its degree is lower than the k threshold. This way described, the particular node needs to be included in the currently examined k-shell. The Reducer therefore collects node K and the k value as a KV pair. The latter outlines the process followed in scenario 2. In scenario 1, the $node_N$ represented as K was not marked meaning that it obviously has a degree larger than k and does not fulfil the criteria to get pruned and included in the current k-shell. So it has to be included in the next MapReduce round of MR-SD. Although this scenario seems as a trivial one, in the sense that it has to be only collected as a KV pair as is, quite more work needs to be done. MR-SD dictates here that the Reducer needs to check if the node couples with any additional information (i.e. attachedInfo); if so, we move on to scenario 3. Scenario 3 shows that one or more neighbors of the $node_N$ under investigation were previously pruned in this pruning round. The neighbors that need to be deleted from the 1-hop neighborhood of node K are included in the attached information. After removing the nodes from the neighborhood, the degree of the $node_N$ shrinks consequently. The $node_N$ and the neighbors are now paired again to a KV and send back to the master in the $G_{remaining}$ output file. However, should the neighborhood be now an empty set, the $node_N$ is assigned to the k-shell and is collected immediately along with its coreness.

It is indisputable that the pruning part of the MR-SD indeed manages to generate the k-cores as long as the k value is correctly updated and effectively disseminated by the master node. Let us explain how the master maintains the progress and the termination of the MapReduce-based k-shell decomposition and converges finally to the correct k-cores.

Each round of MR-SD examines all nodes of the input network to either assign a coreness or to push them to the next round. Once all nodes are parsed, i.e., a round of MR-SD finishes, then one of the following options are followed:

- If new additions to the current k-shell appeared during the pruning round, then the master receives the $Cores_k$ file, including the IDs of the $nodes_N$ that have been added to the current k-core, and the $G_{remaining}$ file with the remaining network. Of course, k-shell decomposition demands that the k value stays the same for another round.
- It is possible that there are no other $nodes_N$ left after the pruning of the network. In this case the master node receives only the $Cores_k$ file and termination is detected; no other $nodes_N$ are left for the next round and all intermediate k-cores are merged into a final output file (see Algorithm 2 variable named k-cores).
- If only $G_{remaining}$ is returned, this means that none of the $nodes_N$ got deleted during the latest pruning round. The master node increases immediately the k value and initiates another round of MR-SD.

In order to understand the functionality of MR-SD we provide a sample graph and an example of the network pruning. The network shown in Figure 6 is the sample graph that we will use to show how MR-SD deconstructs the network into its k-shells; we will describe in details the first pruning round of our proposed solution. What the k-shell decomposition algorithm would do in the first iteration, is to discover that $nodes_N$ H, J and K belong to the *1*-shell. Below you can see how MR-SD manages to converge to the same outcome.

Let us assume that our Hadoop cluster maintains the MapReduce job by assigning it to three Mappers and two Reducers, and that Algorithm 1 has already calculated the 1-hop neighborhood for each $node_N$ in the network of Figure 6.

Figure 6. Example network (left) and its MR-SD k-shell decomposition (right)

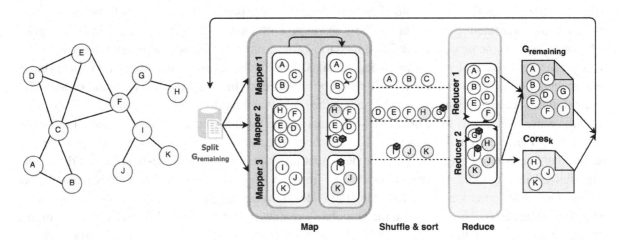

Initialization Phase

The master node sets the initial *k* value to 1 and the $G_{remainig}$ file is thought to be the input graph here, while the network is split to independent chunks and is distributed to the Mappers as show in Figure 6.

Map Phase

Mapper1 receives nodes$_N$ A, B and C, but none of them is of degree less or equal than 1. Thus, Mapper1 collects A, B and C along with their 1-hop neighbors as KV pairs. The chunk that Mapper2 receives, contains nodes D, E, F, G and H. The degree of node$_N$ H is obviously 1 and therefore it gets marked in order to get pruned in the Reduce phase. The Mapper needs also to attach additional information to every 1-hop neighbor of node H, here node G gets the additionalInfo assigned. The same occurs in Map performed by Mapper3. Nodes J and K have degree 1 and get marked, and node I gets the additionalInfo.

Reduce Phase

The two Reducers receive a piece of the network and all necessary information about the alterations that need to be done, according to the preceding Map tasks. Let's say that Reducer1 and Reducer2 obtain nodes A, B, C, D, E, F and G, H, I, J, K respectively. The job of Reducer1 is quite easy; none of the nodes is neither marked nor has additional information attached. Therefore, they are all collected as KV pairs and added to the $G_{remaining}$ network. Reducer2 on the other hand, collects the marked nodes H, J and K along with their coreness (*k* value) as KV pairs into the $Cores_k$ file. This way they are deleted from the network. Moreover, nodes I and G come coupled with the attachedInfo meaning that the Reducers will exclude H, J and K from their 1-hop neighborhood for the rest of the decomposition. Both Reducers ensure that I and G have no empty neighborhoods after the deletions and collect them along with their updated 1-hop neighborhood as KV pairs into the $G_{remaining}$ network.

The MapReduce job is now completed and master node retrieves both the $G_{remaining}$ and the $Cores_k$ files from the cluster. Since both are existing, MR-SD indicates that another pruning round should be forced with the same *k* value and with the updated $G_{remaining}$ as input network.

4. EXPERIMENTAL EVALUATION

In this section we analyse the experimental settings and their outcomes. We also compare the results performed for real-world datasets on a Hadoop cluster with different system settings. The performance for each case is also presented in details. We need first to present the datasets and give an overview of the Hadoop cluster characteristics.

4.1 The Evaluation Platform

Our proposed solution manages to retrieve the *k*-cores of a network in a distributed and parallel way over a collection of connected machines using commodity hardware. Our testing Hadoop cluster comprises five $node_c$, a master and four slave nodes, all offering storage and computational power to the cluster. In means of storage each $node_c$ has a disk capacity of 42GB and their memory is 12GB of RAM each. Another important feature we find in the $nodes_c$ is that they are a blade-based 8-core CPU. The connection between the parts of the cluster supports a 10-gigabit Ethernet network. Finally, each $node_c$ is running CentOS. We performed several experiments, with various settings and during those, no significant interference from any other workloads appeared.

4.2 The Experimental Setting

After describing the hardware part of our experimental platform it is important to have an overview on the datasets used in the experiments as well as on the different settings. Finally, we present the performance measures we used to evaluate our algorithm and show its advantages and its tradeoffs in each case.

It is important to explain why we are not presenting results of other solutions mentioned in Section 2. The reason behind this is that our proposed solution is a novel one in the literature and has therefore no competent approaches. However, we tried algorithms of (Batagelj & Zaversnik, 2002) and (Cheng et al., 2011), but they run out of memory as the input graphs were too large for their purpose; they never finished the computations.

4.2.1 The Data Sources

To test efficiently the MR-SD algorithm we chose eight different real-world networks, varying from small networks to really large sized ones comprising by a few millions nodes. The input graphs are freely offered by Stanford (visit: https://snap.stanford.edu/) and by Gephi (visit: https://github.com/gephi/gephi/wiki/Datasets). Table 1 shows details of the networks regarding the number of the nodes and their connecting edges, but also the number of the jobs required to retrieve their *k*-cores.

Table 1. The datasets used in the experimentation phase

Experiment	Social Network Name	Number of Nodes	Number of Edges	Number of Jobs
1	Autonomous systems AS-733	6474	13895	61
2	Protein Interaction Network in budding Yeast	2361	7182	74
3	Amazon product co-purchasing network	334863	925872	87
4	Deaseasome	7533	22052	118
5	DBLP collaboration network	317080	1049866	360
6	Autonomous systems by Skitter	1696415	11095298	1305
7	LiveJournal online Social Network	3997962	34681189	3363
8	Orkut online social network	3072441	117185083	5918

4.2.2 The Hadoop Settings

All experiments were conducted in the same cluster but with different Hadoop settings. In the first set of experiments, the Map capacity was set to 10 and the Reduce capacity also. This resulted in an average of 4 tasks per computing node.

However, our aim was to try to improve the performance of our algorithm. Having that in mind, we chose to tune the capacity of the Map and Reduce tasks for each node in the cluster until we accomplish to have a cluster with more power. To this end, and after forcing a bunch of fluctuations in the capacity, we finally maintained a cluster with nodes that were able to handle a system with up to 200 Maps and 200 Reduce tasks. Our algorithm could now exploit twenty times more capacity than the first experimentation phase. This also means that each node$_c$ can undertake now an average of 80 tasks. Consequently, using the different Hadoop settings we were able to achieve significant speedup for our proposed solution as presented in Subsection 4.3.2.

In Table 2 you can see the two different clusters used in our experiments. HC1 denotes here on the Hadoop Cluster 1 and HC2 is the second Hadoop Cluster, the one with the higher capacity.

4.2.3 The Performance Measures

In order to address the performance improvements of our proposed solution but also to show its tradeoffs, measures had to be chosen to be able to quantify them. The best fits for this purpose are the following:

1. The Speedup: It is the speedup that appears as we raise the cluster's capacity.
2. The Map Execution Time per job (sec): It is the time spent to execute a Map phase during each job.

Table 2. Hadoop cluster settings used during the experimentation phase

Hadoop Cluster Name	Map Task Capacity	Reduce Task Capacity	Average Tasks per Node
HC1	10	10	4
HC2	200	200	80

3. The Reduce Execution Time per job (sec): It is the time spent to execute a Reduce phase during each job.
4. The Total Execution time (sec): It is the total execution time spent for the *k*-shell decomposition including initializations, communications over the network between the nodes and any other additional computational or communication costs that may occurred from the beginning to the end of the decomposition.
5. The Average CPU time spent (sec): It is the time spent solely by the CPU

4.3 The Obtained Results

In order to have a better overview of the obtained results, they are presented in a common graph for both experimental settings used for this work. This way they can be compared easily and any performance improvements can be observed in a more straight forward way. Moreover, in this section, we explain the impact that different features of the system on the aforementioned measures have.

4.3.1 The Impact of the Network Size on the Speedup

In order to give a better overview of the speedup we achieved we present the results in two different plots; one plot shows the results for the largest graphs used in the experiments and another that highlights the speedup achieved in smaller ones. As we can see in Figure 7, when the size of the networks is large then by increasing the MapReduce capacity of the Hadoop cluster we achieve a great speedup in the calculations of MR-SD. More specifically, the speedup we observed ranges from approximately 42% up to almost 63%. The improvements are achieved by distributing more tasks to each node. Therefore, each worker node undertakes more Map tasks and in all of the experiments more Reduce tasks. The Reduce tasks where now split into smaller jobs, thus the pruning of the network was done in more parallel tasks and this is what seems to boost the calculations of MR-SD.

When the size of the network is relatively smaller than the above, then the speedup of MR-SD is much less. We chose to show for example, experiments 1 and 5. As we can see, the improvement is measured to be approximately 3.3% and 8.5% respectively. However, this is somehow expected, as the Map and Reduce tasks are now split into more, smaller tasks. Since the MapReduce jobs in these cases where from the beginning small ones, this added some additional configuration time to the executions and the

Figure 7. Speedup of MR-SD for small to medium networks (left) and for large networks (right)

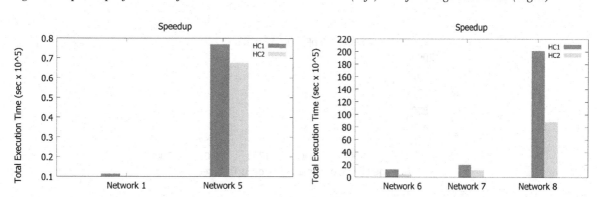

executions themselves took just some seconds. Therefore, the improvement that we observe is not that high as for small to medium networks.

Finally, we have to mention that the execution time depends also on the number of edges of the network, but is not affected greatly by the number of its nodes (see Figure 9). The more edges in a network the denser it tends to be. The latter can lead to a high number of pruning rounds and greater execution time in each round of MR-SD.

Either way, the goal of MR-SD is to maintain k-shell decomposition of networks that are large sized, in a distributed and parallel fashion over a cluster of machines, and this is exactly was is achieved here.

4.3.2 The Average Execution MapReduce Times and the Average CPU Time

We can observe from the plot in Figure 8 that the averaged execution times for Map and Reduce tasks are significantly lower in HC2 than the values appearing in the first cluster, HC1. This is related to the fact that all tasks are split into small chunks and each worker node processes more chunks in parallel. As a result, the average time spent solely by the CPU to perform the calculations in a Hadoop Cluster with more capacity (i.e. the HC2) is also lower than in the cluster with the default Hadoop settings (i.e. the HC1). Detailed breakdown of the execution times are depicted in Figures 11 and 12.

4.3.3 Impact of the Machine Load

As mentioned in Subsection 3.1.3 performing a k-shell decomposition of a network is a highly iterative process. Each pruning round includes some computations performed by each worker node that is assigned a MapReduce task. As a consequence, the vast amount of information used for storing a network graph requires a huge workload until a major part of the nodes is removed. As seen in Figure 13, the first rounds of MR-SD demand a higher CPU time than the last ones in most cases, especially in cases where the input graph is very large-sized. Another important observation is that the time solely spent by the CPU to perform the computations is significantly lower for the decomposition of large networks. However, in each case its graphical representation follows the same trend in both categories of networks, as depicted in Figure 13.

The enormous quantity of data needed to describe large networks, affects also the memory footprint of MR-SD during the pruning rounds. Both the Virtual memory and the Physical memory demands are

Figure 8. Average execution time per map task vs. per reduce task

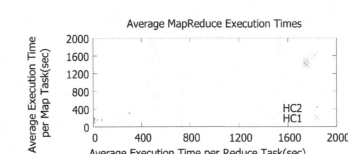

Figure 9. Average CPU time vs. number of nodes per experiment. Blue lines represent results for HC1 and red lines HC2 results

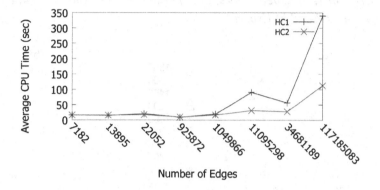

Figure 10. Memory footprint of the experiments per cluster, average physical memory vs. average heap usage

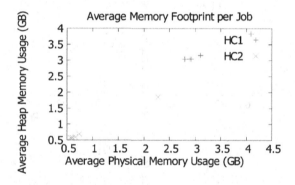

higher for large networks. However, creating Hadoop clusters with increased capacity (like HC2) lowers also the memory requirements during the computations of MR-SD. The memory workload is presented in a plot in Figure 10.

4.3.4 Impact of Network Density

The number of the edges in a network determines the network density level. The more edges appear in a network the denser it tends to be. MR-SD is affected by the network density and by its size. Figure 7 shows that MR-SD k-shell decomposition method demands a greater execution time for networks with some millions of nodes and a larger memory than the time and memory needed to decompose smaller networks to its cores.

The aforementioned is obvious in both clusters we used, HC1 and HC2. For example, you can refer to Figure 7, Figure 9 and Figure 13 to see the execution time of experiment 8, which is a dense and large network, and compare the result with those of experiment 1, which is a smaller and sparser network graph. You can also see how differently MR-SD behaves in the two clusters for the same network, in means of less computation time in HC2.

Figure 11. Average execution time of the map task during each round of MR-SD. The red lines represent results of HC1 and the green lines the results of HC2 for the same dataset. The experiments are the following: a) Experiment 1, b) Experiment 2, c) Experiment 3, d) Experiment 4, e) Experiment 5, f) Experiment 6, g) Experiment 7 and h) Experiment 8

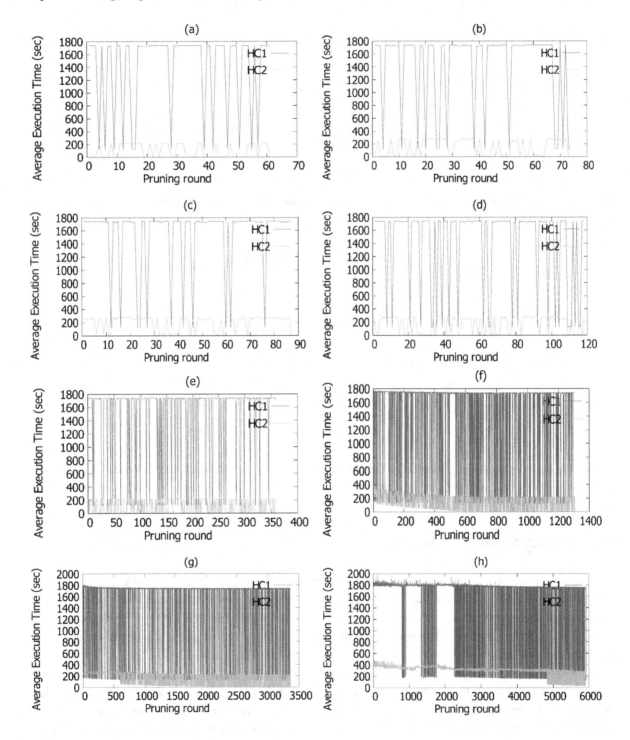

Figure 12. Average execution time of the reduce task during each round of MR-SD. The blue lines represent results of HC1 and the orange lines the results of HC2 for the same dataset. The experiments are the following: a) Experiment 1, b) Experiment 2, c) Experiment 3, d) Experiment 4, e) Experiment 5, f) Experiment 6, g) Experiment 7 and h) Experiment 8.

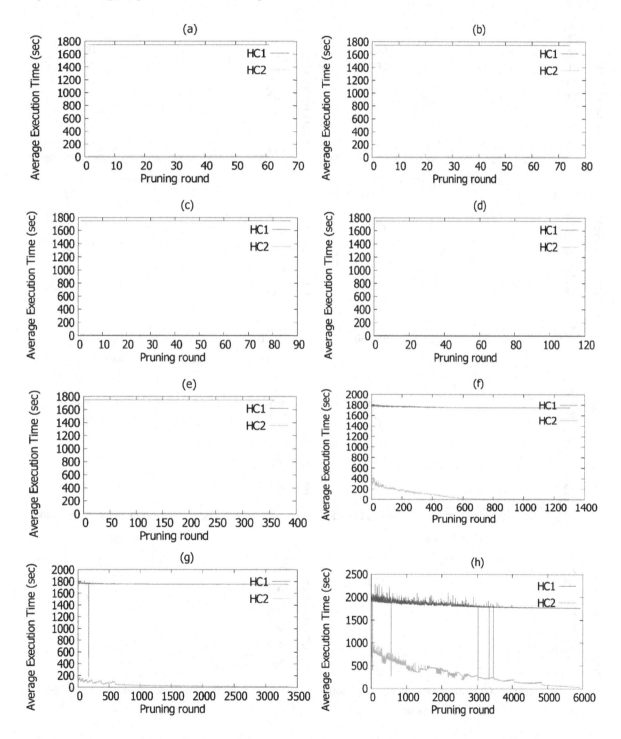

Figure 13. Total CPU time spent per round of MR-SD. The red lines represent results of HC1 and the green lines the results of HC2 for the same dataset. The experiments are the following: a) Experiment 1, b) Experiment 2, c) Experiment 3, d) Experiment 4, e) Experiment 5, f) Experiment 6, g) Experiment 7 and h) Experiment 8.

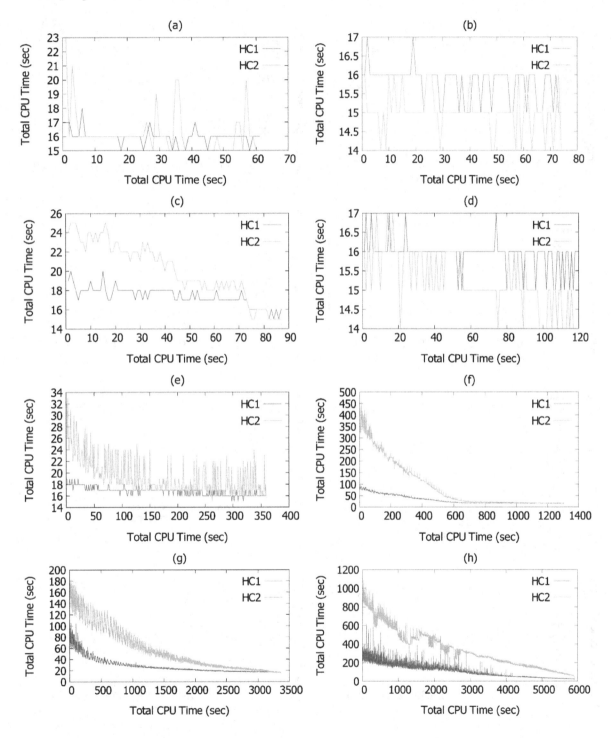

4.3.5 Impact of the Number of VMs

For the experimentation and evaluation phase of MR-SD, we constructed a Hadoop cluster comprising one master and four slave nodes. The networks we chose for testing MR-SD, ranged from small to extremely large. In each experiment, the worker nodes were assigned a part of the network to perform the computations and the pruning. Table 3 shows the number of Map and Reduce tasks performed on the cluster per round on average. When the size of the network is large, this means that all nodes$_c$ have to run more than one task during the pruning rounds of MR-SD. Since we increased the Map and Reduce capacity this also means that in HC2 each node of the cluster undertakes more Map and Reduce tasks than in the first cluster setting. In both clusters, when the network graph was extremely large, as in experiment 8, the worker nodes performed over 30 Map tasks in the first pruning rounds and a number of 8-10 Reduce tasks in HC2. This means that each node of HC1 and HC2 maintained a large number of Map and Reduce tasks during each iteration of MR-SD causing therefore greater time than in other smaller graphs. For smaller networks, although the number of the distributed tasks increased, no significant overhead occurred.

The important observation here is that MR-SD manages to retrieve the k-cores even with great workload. In case of HC2, our approach distributes efficiently a larger number of tasks and performs significantly better, although each node maintains more work on average. This could lead to even better results, when considering using larger Hadoop infrastructures so that all jobs are disseminated more efficiently.

5. CONCLUSION AND FUTURE WORK

Nowadays, k-shell decomposition of Online Social Networks is a key component of Social Network Analysis, as it can be applied in diverse areas. k-core decomposition, as it is also called, has been used

Table 3. Average map and reduce task during each experiment presented for both cluster settings

#	Experiment Name	HC1 setting per round		HC2 setting per round	
		Avg. Map Tasks	Avg. Reduce Tasks	Avg. Map Tasks	Avg. Reduce Tasks
1	Autonomous systems AS-733	2	1	8	8
2	Protein Interaction Network in budding Yeast	2	1	8	8
3	Amazon product co-purchasing network	2	1	8	8
4	Deaseasome	2	1	8	8
5	DBLP collaboration network	2	1	8	8
6	Autonomous systems by Skitter	2.036782	1	8	8.016949
7	LiveJournal online Social Network	2.433541	1	8	8.016949
8	Orkut online social network	9.226935	1	11.01284	8.680973

for discovery of influential spreaders, for Internet topology modelling, for community detection or as a centrality measure. Many algorithms have been prosed for the computation of a network's *k*-shells for weighted and unweighted and for static or slowly changing networks. However, none of the existing solutions are suitable for the computation of the *k*-cores on huge clusters when the size of the input network is extremely large. Modern infrastructures, like those operated by Google or Facebook, are programmed by high performance MapReduce-type frameworks. Motivated by the above, we designed a MapReduce-based distributed *k*-shell decomposition algorithm for large online social networks, that is able to maintain the *k*-cores efficiently even for networks that consist of several millions of nodes and edges. We analyzed all challenges we faced in the design of a distributed and parallel solution for the *k*-shell computation, which is in general a highly iterative algorithm. MR-SD, as we called our solution, is implemented to run on Hadoop clusters following the MapReduce paradigm. We evaluated our algorithm's behavior for eight real-world online social networks, diverse both in size and in density, and assessed its performance for two different Hadoop cluster settings. The cluster was constructed by a master node and four slave nodes, but with different Map and Reduce capacities in the experimentations. As performance measures for our algorithm, we used CPU, Memory and speedup footprints. Finally, we extensively analyzed the advantages of MR-SD running on modern clusters.

As a future work, we plan to optimize the communications' workload between the nodes of the cluster. We also want to run experiments based on MR-SD on commercial modern MapReduce-based clusters, to highlight is scalability. There we will be able to achieve an even better performance and probably a greater speedup. Finally, it is of our interest, to create other versions of MR-SD in order to decompose a weighted or slowly changing network to its *k*-shells too.

REFERENCES

Aksu, H., Canim, M., Chang, Y.-C., Korpeoglu, I., & Ulusoy, O. (2013). Multi-Resolution Social Network Community Identification and Maintenance on Big Data Platform. *Proceedings of the IEEE Conference on BigData*, 102-109. doi:10.1109/BigData.Congress.2013.23

Basaras, P., Katsaros, D., & Tassiulas, L. (2013). Detecting Influential Spreaders in Complex, Dynamic Networks. *IEEE Computer Magazine, 46*(4), 26-31.

Batagelj, V., & Zaversnik, M. (2002). *An O(m) Algorithm for Cores Decomposition of Networks*. University of Ljubljana, Department of Theoretical Computer Science. http://arxiv.org/abs/cs.DS/0310049

Bonchi, F., Gullo, F., Kaltenbrunner, A., & Volkovich, Y. (2014). Core Decomposition of Uncertain Graphs. *Proceedings of the ACM Conference on Knowledge Discovery and Data Mining*, 1316-1325.

Carmi, S., Havlin, S., Kirkpatrick, S., Shavitt, Y., & Shir, E. (2007). A Model of Internet Topology Using k-Shell Decomposition. *Proceedings of the National Academy of Sciences of the United States of America, 104*(27), 11150–11154. doi:10.1073/pnas.0701175104 PMID:17586683

Cheng, J., Ke, Y., Chu, S., & Ozsu, M. T. (2011). Efficient Core Decomposition in Massive Networks. *Proceedings of the IEEE International Conference on Data Engineering*, 51-62.

Dean, J., & Ghemawat, S. (2004). MapReduce: Simplified Data Processing on Large Clusters. *Proceedings of USENIX Conference on Operating System Design and Implementation*, 137-150.

Eidsaa, M., & Almaas, E. (2013). s-Core Network Decomposition: A Generalization of k-Core Analysis to Weighted Networks. *Physical Review E: Statistical, Nonlinear, and Soft Matter Physics*, *88*(062819). PMID:24483523

Garas, A., Schweitzer, F., & Havlin, S. (2012). A k-Shell Decomposition Method for Weighted Networks. *New Journal of Physics*, 14.

Khaouid, W., Barsky, M., Srinivasan, V., & Thomo, A. (2015). k-Core Decomposition of Large Networks on a Single PC. *Proceedings of the VLDB Endowment*, *9*(1), 13–23. doi:10.14778/2850469.2850471

Miorandi, D., & de Pellegrini, F. (2010). k-Shell Decomposition for Dynamic Complex Networks. *Proceedings of the IEEE Conference on Modeling and Optimization in Mobile, Ad Hoc, and Wireless Networks*, 488-496.

Montesor, A., de Pellegrini, F., & Miorandi, D. (2012). Distributed k-Core Decomposition. *IEEE Transactions on Parallel and Distributed Systems*, *24*(2), 288–300. doi:10.1109/TPDS.2012.124

Sariyuce, A. E., Gedik, B., Jacques-Silva, G., Wu, K.-L., & Catalyurek, U. V. (2013). Streaming Algorithms for k-Core Decomposition. *Proceedings of the VLDB Endowment*, *6*(6), 433–444. doi:10.14778/2536336.2536344

Sariyuce, A. E., Gedik, B., Jacques-Silva, G., Wu, K.-L., & Catalyurek, U. V. (2016). Incremental k-Core Decomposition: Algorithms and Evaluation. *The VLDB Journal*, *25*(3), 425–447. doi:10.1007/s00778-016-0423-8

Seidman, S. B. (1983). Network structure and minimum degree. *Social Networks*, *5*(3), 269–287. doi:10.1016/0378-8733(83)90028-X

Shin, K., Eliassi-Rad, T., & Faloutsos, C. (2016). CoreScope: Graph Mining using k-Core Analysis - Patterns, Anomalies and Algorithms. *Proceedings of the IEEE Conference on Data Mining*, 469-478. doi:10.1109/ICDM.2016.0058

Wen, D., Qin, L., Zhang, Y., Lin, X., & Yu, J. X. (2016). I/O Efficient Core Graph Decomposition at Web Scale. *Proceedings of the IEEE International Conference on Data Engineering*, 133-144. doi:10.1109/ICDE.2016.7498235

Wu, H., Cheng, J., Lu, Y., Ke, Y., Huang, Y., Yan, D., & Wu, H. (2015). Core Decomposition in Large Temporal Graphs. *Proceedings of the IEEE International Conference on Big Data*, 649-658.

Chapter 9
Parallelizing Large-Scale Graph Algorithms Using the Apache Spark-Distributed Memory System

Ahmad Askarian
University of Texas at Dallas, USA

Rupei Xu
University of Texas at Dallas, USA

Andras Farago
University of Texas at Dallas, USA

ABSTRACT

The rapidly emerging area of Social Network Analysis is typically based on graph models. They include directed/undirected graphs, as well as a multitude of random graph representations that reflect the inherent randomness of social networks. A large number of parameters and metrics are derived from these graphs. Overall, this gives rise to two fundamental research/development directions: (1) advancements in models and algorithms, and (2) implementing the algorithms for huge real-life systems. The model and algorithm development part deals with finding the right graph models for various applications, along with algorithms to treat the associated tasks, as well as computing the appropriate parameters and metrics. In this chapter we would like to focus on the second area: on implementing the algorithms for very large graphs. The approach is based on the Spark framework and the GraphX API which runs on top of the Hadoop distributed file system.

DOI: 10.4018/978-1-5225-2814-2.ch009

INTRODUCTION

Spark is an open source, in-memory big data processing framework in a distributed environment. It started as a research program in 2009 and became an open source project in 2010. In 2014 it was released as an Apache incubator project (Xin et al, 2013).

Spark is evolved from Hadoop MapReduce so it can be run on Hadoop cluster and data in the Hadoop distributed File System (HDFS). It supports a wide range of workloads, such as Machine Learning, Business Intelligence, streaming and batch processing. Spark was created to complement, rather than replace Hadoop. The Spark core is accompanied by a set of powerful, higher-level libraries which can be used in the same application. These libraries currently include SparkSQL, Spark Streaming, MLlib (for machine learning), and GraphX, as shown in Figure 1.

In order to efficiently use the processing resources of a cluster, Spark needs a cluster resource manager. Yet Another Resource Negotiator (YARN) is a Hadoop processing layer that contains a resource manager and a job scheduler. Yarn allows multiple applications to run on a single Hadoop Cluster. Figure 2 illustrates how Spark uses Yarn as a distributed resource manager (Vavilapalli et al, 2013).

Figure 1. Spark full stack

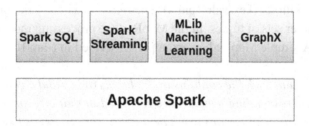

Figure 2. Yet Another Resource Manager

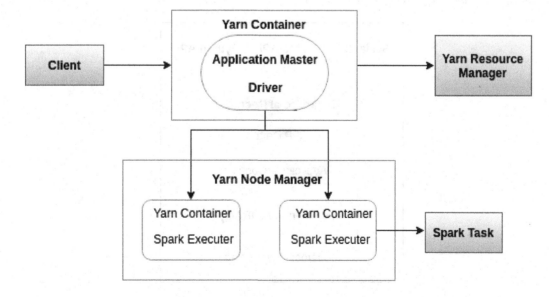

Although Spark is designed for in-memory computation, it is capable of handling workloads larger than the cluster aggregate memory. Almost all the Spark built-in functions automatically split to local disks when the working data set does not fit in memory. In the next two section we outline the difference between Spark and MapReduce, as well as the concept of Resilient Distributed Dataset (RDD) in Spark (Meng, Bradley et al, 2016).

APACHE SPARK VS. HADOOP MAPREDUCE

Apache Spark improvements over Hadoop MapReduce are characterized by efficiency and usability, as shown in Figure 3. In order to improve efficiency, it offers in-memory computing capability, which can provide a fast running environment for applications that need to reuse and share data across computations. Having different languages with integrated APIs, such as Java, Scala, Python and R, improve Spark's usability, as compared to MapReduce.

Next we explain the Hadoop Mapreduce with an example, and then discuss how Spark can improve the efficiency for implementing more complex algorithms (Xin, Deyhim et al, 2014).

MapReduce is a programming model, and an associated implementation, which allows massive scalable data processing across hundreds or thousands of servers. MapReduce refers to two separate and distinct tasks, needed for big data processing. The first one is the *map task,* which converts a set of data to another set of data called tuples (key/value pairs). The *reduce task* takes the map output and combines those data tuples into smaller sets of tuples. In the MapReduce processing model the reduce task always runs after the map task. A simple MapReduce example, described in (ibm01, 2011) is the following.

Assume you have five files, and each file contains two columns (a key and a value in Hadoop terms) that represent a city and the corresponding temperature recorded in that city for the various measurement days. Of course, the real world applications won't be quite so simple, as it's likely to contain millions or

Figure 3. Apache Spark efficiency and usability

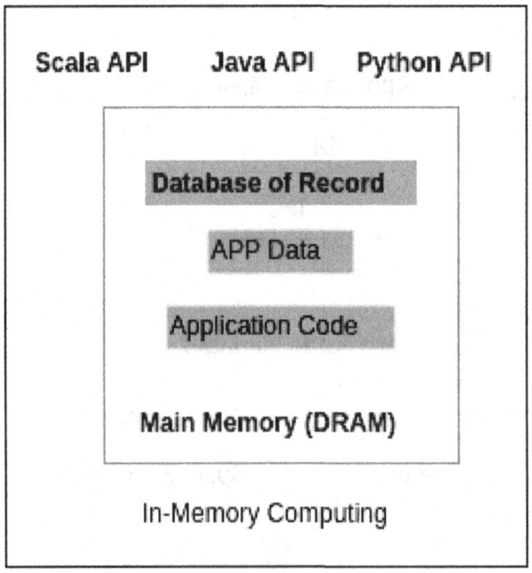

even billions of rows, and they might not be neatly formatted rows at all; in fact, no matter how big or small the amount of data you need to analyze, the key principles we're covering here remain the same. Either way, in this example, city is the key and temperature is the value as shown in Figure 4.

Out of all the data we have collected, we want to find the maximum temperature for each city across all of the data files (note that each file might have the same city represented multiple times). Using the MapReduce model, we can break this down into five map tasks, where each mapper works on one of the five files and the mapper task ges through the data and returns the maximum temperature for each city. For example, the results produced from one mapper task for the data above are shown in Figure 5.

Let us assume the other four mapper tasks (working on the other four files not shown here) produced the intermediate results which are illustrated in Figure 6.

All five of these output streams would be fed into the reduce tasks, which combine the input results and output a single value for each city, producing a final result set, as illustrated in Figure 7.

As an analogy, you can think of the map and reduce tasks as the way a census was conducted in Roman times, where the census bureau would dispatch its people to each city in the empire. Each census taker in each city would be tasked to count the number of people in that city and then return their results to the capital city. There, the results from each city would be reduced to a single count (sum of all cities) to determine the overall population of the empire. This mapping of people to cities, in parallel, and then combining the results (reducing) is much more efficient than sending a single person to count every person in the empire in a serial fashion.

Some applications, such as implementing large scale graph algorithms in a social network, are more complex than just one path of Map and Reduce. They require multiple operations over a same data sets. In MapReduce no sharing data across time stamps or iteration is available (Zaharia et al, 2012). Let's take a look at the PageRank example in MapReduce which requires multiple iteration, see Figure 8.

The algorithm starts with data in HDFS and then does one step on MapReduce (iteration 1). Then to share the data with the next step it has to write it back into HDFS again. After that, in the next iterations of PageRank, the data must be loaded back, and the algorithm is continued.

Spark has a computation model in which after each iteration the data will be stored in memory, and it is available to be processed in the next steps as illustrated in Figure 9.

In Spark, instead of thinking in terms of map and reduce functions, we think in terms of distributed data sets. This is what essentially distinguishes Spark from Hadoop Mapreduce. The data abstraction in Spark is called *Resilient Distributed Dataset (RDD),* consisting of parallel collections of Scala objects. In the next section, RDD is explained in more details, based on (Bourse et al, 2014.).

RESILIENT DISTRIBUTED DATASET (RDD)

RDD is a logical reference of a dataset which is paralleled among many processors in the cluster. RDD is *resilient,* meaning that if data in memory is lost, then it can be recovered. It is *distributed,* which means processing across the cluster, and the dataset can come from a file, or be created by a program. Basically, RDD is a fundamental unit of data in Spark, forming an immutable dataset. It contains two different operations, called *Transformation* and *Action.* Transformation creates a new RDD based on an existing one, while Action returns a value from an RDD. Figure 10 illustrates Transformation and Action for an existing RDD (Zaharia et al, 2012).

Figure 4. Cities information

```
Toronto, 20
Whitby, 25
New York, 22
Rome, 32
Toronto, 4
Rome, 33
New York, 18
```

Figure 5. Maximum temperature for each city

(Toronto, 20) (Whitby, 25) (New York, 22) (Rome, 33)

Figure 6. Output of the mapper task

(Toronto, 18) (Whitby, 27) (New York, 32) (Rome, 37)(Toronto, 32)

(Whitby, 20) (New York, 33) (Rome, 38)(Toronto, 22) (Whitby, 19)

(New York, 20) (Rome, 31)(Toronto, 31) (Whitby, 22) (New York, 19)

(Rome, 30)

Figure 7. Output of the reduce task

(Toronto, 32) (Whitby, 27) (New York, 33) (Rome, 38)

Figure 8. A Multi-Iteration Algorithm In MapReduce

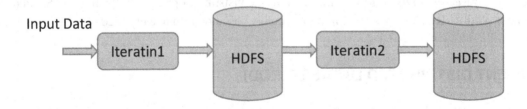

Figure 9. Multi-Iteration Algorithm in Spark

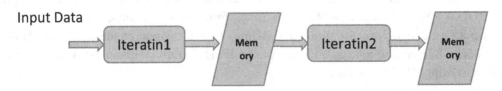

Figure 10. RDD Transformation and Action

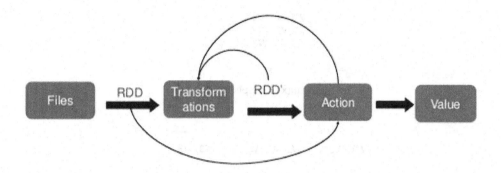

RDD Transformation includes parts called filter, map, union, and others. Actions includes reduce, collect, count, etc. The main advantage of RDDs is that they are simple and well understood, because they deal with concrete classes, providing a familiar object-oriented programming style with compile-time type-safety. For example, given an RDD containing instances of Person we can filter by age by referencing the age attribute of each Person object as illustrated in Figure 11.

The transformations are only computed when an action requires a result to be returned. In this example, when an action like count is called, we will be returned the Persons objects belonging to persons older than 21.

Pair RDD is a special form of RDD, in which each element must have a key-value pair (two element tuple). Pair RDD is important because of the traditional map-reduce algorithms for parallel processing which is based on key and value pairs. Figure 12 shows the word count example which is implemented using pair RDD in Spark. First step is creating an RDD based on input data then split the RDD based on the words space. After having an RDD corresponding to each word, a pair RDD can be created with the word as the key and number one as the value. Then reducing the pair RDDs based on the key returns the word count.

COMPUTATION TIME OF SPARK AND MAPREDUCE

MapReduce has been the centerpiece on Hadoop for batch processing for long time. Map and reduction operations are happen independently and in parallel. In practice parallel performance is limited by the number of independent data sets and the number of processing powers, which in most cases are CPUs. Also, MapReduce doesn't have efficient primitives for data sharing between steps which results in being slow as states between steps goes to distributed file system. While MapReduce is simple, it needs more

Figure 11. Filter by age in an RDD

```
rdd.filter(_.age > 21)
```

Figure 12. Word Count example, using Spark

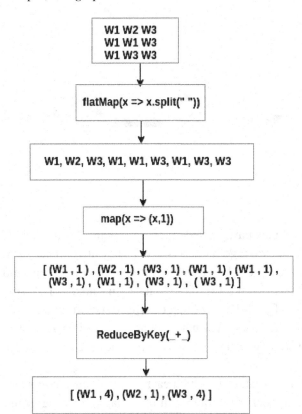

communication or I/O. By using RDD in Spark, MapReduce algorithm is gets sped up especially for data processing in an iterative mode. One of the examples in which iteration plays an important rule is logistic regression. Table 1 shows the computation time for logistic regression in Spark and MapReduce.

As shown in table 1, Spark can run a program up to 100x faster than Hadoop MapReduce in memory(Zaharia et al, 2012).

GRAPHX API FOR SPARK

Graph-based algorithms are becoming very important for solving numerous problems in data-intensive applications, including search engines, recommendation systems, financial analysis, and many others. As these problems grow in scale, computational and memory requirements of the processing algorithms

Table 1. Running time for Spark vs. MapReduce

Big Data processing tool	Running time (s)
Apache Spark	0.9
MapReduce	110

rapidly become a bottleneck. To avoid such a bottleneck, parallel computing resources are required. Graphx is a new component in Apache Spark for graph parallel processing, which extends the Spark RDD by introducing the concept of *Property Graph*. The Property Graph is a directed multigraph, that is, a directed graph with potentially multiple parallel edges sharing the same end vertices. There also *properties* attached to each vertex and edge. GraphX is a native property graph processor. It allows all vertices and edges to have their own properties(Bourse et al, 2014.; Abu-Doleh, et al, 2015; Hinge et al, 2015).

GRAPH PARTITIONING IN SPARK

Graph partitioning algorithms are designed to minimize communication and balance the computation among multiple processors. Partitioning the graph data and balancing the computation on a distributed cluster of machines is a common approach to scale-out computations for large scale input graph data. Iterative computations on input graph data, for instance the PageRank systems, are well known use cases for graph partitioning. The quality of graph partitioning depends on balancing the processing load across machines and minimizing the communication cost inside the cluster (Bourse et al, 2014.). There are two main approaches for partitioning a graph among different machines. They are called *vertex cut* and *edge cut*. Graphx implements the vertex cut approach to ensure one edge is assigned to one partition. In this case one vertex can be shared across partitions. This strategy moves the network communication from edges to vertices. In order to ensure vertices are partitioned in a most efficient way for a particular algorithm, Graphx provides a number of strategies, which are illustrated in Figure 13.

The choice between the partition strategies is based upon the algorithm and the graph structure. The strategy called EdgePartition1D ensures that all edges with the same source are partitioned together, so the edges that belong to a particular partition have the same source. For applications, such as counting the outgoing edges which the operation aggregated to the source, each partition has all the data needed on an individual machine. In this case the network traffic among different machines is minimized. On the other hand, for graphs with power-law structure, a few partitions may receive a significant proportion of the total number of edges (Hcyu, 2015). Figure 14 shows the EdgePartition1D source code in Scala.

Figure 13. Graph partitioning strategy

```
graph.partitionBy(PartitionStrategy.EdgePartition1D)
graph.partitionBy(PartitionStrategy.EdgePartition2D)
graph.partitionBy(PartitionStrategy.CanonicalRandomVertexCut)
graph.partitionBy(PartitionStrategy.RandomVertexCut)
```

Figure 14. EdgePartition1D implementation

```
case object EdgePartition1D extends PartitionStrategy {
    overridedef getPartition(src:VertexId, dst:VertexId, numParts:PartitionID):PartitionID = {
    val mixingPrime:VertexId = 1125899906842597L
    (math.abs(src * mixingPrime)% numParts).toInt
    }
}
```

A large number called mixingPrime is used to balance the partitions. EdgePartition2D uses both source vertices and destination vertices to calculate partitions. Figure 15 shows the source code for EdgePartition2D.

The *RandomVertex Cut* strategy splits the graph based on both source and destination vertices, which can help to create a more balanced partition. This strategy may affect the runtime performance due to the increase in the amount of network communication. In this case even the edge that connects the same pair of nodes may be spread among two machines based on the direction of the edge. Figure 16 illustrates the source code of Random Vertex Cut.

The strategy *Canonical Random Vertex Cut* partitions the edges regardless to the direction, so the edges sharing both a source and a destination will be partitioned together. Figure 17 shows the source code for this partitioning strategy.

In the next section we show an example, which is based on a property graph in a paper citation network (see http://snap.stanford.edu/data/cit-HepTh.html). The network is created from the publication information available for ArXiv High Energy Physics Theory category (Malak, Eeast, 2016).

Figure 15. EdgePartition2D implementation

```
case object EdgePartition2D extends PartitionStrategy {
  overridedef getPartition(src:VertexId, dst:VertexId, numParts:PartitionID):PartitionID = {
    val ceilSqrtNumParts:PartitionID =  math.ceil(math.sqrt(numParts)).toInt
    val mixingPrime:VertexId = 1125899906842597L
    val col:PartitionID = (math.abs(src * mixingPrime)% ceilSqrtNumParts).toInt
    val row:PartitionID = (math.abs(dst * mixingPrime)% ceilSqrtNumParts).toInt
    (col * ceilSqrtNumParts + row)% numParts
  }
}
```

Figure 16. Random Vertex Cut implementation

```
case object RandomVertexCutextends PartitionStrategy{
  override def getPartition(src:VertexId, dst:VertexId, numParts:PartitionID):PartitionID = {
    math.abs((src, dst).hashCode())% numParts
  }
}
```

Figure 17. Canonical Random Vertex Cut implementation

```
case object CanonicalRandomVertexCut extends PartitionStrategy {
  overridedef getPartition(src:VertexId, dst:VertexId, numParts:PartitionID):PartitionID = {
    if(src &lt; dst) {
      math.abs((src, dst).hashCode()) % numParts
    } else {
      math.abs((dst, src).hashCode()) % numParts
    }
  }
}
```

Paper Citation Network Example

The first few lines in the text file containing all the citation information is shown in Figure 18.

After the comment lines, which begin with #, each line represents one edge of the graph. For example the first edge starts from a vertex identified by 1001 to another one identified by 9304045. Each vertex is keyed by a *unique* 64-bit long identifier (VertexID). Similarly, edges have corresponding source and destination vertex identifiers. In the context of a paper citation network, the second paper in the older one being cited by the newer paper. This format of a text file is recognized by GraphX. The next step is the creation of the RDD, based on the edges and vertices data. For this purpose SparkContext should be constructed. Figure 19 shows the source code for loading the graph data, and creates an immutable value called paperCitationGraph (Malak, Eeast, 2016).

GraphLoader is an object in GraphX library which contains a method called edgeListFile. This can load a graph from a text file in edge-list format and it uses two methods. The first one is SparkContext (sc) and the second one is the file that contains the graph property information. Now the graph is ready to be processed in a distributed environment. Finding the most-referenced paper is a well-known problem in a paper citation network. The following steps, as illustrated in Figure 20, can find such a paper in a distributed way using Spark/Graphx library by calling inDegree and reduce methods.

In the first step, an RDD of vertexID and in-degree pairs proceeds from the inDegree method. Figure 21 shows the details.

Figure 18. Text file containing the citation information

```
# Directed graph (each unordered pair of nodes is saved once): Cit-HepTh.txt
# Paper citation network of Arxiv High Energy Physics Theory category
# Nodes: 27770 Edges: 352807
# FromNodeId To NodeId
1001 9304045
1001 9308122
1001 9309097
1001 9311042
1001 9401139
1001 9404151
    .
    .
    .
```

Figure 19. Loading a graph in Spark

```
import org.apache.spark.SparkConf

import org.apache.spark.SparkConf

import org.apache.spark.SparkConf

val paperCitationGraph = GraphLoader.edgeListFile(sc, "cit-HepTh.txt")
```

Figure 20. inDegree and reduce in Graphx API

```
1- val numOfCitation = paperCitationGraph.inDegrees
2- val mostRefPaper =numOfCitation.reduce( (x,y) => if (x._2 > y._2) x else y )
```

Figure 21. inDegrees method in GraphX producing key-value pairs

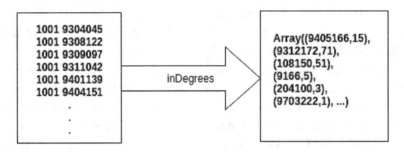

In the second step, each RDD uses a reduce method which takes a function as an input. The function receives two elements from the RDD and returns a single value. The function would be called repeatedly on pairs of elements (RDD) from the reduce method, until only a single value is left. The single value is returned from the reduce method in step 2. Figure 22 illustrates the second step.

The result is: Paper ID 9711200 was cited by 2414 other papers, making it the most cited paper.

Finding PageRank in Social Network Using Apache Spark

The PageRank algorithm can be used to measure the influence of vertices in any social network, although originally it was developed to support Google search. We are using the same data set as the previous section. First let us see how vertices data look like, Figure 23.

As illustrated in Figure 23, all vertices are key-value pairs, where key is the vertex ID and the value is 1. In GraphX all vertices and edges have their own properties, and the arising graph is called property graph. In the considered case the value 1 is the property for all vertices, which is attached to them by the GraphLoader.edgeListFile() method. Now in order to calculate the rank of each vertex, we have to change

Figure 22. reduce(Function) method in GraphX producing a single key value pair

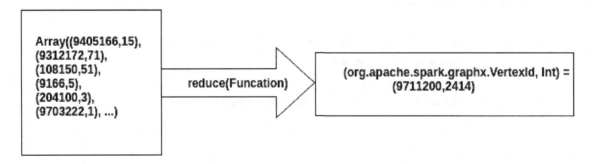

Figure 23. Vertices in the paperCitationGraph

```
paperCitationGraph.vertices.take(6)

Array[(org.apache.spark.graphx.VertexId, Int)] =
Array((9405166,1),
(9312172,1),
(108150,1),
(9166,1),
(204100,1),
(9703222,1))
```

each vertex property to match the corresponding PageRank. The idea of immutable data set implies that the graph property does not change. So a new property graph must be created to express the PageRank property. This is a key Spark concept, the existing RDDs (in this case graph structure) are not updated. Instead, a transformation takes place on an existing RDD to create a new RDD. Figure 24 illustrates two graph properties before and after applying the PageRank method (transformation).

PageRank is a link analysis algorithm that outputs a probability distribution, which can be used to represent the likelihood of a page being referenced. So the new graph has a property of type Double. The code for PageRank calculation in the paper citation network is shown in Figure 25.

Figure 24. PageRank transformation that creates a new property graph

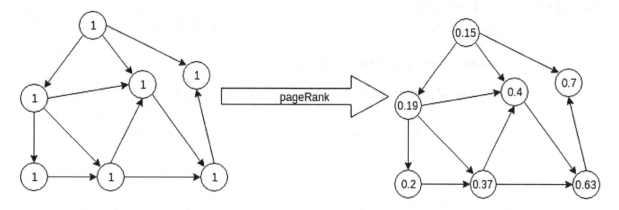

Figure 25. PageRank method in Spark using GraphX library

```
val pr = paperCitationGraph.pageRank(0.01)
val vertices = pr.vertices

vertices: org.apache.spark.graphx.VertexRDD[Double] =
VertexRDDImpl[1019] at RDD at VertexRDD.scala:57
```

The next step is to run the reduce method with an appropriate function to find the vertex with the highest PageRank, see Figure 26.

Finally, we get the result that, according to the PageRank algorithm, paper ID 9207016 is the most influential one.

Finding Connected Components Using Apache Spark

A connected component of a graph is a set of vertices such that every vertex is reachable from every other vertex. Connected component can identify isolated members in social networks, and can also approximate clusters. Figure 27 shows an example of connected components in a graph.

Figure 28 illustrates the network construction, based on RDD collections (vertices and edges).

Using the code provided in Figure 29 allows the detection of connected components in the network above.

Triangle Counting Using Apache Spark

Counting the number of triangles in a large graph is frequently used in complex network analysis such as spam detection and uncovering hidden structures in link recommendation (Malak, Eeast, 2016; Leskovec, 2009. A triangle consists of three vertices that all connected with edges. A social network which contains more triangles usually has tighter connections. The TriangleCount method in spark counts triangles passing through each vertex using the following steps.

Figure 26. The most influential paper

```
vertices.reduce( (x,y) => if (x._2 > y._2) x else y )

(org.apache.spark.graphx.VertexId, Double) = (9207016,82.26069672332562)
```

Figure 27. Finding connected components

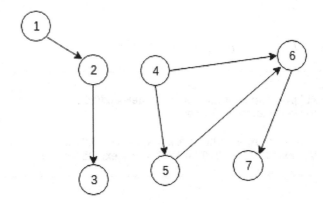

Figure 28. Network construction based on RDD collections

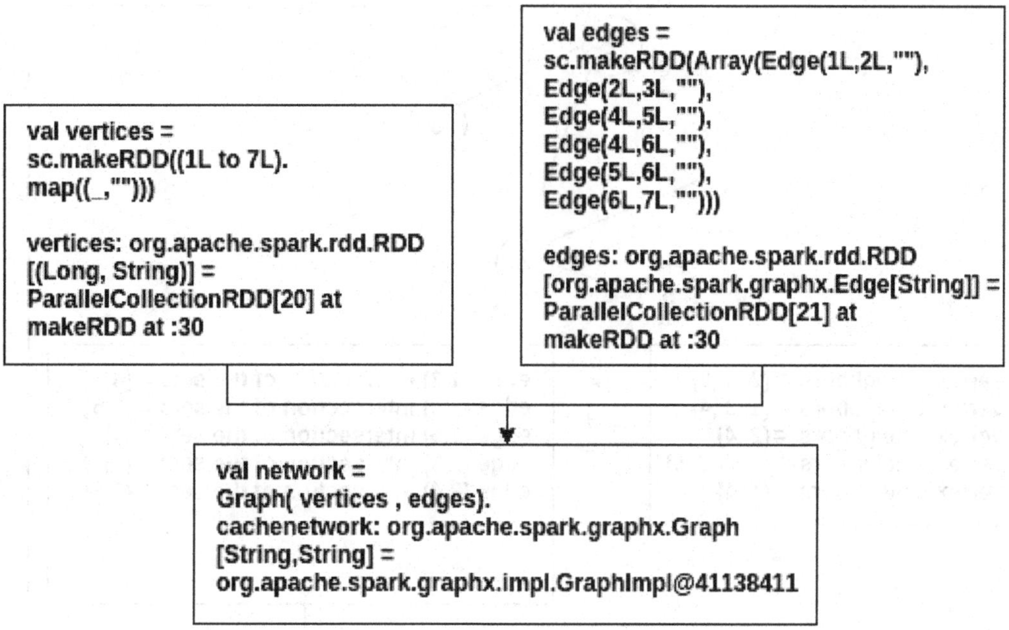

```
val vertices =
sc.makeRDD((1L to 7L).
map((_,"")))

vertices: org.apache.spark.rdd.RDD
[(Long, String)] =
ParallelCollectionRDD[20] at
makeRDD at :30
```

```
val edges =
sc.makeRDD(Array(Edge(1L,2L,""),
Edge(2L,3L,""),
Edge(4L,5L,""),
Edge(4L,6L,""),
Edge(5L,6L,""),
Edge(6L,7L,"")))

edges: org.apache.spark.rdd.RDD
[org.apache.spark.graphx.Edge[String]] =
ParallelCollectionRDD[21] at
makeRDD at :30
```

```
val network =
Graph( vertices , edges).
cachenetwork: org.apache.spark.graphx.Graph
[String,String] =
org.apache.spark.graphx.impl.GraphImpl@41138411
```

Figure 29. Finding connected components

```
network.connectedComponents.
vertices.map(_.swap).
groupByKey.map(_._2).collect

Array[Iterable[org.apache.spark.graphx.VertexId]] =
Array(CompactBuffer(4, 5, 6, 7),
CompactBuffer(1, 2, 3))
```

Step 1: Find the set of neighbors for each vertex.

Step 2: For each edge find the intersection of the sets and send the count to both vertices

Step 3: Find the sum at each vertex and divide by two since each triangle is counted twice.

Figure 30 illustrates the process.

In order to use the TriangleCount method in Spark, the graph has to meet two requirements. First, the graph has to be partitioned by one of the partition strategy options, described in Section 3-1. Second, if there are any duplicate edges, they have to point in the same direction. To ensure the latter requirement, all edges must be in canonical order, pointing from the lower-numbered vertex ID to the higher numbered vertex ID.

Let us consider the Slashdot social network (Malak, Eeast, 2016). to find the number of triangles in a large scale network. Slashdot is a technology news related website which has a specific user community. The website features user-submitted and editor-evaluated current, primarily consisting of technology

Figure 30. Triangle counting algorithm

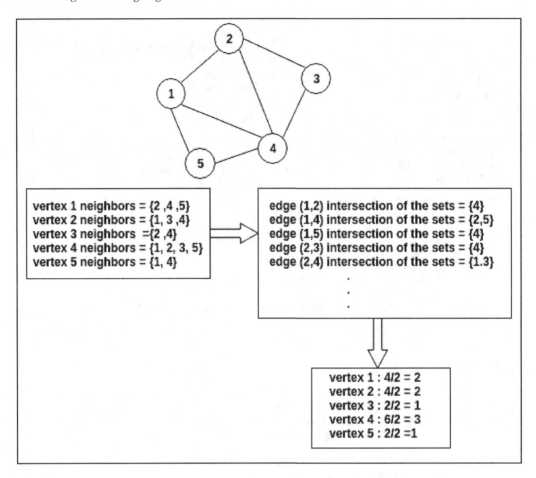

related news. In 2002 Slashdot introduced the Slashdot Zoo feature which allows users to tag each other as friends or foes. The network contains friend/foe links between the users. The network was recorded in November 2008 (Malak, Eeast, 2016). Table 2 shows the data set statistics.

Figure 31 shows the steps including the source code for counting number of triangles in the Slashdot social network.

As shown in the figure above, the number of triangles are 1352001, 61376, 10865, 3935, 1384, 786 and 658 for each of seven subgraphs ((0 to 6).map), respectively, in the social network (Malak, Eeast, 2016; Kolountzakis, Miller, Peng, Tsourkakis, 2012).

SUMMARY

In this chapter we introduced Apache Spark as a replacement for Hadoop Mapreduce. Efficiency of Spark, as a result of in-memory processing, makes it a popular big data processing engine. It also has high usability, due to different programming language APIs. There is a large collection of algorithms that cannot be implemented using only one iteration of Map and Reduce functions. Notably, graph processing

Table 2. Slashdot social network statistics

Number of Nodes	77360
Number of Edges	905468
Nodes in largest WCC	77360 (1.000)
Edges in largest WCC	905468 (1.000)
Nodes in largest SCC	70355 (0.909)
Edges in largest SCC	888662 (0.981)
Average clustering coefficient	0.0555
Number of triangles	551724
Fraction of closed triangles	0.008184
Diameter (longest shortest path)	10
90-percentile effective diameter	4.7

Figure 31. Triangle Counting in Slashdot social network

```
val socNetwork = GraphLoader.edgeListFile(sc, "soc-Slashdot0811.txt")
socNetwork:
org.apache.spark.graphx.Graph[Int,Int] =
org.apache.spark.graphx.impl.GraphImpl@7f92f443
```

```
val socNetwork2 = Graph( socNetwork.vertices , socNetwork.edges.
map(e => if (e.srcId < e.dstId) e else new Edge(e.dstId , e.srcId, e.attr))).
partitionBy(PartitionStrategy.RandomVertexCut)

socNetwork2:
org.apache.spark.graphx.Graph[Int,Int] =
org.apache.spark.graphx.impl.GraphImpl@4265a08d
```

```
val socNetwork2 = Graph( socNetwork.vertices , socNetwork.edges.
map(e => if (e.srcId < e.dstId) e else new Edge(e.dstId , e.srcId, e.attr))).
partitionBy(PartitionStrategy.RandomVertexCut)
socNetwork2: org.apache.spark.graphx.Graph[Int,Int] =
org.apache.spark.graphx.impl.GraphImpl@4265a08dscala>
(0 to 6).map(i => socNetwork2.subgraph(vpred =
            (vid,_) =>
            vid >= i*10000 && vid < (i+1)*10000).
triangleCount.vertices.
map(_._2).reduce(_ + _))

scala.collection.immutable.IndexedSeq[Int] =
Vector(1352001, 61376, 10865, 3935, 1384, 786, 658)
```

algorithms fall in this category. Apache Spark improves efficiency of implementing such algorithms using in-memory processing. Essentially, after one iteration of Map and Reduce, the results are ready, and available in memory for the next iteration. Spark can be 100 times faster than Hadoop Mapreduce for machine learning algorithms, such logistic regression (Zaharia et al, 2012). A fundamental processing unit in Spark is RDD, instead of one path of Map and Reduce functions. RDD is an immutable distributed data set across the cluster which is resilient to data storage failure. Data processing algorithms can be implemented using transformations and actions on each RDD. Transformations will create series of RDDs. As a result of immutability, each one of them can be recalculated from the previous one.

Graphx is a new component in Spark for implementing graph algorithms in a distributed environment. Graphx extends the Spark RDD by introducing a new graph abstraction in terms of a distributed dataset, attached to vertices and edges. In this chapter three important social network algorithms have been introduced using Graphx library in Apache Spark. The first one is finding PageRank in a social network, the second one is finding connected components, and the last but not least is the triangle counting algorithm. In all the three applications we have illustrated the steps via appropriate examples.

REFERENCES

Abu-Doleh, A., & Çatalyürek, Ü. V. (2015, October). Spaler: Spark and GraphX based de novo genome assembler. In *Big Data (Big Data), 2015 IEEE International Conference on* (pp. 1013-1018). IEEE.

Bourse, F., Lelarge, M., & Vojnovic, M. (2014, August). Balanced graph edge partition. In *Proceedings of the 20th ACM SIGKDD international conference on Knowledge discovery and data mining* (pp. 1456-1465). ACM.

hcyu. (2015). *GraphX triangle counting*. Retrieved October 13, 2015 From http://note.yuhc.me/2015/03/graphx-triangle-count-label-propagation/

Hinge, A., & Auber, D. (2015, July). Distributed Graph Layout with Spark. In *2015 19th International Conference on Information Visualisation* (pp. 271-276). IEEE. doi:10.1109/iV.2015.56

ibm01. (2011). *About MapReduce*. Retrieved June 13, 2011 From https://www-01.ibm.com/software/data/infosphere/hadoop/mapreduce/

Kolountzakis, M. N., Miller, G. L., Peng, R., & Tsourakakis, C. E. (2012). Efficient triangle counting in large graphs via degree-based vertex partitioning. *Internet Mathematics*, *8*(1-2), 161–185. doi:10.1080/15427951.2012.625260

Leskovec, J., Lang, K. J., Dasgupta, A., & Mahoney, M. W. (2009). Community structure in large networks: Natural cluster sizes and the absence of large well-defined clusters. *Internet Mathematics*, *6*(1), 29–123. doi:10.1080/15427951.2009.10129177

Malak, M. S., & East, R. (2016). *Spark GraphX in action*. Academic Press.

Meng, X., Bradley, J., Yuvaz, B., Sparks, E., Venkataraman, S., Liu, D., & Xin, D. et al. (2016). Mllib: Machine learning in apache spark. *JMLR*, *17*(34), 1–7.

Vavilapalli, V. K., Murthy, A. C., Douglas, C., Agarwal, S., Konar, M., Evans, R., & Saha, B. et al. (2013, October). Apache hadoop yarn: Yet another resource negotiator. In *Proceedings of the 4th annual Symposium on Cloud Computing* (p. 5). ACM. doi:10.1145/2523616.2523633

Xin, R., Deyhim, P., Ghodsi, A., Meng, X., & Zaharia, M. (2014). *GraySort on Apache Spark by Databricks*. GraySort Competition.

Xin, R. S., Gonzalez, J. E., Franklin, M. J., & Stoica, I. (2013, June). Graphx: A resilient distributed graph system on spark. In *First International Workshop on Graph Data Management Experiences and Systems* (p. 2). ACM. doi:10.1145/2484425.2484427

Zaharia, M., Chowdhury, M., Das, T., Dave, A., Ma, J., McCauley, M., & Stoica, I. et al. (2012, April). Resilient distributed datasets: A fault-tolerant abstraction for in-memory cluster computing. In *Proceedings of the 9th USENIX conference on Networked Systems Design and Implementation* (pp. 2-2). USENIX Association.

Chapter 10
Link Prediction in Social Networks

Sovan Samanta
Tamralipta Mahavidyalaya, India

Madhumangal Pal
Vidyasagar University, India

ABSTRACT

Social network is a topic of current research. Relations are broken and new relations are increased. This chapter will discuss the scope or predictions of new links in social networks. Here different approaches for link predictions are described. Among them friend recommendation model is latest. There are some other methods like common neighborhood method which is also analyzed here. The comparison among them to predict links in social networks is described. The significance of this research work is to find strong dense networks in future.

1. INTRODUCTION

Every kind of social group can be represented in terms of units or actors, composing this group and relations between these units. This kind of representation of a social structure is called Social Network. In a social network, every unit, usually called ``social units'' like a person, an organization, a community, and so on, is represented as a node. A relation between two social actors is expressed by a link. So every social network can be represented by a graph. The recent research on networks, a huge amount of attention has been devoted to social networks and its structures whose vertices represent people or other organization in a social network, and whose edges represent influence between vertices or collaboration. Examples of social networks include the set of all researchers in a particular subject such that edges are joined who have co-authored papers; a collection of businesspersons such that edges are joined who have shared together on a board of directors. Social networks are highly data based objects; they increase and change rapidly over time through the addition of new vertices and edges. Understanding the pattern by which they are joined is an important question that is still not answered, and it creates the motivation for this chapter here. This chapter will discuss about link prediction problem in social network. Suppose, a

DOI: 10.4018/978-1-5225-2814-2.ch010

snapshot of a social network is given at time, accurately prediction of the edges will be proposed such that the edges will be joined to the network during the interval from that time to a given future time. Suppose, a co-authorship network is considered among researchers. There are certainly many reasons, that why two researchers who have never written a paper together, will write a paper in the next years: they may be geographically close when any of them changes institutions. Such types of collaborations can be hard to predict. Our goal is to make this prediction precisely, and to compare which measures in a network solve to the most accurate link predictions. The problem of link prediction across associated networks include anchor link prediction problem and link transfer through associated heterogeneous networks. This chapter summarizes recent growth about link prediction and survey of all the prevailing link prediction techniques. There are many problems to predict accurate links. First of data sparse, missing data or relationship is one of the main obstacle of the system. Imbalance is another possibility for researchers. There are so many possibilities with few choices. Link prediction problem is referred as inaccurate problem due to low accuracy in practice. Another obstacle is accuracy with scalability. Appropriate modelling is required for good prediction.

As part of the recent survey of research on large, complex networks and their properties, some amount of attention has been devoted to the computational analysis of social network structures. The availability of large, detailed datasets encoding such networks has stimulated extensive study of their basic properties, and the identification of recurring structural features. Social networks are highly dynamic objects; they grow and change quickly over time through the addition of new edges, signifying the appearance of new interactions in the corresponding social structure. Understanding the mechanisms by which they evolve is a fundamental question that is still not well understood, and it forms the motivation for our work here. Some basic computational problem underlying social network evolution, the link prediction problem are studied here.

The motivation of this chapter is recommending new friends in online social networks, suggesting interactions between the members of a company/organization that are external to the hierarchical structure of the organization itself, predicting connections between members of terrorist organizations who have not been directly observed to work together, suggesting collaborations between researchers based on co-authorship. Given the links in a social network at time t or during a time interval I, to predict the links that will be added to the network during the later time interval from time t to some given future time. This chapter will discuss different types of methodology and techniques applied to find link prediction in a social network.

2. RELATED WORK AND MOTIVATION

The work of Barabasi et al. (2002), Jin et al. (2001), and Davidsen et al.(2002) on collaboration networks, or the survey of Newman are some examples on this topic. The link prediction problem is co-related to the problem of missing links from a given network. Among them, graph theoretical method is easy and effective to learn. Samanta and Pal (2015) also studied link prediction in telecommunication network assuming it as a fuzzy graph theory.

Han and Kamber (2006) shows that data mining refers to extracting information from large data sets. The term data mining should have been more appropriately named as "Knowledge mining from data". Similarly, Zhu and Davidson (2007) described that there is an analysis of large quantities of data in order to discover meaningful patterns and rules. Data Mining (Zernik, 2010) is about resolving problems by analyzing data already present in the databases. Data mining tasks can be categorized into two categories descriptive and predictive. Descriptive mining tasks (Jain and Srivastava, 2013) focus on general properties of the data in the database. Predictive mining tasks focus on the current data in order to make predictions. The purpose of a data mining determination is normally either to produce a descriptive model or a predictive model. Graphs (Patel and Prajapati, 2013) become important increasingly in modelling composite structures like circuits, chemical compounds, images and social networks. The graph representation is basically used in pattern recognition and machine learning. Graph mining has become a key technique because of the increasing demand on the analysis of huge amounts of structured data in data mining. A Social network (Sharma, Sharma and Khatri, 2015) consists of a group of people and Links between them. These connections can be any type of social link that makes a relationship between two people. Social networks are popular way to mock-up the interactions among the people in a group or community. Social networks are highly vital in nature. They can grow and change as time variations, they can be visualized as graphs, in which a vertex denoted as a person in some group, and link represents some form of association between the consequent persons (Barabasi, 2002).

Given in Figure 1 of the topology of a social network at period t, than it is need to predict the topology from period t to upcoming period t ' where t'>t. Assuming that the number of nodes does not change. Lada. A. Adamic and Eytan Adar, 2003 anticipated the metric of similarity between two pages. It calculates the probability when two individual homepages are strongly related. It computes features that are shared among nodes and then defines the similarity involving them. Liben-Nowell and Kleinberg, 2007 introduced a model based on node similarity for link prediction. There are numerous categories of node similarity. First, one is the neighborhood-based similarity like common neighbors of two nodes and the other one similarity based on a path, which tries to resolve the shortest path distance concerning two nodes. So link prediction can be categorized into two classes, first is to the problem of identifying existing yet unknown links and predicting links that may come into sight in the future. M. E. J. Newman used the concept of clustering & preferential attachment in rising networks.

3. METHODS FOR LINK PREDICTION

Given a snapshot of a social network at time t, we find to accurately predict the edges that will be added to the network during the interval from time t to a given future time t'. In effect, the link prediction problem indicates to what extent can the evolution of a social network be modelled using features intrinsic to the network itself? Consider a co-authorship network among scientists, for example. There are many reasons, exogenous to the network, why two scientists who have never written a paper to-

Figure 1. Link prediction after certain time

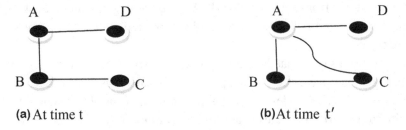

(a) At time t   (b) At time t'

Figure 2. Flowchart of literature review of link prediction

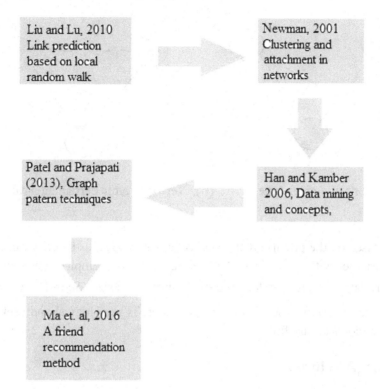

gether will do so in the next few years: for example, they may happen to become geographically close when one of them changes institutions. Such collaborations can be tough to predict. But one also senses that many new collaborations are hinted at by the analysis of the network: two scientists who are close" in the network will have colleagues in common, and will travel in similar circles; this suggests that they themselves are more likely to collaborate in the near future. The goal is to make this intuitive notion precise, and to understand which measures of proximity" in a network lead to the most accurate link predictions. A number of proximity measures lead to predictions that outperform chance by factors of 40 to 50, indicating that the network topology does indeed contain latent information from which to infer future interactions are defined. Moreover, certain subtle measures involving infinite sums over paths in the network often outperform more direct measures, such as shortest-path distances and numbers of shared neighbors.

There are various kinds of methods are available to find the link prediction.

3.1 Common Neighbour (CN) Index

Neighbourhood based link prediction is one of them. Suppose $N(x)$ is the set of neighbours of x. Based on the idea that links are formed between nodes who share many common neighbours, this method is developed. $Score(x; y) = N(x) \cap N(y)$. That is more the score implies more the chances to predict links. How likely a neighbour of x is to be a neighbour of y and vice versa is measured by

Figure 3. Link prediction representation by common neighborhoods

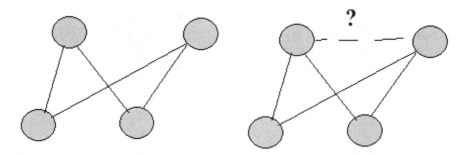

(a): Network at a given time   (b): Network after certain interval of time

different formula. Based on the premise that a new edge has node x as its endpoint is proportional to i.e., nodes like to form ties with `popular' nodes. Researchers found empirical evidence to suggest that co-authorship is correlated with the product of the neighbourhood sizes $Score(x; y) = |N(x)|.|N(y)|$. This score is also used in certain cases. While the first score is very logical and useful to predict. For some cases, both the scores are useful.

3.2 Adamic-Adar (AA) Index

The Adamic-Adar index weighs the importance of a common neighbour v by the rarity of relationships between other nodes and v. Finally, the preferential attachment link prediction score is the product of the degrees of u and v. When it is observed especially poor performance for this predictor in phone, using in-degree, out-degree, and their sum but it is observed only minor differences. The Adamic-Adar index is calculated as follows.

$$AA(x, y) = \sum_{w \in N(x) \cap N(y)} \frac{1}{\log|N(w)|}$$

where $N(u)$ is the neighbour of u.

3.3. A Friend Recommendation Model

An important subject in analysing link prediction is that the structural properties of networks have significant impacts on the performance of algorithms. Therefore, how to improve the performance of link prediction with the aid of structural properties of networks is an essential problem. Nodes are preferentially linked to the nodes with the weak clique structure (PWCS). Based on this PWCS phenomenon, a local friend recommendation (FR) index to facilitate link prediction is proposed. Some experiments show that the performance of FR index is better than some famous local similarity indices, such as Common Neighbour (CN) index, Adamic-Adar (AA) index and Resource Allocation (RA) index. PWCS can give rise to the better performance of FR index in link prediction. A mixed friend recommendation index (labelled MFR) is proposed by utilizing the PWCS phenomenon, which further improves the accuracy of link prediction.

3.4 Katz Measure

There is another way of measure as Katz_ measure. Here sums are taken over all possible paths between x and y, giving higher weight to shorter paths. There are two possibilities of measure. Variants of the Katz measure are considered in (a) unweighted paths, (b) weighted paths. The calculation is given as follows:

$$K\left(u, v\right) = \sum_{l=1}^{\infty} \beta^{l} . \mid paths_{u,v}^{l} \mid$$

Figure 4. Strong connection and weak connection

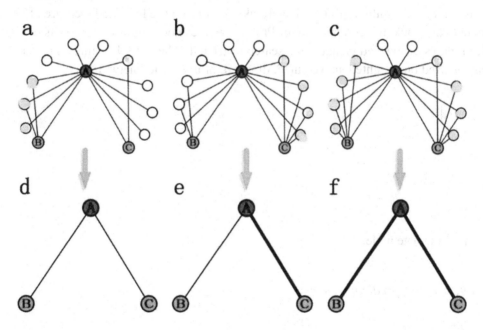

Figure 5. A friend recommendation model

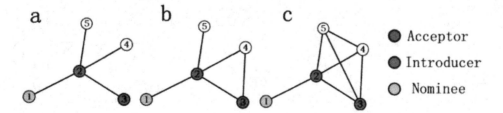

Here, beta value is more for shortest common paths and lesser for longer common paths and l denotes the distance of the paths. Most unsupervised methods either generate scores based on node neighbourhoods or path information. The common neighbours predictor is the number of neighbours, or out-degree neighbours in our directed network, that are shared by nodes u and v. Jaccard's coefficient simply divides the number of common neighbours by the number of total neighbours. From the path-based methods, the unweighted Katz is employed. This had better, more stable performance in the networks than the weighted variant. This method contributes each path to a sum with an influence damped in exponential proportion to its length, l, using the parameterβ. β = 0.005 and, for performance reasons, examination of the measure such that l ≤ 5 is taken.

3.5. The Prop Flow Method

The Prop Flow Method is another interesting link prediction method. A new unsupervised prediction method on networks, Prop Flow, which corresponds to the probability that a restricted random walk starting at u ends at v, using link weights as transition probabilities. The restrictions are that the walk terminates upon reaching v or upon revisiting any node including u. The walk selects links based on their weights. This produces a score S_{ij} that can be taken as an estimation of the likelihood of new links.

Prop Flow is somewhat similar to Rooted PageRank, but it is a more localized measure of propagation. Unlike Rooted PageRank, the computation of Prop Flow does not require walk restarts or convergence but simply employs a modified breadth-first search restricted to height l. It is thus much faster to compute. It may be used on weighted, unweighted, directed, or undirected networks.

$$d\left(u, v\right) = \left|1 - \alpha\right|^{\left|t_u - t_v\right|}$$

$$T_{Flow}\left(u, v\right) = T_{Flow}\left(a, u\right) . \frac{w_{uv}}{\sum_{k \in N\left(u\right)} w_{uk}} . d\left(u, v\right)$$

where, a is intermediate node.

Figure 6. Katz beta link prediction method

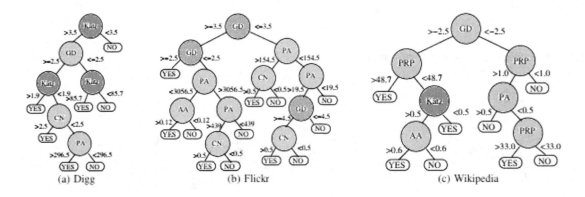

    (a) Digg   (b) Flickr   (c) Wikipedia

4. COMPARISON OF THE METHODS

There are several methods to predict the links between any two nodes in social networks. Some of the useful methods are described here. In CN index method, number of common neighbourhoods is assumed and have been utilized in the formula. In, AA-index method, sum of inverses of logarithm of common neighbourhoods, has been calculated. The error of CN method has been modified in AA-index method. Friend recommendation method is a realistic method based on social structure. Katz measure method depends on paths connecting two target nodes. This actually, generalization of CN method. Here, direct neighbourhood and indirect neighbourhoods of different lengths have been taken for consideration. T_flow method is another important method, which involves the distances of the target nodes. So all the existing methods involve some kinds of direct neighbours or paths.

5. CONCLUSION

This chapter is based on social networks, which predict the exact connection between links and measure normal kinds of measurements for proficient link prediction. Link prediction is concerned with the problem of predicting the survival of links among vertices in a social network. Link prediction techniques can provide a very efficient way for discovering useful knowledge from existing information. Common neighbourhood method and friend recommendation methods are most useful and perfect method. These two concepts can be mixed and the researchers can improve the current prediction systems. Katz measure and T_Flow methods are to be modified to enhance the chances of prediction to higher label. In our future study, these topics would be considered. In addition, these data are based on crisp data. However, nowadays, uncertainty exists in every system parameters. Many authors are working on fuzzy social networks. Thus, the link prediction in fuzzy social network is meaningful in current study. We will focus on this new topic and its related topic.

REFERENCES

Barabasi, A. L., Jeong, H., Neda, Z., Ravasz, E., Schubert, A., & Vicsek, T. (2002). Evolution of the social network of scientific collaboration. *Physica A, 3-4*(3-4), 590–614. doi:10.1016/S0378-4371(02)00736-7

Han, J., & Kamber, M. (2006). Data Mining: Concepts and Techniques (2nd ed.). Academic Press.

Jain & Srivastava. (2013). Data Mining. *International Journal of Research in Engineering and Technology, 2*(11).

Jeh, G., & Widom, J. (2000). SimRank: A Measure of Structural Context Similarity. *The ACM SIGKDD International Conference on Knowledge Discovery and Data Mining*, 538-543.

Kossinets, G. (2006). Effects of missing data in social Networks. *Social Networks, 28*(3), 247–268. doi:10.1016/j.socnet.2005.07.002

Lada, A., & Adar, E. (2003). Predicting missing links via local information. *Social Networks, 25*(3), 211–230.

Leicht, Holme, & Newman. (2006). Vertex similarity in networks. *Phys. Rev. E., 73*, 26-120.

Liu, W., & Lu, L. (2010). Link prediction based on local random walk. *Europhysics Letters Association., 89*(5), 1–12.

Newman, M. E. J. (2001). Clustering & preferential attachment in growing networks. *Physical Review Letters E. Physical Review E: Statistical, Nonlinear, and Soft Matter Physics, 64*(2), 1–13. doi:10.1103/PhysRevE.64.025102

Newman, M. E. J. (2001). The structure of scientific collaboration networks. *Proceedings of the National Academy of Sciences of the United States of America, 98*(2), 404–409. doi:10.1073/pnas.98.2.404 PMID:11149952

Newman, M. E. J. (2003). The structure and function of complex networks. *SIAM Review, 45*(2), 167–256. doi:10.1137/S003614450342480

Nowell, D. L., & Kleinberg, J. (2007). The link-prediction problem for social networking. *Journal of the American Society for Information Science and Technology, 58*(7), 1019–1031. doi:10.1002/asi.20591

Patel, H. J., Prajapati, R., Panchal, M., & Patel, M. J. (2013). A survey of graph pattern mining algorithm and techniques. *International Journal of Application or Innovation in Engineering & Management, 2*(1), 125–129.

Salton, G., & McGill, M. J. (1983). *Introduction to Modern Information Retrieval*. Auckland, New Zealand: MaGraw-Hill.

Samanta, S., & Pal, M. (2014). A New Approach to Social Networks Based on Fuzzy Graphs. *Turkish Journal of Fuzzy Systems, 5*(2), 78–99.

Samanta, S., & Pal, M. (2013). Telecommunication System Based on Fuzzy Graphs. *Journal of Telecommunications System & Management, 3*(1), 1–6.

Sharma, D., Sharma, U., & Khatri, S. K. (2014). An experimental comparison of the link prediction techniques in social networks. *International Journal of Modelling and Optimization, 4*(1), 21–24. doi:10.7763/IJMO.2014.V4.341

Zernik, J. (2010). Data Mining as a Civic Duty–Online Public Prisoners Registration Systems. *International Journal on Social Media: Monitoring, Measurement Mining, 1*(1), 84–96.

Zhu, X., & Davidson, I. (2007). Knowledge Discovery and Data Mining: Challenges and Realities. Academic Press.

Chapter 11
Visualizing Co–Authorship Social Networks and Collaboration Recommendations With CNARe

Michele A. Brandão
Universidade Federal de Minas Gerais, Brazil

Guilherme A. de Sousa
Universidade Federal de Minas Gerais, Brazil

Matheus A. Diniz
Universidade Federal de Minas Gerais, Brazil

Mirella M. Moro
Universidade Federal de Minas Gerais, Brazil

ABSTRACT

Studies have analyzed social networks considering a plethora of metrics for different goals, from improving e-learning to recommend people and things. Here, we focus on large-scale social networks defined by researchers and their common published articles, which form co-authorship social networks. Then, we introduce CNARe, an online tool that analyzes the networks and present recommendations of collaborations based on three different algorithms (Affin, CORALS and MVCWalker). Through visualizations and social networks metrics, CNARe also allows to investigate how the recommendations affect the co-authorship social networks, how researchers' networks are in a central and eagle-eye context, and how the strength of ties behaves in large co-authorship social networks. Furthermore, users can upload their own network in CNARe and make their own recommendation and social network analysis.

1. INTRODUCTION

Social networks represent individuals and the interactions among them, and studying such networks allows to discover different social patterns (Ahmed & Chen, 2016; Brandão & Moro, 2017). For instance, Chang & Chin (2011) study factors that affect user intention to use a social network game, and Pettenati & Cigognini (2007) use social networks theories to elaborate new e-learning practices. Furthermore, the social networks features can also be used to improve the quality of recommendation algorithms, such as those for friends, music, books and collaborators (He & Chu, 2010; Tang, Hu & Liu, 2013).

DOI: 10.4018/978-1-5225-2814-2.ch011

Specifically, recommending collaborators is a specific type of people recommendation in which the main goal is to recommend a pair of individuals to collaborate in a determined context. For instance, Surian et al., (2011) extract information from Source forge[1] and build a developer collaboration network. Then, they propose a new algorithm to recommend developers candidate to projects in Source forge. Likewise, Protasiewicz et al., (2016) propose an architecture to recommend reviewers to evaluate researchers' proposals and publications. In this context, this chapter focuses on recommendation of co-authors by considering algorithms that use information available in co-authorship social networks. A co-authorship social network is a type of social network in which nodes are authors and edges represent that they have publications in common.

Advances in collaboration recommendation algorithms have shown the potential to improve researchers' productivity and their groups through establishing new research connections (Brandão et al., 2013; Lopes et al., 2010; Xia et al., 2014). The recommendation strategies include analyses of the topological features from the co-authorship social networks, semantic properties of the relationship between researchers and math formalizations. Such algorithms provide as result a recommendation list with the top ranked researchers that may collaborate with another researcher.

Besides characteristics of the recommendation algorithms, another relevant aspect of a full system is the visualization of the recommendations results. Generally, the recommendations are presented in sorted lists (according to the recommendation function's result). For instance, Confer (used in IJCAI-16[2]) is a tool that uses recommendation approaches in order to help conference attendees to find talks and papers, to discover people with common interest and manage their time in the conference (Zhang, Bhardwaj & Karger, 2016). It presents the recommendations as a list, and the users can attribute a star to each recommended item. However, these lists are often not enough to understand how the result was defined or to verify the potential of the recommendations to improve the network as a whole.

Here, the authors present an online tool called CNARe (Co-authorship Networks Analysis and Recommendations) - the pronounce is *scenery* (de Sousa et al., 2015). CNARe helps researchers to choose collaborators through automatic recommendations, visualize recommendations, compare the results from different recommendation algorithms and analyze the impact of the recommended researchers in their current network. The tool implements three recommendation algorithms (Brandão et al., 2013; Lopes et al., 2010; Xia et al., 2014). CNARe also provides other visualizations, for example, comparing the relationship between two or more co-authorship networks from different institutions and analyzing the strength of the co-authorships classified as social link (weak, strong or bridges - a co-authorship that connects researchers from different communities) or random relationship.

After discussing related work on recommender systems and social networks visualizations, the contributions of this chapter are summarized as follows.

- The CNARe architecture and the processes of collecting and building a dataset from the ACM digital library[3].
- The description of the main functionalities and interfaces of CNARe, including the use case diagram and the main features of CNARe's pages.
- The visualizations of large social networks emphasizing the strength of co-authorship links.

2. RELATED WORK

In this section, we discuss the related work on recommender systems focusing on people recommendation and social network visualizations.

2.1 Recommender Systems

There are many recommender systems for different contexts, from social networks to e-commerce. These systems can provide recommendations of items (books, papers, songs) or people (friends, co-workers, partners). For instance, Paraschiv et al. (2016) propose a model that considers semantic overlap to recommend papers (items), and Bagci & Karagoz (2016) use the data available on location-based social networks to recommend friends.

Regarding people recommendation, co-authorship social networks have been used to make research teams more productive. The current version of CNARe implements three recommendations algorithms that combine topological properties from co-authorship social networks with academic metrics: *Affin* (Brandão et al., 2013) considers the shortest path between researchers and the researchers' institutional affiliation; *CORALS* (Lopes et al., 2010) combines the shortest path between researchers and their research area; and *MVCWalker* (Xia et al., 2014) uses a random walk model with three academic metrics (the co-author order in the publication, the time of last collaboration and the collaboration frequency).

Regarding similar tools, there are two more related to CNARe: VRRC, which shows the results of only one recommendation algorithm (Barbosa et al., 2012); and CollabSeer, which recommends researchers considering the co-authorship social networks topology and the interests' areas of a user (Chen et al., 2011). In CNARe, the generated recommendations consider not only the research area of the researchers, but also the affiliation, co-author order in the publication, the last collaboration time and the collaboration frequency. Moreover, CNARe provides various visualizations (ego-network and global social networks) aiming to show how a recommended collaborator may change an existing co-authorship social network of the researchers who received the recommendation.

2.2 Social Network Visualizations

Visualizing social networks may easily provide new insights about users and their interactions in such environment (Viégas & Donath, 2004). In other words, a visualization is more than simply plotting pictures, it may also facilitate learning and generate new knowledge. According to Freeman (2000), there are two ways to create social network images: drawing graphs in which nodes represent individuals and edges are the connections between them, and plotting a matrix in which rows and columns represent people and the number or color intensity in the cells stands for the amount of social interaction (e.g., frequency of message exchange, number of co-authorships, the time of interaction) between people. CNARe presents visualizations in both ways.

Furthermore, there are studies investigating the methods that better provide visualizations of large networks. For instance, Rahman & Karim (2016) compare three layouts (force directed drawing, spherical and clustered graph) and provide insights about the three methods that help to identify the best one according to datasets' properties. In addition, Brandes, Indlekofer & Mader (2012) present different methods to visually explore dynamic social networks. The layout of the visualizations in CNARe is

Force-Layout (Holten & Van Wijk, 2009) from D3.js[4] and it was selected through empirical analysis, as it allows analyzing nodes and their interactions in the best way.

Existing social networks visualization tools allow the analyses of different networks. For example, Pajek is a program package that enables analysis and visualizations of large networks (Mrvar & Batagelj, 2016). Likewise, Network Explorer is a large-network visualization tool that enables users to find clusters of nodes and to identify important nodes in the social network (Guerra-Gomez et al., 2016). CNARe differs from such tools by providing recommendations associated with social network visualizations.

3. CNARe ARCHITECTURE

This section presents how CNARe is built regarding its architecture, data storage and collection, and main functionalities.

Figure 1 illustrates a general view of the main components of CNARe divided in backend and frontend. In the backend, CNARe stores researchers' publications in a SQL database, whose relational schema includes tables for researchers, publications and recommendations, as presented in Figure 2. Each table has B-tree indexes for primary and foreign keys. Other indexes were not created because the performance of the necessary SQL queries is fast enough and could (potentially) harm the performance of inserts, deletes and updates. For each researcher, the recommendations are stored in a table that also identifies what method has generated them. Using data previously stored in the database, the users generate the recommendations for each researcher. However, collaborators can also be recommended in real time when one of the three recommendation algorithm is selected.

Figure 1. CNARe architecture

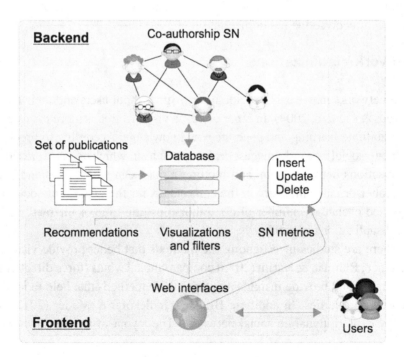

Figure 2. Relational schema of CNARe database: 16 main tables and two associative tables (Publication_has_Researcher and Researcher_has_Area). Relationships are presented using the traditional notation (e.g. Venue has many Publications that must have exactly 1 venue).

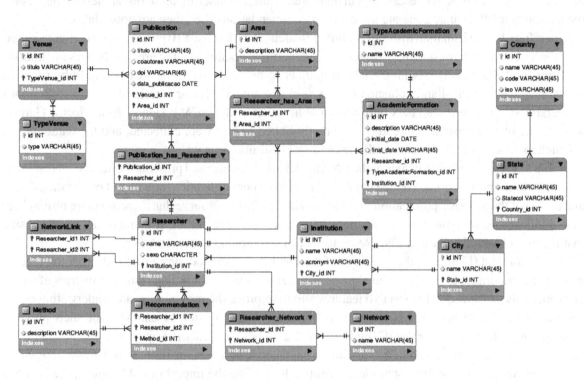

Furthermore, each researcher may belong to more than one co-authorship social network (since a user can add various networks with different clusters, for example, by research group, graduate program, institution, and so on). Finally, it is important to note that publications are in the range [2000-2015] in order to ensure recommendations of researchers that have recent work in the area.

The initial database includes publications from Computer Science. The data collecting procedure uses the snowball sampling strategy (Goodman, 1961) and considers available information in the researchers' page at the ACM digital library. This library was chosen because it presents the area of each publication according to ACM Classification System. Each researcher's page has a list of publications, in which each publication has DOI (Digital Object Identifier System), the co-authors list, the date and location of the publication. From the DOI, the specified URL is accessed to get the research area of each publication and information about each co-author: institution, total number of publications and co-author names (since the co-authors list provides the name in citation format). After inserting the co-authors in the database, a new query is executed to obtain the co-author with the largest number of publications whose page has not been visited yet. Then, the collecting process starts again from the page of such an author.

Initially, the data collecting procedure considers researchers from Brazilian institutions (COPPE/UFRJ, PUC/RIO, UFMG, UFPE, UFRGS, UNICAMP, USP/SC, UFF, USP, UFCG, UFES, UFPR, UFRJ, UFRN, UFSC, UFSCAR, UNB, UNISINOS, PUC/PR, PUC/RS, UFAM, UFBA, UFC, PUC/MG, UCPEL, UFG, UFPA) and international institutions (University of Carnegie-Mellon, of Illinois at Urbana-Champaign, of California - Berkeley, of Singapore, Stanford, Chinese Academy of Sciences, of Southampton, of Los Angeles, Tsinghua, among others)[5].

Reducing the noise in the input of the recommendation algorithms requires to filter the number of researchers. In this case, the noise is given by researchers with few publications, for example, as they may be students or not active researchers in their area. Thus, considering these researchers in the recommendation algorithms may generate not useful recommendations (i.e., they are noise data).

Therefore, for the Brazilian institutions, only researchers with at least 10 publications were considered (such value excludes most students). Regarding international institutions, the previously ones institutions accounts for 100 researchers with the largest number of publications in the ACM digital library. Such researchers were reached and collected from a seed researcher (Hector Garcia-Molina from Stanford University, one of the researchers with more publications in the ACM). Hence, from Hector Garcia-Molina, the other researchers directly or indirectly linked to him were collected, and the database has researchers from other (not mentioned) international institutions as well.

Table 1 summarizes the statistics of the CNARe default database[6] and presents the number of researchers, institutions, publications, average number of co-author per publication, quantity of publications' area and period of the gathered publications as collected in July 2015. Observe that there are more researchers than publications, because most publications have more than one author. It is important to emphasize that this is a default database in CNARe, as users can also upload data themselves.

In the frontend (Figure 1), the three main functionalities of the tool are: visualization of the recommendations according to the three algorithms, visualizations with filters, and results of metrics of social network analysis. Note that the last two features aim to improve the presentation and understating of the recommendations. Moreover, CNARe also allows users to import new researchers and their publications through files in CSV format (Comma Separated Values). In order to import a researcher, the CSV file must have the following columns: researcher name, research area, institution, link to the researcher homepage and the year of the last academic degree. Regarding the import of publications, the user has to inform the following columns in the CSV file: title, publication date, research area, authors and venue. This feature allows anyone with publications to use the tool and build new networks. Next section details the functionalities through examples.

4. DESIGN AND INTERFACES

In order to understand the main functionalities provided by CNARe, Figure 3 shows a use case diagram. Note that we consider our user as a researcher for simplicity, as the tool could be used by a hiring com-

Table 1. Description of the dataset stored in CNARe database.

Collected Data	
#Researchers	6,112
#Institutions	681
#Publications	4,259
Co-authors average	3.98
#Research areas	61
Period	2000 - 2015

Figure 3. Use case diagram: a researcher can execute all actions. The include indicates that those actions depend on the search of a researcher.

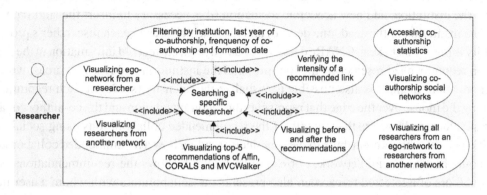

mittee of a department as to make its collaboration network stronger. Next, we detail each functionality (collaboration recommendation, visualizations and filters, and social networks metrics).

4.1 Collaboration Recommendation

Figure 4 shows the initial page for collaboration recommendation. It presents the field to search a researcher from which the user can visualize and compare the top-5 generated recommendations. The comparison is fulfilled in pairs, i.e., three combinations: Affin and CORALS, Affin and MVCWalker, CORALS and MVCWalker. In this example, the ego-network of the researcher is on the left and the recommendations on the right according to Affin and CORALS algorithms.

Figure 4. Main interface of CNARe with recommendations to Mirella M. Moro.

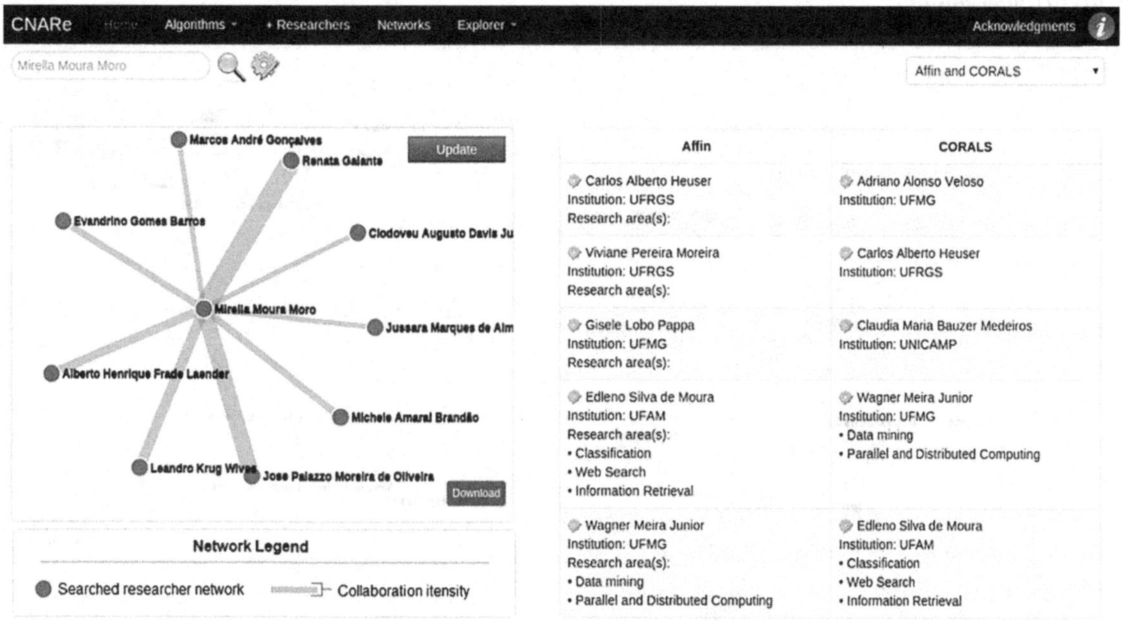

The page also allows to edit or add information about a researcher stored in the database. In order to do so, the user clicks on the editing icon that is in the right side of each researcher name. There, the user can change the institution, add new academic formation (it is necessary to insert the start date, conclusion date, the institution of the academic degree) and the research area in each researcher's profile. Such functionality is important to keep CNARe database updated (e.g., correct old information in the database).

For each recommended researcher, the tool presents the institution and research areas, which allow to know more about them. It is also possible to visualize the intensity (score) of each recommendation when moving the mouse over the edge that represents the recommendation and the co-authors of a recommended researcher, and analyze the strength of the recommended collaborations using social networks metrics. Such visualizations contribute to the user understanding how a recommended collaboration may change a co-authorship social network. For example, Figure 5 shows the recommendations considering the co-authors of a selected researcher, also presents the collaborators with whom a user may have contact by using the recommended researchers as "bridge".

4.2 Visualizations and Filters

In order to visualize the co-authorship social networks, the tool provides two options: ego-network of a researcher (examples in Figures 4 and 5) and global co-authorship network (example in Figure 6). The ego-network presents a researcher with her/his co-authorships, aiming to visualize the current collaborations and the recommended ones. On the other hand, the global networks show an eagle-eye vision of all co-authorships from an institution, a researcher (the relationships among co-authors of a researcher), or a network inserted by user. For instance, a user can visualize a global co-authorship social network of an institution from a recommended researcher.

Figure 5. Green lines represent recommended collaborations: the more intense more has been recommended by the algorithm. The recommendations are generated by clicking in one of the options with the algorithms' name.

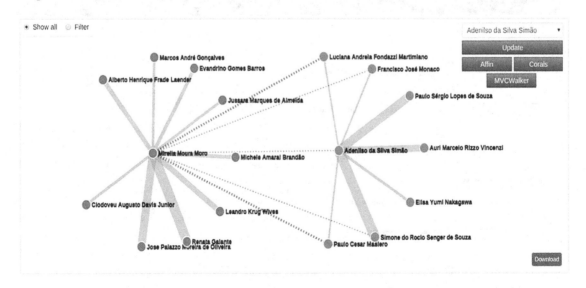

Figure 6. Global network example: in the Visualization Options menu, when the Co-authorship option is selected, a co-authorship matrix is presented instead of the social network. Here, the matrix is in a blue rectangle.

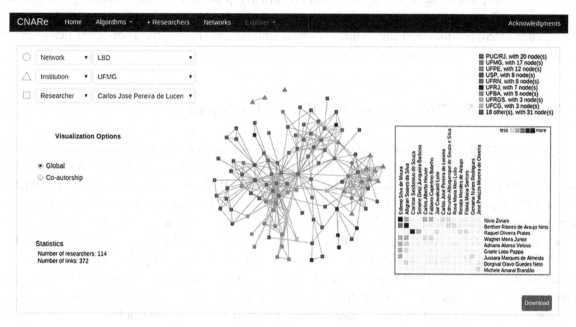

Moreover, CNARe also allows to compare three co-authorship social networks (accessing the option Compare More). This enables, for instance, to analyze which institution of the five recommended researchers has the densest co-authorship network. The visualizations can be personalized through four filters applied to the co-authorships: (1) by institution, it shows only the links of co-authors from a selected institution; (2) the last time that the co-authorship happened, it focuses on co-authorships in a period of years (e.g., the last two years); (3) the co-authorship frequency, it presents the links between researchers that published together a selected number of times (e.g., from 2 to 5 publications in common); and (4) the date of the last academic formation, it allows to consider researchers from similar academic "generations" (e.g., removing researchers who have retired or are too young).

4.3 Social Networks Metrics

CNARe also presents the results for social networks metrics. Considering the ego-networks, it may be hard to find relevant metrics, because the networks are relatively small, with not enough information. For ego-networks, CNARe applies three metrics (Easley & Kleinberg, 2012; Wasserman & Faust, 1994): (1) neighborhood overlap is the number of nodes that are neighbors of both researchers involved in a co-authorship divided by the number of nodes that are neighbors of at least one of the researchers in a co-authorship; (2) clustering coefficient is the probability that two randomly selected co-authors of a researcher are also connected to each other; and (3) affiliation homophily is the measure of the similarity between a pair of researchers considering their institution.

Specifically, the neighborhood overlap metric presents the strength of the recommended links, which allows to analyze if each recommended link will be a bridge (i.e., an edge responsible for connecting different communities and not connected yet) or not. The clustering coefficient and homophily metrics show how the recommendations affect the researchers' networks from different perspectives.

CNARe also presents statistics of the global co-authorship social networks, including the number of nodes in each network (of a researcher, institution or uploaded by a user) and in the global network, the amount of connections and the frequency of co-authorships (Figure 6). These statistics allow to understand the topology of the social networks.

5. ADVANCED SOCIAL NETWORKS VISUALIZATIONS

The goal is now to provide the visualizations of large social networks and distinguish the links according to their strength. Thus, CNARe also allows the visualization of co-authorships from different datasets, such as PubMed[7] (US National Library of Medicine National Institutes of Health), DBLP[8] (Computer Science Bibliography) and APS[9] (American Physical Society), which offer insights on the organization of these different social networks. Table 2 presents the number of nodes and edges in each social network, as collected in April 2016 for PubMed, September 2015 for DBLP, and March 2016 for APS.

The data from PubMed was gathered through the e-utilities offered by the National Center for Biotechnology Information[10]. The e-fetch utility allows to make queries to the NCBI's database. The queries aim to collect data from publications from the most prestigious venues in the health and medical sciences according to h5-index (h-index of those papers published in the last five years (Bornmann & Daniel, 2007)). Likewise, DBLP's dataset was taken from Universität Trier website[11], which is then split into two different datasets (due to its large size): one for the social network considering authors' common articles as the edges, and another considering inproceedings. Regarding the APS, the authors get access to a sample dataset in JSON format[12]. Then, such file was parsed in order to insert the data in a relational database and to build a social network.

In CNARe, the visualizations of those social networks show the edges classified according to their strength. In order to do such classification, an existing algorithm called RECAST *Random rElationship ClASsifier sTrategy* is applied to the social networks. Such algorithm classifies the edges as social links (friends, acquaintances or bridges) or random links (Vaz de Melo et al., 2015). Here, the edges classified as friends are called strong links and acquaintances as weak ones. Bridges and random links maintain the same name.

RECAST considers the temporal aspect of the relationships in the social networks. In a temporal graph, the interactions among individuals change over time (Holme & Saramäki, 2012; Nicosia et al., 2013). Such graph is generated, so that the co-authorships occurring at time step k are represented by a graph $G_k\left(V_k, \varepsilon_k\right)$. Note that V_k is the set of nodes involved in a co-authorship at the *k-th* time step,

Table 2. Description of the large social networks stored in CNARe database.

Dataset	Number of Nodes	Number of Edges
PubMed	443,784	5,550,294
DBLP Articles	837,583	2,935,590
DBLP Inproceedings	945,297	3,760,247
APS	180,718	821,870

whereas ε_k is the set of edges representing the co-authorships during the same time step. Thus, an edge between two nodes i and j ($i, j \in V_k$) exists in ε_k if i and j have published together during time step k. Then, Vaz de Melo et al. (2015) define a time varying representation of the social networks by exploiting a temporal accumulation graph $G_t = (V_t, E_t)$, in which V_t is the set of all nodes and E_t is the set of all edges that are in the social network between time 0 and time step t.

Overall, RECAST classifies an edge as social when two characteristics are present in the relationship: *regularity* and *similarity*. The regularity indicates that a relationship repeats over time, whereas the similarity means that two individuals in a relationship have common neighbors. Such characteristics can be mapped into social network metrics as edge persistence and topological overlap (also known as neighborhood overlap), respectively. Therefore, considering the aggregated temporal graph G_t and a pair of researchers i and j, the two social network characteristics are formally defined as follows.

- **Edge Persistence:** $per_t(i,j) = \dfrac{1}{t} \sum_{k=1}^{t} 1_{[(i,j) \in \varepsilon_k]}$, where $\left[(i,j) \in \varepsilon_k \right]$ is an indicator function that is 1 when the edge (i,j) exists in ε_k at time k, and 0 otherwise.

- **Topological Overlap:** $to_t(i,j) = \dfrac{|\{k \mid (i,k) \in E_t\} \cap \{k \mid (j,k) \in E_t\}|}{|\{k \mid (i,k) \in E_t\} \cup \{k \mid (j,k) \in E_t\}|}$.

Considering such properties, Vaz de Melo et al. (2015) evaluate which combination of values of edge persistence and topological overlap defines a relationship as friends (strong), bridges, acquaintances (weak) or random, and compare the results with a random graph G_t^R (a random version of G_t with the same number of nodes, edges and degree distribution; the only difference is the way that nodes are connected to each other). To do so, they define a parameter called p_{rnd}, the only parameter in RECAST, and identify a feature value $\bar{x}$ for each CCDF, Complementary Cumulative Distribution Function (Zwillinger & Kokoska, 1999), $\bar{F}(\bar{x}) = p_{rnd}$ for the random network G_t^R. The value $\bar{x}$ is a threshold such that if p_{rnd} is setted to some small value, values of edge persistence and topological overlap higher than $\bar{x}$ occur with probability lower than p_{rnd} in a random network. Thus, links with such values are most probably to be social relationships. The parameter p_{rnd} is the expected classification error percentage. In sum, the edges are classified as following: friends when $per(i,j) > \bar{x}_{per}$ and $to(i,j) > \bar{x}_{to}$; bridges when $per(i,j) > \bar{x}_{per}$ and $to(i,j) \le \bar{x}_{to}$; acquaintances when $per(i,j) \le \bar{x}_{per}$ and $to(i,j) > \bar{x}_{to}$; and random otherwise.

In the CNARe page that shows the visualization of the classified edges, the selection of nodes from each dataset can be done by researcher ego-network, publication venue or publication area, enabling comparison of different social networks topology. Also, the representation of co-authorships has been modified through distinct shapes and colors to show different properties, allowing visualization of bridges (a co-authorship that connects researchers from different communities) or classification of co-authorships as weak or strong. Figure 7 presents the visualization of a social network from a venue in the PubMed dataset.

Figure 7. Visualization of PubMed social network from the venue Lancet Medical Journal (London, England). The green edges are strong links, red edges are bridges, purple edges are weak links and dark purple edges are random links. The gray edges are links that do not received any classification.

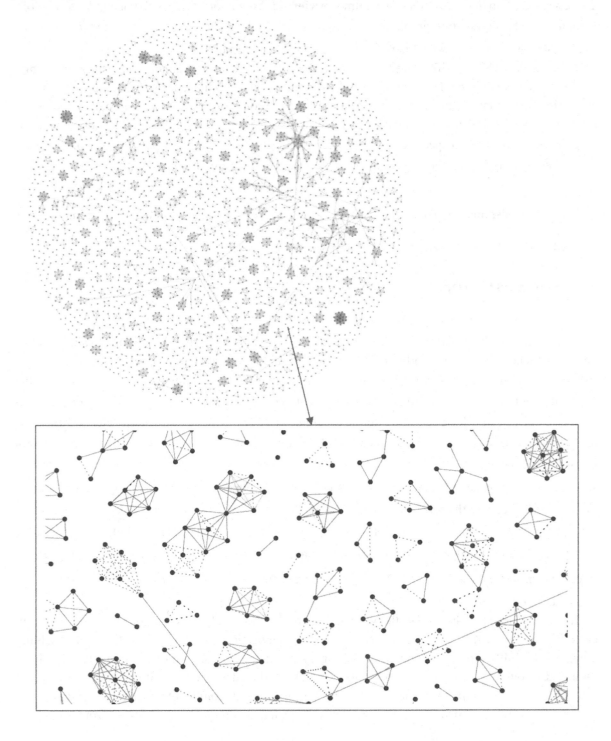

6. CONCLUDING REMARKS

This chapter presented CNARe, an online tool that shows the collaboration recommendations of three different algorithms (Affin, CORALS and MVCWalker). Visualizations and metrics of social networks are also used in order to show how the recommendations may modify researchers' ego networks. The visualizations reveal that new recommended links may work as bridges to co-authorship social networks. All these visualizations represent a step-forward in the collaboration recommendation tools, because CNARe considers three recommendation algorithms instead of only visualizing the results. Furthermore, besides CNARe having initial datasets, others can be easily uploaded. The only requirement is that the data have the fields needed by the recommendation algorithms. Finally, CNARe also provides visualizations of large networks differentiating the edges classified (strong, weak, bridges or random) by RECAST algorithm.

In the future, the authors plan to include other recommendation algorithms and social networks metrics. The next steps also comprise a better differentiation of the edges regarding their strength (i.e., consider algorithms different from RECAST).

ACKNOWLEDGMENT

This work was partially funded by CAPES, CNPq and FAPEMIG – Brazil.

REFERENCES

Ahmed, N. M., & Chen, L. (2016). An efficient algorithm for link prediction in temporal uncertain social networks. *Information Sciences*, *331*, 120–136. doi:10.1016/j.ins.2015.10.036

Bagci, H., & Karagoz, P. (2016). Context-Aware Friend Recommendation for Location Based Social Networks using Random Walk. In *Proceedings of the 25th International Conference Companion on World Wide Web* (pp. 531-536). International World Wide Web Conferences Steering Committee. doi:10.1145/2872518.2890466

Barbosa, E. M., Moro, M. M., Lopes, G. R., & de Oliveira, J. P. M. (2012). VRRC: web based tool for visualization and recommendation on co-authorship network. In *Proceedings of the 2012 ACM SIGMOD International Conference on Management of Data* (pp. 865-865). ACM. doi:10.1145/2213836.2213975

Bornmann, L., & Daniel, H. D. (2007). What do we know about the h index? *Journal of the American Society for Information Science and Technology*, *58*(9), 1381–1385. doi:10.1002/asi.20609

Brandão, M. A., & Moro, M. M. (2017). Social professional networks: A survey and taxonomy. *Computer Communications*, *100*, 20–31. doi:10.1016/j.comcom.2016.12.011

Brandão, M. A., Moro, M. M., Lopes, G. R., & Oliveira, J. P. (2013). Using link semantics to recommend collaborations in academic social networks. In *Proceedings of the 22nd International Conference on World Wide Web* (pp. 833-840). ACM. doi:10.1145/2487788.2488058

Brandes, U., Indlekofer, N., & Mader, M. (2012). Visualization methods for longitudinal social networks and stochastic actor-oriented modeling. *Social Networks*, *34*(3), 291–308. doi:10.1016/j.socnet.2011.06.002

Chang, C. C., & Chin, Y. C. (2011). Predicting the usage intention of social network games: An intrinsic-extrinsic motivation theory perspective. *International Journal of Online Marketing*, *1*(3), 29–37. doi:10.4018/ijom.2011070103

Chen, H. H., Gou, L., Zhang, X., & Giles, C. L. (2011). Collabseer: a search engine for collaboration discovery. In *Proceedings of the 11th annual international ACM/IEEE joint conference on Digital libraries* (pp. 231-240). ACM. doi:10.1145/1998076.1998121

de Sousa, G. A., Diniz, M. A., Brandão, M. A., & Moro, M. M. (2015). CNARe: Co-authorship Networks Analysis and Recommendations. In *Proceedings of the 9th ACM Conference on Recommender Systems* (pp. 329-330). ACM.

Easley, D., & Kleinberg, J. (2012). Networks, crowds, and markets: Reasoning about a highly connected world. *Significance*, *9*, 43–44.

Freeman, L. C. (2000). Visualizing social networks. *Journal of Social Structure, 1*(1), 4.

Goodman, L. A. (1961). Snowball sampling. *Annals of Mathematical Statistics*, *32*(1), 148–170. doi:10.1214/aoms/1177705148

Guerra-Gomez, J. A., Wilson, A., Liu, J., Davies, D., Jarvis, P., & Bier, E. (2016). Network Explorer: Design, Implementation, and Real World Deployment of a Large Network Visualization Tool. In *Proceedings of the International Working Conference on Advanced Visual Interfaces* (pp. 108-111). ACM. doi:10.1145/2909132.2909281

He, J., & Chu, W. W. (2010). *A social network-based recommender system*. Springer.

Holme, P., & Saramäki, J. (2012). Temporal networks. *Physics Reports*, *519*(3), 97–125. doi:10.1016/j.physrep.2012.03.001

Holten, D., & Van Wijk, J. J. (2009). Force-Directed Edge Bundling for Graph Visualization. *Computer Graphics Forum*, *28*(3), 983–990. doi:10.1111/j.1467-8659.2009.01450.x

Lopes, G. R., Moro, M. M., Wives, L. K., & De Oliveira, J. P. M. (2010). Collaboration recommendation on academic social networks. In *International Conference on Conceptual Modeling* (pp. 190-199). Springer Berlin Heidelberg.

Mrvar, A., & Batagelj, V. (2016). Analysis and visualization of large networks with program package Pajek. *Complex Adaptive Systems Modeling*, *4*(1), 1–8. doi:10.1186/s40294-016-0017-8

Nicosia, V., Tang, J., Mascolo, C., Musolesi, M., Russo, G., & Latora, V. (2013). Graph metrics for temporal networks. In *Temporal Networks* (pp. 15–40). Springer Berlin Heidelberg. doi:10.1007/978-3-642-36461-7_2

Paraschiv, I. C., Dascalu, M., Dessus, P., Trausan-Matu, S., & McNamara, D. S. (2016). A Paper Recommendation System with ReaderBench: The Graphical Visualization of Semantically Related Papers and Concepts. In *State-of-the-Art and Future Directions of Smart Learning* (pp. 445–451). Springer Singapore. doi:10.1007/978-981-287-868-7_53

Pettenati, M. C., & Cigognini, M. E. (2007). Social networking theories and tools to support connectivist learning activities. *International Journal of Web-Based Learning and Teaching Technologies*, 2(3), 42–60. doi:10.4018/jwltt.2007070103

Protasiewicz, J., Pedrycz, W., Kozłowski, M., Dadas, S., Stanisławek, T., Kopacz, A., & Gałeżewska, M. (2016). A recommender system of reviewers and experts in reviewing problems. *Knowledge-Based Systems*, *106*, 164–178. doi:10.1016/j.knosys.2016.05.041

Rahman, M., & Karim, R. (2016). Comparative study of different methods of social network analysis and visualization. In *2016 International Conference on Networking Systems and Security (NSysS)* (pp. 1-7). IEEE. doi:10.1109/NSysS.2016.7400702

Surian, D., Liu, N., Lo, D., Tong, H., Lim, E. P., & Faloutsos, C. (2011). Recommending people in developers' collaboration network. In *18th Working Conference on Reverse Engineering* (pp. 379-388). IEEE.

Tang, J., Hu, X., & Liu, H. (2013). Social recommendation: A review. *Social Network Analysis and Mining*, *3*(4), 1113–1133. doi:10.1007/s13278-013-0141-9

Vaz de Melo, P. O., Viana, A. C., Fiore, M., Jaffrès-Runser, K., Le Mouël, F., Loureiro, A. A., & Guangshuo, C. (2015). Recast: Telling apart social and random relationships in dynamic networks. *Performance Evaluation*, *87*, 19–36. doi:10.1016/j.peva.2015.01.005

Viégas, F. B., & Donath, J. (2004). Social network visualization: Can we go beyond the graph. *Workshop on social networks, CSCW*, 4, 6-10.

Wasserman, S., & Faust, K. (1994). *Social network analysis: Methods and applications* (Vol. 8). Cambridge university press. doi:10.1017/CBO9780511815478

Xia, F., Chen, Z., Wang, W., Li, J., & Yang, L. T. (2014). MVCWalker: Random Walk-Based Most Valuable Collaborators Recommendation Exploiting Academic Factors. *IEEE Transactions on Emerging Topics in Computing*, 2(3), 364–375. doi:10.1109/TETC.2014.2356505

Zhang, A. X., Bhardwaj, A., & Karger, D. (2016). Confer: A Conference Recommendation and Meetup Tool. In *Proceedings of the 19th ACM Conference on Computer Supported Cooperative Work and Social Computing Companion* (pp. 118-121). ACM.

Zwillinger, D., & Kokoska, S. (1999). *CRC standard probability and statistics tables and formulae*. Crc Press. doi:10.1201/9781420050264

ENDNOTES

1   Source forge: http://sourceforge.net
2   Confer in IJCAI-16: http://confer.csail.mit.edu/ijcai2016/schedule
3   ACM digital library: http://dl.acm.org
4   D3.js: http://d3js.org
5   In the future, the authors plan to consider other institutions as well.
6   A dump of the relational database is available on http://www.dcc.ufmg.br/~mirella/projs/apoena
7   PubMed: www.ncbi.nlm.nih.gov/pubmed
8   DBLP: dblp.uni-trier.de
9   APS: www.aps.org
10   NCBI: www.ncbi.nlm.nih.gov
11   DBLP XML: dblp.uni-trier.de/xml/
12   APS dataset: journals.aps.org/datasets

Chapter 12
Community Detection in Large-Scale Social Networks:
A Survey

S Rao Chintalapudi
Jawaharlal Nehru Technological University, Kakinada (JNTU-K), India

M. H. M. Krishna Prasad
Jawaharlal Nehru Technological University, Kakinada (JNTU-K), India

ABSTRACT

Community Structure is one of the most important properties of social networks. Detecting such structures is a challenging problem in the area of social network analysis. Community is a collection of nodes with dense connections than with the rest of the network. It is similar to clustering problem in which intra cluster edge density is more than the inter cluster edge density. Community detection algorithms are of two categories, one is disjoint community detection, in which a node can be a member of only one community at most, and the other is overlapping community detection, in which a node can be a member of more than one community. This chapter reviews the state-of-the-art disjoint and overlapping community detection algorithms. Also, the measures needed to evaluate a disjoint and overlapping community detection algorithms are discussed in detail.

1. INTRODUCTION

Social Network Analysis has become an important field of data mining and machine learning. Many complex systems can be represented as networks, where nodes represent actors or entities and links represents interactions or relationships between them. Network Analysis is an emerging area to analyze real world networks like biological networks, road networks, social networks, information networks. With the increase of number and size of the networks, there is a scope for computational techniques that helps in understanding the properties of networks. The networks in the real world are not simply random graphs and most of the real world networks have properties like power law distribution, small world. One of the most interesting properties of networks that can be used in the real world applications

DOI: 10.4018/978-1-5225-2814-2.ch012

is community structure. Community detection is similar to process of clustering in data mining and it is also called as unsupervised learning because grouping can be done without prior knowledge of clusters. Identifying communities has several applications such as classifying people viz., influencers, identifying correlated structures in protein - protein interaction networks, grouping web clients geographically to improve performance, analyzing social networks viz., facebook, twitter, identifying web pages of same thematic category in the hyperlink networks, to understand the connection patterns between scientific papers in citation networks, product recommendation systems for on-line retail sites, political election prediction based on discussions of certain topics on twitter and so on.The rest of the chapter is organized as follows: Section 2 discusses about communities in social networks. Section 3 reviews state of the art disjoint and overlapped community detection algorithms. Section 4 describes datasets both synthetic and real world networks, which are used to evaluate community detection algorithms. Section 5 describes the evaluation measures to test the accuracy of disjoint and overlapped community detection algorithms. Section 6 presents some of the challenges come across in detecting communities were discussed. Section 7 concludes the chapter.

2. COMMUNITIES IN SOCIAL NETWORKS

Community in a social network is a group of nodes that are densely connected and sparsely connected with the rest of the network. It is also defined as collection of nodes with high density of internal links and with low density of external links. A community can also be called as module, cluster or group. Community detection has importance over several disciplines such as biology, statistical physics, sociology, applied mathematics and computer science. Communities are broadly classified into two categories based on node participation. One is disjoint community, where a node can be a member of only one community at most. The other is overlapping community, where a node can be a member of more than one community. In the real world networks, several overlapping communities can exists. For example, in social networks, a person may be a member of family circle, job circle and friend circle at the same time. Hence, the study of overlapping communities is the most relevant concept in real world social networks. The illustration of disjoint and overlapping communities in a sample network is depicted in Figure 1 and Figure 2 respectively.

Figure 1. Example for disjoint communities

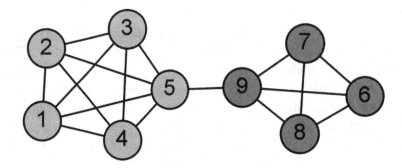

Figure 2. Example for overlapping communities

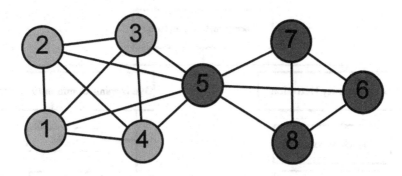

In Figure 1, a sample network with two disjoint communities is depicted (each color represents one community). In Figure 2, a sample network with two overlapping communities is depicted and node 5 is participated in both the communities, hence it is called as overlapping node.

3. COMMUNITY DETECTION ALGORITHMS

Many community detection algorithms have been developed till now, according to their detection capability they are broadly classified into two categories. One is disjoint community detection algorithms and the other is overlapped community detection algorithms. All these algorithms aimed at improving the capability of detecting meaningful communities, while keeping computational complexity as low as possible. The state of the art disjoint and overlapping community detection algorithms discussed in this chapter are listed in Figure 3.

3.1 Disjoint Community Detection Algorithms

In this section, authors presented the popular disjoint community detection algorithms (Lancichinetti et al. 2009; S Rao et al. 2015). Many disjoint community detection algorithms are available but authors considered only significantly important algorithms. If an algorithm is too slow, in that case authors omitted such algorithms.

Edge betweenness algorithm (Girvan et al. 2002) is a hierarchical approach based on edge betweenness. Edge betweenness score is the number of shortest paths in which a given edge is included. The edges connecting communities are expected to have high edge betweenness. In this method, the edges with high edge betweenness score will be removed and so on. This method is computationally intensive as it recalculates the value of edge betweenness for each edge removal. It produces full dendrogram plot but does not indicate where to cut the plot to identify the communities, forcing one need to use modularity score at each level of dendrogram to decide final communities. Also suffers with scalability problem, as authors mentioned the upper limit of the network size is 700 nodes and 3500 edges.

Fast Greedy algorithm (Clauset et al. 2004) is also a bottom-up hierarchical approach. It optimizes the modularity score in a greedy manner. In this method, initially each node belongs to a new community and these communities are merged iteratively based on maximum improvement of modularity score.

Figure 3. List of community detection algorithms

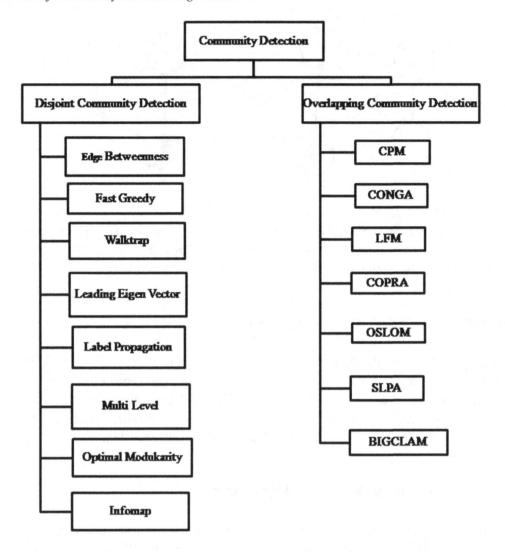

The algorithm stops when there is no improvement in modularity score. It is a faster approach but suffer from a resolution limit that communities below the threshold will always be merged.

Walktrap algorithm (Pons et al. 2005) is implemented based on random walks. The basic idea of this method is that short distance random walks tend to stay in the same community. It is also a hierarchical clustering algorithm. Random walk is a process of traversing nodes at random. It merges separated communities in a bottom up manner based on the results of random walks. This method also uses modularity score to cut the dendrogram as in fast greedy method. Even though it produces accurate results but it is slower than the fast greedy method.

Leading Eigen Vector algorithm (Newman 2006) is a hierarchical method that uses modularity function. The network will be split into two parts whenever modularity increases than the threshold. Splitting can be done based on leading Eigen vector in the modularity matrix and there will be a stop condition to prevent dense communities to be split further. It produces high modularity score than the fast greedy method but slower.

Table 1. Time complexity of disjoint community detection algorithms

Algorithm	Time Complexity	Year
Edge Betweenness	$O(m^2n)$	2002
Fast Greedy	$O(nlog^2(n))$	2004
Walktrap	$O(n^2logn)$	2005
Leading Eigen Vector	$O(n^2)$	2006
Label Propagation	$O(m)$	2007
Multilevel	$O(nlogn)$	2008
Optimal Modularity	$O(n^3)$	2008
Infomap	$O(m)$	2008

Label Propagation algorithm (Raghavan et al. 2007) is an approach that assigns k labels to each node in the network and reassigns label to nodes that are frequent in its neighborhood. It converges as the label of each node is frequent label in its neighborhood. This method is faster but produces different results in each run based on initial configuration. So, one need to run the algorithm several times and build the consensus, but it consumes time.

Multi-Level algorithm (Blondel et al. 2008) implemented based on modularity measure and is a hierarchical approach. It reduces the computation time of the modularity. In this algorithm, first each node is assigned to one community and modularity will be computed for all initial communities. In the next step, each node is removed from the community and moved to other communities iteratively. For each movement calculate modularity gain. If it is a largest positive gain, then assign the node to that community. If not, the node remains in its original community. This iterative process will be terminated until no further improvement in modularity. The time complexity for this algorithm is linear for sparse graphs.

Optimal Modularity algorithm (Brandes et al. 2008) works based on the maximal modularity score. It transforms modularity maximization problem into integer programming problem as it is a NP- complete problem. It can process the networks up to 50 nodes. Hence, it is not suitable for large scale networks.

Infomap algorithm (Rosvall et al. 2008) uses the concepts of information theory. It calculates the shortest description length for each random walk on the network. The description length is computed by the number of bits per node required to encode the path of random walk. It is a serial implementation of map equation. Map equation is used to evaluate quality of graph clustering and tells about the optimal number of communities and optimal assignment of nodes into those communities by using information theory. The parallel implementation of infomap is RelaxMap (Seung hee et al. 2013) that utilizes multi core processing. Time complexities of all the above disjoint community detection algorithms are listed in Table 1, where m represents number of edges and n represents number of nodes. The time complexities of algorithms in Table 1 are for sparse networks.

3.2 Overlapped Community Detection Algorithms

In this section, authors reviewed popular and the state-of-the-art overlapped community detection algorithms in large scale social networks (Xie et al. 2013 ; Harenberg et al. 2014; Chakraborty 2015). The algorithms studied in this section and their characteristics are listed in Table. 2. The time complexities listed in the Table.2 are for the worst case scenario.

One of the most popular method for finding overlapping communities is Clique percolation Method (CPM) proposed by (Palla et al. 2005). It is based on the assumption that a community consists of fully connected subgraphs i.e, Cliques. This method detects overlapping communities by searching for each such subgraph for adjacent cliques that share with it at least certain number of nodes. Given parameter k, the algorithm starts by identifying all cliques of size k. Then a new graph is constructed where all cliques are denoted as nodes and cliques that share k-1 members are connected using edges. Communities are then identified by reporting the connected components of this new graph. A node can be a part of multiple k-cliques at the same time; hence, overlapping communities can be formed. This algorithm is suitable for only networks with densely connected components but it is a computationally intensive approach. CFinder is an implementation of CPM, whose time complexity is polynomial for some applications. However, it fails to terminate in many large social networks and also the communities discovered by CFinder are usually of low Quality. This is like a pattern matching algorithm rather than community detection because it is aimed to find particular structure in the network.

Cluster Overlap Newman Girvan Algorithm (CONGA) (Gregory 2007) is an extension of Girvan and Newman's divisive clustering algorithm that finds overlapping communities and it allows a node to split into multiple communities based on split betweenness. Initially, edge betweenness of edges and split betweenness of nodes are calculated. Then an edge with maximum edge betweenness is removed or a node with maximum split betweenness is split. After completion of this step, recalculate edge betweenness and split betweenness. Repeat the above process until all edges are considered. The calculation of edge betweenness and split betweenness are computationally expensive for large networks. CONGO (Gregory 2008) is a refined version of CONGA, in which local betweenness is used to optimize the runtime of the algorithm.

LFM (Lancichinetti et al. 2009) starts with a random seed node and expands community until the fitness function is maximal. The fitness function used in this algorithm is as in Eq. (1).

$$f(c) = \frac{k_{in}^c}{(k_{in}^c + k_{out}^c)^\alpha} \tag{1}$$

Where k_{in}^c and k_{out}^c are the total number inner and outer links of the community c, and α is the resolution parameter that controls the community size. Once a community is found, the algorithm selects another node that is not yet assigned to any other community. This method is significantly depends on resolution parameter (α) of the fitness function. The time complexity of this algorithm for a fixed α-value is $O(n_c s^2)$ approximately, where n_c is number of communities and s is average size of the communities. The worst-case time complexity of this algorithm is $O(n^2)$.

Community Overlap Propagation Algorithm (COPRA) (Gregory 2010) is an extension of label propagation that allows a node belongs to up to v communities, where v is supplied by the user. Each node is associated with belonging coefficient as in Eq. (2) for indicating strength of community membership. The parameter v controls the maximum number of communities that a node can associate. The time complexity of this algorithm is $O(vm \log(vm / n))$ per iteration. This method produces small size communities for majority of the networks

$$b_t\left(c, x\right) = \frac{\sum_{y \in N(x)} b_{t-1}\left(c, y\right)}{\left|N(x)\right|}$$

(2)

Where x is a node, c is a community identifier and t represents an iteration number. Each propagation step updates node labels to the union of its neighbors and normalizes the sum of belonging coefficients of all neighbors. It is a non deterministic algorithm, so there is a scope to improve determinacy.

Order Statistics Local Optimization Method (OSLOM) (Lancichinetti et al. 2011) checks the statistical significance of a community with respect to a global null model during community expansion. It uses local optimization of fitness function. This algorithm consists of three phases. In the first phase, it identifies significant communities until convergence. In the next phase, the algorithm analyzes the resulting set of communities, trying to detect their internal structure and possible unions. In the final phase, the algorithm detects hierarchical structure of communities. Usually, this algorithm generates more number of singleton communities and outliers. In general, the worst-case time complexity of this algorithm is $O(n^2)$, while the actual time complexity is depends on community structure in the given network.

Speaker-Listener Label Propagation Algorithm (Xie et al. 2011) (Xie et al. 2012) is an extended version of Label Propagation Algorithm (LPA) that detects both disjoint and overlapping communities. This algorithm is developed based on speaker-listener interaction dynamic process. Initially, the memory of each node in the network is assigned with a unique label. That means each node can be considered as a different community. Next, a node is selected as a listener. Each neighbor of the listener randomly selects a label and sends the label to the listener. Neighbors of the Listener now play a role of speakers. Then the listener adds most popular label received to its memory. The above procedure can be repeated until upto maximum number of iterations (T), which is supplied as a parameter to the algorithm. Finally, the post processing based on the labels in the node memories and the threshold r is applied to produce the communities. In the post processing step, the algorithm converts memory of each node into a probability distribution of labels. If the probability of a particular label during the post processing step is less than a given threshold r, then the label is deleted. If a node contains multiple labels, then the node belongs to more than one community, called overlapping node. The smaller value of r produces more

Table 2. Summary of overlapping community detection algorithms

Algorithm	Network Type	Disjoint Communities	Overlapping Communities	Time Complexity	Implementation	Year
CPM	Undirected	No	Yes	*exponential*	C++	2005
CONGA	Undirected	No	Yes	$O(m^3)$	Java	2007
CONGO	Undirected	No	Yes	$O(nlogn)$	Java	2008
LFM	Undirected	No	Yes	$O(n^2)$	C++	2009
COPRA	Undirected	No	Yes	$O(vmlog(vm/n))$	Java	2010
OSLOM	Directed & Undirected	No	Yes	$O(n^2)$	C++	2011
SLPA	Directed & Undirected	Yes	Yes	$O(tm)$	Java	2012
BIGCLAM	Undirected	Yes	Yes	$O(kn^2)$	C++	2013

number of overlapping communities. If the threshold (r) is ≥ 0.5, then the algorithm produces only disjoint communities. The algorithm produces stable results when the iterations are greater than 20.

Cluster Affiliation Model for Big Networks (BIGCLAM) (Yang et al. 2013) is an overlapping community detection algorithm that can process large networks with millions of nodes and edges. It is a model-based community detection algorithm that can detect densely overlapping, hierarchically nested as well as disjoint communities in the massive networks. It is based on the observation that overlaps of communities are more densely connected rather than the non overlapping parts of communities. Non negative matrix factorization is used to develop the model. The main concern of this algorithm is to choosing the number of communities.

4. DATASETS

In this section, the datasets both synthetic and real world datasets used for evaluating community detection algorithms are discussed.

4.1 Synthetic Networks

Random graphs are not sufficient for evaluating community detection algorithms in social networks because they do not have community structure. To study the behavior of the community detection algorithms, one need to have networks with similar properties of social networks such as community structure, power law distribution and so on.

Girvan and Newman (Girvan et al. 2002) were proposed a method to test the community detection algorithms based on planted l-partition model. This network is called as GN Benchmark Network and it is one of the most used benchmark network. It consists of 128 nodes with the equal degree of 16 and four communities with 32 nodes each. This benchmark network has three drawbacks, one is all nodes have equal degree; the second is all communities are of same size and the other is smaller network. These three properties are not there in real world networks as they consist heterogeneous distribution of node degree, community size and more number of nodes. Hence, these networks are not sufficient to test the community detection algorithms.

To overcome the drawbacks of GN benchmark networks, (Lancichenetti et al. 2009) proposed networks by introducing power law distributions of degree and community size. LFR Benchmark networks generator can generate both networks with disjoint communities and networks with overlapped communities. The parameters used in generating LFR benchmark networks are number of nodes (N), average degree ($\bar{k}$), mixing parameter (μ), maximum degree (k_{max}), exponents of the power law distribution (t_1, t_2), minimum community size (C_{min}), Maximum community size (C_{max}), number of overlapping nodes (O_n) and number of memberships of the overlapping nodes (O_m). Mixing parameter is the most influential parameter in LFR benchmark networks and it can be defined as follows.

$$\mu = \frac{\sum_i k_i^{ext}}{\sum_i k_i^{tot}} \tag{3}$$

Where k_i^{ext} and k_i^{tot} are external degree and total degree of a node i. The lower mixing parameter (μ) value generates highly modular communities in the network. To generate overlapping communities the values of the parameters O_m and O_n should be greater than one. The degree distribution of the network is controlled by power laws with exponents t_1 and t_2 respectively. These networks resemble real-world social networks in terms of degree distribution and clustering coefficient. The complexity of this network generator is linear in terms of number of links in the network. Ground truth information will be generated along with the network.

4.2 Real World Social Networks

The actual performance of the community detection algorithms can be observed when the algorithms are tested on real-world social networks such as Karate, Dolphins, Polbooks, football, Jazz, Netscience and Polblogs and so on. These network datasets can be acquired from Newman's personal web page (Newman 2015). The detailed summary of these real world social networks are listed in (Table 3). The large collection of network datasets is also available in Stanford Large Network Dataset Collection (Leskovec et al. 2015). And the most of these networks does not have ground truth information so it is not possible to find accuracy of the algorithm using NMI, ONMI, Omega Index and F-score. Therefore, Modularity proposed by (Newman et al., 2006) and Overlap modularity proposed by (Nicosia et al. 2009) can be used with real world social networks. Three real world social networks Zachary karate club, dolphin network and American football network with their communities are depicted in Figure 4, Figure 5 and Figure 6 respectively.

Figure 4. Communities in karate network

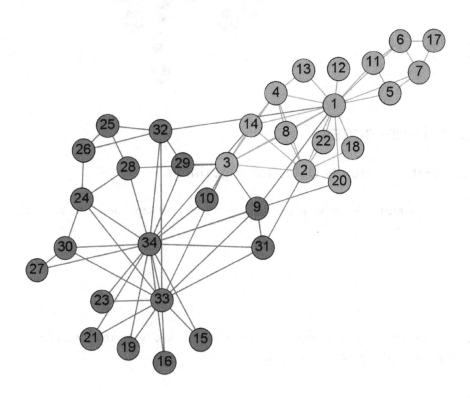

Figure 5. Communities in dolphin network

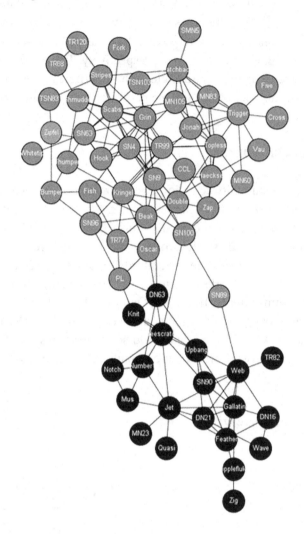

5. EVALUATION MEASURES

5.1. For Disjoint Community Detection Algorithms

Modularity is used to measure how vertices of different types are separated from each other and it can be calculated as follows

$$Q = \frac{1}{2m} \sum_{i,j} A_{ij} - \frac{k_i k_j}{2m}$$
(4)

Here, Q represents modularity, m represents number of edges, A_{ij} represents an entry of adjacency matrix, k_i, k_j represents the degrees of vertex i, j respectively.

Figure 6. Communities in football network

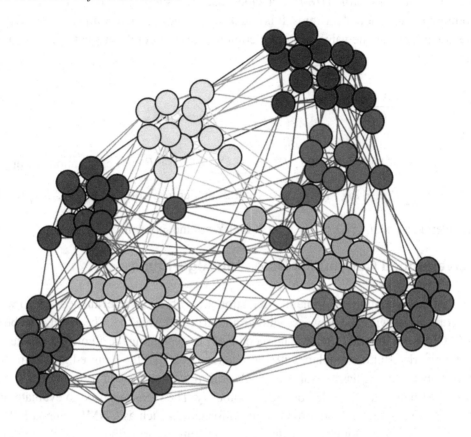

Table 3. Summary of real-world social networks

Dataset	Nodes	Edges	Description
Karate	34	78	Zachary's karate club
Sawmill	36	62	Sawmill Communication network
Dolphins	62	159	Dolphin social network
Lesmis	77	254	Coappearances of characters in Les Miserables
Polbooks	105	441	Books about US Politics
Words	112	425	Adjectives and nouns
Football	115	613	American college football
Jazz	198	2742	Jazz musicians network
Netscience	379	914	Co-authorship Network
Metabolic	453	2025	Metabolic network of C. elegans
Email	1133	5451	Network of e-mail interchanges
Polblogs	1490	16718	Political blogs

Normalized Mutual Information (NMI) is a widely used measure, adopted from information theory to evaluate community detection algorithms. It is equals to 1 if the detected communities and their ground truth are identical whereas the value is 0 if the communities are purely distinct with the ground truth. It can be defined as

$$I_{norm}(X,Y) = \frac{2I(X,Y)}{H(X) + H(Y)} \qquad (5)$$

Where $I(X,Y) = H(X) - H(X \mid Y)$, $H(X) = -\sum_{x} P(x) \log P(x)$ (i.e. Shannon entropy)

$H(X \mid Y) = -\sum_{x,y} P(x,y) \log P(x \mid y)$ (i.e. Conditional entropy of X given Y), $I_{norm}(X,Y) = 1$, if

X and Y are identical and $I_{norm}(X,Y) = 0$, if X and Y are independent.

5.2. For Overlapped Community Detection Algorithms

The accuracy of the overlapping community detection algorithm can be evaluated in two ways. One is to test the algorithm on synthetic networks with ground truth information. The results can be quantified using ONMI, Omega index and F-Score. The second way of evaluating the algorithm is to test with real-world social networks. But the problem with these networks is that the required ground truth information is not available. So, one has to evaluate the algorithm without ground truth information. It can be possible with the quality metric called overlap modularity. The measures used to evaluate overlapping community detection algorithm with ground truth information such as ONMI, Omega Index, F-Score and the measure to evaluate algorithms without ground truth information i.e. overlapping modularity are discussed in the rest of the section. Ground truth information for synthetic networks is available, so one can apply the metrics such as ONMI, Omega Index and F-Score.

The extended version of NMI proposed by (McDaid et al. 2013) is called Overlapping Normalized Mutual Information (ONMI), can be used to evaluate overlapping community detection algorithms. It is defined based on two normalization inequalities, such as max(H(X),H(Y)) is denoted by ONMI$_{MAX}$ and 0.5*(H(X)+H(Y)) is denoted by ONMI$_{SUM}$. ONMI$_{MAX}$ and ONMI$_{SUM}$ can be calculated using Eq. (6) and Eq. (7) respectively. The range of ONMI$_{MAX}$ and ONMI$_{SUM}$ is also in between 0 and 1. If ONMI=1, that means the detected community structure is completely the same with the ground truth community structure. If ONMI=0, then the detected community structure is entirely different from the ground truth community structure. That is, the value of ONMI increases when the accuracy of the detected community structure is improved.

$$ONMI_{MAX} = \frac{I(X:Y)}{\max(H(X), H(Y))} \qquad (6)$$

$$ONMI_{SUM} = \frac{I(X:Y)}{0.5 * (H(X) + H(Y))} \qquad (7)$$

The mutual information I(X:Y) can be calculated as follows.

$$I(X:Y) = \frac{1}{2}[H(X) - H(X \mid Y) + H(Y) - H(Y \mid X)]$$

Where X, Y are two covers, H(X) and H(Y) are the entropy of covers X and Y respectively, H(X|Y) and H(Y|X) are conditional entropies.

Omega Index is also a popular metric to evaluate overlapping community detection algorithms. It is an Overlapping version of Adjusted Rand Index. It is based on pairs of nodes in agreement in two covers. Let C_1, C_2 are two covers, the omega index can be defined as in Eq. (8)

$$\Omega(C_1, C_2) = \frac{\Omega_u(C_1, C_2) - \Omega_e(C_1, C_2)}{1 - \Omega_e(C_1, C_2)} \tag{8}$$

Where $\Omega_u(C_1, C_2)$ represents unadjusted omega index, is the fraction of pairs that belong to same community in both C_1 and C_2.

$$\Omega_u(C_1, C_2) = \frac{1}{M} \sum_j \left| t_j(C_1) \cap t_j(C_2) \right|$$

Where M represents the number of node pairs i.e. *n(n-1)/2* and $t_j(C)$ is the set of pairs of items that appear together in exactly *j* communities in a cover *C*.

$\Omega_e(C_1, C_2)$ is the expected omega index value in the null model and it can be computed as follows.

$$\Omega_e(C_1, C_2) = \frac{1}{M^2} \sum_j \left| t_j(C_1) \right| \cdot \left| t_j(C_2) \right|$$

The above definition of omega index is reduced to Adjusted Rand Index, if the network doesn't have overlapping communities. The range of omega index is 0 to 1, where 1 represents perfect matching. The higher values of omega index represent good similarity between detected and actual covers.

F-score (Xie et al. 2013) is used to evaluate accuracy of overlapping nodes detection and it can be defined as the harmonic mean of precision and recall. The range for F-score is from 0 to 1, where 1 represents best case and 0 represents worst case and the value of F-score is higher when the accuracy of detecting overlapping nodes is higher. It can be computed using Eq. (9).

$$F = \frac{2 \times precision \times recall}{precision + recall} \tag{9}$$

Where

$$recall = \frac{\# Correctly\_det\,ected\_overlapping\_nodes}{\# actual\_overlapping\_nodes}$$

$$precision = \frac{\#Correctly\_detected\_overlapping\_nodes}{\#total\_detected\_overlapping\_nodes}$$

Overlap Modularity is a quality measure that evaluates overlapping community detection algorithms without ground truth information and it is based on belonging coefficients of links. It can be used as both evaluating and detecting overlapping communities in social networks. If $l=(i,j)$ is an edge that belongs to community c, then the belonging coefficient of l can be represented as a function of belonging coefficient of node i and node j to the community c.

$$\beta_{l,c} = F(\alpha_{ic}, \alpha_{jc})$$

Where $F(\alpha_{ic}, \alpha_{jc})$ is an arbitrary function and can be taken as product or average or maximum of α_{ic} and α_{jc}. The expected belonging coefficient of any possible link $l(i,j)$ starting from a node into community c is an average of all possible belonging coefficients of l to community c.

$$\beta_{l(i,j),c}^{out} = \frac{\sum_{j \in V} F(\alpha_{ic}, \alpha_{jc})}{|V|}.$$

Accordingly, the expected belonging coefficient of any link $l(i,j)$ pointing to node j in community c is defined as:

$$\beta_{l(i,j),c}^{in} = \frac{\sum_{j \in V} F(\alpha_{ic}, \alpha_{jc})}{|V|}$$

These belonging coefficients are used as weights for the probability of having a link starting at node i and pointing to node j. Therefore, modularity in the case of overlapped communities can be computed as in Eq. (10).

$$Q_{ov} = \frac{1}{m} \sum_{c \in C} \sum_{i,j \in V} \left[\beta_{l(i,j),c} A_{i,j} - \frac{\beta_{l(i,j),c}^{out} k_i^{out} \beta_{l(i,j),c}^{in} k_j^{in}}{m} \right] \tag{10}$$

Where k_i^{out}, k_j^{in} are the number of outgoing and incoming links of *i* and *j* respectively and *m* is the total number of edges. The overlap modularity is significantly depends on the arbitrary function $F(\alpha_{ic}, \alpha_{jc})$ The higher values of overlap modularity indicates good community detection algorithm. Usually, the modularity above 0.3 indicates good modular structures in the network.

6. CHALLENGES IN COMMUNITY DETECTION

There are several challenges in developing algorithms for community detection. The basic challenge is that there is no universal definition for community. Some of the challenges that can be considered for future research are listed as follows.

- **Scalability:** Nowadays, the size of the real world networks is really large. Most of the existing community detection algorithms are works with small size networks where the number of nodes is multiples of hundreds. The efficiency of the existing algorithms with larger networks is decreasing rapidly and even some algorithms are failed to detect communities. Hence, there is a scope to develop a robust and scalable algorithm to identify communities for large scale social networks.
- **Run Time:** It is another major constraint in graph mining algorithms. Many of the existing algorithms are sequential and having high runtimes. Hence, these algorithms can be paralelleized by utilizing the power of multi threading in java. The performance of these algorithms can be improved further using either high performance computing system (GPU) or Hadoop distributed computing environment or Apache Spark. GPUs are very useful when the runtime of the application is crucial.
- **Dynamic Networks:** The connections between the nodes can be changed dynamically with the time that means the number of edges can be increased or decreased. And also new nodes can be added to the network. Hence there is a scope to develop community detection algorithms for timely evolving networks. These algorithms are very helpful in applications like epidemic spreading.
- **Directed Networks:** The existing algorithms are primarily focused on undirected networks only. Some of these algorithms may work for directed networks, but does not produce good results. So, there is a scope to incorporate edge directionality to work with directed as well as undirected networks.
- **Wide Variety of Networks:** There are several types of networks that are useful in real time such as bipartite networks, attributed networks, weighted networks and so on. Extending the existing algorithms for these networks will be a good contribution for this area.

7. CONCLUSION

In this chapter, authors focused on communities in social networks and described how they can be formed and can be detected. Communities are of two types, based on node participation, one is disjoint communities where a node is a member of only one community, and the other is overlapping community where a node can be a member of more than one community. The disjoint community detection algorithms may not suitable for detecting overlapping communities; hence overlapping community detection algorithms are also discussed. Authors reviewed eight disjoint and eight overlapped community detection algorithms in detail. To evaluate these community detection algorithms, synthetic networks such as GN benchmark network, LFR benchmark networks and real world social networks such as karate, dolphins... etc are discussed in detail. LFR benchmark networks are the good choice for evaluating both disjoint and overlapping community detection algorithms than the GN benchmark networks because they have properties similar to real world social networks. The two popular measures for evaluating the accuracy of disjoint community detection algorithms such as modularity, NMI are discussed where NMI can be used when ground truth information is available, otherwise modularity can be used. The measures used in evaluating disjoint community detection algorithms are not suitable for overlapped community detection algorithms. Hence, authors also included measures for evaluating overlapped community detection algorithms such as ONMI, Omega Index, F-Score and Overlap Modularity. If the ground truth information is available with the network, then one can easily compute ONMI, Omega Index, F-Score, otherwise overlap modularity can be computed for testing the accuracy of the algorithm. Finally, after reviewing all the sixteen state of the art community detection algorithms authors observed that there is a lot of scope in this area to research and the challenges in community detection were also discussed.

REFERENCES

Aggarwal, C. C. (2014). *Data Mining: The Textbook*. Springer International Publishing.

Blondel, V. D., Guillaume, J.-L., Lambiotte, R., & Lefebvre, E. (2008). Fast unfolding of communities in large network. *Journal of Statistical Mechanics*, *2008*(10), 10008. doi:10.1088/1742-5468/2008/10/P10008

Brandes, U., Delling, D., Gaertler, M., Gorke, R., Hoefer, M., Nikoloski, Z., & Wagner, D. (2008). On modularity clustering. *IEEE Transactions on Knowledge and Data Engineering*, *20*(2), 172–188. doi:10.1109/TKDE.2007.190689

Chakraborty, T. (2015). Liveraging disjoint communities for detecting overlapping community structure. *Journal of Statistical Mechanics*, *2015*(5), P05017. doi:10.1088/1742-5468/2015/05/P05017

Clauset, A., Newman, M. E. J., & Moore, C. (2004). Finding community structure in very large networks. *Physical Review E: Statistical, Nonlinear, and Soft Matter Physics*, *70*(6), 066111. doi:10.1103/PhysRevE.70.066111 PMID:15697438

Girvan, M., & Newman, M. E. J. (2002). Community structure in social and biological networks. *Proceedings of the National Academy of Sciences of the United States of America*, *99*(12), 7821–7826. doi:10.1073/pnas.122653799 PMID:12060727

Gregory, S. (2007). An algorithm to find overlapping community structure in networks. In J. N. Kok, J. Koronacki, R. Lopez de Mantras, S. Matwin, D. Mladenic, & A. Skowron (Eds.), *PKDD 2007. LNCS (LNAI)* (Vol. 4702, pp. 91–102). Heidelberg: Springer. doi:10.1007/978-3-540-74976-9_12

Gregory, S. (2008). A fast algorithm to find overlapping communities in networks. In W. Daelemans (Ed.), *ECML PKDD 2008, LNAI* (Vol. 5212, pp. 408–423). Berlin: Springer. doi:10.1007/978-3-540-87479-9_45

Gregory, S. (2010). Finding overlapping communities in networks by label propagation. *New Journal of Physics*, *12*(10), 10301. doi:10.1088/1367-2630/12/10/103018

Harenberg, S., Bello, G., Gjeltema, L., Ranshous, S., Jitendra, H., Ramona, S., … Samatova, N. (2014). Community detection in large-scale networks: a survey and empirical evaluation. *WIREs Comput Stat, 6*, 426-439.

Lancichinetti, A., Fortunato, S., & Kertesz, J. (2009). Detecting the overlapping and hierarchical community structure of complex networks. *New Journal of Physics, 11*(3), 033015. doi:10.1088/1367-2630/11/3/033015

Lancichinetti, A., Radicchi, F., Ramasco, J. J., & Fortunato, S. (2011). Finding statistically significant communities in networks. *PLoS ONE, 6*(4), e18961. doi:10.1371/journal.pone.0018961 PMID:21559480

Leskovec, J., & Krevl, A. (2015). *SNAP Datasets: Stanford Large Network Dataset Collection*. Retrieved November 12, 2015 from http://snap.stanford.edu/data

McDaid, A. F., Greene, D., & Hurley, N. (2013). *Normalized Mutual Information to evaluate overlapping community finding algorithms.* CORRabs/1110.2515

Newman, M. E. J. (2006). Finding community structure in networks using the eigenvectors of matrices. *Physical Review E: Statistical, Nonlinear, and Soft Matter Physics, 74*(3), 036104. doi:10.1103/PhysRevE.74.036104 PMID:17025705

Newman, M. E. J. (2015). *Real world network datasets*. Retrieved October 10, 2015, from http://www-personal.umich.edu/~mejn/netdata/

Nicosia, V., Mangioni, G., Carchiolo, V., & Malgeri, M. (2009). Extending the definition of modularity to directed graphs with overlapping communities. *Journal of Statistical Mechanics, 2009*(03), 03024. doi:10.1088/1742-5468/2009/03/P03024

Palla, G., Derenyi, I., Farkas, I., & Vicsek, T. (2005). Uncovering the overlapping community structure of complex networks in nature and society. *Nature, 435*(7043), 814–818. doi:10.1038/nature03607 PMID:15944704

Pons, P., & Latapy, M. (2005). Computing communities in large networks using random walks. *Computer and Information Sciences-ISCIS 2005*, 284-293.

Raghavan, U. N., Albert, R., & Kumara, S. (2007). Near linear time algorithm to detect community structures in large-scale networks. *Physical Review E: Statistical, Nonlinear, and Soft Matter Physics, 76*(3), 036106. doi:10.1103/PhysRevE.76.036106 PMID:17930305

Rao, S. C., & Krishna Prasad, M. (2015). A survey on community detection algorithms in large scale real world networks. In *Proceedings of 2nd international conference on computing for sustainable global development (IndiaCom 2015)* (pp 1323-1327). New Delhi: IEEE.

Reza, Z., Abbasi, M. A., & Liu, H. (2014). *Social Media Mining: An Introduction*. Cambridge University Press.

Rosvall, M., & Carl, T. B. (2008). Maps of random walks on complex networks reveal community structure. *Proceedings of the National Academy of Sciences of the United States of America, 105*(4), 1118–1123. doi:10.1073/pnas.0706851105 PMID:18216267

Seung-Hee, B., Daniel, H., Jevin, W., Rosvall, M., & Howe, B. (2013). Scalable Flow-Based Community Detection for Large-Scale Network Analysis. In *Proceedings of IEEE International Conference on Data Mining Workshops (ICDMW 2013)* (pp. 303-310). Dallas, TX: IEEE.

Xie, J., & Szymanski, B. K. (2012). Towards linear time overlapping community detection in social networks. In *Proceedings of PAKDD Conf.* (pp. 25-36) Kuala Lumpur, Malaysia: ACM doi:10.1007/978-3-642-30220-6_3

Xie, J., Szymanski, B. K., & Liu, X. (2011). SLPA: Uncovering Overlapping communities in Social Networks via A Speaker-listener Interaction Dynamic Process. In *Proceedings of 11th IEEE International Conference on Data Mining Workshops (ICDM)* (pp. 344-349). Vancouver, BC: IEEE. doi:10.1109/ICDMW.2011.154

Xie, J. R., Kelley, S., & Szymanski, B. K. (2013). Overlapping community detection in networks: The state of the art and comparative study. *ACM Computing Surveys*, *45*(4), 1–43. doi:10.1145/2501654.2501657

Yang, J., & Leskovec, J. (2013). Overlapping Community Detection at Scale: A Nonnegative Matrix Factorization Approach. In *Proceedings of WSDM*, (pp. 587-596). Rome, Italy: ACM. doi:10.1145/2433396.2433471

Chapter 13
Spreading Activation Connectivity Based Approach to Network Clustering

Alexander Troussov
The Russian Presidential Academy of National Economy and Public Administration, Russia

Sergey Vinogradov
The Russian Presidential Academy of National Economy and Public Administration, Russia

Sergey Maruev
The Russian Presidential Academy of National Economy and Public Administration, Russia

Mikhail Zhizhin
Colorado University of Boulder, USA

ABSTRACT

Techno-social systems generate data, which are rather different, than data, traditionally studied in social network analysis and other fields. In massive social networks agents simultaneously participate in several contexts, in different communities. Network models of many real data from techno-social systems reflect various dimensionalities and rationales of actor's actions and interactions. The data are inherently multidimensional, where "everything is deeply intertwingled". The multidimensional nature of Big Data and the emergence of typical network characteristics in Big Data, makes it reasonable to address the challenges of structure detection in network models, including a) development of novel methods for local overlapping clustering with outliers, b) with near linear performance, c) preferably combined with the computation of the structural importance of nodes. In this chapter the spreading connectivity based clustering method is introduced. The viability of the approach and its advantages are demonstrated on the data from the largest European social network VK.

DOI: 10.4018/978-1-5225-2814-2.ch013

1. PROLIFERATION OF TECHNO-SOCIAL SYSTEMS POSES NEW CHALLENGES TO THE STRUCTURAL ANALYSIS OF MASSIVE NETWORKS

The proliferation of techno-social systems has lead to the emergence of massive networks connecting people and various digital artifacts. These networks become more and more multidimensional. Network models of the data have nodes, representing actors, abstract concepts, projects etc. Abstract ideas become foci of interactions leading to the formation of communities of actors, where the same actor typically belongs to many communities simultaneously. This phenomenon requires certain considerations on the approaches to study the structure of such networks, including understanding of local topology – centralization, degree distribution, as well as mezzo- and macro-level structures, such as communities. In this paper the focus is on multidimensional networks, where the nodes represent actors and various artifacts they create and do; however the approach could be useful for other types of networks dimensionalities.

Clustering is one of the most frequently used method in Data Science-related applications; for example, in a recent poll among data scientists clustering is the second most used technique after regression, coming ahead of decision trees/rules, visualization, K-nearest neighbors, principal component analysis, statistics, and text mining (Kdnuggets, 2016).

The sheer volume of Big Data and multidimensionality of the data poses novel challenges for graph-mining. This chapter focuses on the tasks traditionally associated with mining of social networks, but one can expect that the same approach is applicable to analyze the structure of network models of data.

- Centralization, which is ranking the nodes according their structural prominence.
- Communities, such as on-line communities exhibiting some properties of communities of practice. Lave & Wenger (1998) define communities of practice as "groups of people who share a concern or a passion for something they do and learn how to do it better as they interact regularly." This learning that takes place is not necessarily intentional.

Two questions regarding clustering that need to be addressed by future research are:

- Centralization and community detection - how these tasks are related? If useful centralization is possible without community detection?
- Strict partitioning for detection of communities in massive social graphs with multidimensional links is not needed and might be not computationally feasible. Instead, local partitioning or local partitioning or local fuzzy overlapping clustering with outliers might be more appropriate.

Requirements for clustering could be summarized as follows:

- Local overlapping clustering, that is a node, could belong to several clusters. Overlapping, as contrasted with fuzzification, is an unavoidable consequence of multidimensionality. To explain why fuzzification is not an adequate approach for structural discovery in multidimensional networks, let us consider a simple example. Suppose that a person on a social network is classified as *a mathematician*. When the classification is based on fuzzification, new evidences that a person is interested, for instance, in *classical music* should decrease the value of her membership function in the group of mathematicians, while in reality there may be a positive correlation between two interests mentioned above.

- Community detection preferably should be combined with centralization (to discriminate between prominent actors in communities and connectors like brain hunters on LinkedIn);
- Scalability and near-linear performance are non functional, but critical requirements for Big Data systems engineering.

2. ON THE NATURE OF STRUCTURE, STRUCTURES IN DATA

In practice, probably, most of the approaches to the structure in data are based on the intuition from the physical world, and this intuition works well for data with low dimensionality. The algorithmic perspective of finding structures in data is described in (Stein & Nigemman, 1999) and (Mirkin, 2016).

Graph clustering is frequently used for *community detection*, however, the answer to the question *what is community in massive on-line social networks* is not yet known. Communities, such a tribe learning to survive or a group of engineers working on similar problems has been long studied in social sciences. Dozens of communities were introduced. However, transfer on the notion of communities to groups of on-line users is problematic.

- Virtual communities, in contrast with real world communities, don't have face-to-face meetings.
- Recent advances in digital technologies invite consideration of organizing as a process that is accomplished by global, flexible, adaptive, and ad hoc networks that can be created, maintained, dissolved, and reconstituted with remarkable alacrity. The structure and dynamic of virtual communities is different (see Nevidomsky & Troussov, 2010).

By "community", researchers usually mean empirically defined group of users. In many cases such groups do not form communities in any commonly accepted sense of the term. Sometimes, researchers and software developers assume that on-line communities and real-life communities have something in common. In one case (Fildes, 2010) a large company tested their social service on its own intranet. The test passed well, however soon after this service has been introduced to customers, the company was forced to abolish the improvement. The cause of this failure was that the test has been performed inside a single context (company's employees only), while in real life, people participate in multiple contexts (family, work, friends, etc) and play different roles in different contexts. Frequently, people work actively to keep these contexts separate both in real life and virtual communications.

Cliques as defined in graph theory are used to identify closely-knit sets of nodes, although this abstraction per se is too restrictive a notion for most of the tasks related to massive networks.

Social network analysis (SNA), which is the process of investigating social structures through the use of network and graph theories, developed two major approaches for structural analysis – centralization and clustering.

Recently, network science contributed greatly to the development of the notion of structure. Erdős–Rényi model for generating random graphs proved to be not applicable to real world problems. From the point of view of social relations, in these graphs there are no preferences in connections. The results of Stanley Milgram's small-world experiment showed that the average path length for social networks of people in the United States is relatively small to the size of the network. This small-world property was found later in many real life networks. Two major approaches to explain a relatively small diameter of massive real world networks we proposed: Barabási–Albert model (scale free networks) and Watts–

Strogatz model (small world properties). There are observations that in Big Data there is a tendency to the emergence of typical network characteristics. (Snijders et al., 2012).

Methods of structural analysis used in SNA were generalized by Borgatti and Everett through the use of the notion of the network flow. Spreading activation methods constitute generalization of the notion of the network flow. Advantages of such generalization for practical applications, and versatility of these methods were shown in (Maruev et al., 2015). For instance, this paper provides description of the use case, where injection of fuzzy logic into the computational scheme of spreading activation resulted in a significantly improved solution.

3. SPREADING ACTIVATION CONNECTIVITY BASED APPROACH

Mirkin (2016) describes the essence of the clustering as following: "Technically speaking, the idea behind clustering is rather simple, introduce a measure of similarity between entities under consideration and combine similar entities into the same clusters while keeping dissimilar entities in different clusters".

The focus of this chapter is on how to choose the measure of similarity between groups of nodes on networks and how to perform clustering to address the issues raised in (Mirkin, 2016): "First, too many similarity measures and clustering techniques have been invented with virtually no support for a non-specialist user in selecting among them. The trouble with this is that different similarity measures and/ or clustering techniques may, and frequently do, lead to different results. Moreover, the same technique may also lead to different clustering solutions depending on the choice of parameters such as the initial setting or the number of clusters specified. On the other hand, some common data types, such as questionnaires with both quantitative and categorical features, have been left virtually without any substantiated similarity measure. Second, use and interpretation of cluster structures may become an issue, especially when available data features are not straightforwardly related to the phenomenon under consideration. For instance, certain data on customers available at a bank, such as age and gender, typically are not very helpful in deciding whether to grant a customer a loan or not (beyond certain obvious limits).

In many heuristic clustering procedures, the similarity and dissimilarity is measured by number of links. In graph models, clusters have many edges within them, and as little as possible edges between them. In this chapter a measurement model where agglomeration steps take into account the cumulative strength of ties between objects is introduced. The measure is quantified using a generic iterative computational scheme of spreading activation.

3.1 Spreading Activation Methods

Spreading activation, originated in cognitive sciences and later used in various domains of information retrieval and artificial intelligent, in mathematical terms is an the operator on the space of functions on the nodes of the network $T:F(G) \rightarrow F(G)$

T – operator
G – graph model of the network
v – vertice on the graph
F(v) – real or vector function

In spreading activation, the operator is usually computed locally, that is

$$T: F(v) \to F_{img}(v)$$

the value of the function $F_{img}(v)$ depends only on the values of $F(v)$ in the vertice v and its neighbors. In this respect spreading activation computational scheme is *a finite-difference method on the network*, the direct extension of traditional finite difference methods used in the numerical simulation in physics and engineering.

Frequently, the operator T is applied many times, until the convergence to $F_{inf}(v)$ or could be stopped after several iterations.

The viability of this generalization for network mining has been demonstrated previously (Troussov et al., 2009). It has also been shown that popular graph clustering algorithms MajorClust (Stein, B. & Nigemman, O., 1999) and its fuzzified version in (Levner et al., 2007b) could be perceived as the spreading activation method.

The vectorised version of the spreading activation, as a platform for efficient execution of various versions of spreading activation, and applications of this version were introduced in (Troussov et al., 2009b). The method has been described in detail in (Troussov et al., 2011).

Maruev et al, 2015 demonstrated the advantages of the injection of fuzzy logic into the spreading activation iterative computational scheme for the purposes of computation of structural importance of nodes.

3.2 Spreading Activation Connectivity and Its Rationale

Although one can think that spreading activation connectivity could be useful for many applications of network clustering, the primary focus of this chapter is on the detection of community structures in massive multidimensional social networks (for instance, a social graph augmented with the links induced from metadata about users and topics of their posts). This approach could be perceived as generalization of traditional methods of social network analysis to the point where they become methods of complex networks study.

Network flow algorithms are at the heart of centralization methods in social network analysis (Wasserman & Faust, 1994; Hanneman & Riddle, 2005). According to recent observations by Borgatti and Everett (Borgatti, 2005; Everett & Borgatti, 2005; Borgatti & Everett, 2006), all the current approaches to structural importance of nodes in Social Network Analysis, are based on the idea that something is flowing between the nodes across the links. Authors of this chapter hold the view that in many tasks related to the mining of massive networks the structural prominence of nodes, as well as other parameters of local topology indeed could be explained and computed in terms of incoming, outcoming and passing through traffic; the authors also argue that the notions of traffic and network flow could be, and should be, replaced by more general notions of the abstract processes on the networks which happen in the absence of long-distance forces. In other words, the essence of Borgatti and Everett's observation might be useful for mining networks where interactions happen only between neighbors (or, more accurately, other interactions are simply not captured in the network model), where interactions are compared with contact forces in physics as opposed to long range forces (like electric forces); apparently, in some cases these interactions can be explained by "a flow" through the links, and in other cases such an explanation is not possible, not needed, and might be confusing.

Spreading activation connectivity is generalization of network flow algorithms, the advantages of such generalization are shown by Maruev et al, 2015.

Spreading activation connectivity C(A,B) between two sets of nodes A and B on a network could be defined as follows. The initial activation is assigned to nodes from the set A, the activation is propagated to all nodes from the set B, the total sum of the activation on nodes from the set B (possibly normalized to the aggregated activation on the set A). Spreading activation connectivity is based on flexible quantification of cumulative strength of connections between sets of nodes, rather than using shortest paths or particular formulas related to spectral methods (see, for instance, Pelillo & Torsello, 2006) not allowing infusion of fuzzy logic or ideas from cellular automata into the computational scheme.

This measure is not a metric in the mathematical sense since $C(A,B) \neq C(B,A)$. The applicability of such non-symmetric measure could be justified by two types of arguments:

1. Prof. A.A.Kirillov, a fellow of the American Mathematical Society, taught functional analysis at conference room on the 14th floor of the main building of Moscow State University. Speaking about *distance* and *metrics*, he usually warned his students "if someone thinks that the distance between the 1st floor and the 14th floor and the distance between the 14th floor and the 1st floor are the same, he should travel by foot these distances in both directions, upstairs and downstairs, and compare the results".

2. In semantic theory of information retrieval there are notions of "relevance relationship" and "degree of relevance" between texts. However it can be difficult to provide explanations of these notions. There is not a clear answer to the question of whether degree of relevance should have symmetric property (for instance, whether the relevance of a concept to a text is the same as the relevance of the text to the concept).

Clustering on network might require detection of outliers, spreading activation based connectivity is applicable for both tasks.

4. EXPERIMENTAL VALIDATION

The feasibility of spreading activation connectivity based clustering and its usability was validated on the task of clustering 46 million users of the largest European online social networking service VK, originally VKontakte (Panchenko, 2014; VK, 2016). After collecting the data using the official API VK and building the data model (46 million users, their profiles, posts, and 200 million connections), the interest's graph has been constructed. This model represents automatically computed interests of users. Each node in this graph is labeled by a cloud of keywords and represents "the interest", described by keywords. The links between nodes are constructed based both on similarity of interests and social links of users. Each node is provided with the list users who share this interest and are connected by chains of interest and social connections. Therefore the interests' graph, in addition to representing the relations between interests, provides overlapping clustering.

Clusters of users in this validation are the group of users connected by chains of social links and similarity of interests computed based on term frequencies in textual posts. Automatic data curation took 3 days, construction of the multidimensional model (similar interests' graph) – one day, clustering (that is interests' graph construction) – 4 days (on two high performance virtual servers).

The clustering introduced in this paper is based on the same idea as MajorClust algorithm, where on each iteration a node takes the label popular amongst its neighbors. The computational scheme in Major-Clust could be generalized as iterative computational scheme, which could be named "finite-difference method on networks", the same as employed in spreading activation (Troussov et al., 2009). The ideas behind various algorithms based on the same computational scheme might be very different, and computational scheme per se doesn't justify lumping all algorithms employing it into one group "spreading activation method", therefore we prefer to use the term "spreading activation methods".

The performance of the algorithm introduced in this paper is low degree polynomial; algorithm computed interpretable overlapping clustering in 4 days on two servers. The results are presented in several ways, including list of interests sorted by the number of users having this interests, the graph of connected interests, the overlapping clustering of users. All the operation used are "knowledge free", parameters of modelling and algorithm include selection of several thresholds, most notably, thresholds for term frequencies.

4.1 Crawling

Crawling has been done through the official API of the VK social network. The limitations and low performance of this API has been largely overcome by tools, which are outside of the scope of this paper. The collected data include:

- Profiles,
- Lists of friends,
- Text posts,
- Social links between users.

Crawling has been performed in the period 1st of the August 2016 till 2nd of October 2016 by 25 high performance virtual servers. Technical tools used in multilink flexible structure Web crawler, data collection and analytic module include GreenPlum Database (GPDB) from Pivotal, JSONB, HTTP REST/JSON web-service, Nginx, Python3, DigitalOcean, Python scripts and libraries numpy, scipy, graph-tool, sklearn, xgboost.

4.2 Data Curation

On this stage we selected out of 320 millions of profiles only those, which look like profiles of real people from Russian Federation who are active on VK, and whose interests could be detected based on their posts, not on what they claim as their interests, since most of the announced interests are not reliable or could not be interpreted. Examples of such claimed interests include profile of a young lady *"My interests are friends, brother and HIM!"*, and the interest *"It is good that I moved to St.Petersburg"*. We also discarded profiles where names and family names could not belong and could not be transformed to names and surnames or real people.

Since many users registered using non-canonical or deliberately alternated forms of their name, we applied a recurrent neural network to check if names and surnames could be normalized to the form, which could belong to real people. This task has been performed based on the linguistic dictionary, the data base of names and surnames of 4 millions real people, the data base of one thousand pairs of transformation: string to real name.

4.3 Interests' Graph Construction

The last ten textual posts of users were considered as corpora, term frequencies (tf–idf method from *sklearn* library) were used to compute similarity of users' interests. The nodes in the network represent users, links – connection between users.

Construction of Proximity Interests' Graph

A proximity interests' graph has been constructed based on the egocentric networks with radius two for each user. That is the set of similar interests were computed for user and his "friends", and for user and friend-of-friends.

Construction of Interests' Graph

Nodes on this graph represent interests, labeled by the cloud of terms. Each interest has the attribute – number of users who share this interest. The links between interests are induced by the social links between users.

4.4 Experimental Results

The largest European social network VK has 320 million profiles (the data are given at the period of crawling, which is end of summer 2016). After data curation, which includes:

- Only profiles of users from Russian Federation were taken;
- With not empty major fields (city, birth date);
- Active profiles with more than ten posts in 2016;
- With names and surnames which could belong to real people or could be easily transformed to a real name and surname (CNN neural network and the data base of real name-surnames of 4 million individuals and on thousand not-real, but where manual transformation into real one existed)

52 million profiles were obtained.

Most of the profiles have non-empty field "Interests". As one could expect, information in these fields can't be easily interpreted or taken for granted for the sociological or demographic applications. The content of the posts is a better predictor of user interests. Using unsupervised and knowledge free natural language processing of all posts 80 thousand most popular interests were computed, after manual inspection of the top interests we assigned labels to top interests, which include music, sport, cars, computers, psychology (we found that this discipline is popular on the Russian part of the Internet), sex, children. These manually created labels are shown on figures below for interpretation purposes.

The graph for data mining has been built, where the nodes are 46 million profiles where at least one of the 80 thousand precomputed interests has been detected. Each node has been assigned a link to other

Figure 1. The results of clustering showing 4 thousand interests and their connection. Each interest is represented by one or more nodes, the size of the node is proportional to the number of profiles falling into the category. For example, of two big nodes related to computers, don't have much connections, since one of them could be interpreted as computers in the context of engineering and science, and the other node is related to games in entertainment.

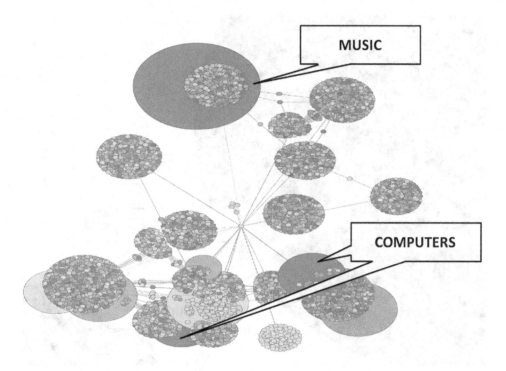

nodes based on the social connections in its egocentric network with radius two (which includes *friend* and *friends-of-friends*. A link has been assigned based on the existence of common interests.

A spreading activation connectivity based algorithm has been applied. For the interpretational purposes, the results of clustering are better to be viewed as the network of interests and the relation between interests; a profile could belong to unlimited number of "interests", importance of the interests could be quantified and assessed in the number of users which falls into the category, the strength of the connections between interests can be measured as the number of profiles which simultaneously fall into both categories.

Clustering has been performed for 80 thousand interests with 3 million connections between them. For explanatory purposes we show the figures for 4 thousand out of 80 thousand interests.

Although, as we noted before, the most populated interests are *music, computers, children*, etc., most of the user profiles falls simultaneously into several interest categories. The top ten most populated intersections of interests in decreasing of popularity order are *{recreation, outdoor activity, nature} {travel, children, internet}, {skiing, music, mountain skiing, foreign languages}, {vacations, people, outdoor activities}, {cars, snowboarding, business}, {computers, cars}, {soccer, vacations, cars}, {basketball, cars, business}, {cars, sport}, {psychology, arts}*. In top 50 one can find the following combinations in decreasing order: *{fishing, sport, music},{fishing, skiing, nature},{sex, internet, sport, business},{cars,*

Figure 2. A fragment from Figure 1 showing that each big group of interests, like music, has very granular and fragmented structure, which could be mined for sociological, demographic, advertisement ranking, and other applications to analyze each particular profile. At the same time, this combination of macro-, mezzo, and micro-level clustering, allows to what is common for most applications of Big Data – it is frequently easier to predict agent behavior than to explain it.

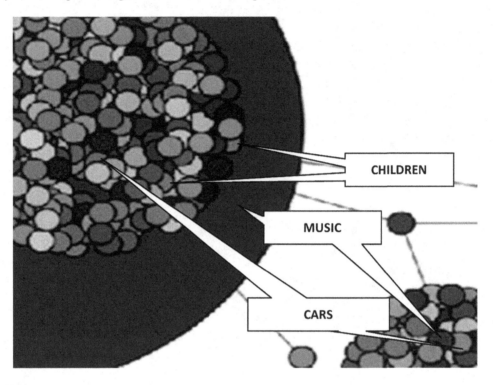

girls},{dancing, theater, fitness, sport, work},{computers, games, computer games},{billiards, cats}, {photography, travels, summer, life, music, family},{photography, cinema, architecture, photo, music, design}

5. CONCLUSION

A novel approach to clustering on network has been introduced. The viability of approach has been demonstrated by its application to obtain clustering structure of the largest European social network VK. Methods of data modeling and clustering described in this chapter were capable of automatically creating a network of overlapping clusters from mega level down to smallest clusters up to a certain threshold of term frequencies used to detect similarity of interests. Most of the user profiles fall simultaneously into one or several automatically detected interest's categories. Popular interest's categories, like *music, computers, children*, etc.; and more fine grained categories like *{travel, children, internet}, {skiing, music, mountain skiing, foreign languages}, {dancing, theater, fitness, sport, work},{computers, games, computer games},{billiards, cats}.*

Authors of the chapter agree that: *The general opinion among specialists is that clustering is a tool to be applied at the very beginning of investigation into the nature of a phenomenon under consideration, to view the data structure and then decide upon applying better suited methodologies.* (Mirkin, 2016). The results of the clustering are easy to visualize at any level of granularity, visualization provides support to specialists and non-specialists via labels, which are sets of automatically created keywords from users' posts.

ACKNOWLEDGMENT

We thank Barry Feeney of ITT Dublin and Robert John Freeman for comments that improved the manuscript.

REFERENCES

Anderson, J. (1983). A Spreading Activation Theory of Memory. *Journal of Verbal Learning and Verbal Behavior*, *22*(3), 261–295. doi:10.1016/S0022-5371(83)90201-3

Borgatti, S. (2005). Centrality and network flow. *Social Networks*, *27*(1), 55–71. doi:10.1016/j.socnet.2004.11.008

Borgatti, S., & Everett, M. (2006). A graph-theoretic perspective on centrality. *Social Networks*, *28*(4), 466–484. doi:10.1016/j.socnet.2005.11.005

Breunig, M., Kriegel, H., Ng, R., & Sander, J. Identifying Density-Based Local Outliers. *Proceedings of the 2000 ACM SIGMOD International Conference on Management of Data,* 93–104. doi:10.1145/342009.335388

Chen, C. H. (Ed.). (1996). *Fuzzy Logic and Neural Network Handbook*. McGraw-Hill, Inc.

Collins, A. M., & Loftus, E. F. (1975, November). A spreading-activation theory of semantic processing. *Psychological Review*, *82*(6), 407–428. doi:10.1037/0033-295X.82.6.407

Crestani, F. (1997). Application of Spreading Activation Techniques in Information Retrieval. *Artificial Intelligence Review*, *11*(6), 453–482. doi:10.1023/A:1006569829653

Daelemans, W., & Bosch, A. (2005). *Memory-Based Language Processing*. Cambridge University Press. doi:10.1017/CBO9780511486579

Everett, M. G., & Borgatti, S. P. (2005). Extending centrality. In P. J. Carrington, J. Scott, & S. Wasserman (Eds.), *Models and Methods in Social Network Analysis* (pp. 181–201). Cambridge University Press. doi:10.1017/CBO9780511811395.004

Fildes, J. (2010). *Google admits Buzz testing flaws*. BBC News.

Goldstein, M., & Uchida, S. (2016). A Comparative Evaluation of Unsupervised Anomaly Detection Algorithms for Multivariate Data. *PLoS ONE*, *11*(4). doi:10.1371/journal.pone.0152173 PMID:27093601

Hanneman, R. A., & Riddle, M. (2005). *Introduction to social network methods*. Riverside, CA: University of California, Riverside. Retrieved from http://faculty.ucr.edu/~hanneman/

Judge, J., Sogrin, M., & Troussov, A. (2007). Galaxy: IBM Ontological Network Miner. *Proceedings of the 1st Conference on Social Semantic Web (CSSW)*.

Kinsella, S., Harth, A., Troussov, A., Sogrin, M., Judge, J., Hayes, C., & Breslin, J. G. (2008). Navigating and Annotating Semantically-Enabled Networks of People and Associated Objects. In T. Friemel (Ed.), *Why Context Matters: Applications of Social Network Analysis* (pp. 79–96). VS Verlag. doi:10.1007/978-3-531-91184-7_5

Lave, J., & Wenger, E. (1998). *Communities of practice: Learning, meaning, and identity*. Academic Press.

Maruev, S., Stefanovsky, D., Frolov, A., Troussov, A., & Curry, J. (2014a). Deep Mining of Custom Declarations for Commercial Goods. *Procedia Economics and Finance, 12*, 397–402.

Maruev, S., Stefanovskyi, D., & Troussov, A. (2015). "Semantics of Techno-Social Spaces", in the. In J. Zizka & F. Darena (Eds.), *Modern Computational Models of Semantic Discovery in Natural Language*. IGI Global. doi:10.4018/978-1-4666-8690-8.ch008

Mirkin, B. (2016). Clustering: A Data Recovery Approach (2nd ed.). Chapman & Hall/CRC Computer Science & Data Analysis.

Morton, K. W., & Mayers, D. F. (2005). *Numerical Solution of Partial Differential Equations, An Introduction*. Cambridge University Press. doi:10.1017/CBO9780511812248

Nevidomsky, A., & Troussov, A. (2010). Structure and Dynamics of Enterprise 2.0 Communities. *Web Science Conference 2010 (WebSci10)*.

Panchenko, A. (2014). *Working with FB and VK Data*. Academic Press.

Pelillo, M., & Torsello, A. (2006). Payoffmonotonic game dynamics and the maximum clique problem. *Neural Computation, 18*(5), 1215–1258. doi:10.1162/neco.2006.18.5.1215 PMID:16595063

Rübenkönig, O. (2006). *The Finite Difference Method (FDM) - An introduction*. Albert Ludwigs University of Freiburg.

Snijders, C., Matzat, U., & Reips, U.-D. (2012). 'Big Data': Big gaps of knowledge in the field of Internet. *International Journal of Internet Science, 7*, 1–5.

Stein, B., & Nigemman, O. (1999). On the nature of structure and its identification. Lecture Notes in Computer Science, 1665, 122–134.

Troussov, A., Darena, F., Zizka, J., Parra, D., & Brusilovsky, P. (2011). Vectorised Spreading Activation Algorithm for Centrality Measurement. *Acta Universitatis Agriculturae et Silviculturae Mendelianae Brunensis, 59*(7), 469-476.

Troussov, A., Levner, E., Bogdan, C., Judge, J., & Botvich, D. (2009). Spreading Activation Methods. In A. Shawkat & Y. Xiang (Eds.), *Dynamic and Advanced Data Mining for Progressing Technological Development*. IGI Global.

Troussov, A., Parra, D., & Brusilovsky, P. (2009b). Spreading Activation Approach to Tag-aware Recommenders: Modelling Similarity on Multidimensional Networks. *Proceedings of Workshop on Recommender Systems and the Social Web at the 2009 ACM conference on Recommender systems, RecSys '09.*

VK. (2016). Retrieved from https://en.wikipedia.org/wiki/VK_(social_networking)

Wasserman, S., & Faust, K. (1994). Social Network Analysis: Methods and Applications. Cambridge, UK: Cambridge University Press.

Chapter 14
Scalable Method for Information Spread Control in Social Networks

Michal Wojtasiewicz
Polish Academy of Sciences, Poland

Mieczysław Kłopotek
Polish Academy of Sciences, Poland

ABSTRACT

In this chapter, scalable and parallelized method for cluster analysis based on random walks is presented. The aim of the algorithm introduced in this chapter is to detect dense sub graphs (clusters) and sparse sub graphs (bridges) which are responsible for information spreading among found clusters. The algorithm is sensitive to the uncertainty involved in assignment of vertices. It distinguishes groups of nodes that form sparse clusters. These groups are mostly located in places crucial for information spreading so one can control signal propagation between separated dense sub graphs by using algorithm provided in this work. Authors have also proposed new coefficient which measures quality of given clustering with respect to information spread control between clusters. Measures presented in this paper can be used for determining quality of whole partitioning or a single bridge.

1. INTRODUCTION

The most common way to grasp real world phenomena is to distinguish objects (elements, entities) and relations (interactions etc.) between them. From a global perspective the entities and their relations form networks. The distribution of relations is usually not uniform and hence some structures of elements and their relations may be distinguished. Mining such structures has the potential of discovering new knowledge about the network or its parts or even members. One of the basic ways of network mining is splitting of the network or rather its representation as a graph, into clusters. Clusters are groups of nodes which are interconnected in a way distinguishing them from the surrounding network. These groups or subsets of nodes are usually characterized by a denser set of relations. Such subsets (clusters) can be

DOI: 10.4018/978-1-5225-2814-2.ch014

interpreted in various ways. This creates a necessity for algorithms that can cope with diversity of possible meanings. Commonness of networks in everyday life (e.g. the Internet, data sets of citings) implies using advanced methods to analyze them. The most common and natural coding method for networks are graphs. Graph structure and the way of information spread in networks are the most interesting fields of research in social network community detection. In this paper scalable method of cluster analysis based on random walks is presented. The method divides a graph into subsets, where some of them can be used for information spread control. The main aim of the algorithm presented in this paper is to detect dense subgraphs which can be interpreted as tight communities and to detect relatively sparse subgraphs interconnecting them called *bridges*, as they are deemed to bridge information spread between the tight communities. The method provides clustering sensitive to vertices assignment uncertainty. As a result of introduced Parallelized Locally Aggregated Random Walks (ParaLARW) algorithm one receives division which distinguishes sparse groups of nodes responsible for signal transfer between clusters.

2. RELATED WORK

So far many algorithms for detecting communities in networks have been developed. Among most popular and most frequent used techniques one has to distinguish four categories: *bisection methods*, *hierarchical methods*, *combinatorical methods* and *spectral methods* [Fortunato, 2010]. Because of the diversity of cluster analysis problems, each of the areas is used in different situations. Choice of a method of identifying clusters should be made so that the available knowledge about the data could be used the most effectively. In practical tasks one mostly deals with very large graphs, which frequently consist of hundreds of thousands nodes and millions of edges. In such situations there is a limited number of methods which provide a solution in a reasonable time. This is because of complexity problems and difficulty of finding dense sets in large networks. An initial analysis, e.g. estimation of expected number of dense sets, is hard to perform as well. These are the reasons why hierarchic methods are mostly preferred in such situations. The most efficient algorithms operate on smaller sets and then aggregate results with a determined stop condition [Blondel et al., 2008][Pons and Latapy, 2005][Clauset et al., 2004]. In this paper authors introduced a parallelized version of hierarchic, scalable algorithm of cluster analysis which was firstly proposed in [Wojtasiewicz and Ciesielski, 2014]. This algorithm returns a very special partition. Among standard clusters one can distinguish subgraphs which are sparse and cannot be clearly assigned to any dense clusters. These special subgraphs enable control of signal propagation between clusters. Such a situation is connected to a feature of the MCL algorithm and it was fully discussed in section 2.1. Many of articles speaking about modeling or controlling the information spread in networks focus on greedy selection of vertices that have the highest influence in graph [Kempe et al., 2005]. The main problem with such an approach is that user starts with one the most influential vertex and then searches for the most influential node in given neighborhood. It can be easily seen that this kind of thinking produces very local results. Additionally it is very probable that first most influential vertex is deep in cluster. Finding few most influential nodes in social networks in that way does not solve problem of signal propagation between clusters. The author of [Doerr et al., 2012] noticed that vertices of high degree gather more information in their neighborhood, while vertices of lower degree quickly transfer information inside the graph. Similar behavior occurs in clusters obtained via MCL algorithm, as we point at in 2.1. It was noticed, that in dense subsets information is transferred relatively fast. It happens because such subsets have many internal edges and a few on the outside. That creates the problem of communication between the clusters, which should be solved by initiating signal transfer on the boundaries of the clusters. This is what ParaLARW does. An interesting approach for identifying influential vertices was presented in [Aggarwal et al., 2014]. Authorsanalyzed dynamic social networks and they developed algorithm which assigns *dynamic influential value*. This coefficient is based on a probability of spreading influence through time. It is calculated in a greedy way so there is again problem with local optimum. Because it takes into account information from future states of a network it is useless in static analysis. In work [Ju et al., 2013] authors introduced approach in which there can be more than one type of influence. Every node can have an *opinion* which is continuous function of time. Despite that interesting approach authors assume that influence of node is given by its degree. This assumption is too strong. It is easy to imagine that vertex can have small degree but signal started in this vertex will propagate very fast. This will happen in situation when such a node is connected to several dense clusters. In every work mentioned above vertices were considered separately. Algorithm introduced in this paper provides division in a graph where some groups of vertices can be used for signal diffusion control.

2.1 MCL Feature

During work on the scalable modification of Markov Clustering Algorithm (MCL) a very interesting feature was revealed. The figure 1 shows behavior of the algorithm in a situation of three vertices.

In the figure 1 result of the standard MCL algorithm can be seen. Despite that there is no distinction between these three nodes, the method has found two clusters. It happened because probability mass ran out very fast from vertex *3* to other vertices. It should be noticed that there are several edges between vertex *3* and vertices *1* and *2*. This is why the MCL method decided to mark vertex *3* as a different subgraph in a sense of probability mass distribution. Role of a node *3* is to transfer random walker between

Figure 1. MCL feature. Nodes 1 and 2 were pushed into one cluster and node 3 into a second one.

Feature of MCL Based on Random Walks

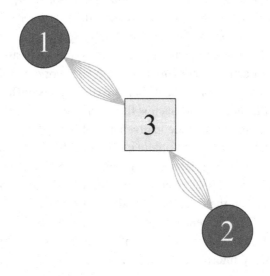

vertices *1* and *2*. It is not hard to imagine that nodes from figure 1 can be groups of vertices. If one of the groups hidden underneath vertex *3* forms a sparse cluster and its neighboring clusters are dense then vertex *3* is a bridge candidate according to the definition 3. from section 3. As can be seen in section 5.1 bridges play important role in information spread through networks. If one wants to reach as many units as possible in shortest possible time then it is not recommended to start in a node located deep in a dense cluster. In a such situation signal will need a lot of time to travel between different clusters. The best way is to identify bridges (if they exist) and initiate signal in one or some of them. On the other hand removing bridges adjacent to a considered cluster will make leaving that cluster more difficult. One can control signal propagation over a graph by simply opening and closing information flow through bridges.

2.2 Random Walks in MCL Algorithm

Markov Clustering Algorithm relies on performing sequences of one-step random walks. To fully understand how MCL works one needs to get familiar with several definitions.

Definition 1

Markov chain is a stochastic process that satisfies *Markov property*.

Definition 2

Markov property for discrete-time markov chain is defined as follows:

$$P(X_{n+1} = y \mid X_0 = x_0, X_1 = x_1, ..., X_n = x_n) = P(X_{n+1} = y \mid X_n = x_n)$$

where $\mathbf{X} = (X_0, X_1, ..., X_n)$ is Markov chain and $(x_0, x_1, ..., x_n, y)$ is a sequence of states. It is also called memorylessness property.

As can be seen in definition 2. future values of states in discrete-time Markov chain depend only on current values. It means that using such an approach one does not have to consider the whole past of simulated stochastic process. That property makes random walks an interesting tool for large and very large graphs exploration. MCL is strongly based on that property. It repeatedly calculates transition probabilities of one-step random walk. After each step all probabilities are raised to the power of inflation parameter. That trick implies larger difference between small and big probabilities. It allows random walker to distinguish regions characterized by large transition probabilities. MCL should be recognized as a sequence of very short random walks of different Markov chains. Every chain starts with joint probability distribution obtained by exponentiation of transition probabilities from a previous chain. In other words MCL is a chain of Markov chains. In work [van Dongen, 2000] author explained why he used the inflation trick. He realized that a simple chain cannot provide a final partition because probability mass is spread along the whole graph without significantly concentrated regions. Usage of inflation between particular steps of random walk results with better distinction of regions where probability mass can form a cluster. Interesting modification of original MCL is to perform more steps in each Markov chain. In such an approach a chain from a single stage of MCL will have larger impact and probably will result with more accurate clustering. However, the modification could also result with slower convergence what can be crucial in on-line clustering. That direction will be a part of future work.

Another interesting idea is to adjust value of inflation with respect to current probability distribution. In situations where joint distribution is similar to uniform an inflation parameter should be different than in case of distributions consisting of several highly probable regions. Large value of inflation can result with unnatural or useless division into very small or even single node clusters. On the other hand small value could not assure any division at all or it might require

a long time for convergence. Additionally it is not clear how such a parameter should be set. Information about base statistics of transition probability distributions can improve adjustment of inflation parameter and this research direction also will be part of future work.

3. PARALARW ALGORITHM

Popular way of dealing with a complex problem is to divide it into smaller parts. The point of this process is to minimize the complexity without losing key data. One has to find optimal trade-off between global and local approach. The algorithm presented in this paper is an answer to a problem of scalability of MCL method [van Dongen, 2000]. That algorithm relies on simulating random walks on a network. The MCL procedure comes down to multiplication of stochastic matrices. There are several computational problems related. The most significant is the multiplication of very large matrices. Because of that one has to have a huge amount of operation memory and computational power. At the beginning of the process stochastic matrix is sparse but it becomes dense quickly, after several steps. As the matrix gets more and more dense the operation memory starts to become insufficient. It regards even small graphs. The solution suggested in this paper is based on execution computations on specific subsets of graph. Dense subsets are separated using the MCL algorithm locally and then the aggregation step is performed. This is a hierarchic method which results with multilevel clustering. Such a division has an important advantage. Among selected clusters there are subgraphs which are not dense in a sense of a number of internal edges. Authors have named these sparse subgraphs *bridges candidates* which were defined in section 4.

3.1 Scheme

In this section authors recall a scheme of the LARW algorithm proposed in [Wojtasiewicz and Ciesielski, 2014]. The scheme consists of three main steps which are discussed briefly below and can be seen in figure 2.

1. Find spanning tree T(G) of a given graph G. Now find vertex v which fulfills condition:

$$V(T(G))_{min} = \operatorname*{argmin}_{u \in V(T(G))}(\deg(u)) \tag{1}$$

Figure 2. Flowchart of LARW algorithm

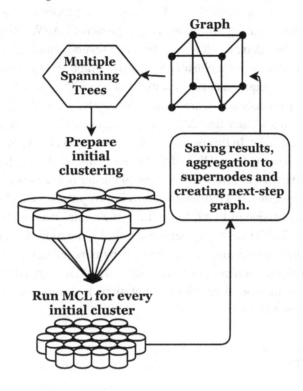

$$v = \underset{w \in G}{\mathrm{argmax}}(\deg(w) : w \in V(T(G))_{\min}) \tag{2}$$

where V (T(G)) is set of all vertices in graph G and deg(v) is a degree of vertex *v*. Next, cut out neighborhood of rank *r* of found vertex *v*. Save the rest of a graph as G0. Repeat this step for all next G0 until reaching situation when all nodes are assigned to some neighborhood. This first clustering will be called *initial clustering*.

2. Apply the MCL method for every cluster in initial clustering. Save received results.
3. Aggregate every cluster from second step to one *supernode*. Create a new graph from supernodes and assign transition probabilities between them as a sum of probabilities between vertices from considered clusters. The whole procedure has to be repeated until graph becomes a separated set of supernodes. The ranks of neighborhoods are chosen arbitrary once for all runs of the algorithm. In future authors will investigate procedure with adaptive choice of neighborhoods orders.

The first step of the scheme above contains an important rule for choosing vertices. This rule should cause a situation where vertices chosen firstly are located near borders of clusters. Neighborhood of that vertex probably consists of vertices from different clusters.

The MCL algorithm should find out that a certain initial cluster has to be divided according to borders of actual dense subsets. Aggregation of clustering which results in grouping vertices into a supernode is a typical technique of hierarchic algorithms. As one can see proposed algorithm returns multilevel clustering with more and more coarse partitioning. After one run of LARW [Wojtasiewicz and Ciesielski, 2014] one can choose the most adequate clustering between several obtained. The main idea of the algorithm is to recognize the location of true clusters border in a graph and then divide initial clusters along them. Local approach satisfies requirement of scalability of algorithm for large datasets. Hierarchic way ensures that vertices near to a border which are from different clusters will be still separated. The LARW performs tens or hundreds times faster than MCL [van Dongen, 2000] for large sets and that advantage becomes higher with larger graphs. In this paper the parallel version of LARW was introduced. Because of structure of the algorithm second step (*Run MCL for every initial cluster*) from figure 2 can be easily done in parallel manner. Every run of MCL on any initial cluster is independent from the others so they can be performed by different thread. Firstly introduced in [Wojtasiewicz and Ciesielski, 2014] LARW algorithm is a single thread version of ParaLARW. Table 1 contains running times in seconds for every part of LARW and ParaLARW. Times were measured only for the most demanding first stage of algorithms. It means before any aggregation. As can be seen by parallelization of LARW one can achieve even 30% profit of a running time. Of course such method should be applied only to large graphs where time needed for proper initialization of parallel computations is significantly smaller than time needed for multiplying stochastic matrices.

4. BRIDGES QUALITY

In this section the new clustering quality coefficient is presented. Until now many different coefficients were developed and considered [da F. Costa et al., 2007]. A significant number of them is concentrated on measuring how density of clusters.

The most frequently used is so called *modularity* [Newman, 2006]. Value of modularity measures how far is a certain cluster from a random graph. In this paper authors proposed a new coefficient which was developed to measure quality of found bridges. It is clear that some bridges will be more important in a sense of information spread in network. Proper measurement of bridges quality will allow to choose a clustering which is the best for information diffusion control. Well defined coefficient should take

Table 1. Table of running times.

Graphs	Initial clustering	Single thread MCL	Triple thread MCL	Aggregation
Snapshot	507.75	1006.25	694.6	359.82
Gnutella	270.46	30.32	22.64	129.95
HepPh	71.52	23.76	16.81	31.19
HepTh	51.81	20.87	14.62	22.37
Coautorship	36.21	15.92	13.46	3.03
Polblog	0.12	8.97	9.85	0.2
Football	0	0.28	0.58	0.01
Lesmis	0	0.2	0.52	0
Dolphins	0	0.2	0.55	0.2
Zachary	0.02	0.21	0.53	0.02

into account three important factors: a probability that signal will travel between two clusters through given bridge (P_{bridge}), density of neighboring clusters (ds) and fraction of bridge vertices which directly participate in signal transfer (F_{bridge}). Together with introduction of a new coefficient, the definition of a bridge is needed. Intuitively bridges are subgraphs which have fewer internal edges than external ones. Additionally they have at least two neighboring clusters and at least two of those clusters are dense. Of course bridges should connect dense clusters stronger than edges that connect them directly. Formally, they are specified by Definition 3 as follows.

Definition 3

Among clusters one can distinguish two categories:

1. Dense cluster with $ds_C > 0.5$ where ds of cluster C is defined as a number of edges within cluster divided by half of sum of degrees in the cluster.
2. The remaining ones which may be called sparse ones.

Among the sparse clusters one can distinguish bridge candidates that is ones with two or more neighboring dense clusters. For the bridge candidates statistics P_{bridge}, F_{bridge} and ds_{bridge} were defined as follows:

$$P_{bridge} = \frac{E_{bridge}(C_1, C_2, \ldots, C_k)}{E_{inter}(C_1, C_2, \ldots, C_k) + E_{bridge}(C_1, C_2, \ldots, C_k)} \tag{3}$$

$$F_{bridge} = \frac{V(bridge) - V(bridge)_{iso}}{V(bridge)} \tag{4}$$

$$ds_{C_j} = \frac{2E(C_j)}{\sum_{v \in V(C_j)} \deg(v)} \tag{5}$$

$$ds_{bridge} = \frac{1}{k} \sum_{i=1}^{k} ds_{C_i} \tag{6}$$

where $E_{inter}(C_1, C_2, \ldots, C_k)$ is a number of edges which directly connect dense clusters $C_1, C_2, \ldots, C_k$ (these clusters are all the dense neighbors of the bridge candidates), $E_{bridge}(C_1, C_2, \ldots, C_k)$ is a number of edges which connect bridge to its neighboring dense clusters, $V(bridge)_{iso}$ is number of bridge candidate vertices which are not directly connected to dense clusters, $V(bridge)$ is a number of all vertices which form given bridge candidate and deg is a degree of a given vertex.

Bridge candidate for which $P_{bridge} > 0.5$ will be called bridge. All bridges considered in further part of this paper follow definition 3. The measure of bridge quality, InfoSpred$_{bridge}$, will be introduced.

$$InfoSpread_{bridge} = 3 \frac{P_{bridge} \cdot ds_{bridge} \cdot F_{bridge}}{P_{bridge} + ds_{bridge} + F_{bridge}} \tag{7}$$

Intuitively, a dense cluster is one that would capture a random walker within it for a large number of steps. They may be viewed as tight communities. A bridge would participate in the transfer of a random walker between two dense clusters on the rare occasions when he leaves a dense cluster. P_{bridge} shows how often random walker will travel through bridge if such transfer occurs. F_{bridge} tells about importance of internal nodes of bridge candidate for such a transfer. ds_{bridge} expresses how difficult it is for random walker to escape the dense clusters that bridge candidate connects. These three quantities characterize different aspects of being a connection between communities. All three measures range from 0 to 1. As a consequence, also InfoSpread$_{bridge}$ lies in the same range. To compare two different clusterings one can use sum of InfoSpread values over all bridges. Such measure was shown in table 4. In future work authors will use values of InfoSpread not only to determine which bridge candidates are proper bridges but also to aggregate them. Such a procedure results in a smaller number of bridges but they have a more important role in information transfer. The rest of bridge candidates will be joined to dense clusters in order to maximize the value of modularity.

5. RESULTS

5.1 Clustering Quality

In this section we compare the proposed ParaLARW algorithm with three methods: Louvain algorithm [Blondel et al., 2008], Walktrap [Pons and Latapy, 2005] and FastGreedy algorithm [Clauset et al., 2004]. These three methods maximize modularity coefficient [Newman, 2006]. Louvain method is a hierarchic, greedy algorithm. It aggregates neighboring vertices in order to maximize modularity. Walktrap works similarly to Louvain but distances between vertices are calculated using short random walks. Walktrap uses gain of modularity as a stop condition of aggregation step. The FastGreedy method is very similar to Louvain algorithm. The main difference is that Louvain is a multi-level (hierarchic) clustering method. Because of that FastGreedy results with slightly different partitioning. However, authors noticed that running time needed to receive results with the FastGreedy method is significantly smaller and this is because of tricky use of special data structures and clever algorithm implementation. Because ParaLARW results in multilevel clustering, a partition which corresponds to the highest value of modularity was chosen. For evaluation authors used datasets listed in table 2 and one can see there a number of vertices ($V(G)$) and edges ($E(G)$) of chosen graphs. All of datasets can be found on [Newman, 2012] or [University, 2012]. In table 4 authors presented four values: modularity [Newman, 2006], assortativity [da F. Costa et al., 2007], number of found bridges and values of sum of InfoSpread Coefficient introduced in section 4. These are important statistics to measure quality of resulted clusterings. Authors have investigated four values of rank r which determines neighborhoods: 1, 2, 3, 4 and four values of inflation as well. These values are 1, 1.25, 1.5, 2. Previous analysis showed that setting larger values of inflation

Table 2. Table of graphs descriptions.

Graphs	#V(G)	#E(G)
Slashdot	82144	500481
Gnutella	62586	147892
HepPh	34546	420877
HepTh	27769	352285
Coauthorship	16264	47594
Polblog	1490	16726
Football	115	615
Lesmis	77	254
Dolphins	62	159
Zachary	34	75

returns very fine clustering. In table 4 one can see statistics of clustering which is characterized with the highest value of modularity.

As can be seen in table 4 for almost every graph, values of modularity and assortativity are lower in case of ParaLARW algorithm. Other three algorithms are aimed at modularity maximization so it is hard to compete in that field. However, after analysis of the last two columns (number of found bridges and value of InfoSpread) of table 4 one will see that ParaLARW almost always outperforms other algorithms. It is worth to mention that authors have chosen ParaLARW clustering with highest value of modularity. Probably there can be found a partitioning with lower modularity but higher value of the InfoSpread Coefficient. Interesting thing is that Louvain and FastGreedy algorithm did not find almost any bridges at all. It is because they are greedy algorithms strictly aimed to modularity maximization. Second interesting observation is that if ParaLARW did not find a bridge no other algorithm did. It is quite clear that for small graphs it is very difficult to distinguish any vertices which lie between subgraphs and transfer random walker between dense clusters. Only one algorithm is really devoted to detect bridges and it is Walktrap. This method is based on random walks as well but it is aimed to maximization of modularity rather than InfoSpread. However, Walktrap finds more bridges in case of HepTh network. It is related to the fact that Walktrap has tendency to result in clustering generated by neighborhoods of hubs – vertices of a very high degree. After analysis of structure of networks HepTh and HepPh authors realized that these two cicition networks have very skew degree distribution. It means that there are a few hubs and the rest are vertices with relatively small degree. In such a situation the Walktrap distinguishes large subgraphs with many internal edges generated by hubs and at the same time cuts off vertices which are between neighborhoods of these hubs. There is a significant difference between ParaLARW and Walktrap in ways of finding bridges. It is because Walktrap uses short random walks only to calculate distances between pairs of nodes while ParaLARW simulates random walk to determine approximated transfer probability distribution. As was shown in section 2.1 the MCL algorithm is able to distinguish groups of vertices which are responsible for information transfer between dense clusters. In future authors will investigate different ways of determining initial clustering which has important role in applying MCL locally. The proposed method clearly finds proper bridges which is shown more precisely in section 5.2.

5.2 Signal Initialization

Possible way of analyzing bridges influence is to simulate how fast signal discovers a graph when it was started in a bridge against signal initialization inside a cluster. To do such simulation Markov Chain was involved again. For every bridge authors did the same procedure:

1. Identify bridge and cut out subgraph induced by vertices from considered bridge and adjacent clusters. Call that subgraph G_{sub}. Set of neighboringclusters does not contain other bridges.
2. Simulate signal propagation by multiplying stochastic matrices (related to G_{sub}) 1, 2, ..., d times where d is diameter of G_{sub}. For every cluster and bridge in G_{sub}, in every step calculate how much information was spread outsidethem in certain number of steps.

The simulation performed in step 2. was done by calculating fraction of positivetransition probabilities from given cluster to the rest of analyzed subgraph G_{sub}.Fractions were calculated for every step of a random walker. Now it is enough to compare fractions of positive probabilities derived from bridge and the ones derived from its neighboring clusters. To receive proper value for whole graph authors calculated two average fractions of positive probabilities, over all found bridges and over all neighboring dense clusters, for every step of random walker. Every bridge has its G_{sub} with neighboring dense clusters. Then for every step of random walker average differences of the fractions were calculated. Of course number of steps as well as the diameter can be different in different G_{sub}. Therefore calculated difference is a measure of an average coverage difference calculated for every step of random walker, for different signal initializations spots. Figure 3 shows results of ParaLARW bridges impact. Simulations were provided for datasets where at least one ParaLARW bridge was found. Figure 3 presents a potential of signal diffusion by using ParaLARW bridges for three datasets. It proves that initialization of a signal in a bridge leads to higher coverage of a network than initialization in any other neighboring dense cluster. All coverage differences are non-negative which means that signal started in a bridge explores graph faster. However, two of these graphs are only for academic research and are not interesting in a sense of practical usage. Interesting fact is that random walker has to perform more steps to achieve highest coverage difference in case of larger graph. It is due to size of clusters which build analyzed graph. If clusters are larger then signal started inside one of them will visit more nodes in first several steps.

Intuitively signal will propagate fast inside dense subgraphs. As can be seen in figures 4 and 8 random walker travels faster when the value of InfoSpread Coefficient is significantly higher.

It means that proposed coefficient truly measures quality of a clustering with respect to its potential of information spreading. Clearly, with higher value of the InfoSpread for ParaLARW partitioning, faster exploration in several initial steps of networks Coauthorship and Slashdot is achieved. Such a behavior is preserved also for HepTh but with advantage for Walktrap (figure 5). In the case of HepPh (figure 6) the values of InfoSpread are very similar for Walktrap and ParaLARW but Walktrap bridges seem to be located more properly. It can be related to the fact that Walktrap results with larger clusters and it is very difficult to transfer random walker between dense clusters. Additionally Walktrap clustering has higher value of the modularity. An important conclusion appears. The ParaLARW does not work very well for citation networks. In near future it will be improved in this direction. The best performance of ParaLARW can be seen in figure 7. The difference between proposed method and Walktrap is huge. It is worth mentioning that both sum of InfoSpread and modularity are higher in case of ParaLARW. There is no need to provide comparison with Louvain or FastGreedy algorithms because these methods hardly

Table 3. Table of clustering results.

Graphs	Algorithm	Modularity	Assortativity	Found bridges	InfoSpread
Slashdot	Louvain	0.335	0.449	1	0.364
	ParaLARW	0.157	0.163	534	102.31
	Walktrap	0.186	0.265	123	66.03
	FastGreedy	0.319	0.469	1	0.327
Gnutella	Louvain	0.5	0.53	0	0
	ParaLARW	0.407	0.408	1501	556.953
	Walktrap	0.356	0.494	199	75.967
	FastGreedy	0.505	0.562	0	0
HepPh	Louvain	0.723	0.803	0	0
	ParaLARW	0.372	0.399	53	27.1
	Walktrap	0.681	0.775	41	26.036
	FastGreedy	0.526	0.857	0	0
HepTh	Louvain	0.657	0.723	0	0
	ParaLARW	0.328	0.38	71	39.55
	Walktrap	0.566	0.613	276	160.622
	FastGreedy	0.506	0.76	0	0
Coauthorship	Louvain	0.84	0.866	0	0
	ParaLARW	0.666	0.674	140	83.2
	Walktrap	0.742	0.78	20	10.128
	FastGreedy	0.78	0.873	0	0
Polblog	Louvain	0.427	0.843	0	0
	ParaLARW	0.412	0.828	0	0
	Walktrap	0.426	0.851	0	0
	FastGreedy	0.427	0.847	0	0
Football	Louvain	0.605	0.674	0	0
	ParaLARW	0.601	0.66	0	0
	Walktrap	0.603	0.671	0	0
	FastGreedy	0.55	0.671	0	0
Lesmis	Louvain	0.556	0.702	0	0
	ParaLARW	0.528	0.66	0	0
	Walktrap	0.521	0.714	0	0
	FastGreedy	0.5	0.652	0	0
Dolphins	Louvain	0.519	0.679	0	0
	ParaLARW	0.455	0.538	1	0.411
	Walktrap	0.489	0.735	0	0
	FastGreedy	0.496	0.621	0	0
Zachary	Louvain	0.415	0.6	0	0
	ParaLARW	0.401	0.56	1	0.595
	Walktrap	0.346	0.545	0	0
	FastGreedy	0.387	0.621	0	0

Figure 3. Signal Initialization with ParaLARW

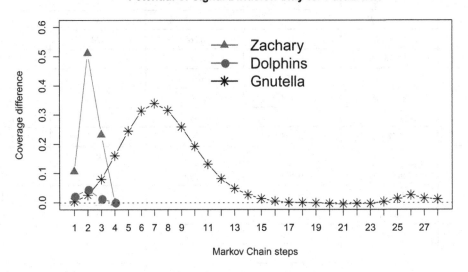

Figure 4. Signal Initialization in Coauthorship network with ParaLARW and Walktrap

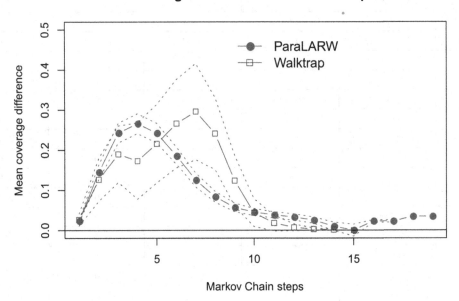

Figure 5. Signal Initialization in HepTh network with ParaLARW and Walktrap

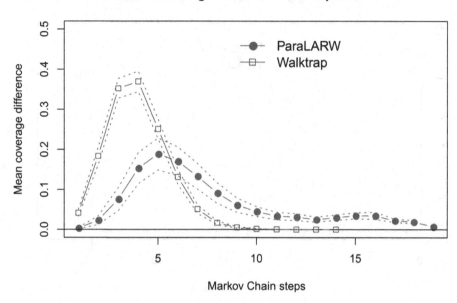

Figure 6. Signal Initialization in HepPh network with ParaLARW and Walktrap

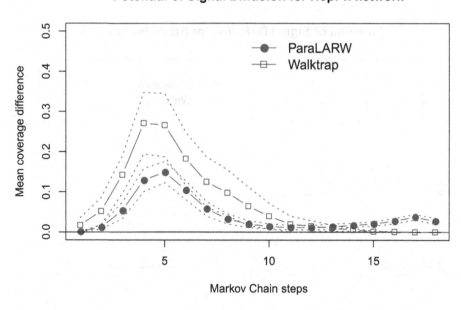

Figure 7. Signal Initialization in Gnutella network with ParaLARW and Walktrap

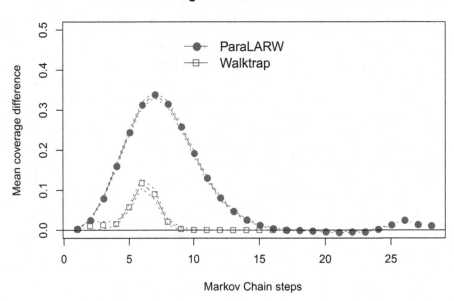

Figure 8. Signal Initialization in Slashdot network with ParaLARW and Walktrap

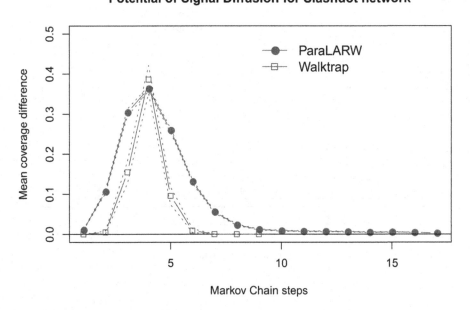

found any bridges and their values of InfoSpread are significantly smaller. Detailed analysis shows that sum of InfoSpread is related to dynamics of signal propagation in first steps while value of modularity determines maximal coverage differences. It is intuitive. If value of sum of InfoSpread is high there are a lot of good bridges which means that signal started in one of them will propagate quickly. In the same time value of modularity shows how well separated are dense clusters. In case of high value of modularity it is very hard for random walk to get out of dense cluster. That is why higher value of modularity implies higher maximal coverage difference. These two statistics should be considered jointly while analyzing bridges potential of information dispersion. Both algorithms resulted with statistically significant difference in coverage but for almost every set confidence intervals are wider for Walktrap. Authors provided estimation quality with significance level equal 5%. Less acurate estimation for graphs HepPh and Coauthorship implies that there is hardly a difference between coverages achieved by ParaLARW and Walktrap, even if Walktrap results with higher mean. The rest of sets are characterized by good estimation with narrow confidence intervals.

5.3 Bridges Characteristics

In this section authors described basic statistics of ParaLARW bridges for the most interesting graphs. Relationship between size of a bridge and InfoSpread Coeffient was analyzed as well. Firstly it is important to check what percentage of bridge candidates is in fact true, useful bridges.

As can be seen in table 4 only citation graphs have percentage of true bridges below 50%. The best result can be seen in row with Gnutella set what is very consistent with signal propagation from figure 7. Next interesting question is whether size of a bridge is correlated with value of InfoSpread Coefficient. Authors investigated occurrence of such a dependency by constructing simple linear model and analyzing significance of coefficient of explanatory variable which is InfoSpread. In figure 9 one can see the relation between InfoSpread Coefficient and size of a bridge. As can be seen in figure 9 InfoSpread Coefficient favors smaller bridges in case of Coauthorship set. Detailed statistics for all sets were placed in table 5.

Table 5. shows what can be seen in figure 9. Higher values of InfoSpread Coefficient correspond to smaller sizes of bridges. One can see that when taking 5% of significance level citations networks do not have this property. Figures 10a and 10b show relation in case of graphs HepTh and HepPh respectively. An interesting observation is that structures of bridges in both cases are totally different. In case of HepTh all bridges are small except one. This single bridge on the other hand is very big. In second case sizes of bridges are very different and do not concentrate on small or high values of InfoSpread Coefficient. Such a correlation between bridge size and InfoSpread can be induced by fact that InfoSpread consists partially of information how many nodes of given bridge directly take part in signal transfer. In smaller

Table 4. Table of fraction of true bridges

Graph	Bridge candidates	Bridges	Percent
Coauthorship	252	140	55.56%
HepTh	815	71	8.712%
HepPh	944	53	5.61%
Gnutella	1501	1501	100%
Slashdot	743	534	71.87%

Table 5. Table of coefficients of linear models

Graph	Coefficient	p-value
Coauthorship	-5.439	0.00462
HepTh	-302.3	0.0913
HepPh	-5.317	0.186
Gnutella	-66.73	0
Slashdot	-48.596	0

bridges larger fraction of vertices will take part in signal propagation. That is why authors investigated correlation between size of a bridge and every component of InfoSpread Coefficient. For this purpose authors built one linear model for each set but this time every model has three explanatory variables. Each variable is a part of InfoSpread. Such a model will show which part is the most significant in sense of explaining size of a bridge.

Tables 6 and 7 show very interesting results. Only in case of Coauthorship network part of InfoSpread which corresponds to fraction of nodes is significant with the 5% level of significance. The second very

Figure 9. Dependency between InfoSpread and size of a bridge for Coauthorship network

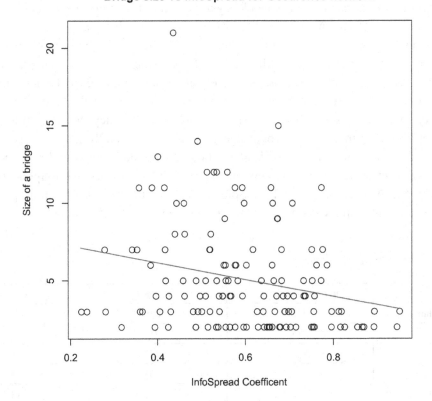

Table 6. Table of detailed coefficients of linear models, part 1.

	Graphs					
	Coauthorship		HepTh		HepPh	
	Coefficent	p-value	Coefficent	p-value	Coefficent	p-value
Probability	-4.175	0.03	-142	0.317	-2.974	0.33
Density	4.714	0.227	-706.9	0.026	-2.954	0.584
Fraction	-4.427	0.004	132.7	0.421	-3.631	0.391

Table 7. Table of detailed coefficients of linear models, part 2.

	Graphs			
	Gnutella		Slashdot	
	Coefficent	p-value	Coefficent	p-value
Probability	-371.273	0	-10.882	0
Density	-121.062	0	2.117	0.035
Fraction	-5.28	0.363	-0.655	0.513

Figure 10. InfoSpread vs bridge size for HepTh

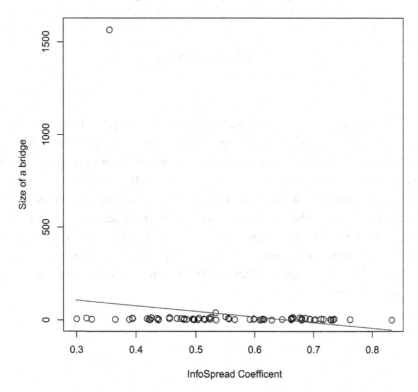

Figure 11. InfoSpread vs bridge size for HepPh

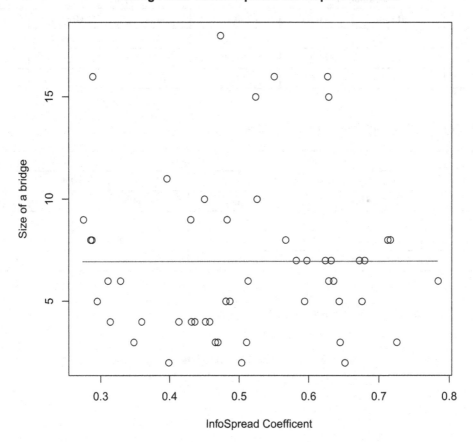

interesting observation is that in every model coefficient related to probability that signal will flow through bridge is negative. It means that smaller bridges transfer more information between neighboring dense clusters. This is exactly what InfoSpread should measure. It should distinguish bridges which are small and very influential. Conclusion of this section is that InfoSpread favors small bridges and for constant density and fraction, smaller bridges are characterized by higher probability of transferring information. In addition authors checked Pearson's correlation coefficient and any two pair of variables for any set were not correlated. For almost every pair correlation value was smaller than 0.3. Only for Slashdot set correlation between density and probability is equal 0.55, what is still not a high value. Of course because of high values of p-value, coefficients for HepTh and HepPh show that proposed values do not explain size of the bridges.

6. CONCLUSION

This section contains a discussion of results received in sections 5.1 and 5.2. As can be seen in table 3 ParaLARW returns clustering with lower modularity, however it has a big advantage in detecting subgraphs responsible for information transfer between clusters. Authors have introduced new measure, InfoSpread Coefficient, which is useful for determining quality of found *bridges*. This new measure takes into account three most important properties of a bridge: P_{bridge}, F_{bridge} and ds_{bridge}. InfoSpread can rank bridges for optimization purposes like a signal initialization cost. In figures presented in section 5.2 one can clearly see that bridges have a serious impact on information dispersion over a network. Especially in case of large networks like Slashdot or Gnutella one can see that difference in coverage is significant. It can be seen that after several steps signal started in a dense cluster is trapped inside cluster while signal initialized in a bridge discovers more and more nodes. After some steps coverages become similar but these first several steps are the most important. This is because of possible optimization of signal initialization cost and importance of time necessary for reaching certain number of nodes or communities. It is clear that removing bridges from graph will significantly reduce potential of information transfer between clusters. This is because most of paths between dense clusters go through bridges. ParaLARW (Parallelized version of LARW) is significantly faster (for large networks) than non-parallelized version. One can see in table 1 that running time gain can achieve even 30% for the most demanding stage of the ParaLARW clustering process. Next modifications of ParaLARW will allow to achieve better results for citation networks which have very skew nodes degrees distribution.

7. FUTURE WORK

In this section future directions of research are presented. As can be seen in table 1 time needed to perform the initial clustering can be really high in comparison to main part which is MCL run. One can solve this problem by providing adequate initial partitioning without building multiple spanning trees. Probably a proper sequence of neighborhoods can be determined with just one spanning tree. In future authors will investigate more ideas for providing initial clustering. The second direction of future work is proper aggregation of neighboring bridges. As can be seen in table 4 in some cases ParaLARW finds a lot of bridges. Part of them could be aggregated to one bridge by maximization of InfoSpread Coefficient. Proper bridges should be maximally influential so appending two less important bridges to one more influential can have significant impact on information spread control. Third important field of future research is a different way of aggregation clusters to a supernode. One can construct a supernode from more than one cluster resulted from MCL. It could gain profit if one will aggregate more than one cluster what will maximize modularity. Another very important area of research is using random walks to detect bridges in any partitioning. If one has already derived clustering which satisfies some conditions then only need is to find proper bridges for information spread control. Such an approach will save time needed for reiteration of cluster analysis and will maintain important features of partitioning, like high value of modularity.

ACKNOWLEDGMENT

The paper is co-founded by the European Union from resources of the European Social Fund. Project PO KL "Information technologies: Research and their interdisciplinary applications", Agreement UDA-POKL.04.01.01-00-051/10-00.

REFERENCES

Aggarwal, C., Lin, S., & Yu, P. S. (2014). On influential node discovery in dynamic social networks. *SDM*, 636-647.

Blondel, V. D., Guillaume, J.-L., Lambiotte, R., & Lefebvre, E. (2008). Fast unfolding of communities in large networks. *Journal of Statistical Mechanics*, *2008*(10). doi:10.1088/1742-5468/2008/10/P10008

Clauset, A., Newman, M. E. J., & Moore, C. (2004). Finding community structure in very large networks. *Physical Review E: Statistical, Nonlinear, and Soft Matter Physics*, *70*(6), 066111. doi:10.1103/PhysRevE.70.066111 PMID:15697438

da F. Costa, L., Rodrigues, F. A., Travieso, G., & Boas, P. R. V. (2007). Characterization of complex networks: A survey of measurements. *Advances in Physics*, *56*(1), 167 – 242.

Doerr, B., Fouz, M., & Friedrich, T. (2012). Why rumors spread fast in social networks. *Communications of the ACM*, *55*(6), 70–75. doi:10.1145/2184319.2184338

Fortunato, S. (2010). *Community detection in graphs*. Complex Networks and Systems Lagrange Laboratory ISI Foundation.

Ju, C., Cao, J., Zhang, W., & Ji, M. (2013). Influential node control strategy for opinion evolution on social networks. Academic Press.

Kempe, D., Kleinbergy, J., & Tardosz, E. (2005). Influential nodes in a diffusion model for social networks. *LNCS*, *3580*, 1127–1138.

Newman, M. (2012). Retrieved from http://www-personal.umich.edu/ mejn/netdata/

Newman, M. E. J. (2006). Modularity and community structure in networks. *Proceedings of the National Academy of Sciences of the United States of America*, *103*(23), 8577–8582. doi:10.1073/pnas.0601602103 PMID:16723398

Pons, P., & Latapy, M. (2005). *Computing communities in large networks using random walks*. arXiv:physics/0512106

Stanford University. (2012). Retrieved from http://snap.stanford.edu/data/

van Dongen, S. M. (2000). *Graph clustering by flow simulation* (PhD thesis). Universiteit Utrecht.

Wojtasiewicz, M., & Ciesielski, K. (2014). Identifying bridges for information spread control in social networks. In *Lecture Notes in Computer Science: Vol. 8852. Workshop on Social Influence* (pp. 390–401). Berlin: Springer.

Chapter 15
The Eternal-Return Model of Human Mobility and Its Impact on Information Flow

Martine Collard
University of the French West Indies, France

Philippe Collard
University of Nice – Sophia Antipolis, France

Erick Stattner
University of the French West Indies, France

ABSTRACT

Human motions determine spatial social contacts that influence the way information spreads in a population. With the Eternal-Return model, we simulate an artificial world populated by heterogeneous individuals who differ in their mobility. This mobility model is synthetic but it represents regular patterns and it integrates the principles of periodicity, circular trajectory and variable amplitude of real patterns. We use a multi-agent framework for simulation and we endow agents with simple rules on how to move around the space and how to establish proximity-contacts. We distinguish different kinds of mobile agents, from sedentary ones to travelers. To summarize the dynamics induced by mobility over time, we define the mobility-based "social proximity network" as the network of all distinct contacts between agents. Properties such as the emergence of a giant component are given insight in the process of information spreading. We have conducted simulations to understand which density threshold allows percolation on the network when the mobility is constant and when it is varying.

INTRODUCTION

Spatial diffusion of an information whatever is the kind of information, knowledge, rumor, diseases or numeric viruses for instance, can be modeled with common principles. Related works (Eubank, Anil Kumar, & Marathe, 2008; De & Das, 2008; Borner, Sanyal, & Vespignani, 2007) have tend to show

DOI: 10.4018/978-1-5225-2814-2.ch015

that these dissemination phenomena present very analogous characteristics indeed. This field has been well studied for years with a particular emphasis on epidemics since real datasets and simulation tools are available in this domain. But researches are generally restricted to studies on diffusion phenomena according to static network properties or virtual dynamics models. Few attention has been paid until very recently on social agents mobility and its impact on network dynamics and on information spread while mobility is obviously an important dimension in social practices. New societal challenges like urban planning or traffic management need to get a better knowledge of user motion patterns and user behavior in their environment.

Human mobility may induce deep modifications in social links among persons and thus variations on the information spreading. The phenomenon depends on the kind of mobility and on the kind of social relationship underlying the network. In most works, the mobility considered is spatial and the social behavior is realized by the ability for an individual to have a direct contact via spatial proximity. Proximity has been studied for years and it has been shown that it plays an important role on social communications. Individuals who share a close space should be more likely to develop friendship or other social even on-line relationships (Hall, 1963; Eveland & Bikson, 1986; Huang, Shen, Williams, & Contractor, 2009) and to create dynamics contact graphs (Toroczkai & Guclu, 2007).

But the lack of general tools to track individual locations has been an obstacle to extract any knowledge on human mobility from real situations. Synthetic mobility models like the random walk (RW) model and derivatives like the random waypoint (RWP) model were mostly studied for designing mobile ad hoc networks (Manets) and communication protocols (Camp, Boleng, & Davies, 2002; Chaintreau et al., 2005; Amor, Bui, & Lavallée, 2010). The RW model was intended to represent the movement of living beings considering that an individual moves from its current location to a new location by randomly choosing his direction and his speed until a given time or until its next location. The random way point (RWP) model is a variation of the RW model and was widely used. In this model, each individual chooses randomly a destination and a speed in the available space. But studies on RWP showed non realistic features (Bai, Sadagopan, & Helmy, 2003; Yoon, Noble, Liu, & Kim, 2006) and other variations like the Levy-walk models (A. M. Edwards, 2007) were proposed. Camp et al. (Camp et al., 2002) have provided a good survey of these models and their impact on adhoc network protocol performances.

Recent results (M. C. Gonzalez, 2008; Song, Qu, Blumm, & Barabási, 2010; Belik, Geisel, & Brockmann, 2011) have challenged the assumed random motion of human trajectories showing that they exhibit regular returns and reproducible patterns. Jardosh et al (Jardosh, Belding-Royer, Almeroth, & Suri, 2003) have noticed indeed that "people on college campuses, at conferences and in shopping areas generally do not move in random directions". Rhee et al (Rhee et al., 2011) showed obvious deviations between Levy walks and human walks even if they have similar statistical behaviours. And in (Kim & Kotz, 2006), Kim et al. figured outdoor walks of pedestrians as segment lines that suggest regular returns to previous locations. It has appeared indeed that in contrast with random walk models, concrete schemes found in real user traces follow patterns with cyclic spatio-temporal regularities and amplitudes more or less strong. For instance, Camp et al. (Camp et al., 2002) described an urban mobility model including regular patterns. On the basis of real observations, Daude and Eliott (Daude & Eliot, 2005) simplify the periodic behavior by proposing three simplified models among which two are circular. By studying traces of mobile phones, Gonzales et al. (M. C. Gonzalez, 2008) confirm the periodicity and the heterogeneity of the mobility in their amplitude by highlighting the common tendency of human agents to travel on short distances and to return to frequent locations with some occasional longer travel paths. More recently, Belik et al. (Belik et al., 2011) have even demonstrated that the time spent away from these locations was a relevant variable of a global outbreak threshold on a network.

In fact both random features and regular patterns seem to be observed into human trajectories. This sharp contrast between regular and random patterns observed may be due to the context in which experiments are conducted, and mainly to spatial and temporal scales of human motions at which observations are done. Regarding spatial granularity, studies on mobilty were done in various contexts: air transportation data, pedestrian walks over a urban area either by foot, by bus or by car, bank notes movements or mobile phone data. Regarding time, studies are conducted either on a daily or weekly scale or over several months or years depending on the field. Finally as noticed by Brockmann (Brockmann, 2010), there is no complete study on human mobility with all spatial motion scales. It has been shown that as expected, on a daily or monthly scale, persons are located on some individual locations most of the time and that they move mainly between these locations (Brockmann, 2010; M. C. Gonzalez, 2008; Belik et al., 2011). In this work, we are mostly interested in this kind of situations in order to study the impact of human mobilty on diffusion when the information is transmitted by proximity between individuals like people moving around a small set of salient locations (home, work, school, sport, etc) most of their time. The Eternal Return (ER) model that we defined, represents regular patterns. It integrates at once the principles of periodicity, circular trajectory and variable amplitude that allows to distinguish agents that are travelers and other ones that are sedentaries.

Starting from the principles of circularity and regularity in human trajectories, we investigate in this paper dependency relationships between mobility, social behavior and information dissemination on social networks on the basis of the mobility model called Eternal-Return (ER) we introduced previously (Collard, Collard, & Stattner, 2012) for studying percolation. The ER model integrates regular returns. It is synthetic and minimal in order to focus on the impact of some mobility parameters only. Nevertheless we show how much and why individual mobility may have an impact on (i) social behavior at an individual level and (ii) afterwards at a global level on emerging dissemination processes through social links when these links need spatio-temporal co-occurrence. Agent mobility may induce deep modifications in social links among agents and thus variations on the information spreading. The phenomenon depends on the kind of mobility and on the kind of social relationship underlying the network. The mobility considered here is geographic and the social behavior is realized by the ability for an agent to have a direct contact via spatial proximity. Social links between agents are solely defined by direct physical contact. And a physical contact is supposed to be induced by proximity only. The mobility model we propose aims only at replicating salient mechanisms with few parameters introduced into simulations. Another motivation for us has been to study their potential action of emergence. Despite its simplicity, this social behavior model gives a true interpretation of the real world where each individual has generally social contacts with only a closed and small fraction of the entire population (Crooks, Hudson-Smith, & Dearden, 2009). An agent is considered to have a social contact with another one if and only if this agent is located in his narrow neighborhood.

While basic, this situation takes on important social meaning since it happens when roads are crossing and two people meet in a limited spatio-temporal space. In this case, social relationships are rarely meaningless. Each one is likely to transmit an information, a rumor or an infectious disease to others standing in the same reduced space. The ER model integrates at once the principles of periodicity, circular trajectory and variable amplitude that allows to distinguish agents that are travelers and other ones that are sedentary. It infers the Social Proximity Network which is both minimal and dynamic: minimal because one link concerns two agents only and has no incidence for the couple as such and dynamic because information about links is casual and volatile. Emergence of direct contacts in social groupings is depending on agent neighborhood topology that is itself relying on agent mobility. We have modeled a spatio-temporal cooccurrence social system on which we planned to study in depth the impact of agent mobility as a main parameter.

One of the main important challenges in this field of social networks is to scale up from the individual to the population level in order to understand how individual properties and inter-individuals patterns infer global structures or tendencies and how they have an impact on social phenomena like spatial grouping, motion in urban environments or information flow. Beyond static patterns, the role of network dynamics is a key issue and is a very emergent research field (Gross, D' Lima, & Blasius, 2006; Read, Eames, & Edmunds, 2008; Christensen, Albert, Grenfell, & Albert, 2010). In this work, first of all, we consider the point of view of a percolation process in order to know when the connectivity of the network is ensured. Then we consider the information flow from the point of view of information diffusion. Studying the diffusion process allows to find conditions under which an information may be spread depending on different parameters such as the probability for an agent to get the information from another. We have based the study on the standard epidemic diffusion model SIR (Susceptible, Infected, Recovered). Models of information diffusion are very much similar whatever can be the nature of the information. The mathematical approach of compartment models for epidemics modeling like SIR fits other cases such as knowledge or rumor spreading. These models consider that individuals switch from a state to another with a given probability. The transitions Susceptible to Infected and Infected to Recovered defined for epidemics are obviously analogous to Innovator to Incubator and Incubator to Adopter transitions in knowledge diffusion as underlined by Borner et al. (Borner et al., 2007). Network based models (Gross et al., 2006; Christensen et al., 2010; Stattner, Collard, & Vidot, 2011) have extended compartment models more appropriately to understand diffusion process since they involve individuals (nodes) and contact links (vertices) among them.

In our approach, network dynamics is induced by agent mobility. Each agent is characterized by his own mobility that represents his way to move. For ex-ample, low mobility should characterize sedentary agents while high mobility should be the prerogative of travelers. A sedentary agent moves only within his immediate vicinity, while a traveler explores a large area before returning to its place of residence. We study how this kind of mobility as an impact on physical proximity. Our work is composed of three complementary parts on: (i) the ER synthetic mobility model properties with strong results that demonstrate its relevance. We define the ER agent mobility model and the simulation tool we implemented. Simulations allow to check that is in compliance with well known properties in geographic patterns. (ii) the mobility-based Social Proximity Network (mSPN) built by proximity relationships and agent ER mobility over time. We conduct experiments that point out the influence of both density of agents and mobility on the ability for an agent to have spatial contacts. We distinguish two types of agents, traveler and sedentary, according to their mobility and we study their interplay regarding proximity. (iii) the impact of mobility on percolation and diffusion phenomena since we highlight the impact of agent mobility on percolation critical thresholds and on information spreading through an mSPN.

The remaining of the paper is organized in the following way: the 1st section is devoted to the ER model, the 2nd section presents the social network induced by the agent mobility, the 3rd section focuses on critical thresholds that allow network connectivity under mobility and the fourth section presents our results on the impact of agent mobility on a diffusion process.

ETERNAL-RETURN MODEL OF MOBILITY

The Eternal-Return (ER) model defines a kind of spatio-temporal mobility that represents the way people behave when they move from place to place. The concept of mobility seems to have multiple meanings. In this study, we rather consider mobility as circulation that is motion of individuals like pedestrians in an urban or inter-urban space. The ER mobility model is defined in order to simulate the tendency of humans to return to the location they visited earlier. This mobility is typical of homework motions. Although the ER model of mobility is freely inspirited and restrictive, it is sufficient to express truly the fact that some agents go across large spaces while others are confined in a small areas: sedentary agents (resp. travelers) are defined by low (resp. high) mobility. It can be considered as a simple representation of pedestrians moving around their "world". Each agent has its own location that is updated when he is moving forward. He has a heading that indicates the direction he is facing and he will follow to move straightforward.

The agent heading is a value between 0° and 360°. At each time step, each agent moves straight on for one unit. Thereby the speed is constant and identical for all the agents. In each time-step-slice, we determine the new position for an agent on the basis of his current position and his mobility.

The ER model defines agents trajectory as a regular polygon, with one vertex at each time-step. The amount an agent ai turns at a corner is his constant exterior angle (noted αi). Walking all the way round the polygon, an agent makes one full turn. The sum of exterior angles in his trajectory is equal to 360°. Let us note fTL_i (stands for fullTurnLength) the length of the path polygon size-an agent ai has to follow to come back to a given position. fTL_i is thus the number of time-steps needed to make one full turn. Moreover we assume each agent have his own direction d_i i.e. he walks around his polygon either clockwise or counter-clockwise: in the first case $d_i = -1$ otherwise $d_i = +1$.

For each agent the fullTurnLength is a fixed number uniformly set at random during the initialisation process in the range [3, 360]. Finally, we normalize this value by dividing it by its maximum value.

For each agent a_i, we define his mobility μ_i by the following equation:

$$\mu_i = d_i . fTL_i / 360 \tag{1}$$

So the relation between the mobility and the exterior angle is:

$$\mu_i . \alpha_i = 1 \tag{2}$$

With these hypotheses, mobility μ_i is a non-zero real number in the range $[-1, +1]$, and the absolute value of the exterior angle α_i varies from 1° to 120°. As a consequence, least mobile agents move on a tiny triangle and most mobile agents move on a big polygon of 360 sides. The borderline case of mobility is for $\alpha = 0$ (i.e. $\mu = \infty$) and corresponds to a linear trajectory.

Algorithm 1 describes the ER mobility process: depending on its location and its mobility μ_i, each agent defines its own motion. We assume in the ER model a simple situation in which each agent has an invariable mobility. Agents walk around regular polygons and, as each one has the same speed, their only characteristic parameter is their mobility. As a consequence, the local behavior of each mobile agent is deterministic and periodic. Figure 1 gives an illustration of trajectories of agents each with its own mobility. As there are many agents and so many periods which interact together, it is difficult to predict when and where agents will cross in a same vicinity.

To clarify the terminology and allow to simplify the analysis, according to mobility, we define two typical class of agents: the traveler and the sedentary agents. Sedentary agents (resp. travelers) are defined by low (resp. high) fullTurnLength.

Algorithm 1. MakeMove

```
{Make agents move according to their mobility}
for agent a_i in agents do
    turn right by (1/m_i) degrees
    move forward for one step
end for
```

The Eternal-Return model has been implemented with the NetLogo multiagent programmable modeling environment (Wilensky, 1999). The space is a 2-dimensional grid connected circularly so that the model is similar to a 2-D cellular automata model where the "world" includes numerous agents embedded on a toroidal grid.

Simulations are performed on a L1xL2 lattice as described in (Collard et al., 2012). The agent density δ (number of people per area unit) is a parameter of the model. At the initial step t = 0, agents are randomly distributed across the unbounded grid.

Several agents may stand on a same cell at the same time. A mobility coefficient is assigned to each agent according to an uniform random distribution defined on the fullT urnLength. All reported results are based on the mean of 100 runs.

MOBILITY-BASED SOCIAL PROXIMITY NETWORK

In this section we study the system resulting from activating ER agent motions: the network of all distinct contacts between agents which features are influenced by mobility and density parameters. In the following we first define this network, then we focus on the number of social contacts per agent.

Dynamic Social Networking

In the ER Model, agents are assimilated as nodes of the social network and their social links are generated by spatial proximity. This kind of interactions, based on geographical proximity of individuals takes on much interest since it is an abstract generalization of multiple effective contacts such as physical contact, exchange of words, participation in the same event or attendance at the same place.

Mobility is a core parameter in spatial agent-based models, because it sets the agent neighborhood configuration and so the ability for an agent to establish a contact with another agent. In the ER model, mobility allows agents to explore areas more or less important of their geographical environment and a fortiori to generate more or less proximity contacts as shown in the following section. Indeed, we suppose that two agents come into contact when they are geographically close enough, i.e. the proximity distance between them is less than or equal to 1. On Figure 2, we show how instantaneous proximity contacts occur and evolve in the ER Model. At t_1 no individual is close enough to create a contact. At t_2, agents 1 and 2 are sufficiently close to come into contact. At t_3, this contact is deleted while a new contact is

Figure 1. Agent's trajectory: density = 2% at time 40 with mixed mobility

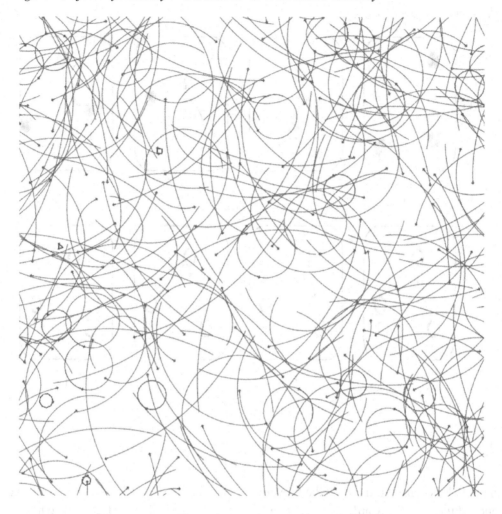

created between agents 1 and 3 who become close enough. At t_4, no individual comes into contact, so all links are removed. Thus individual mobility leads to a network of contacts, which dynamics is a very significant feature, since each time agents are in motion, new contacts are created while others are deleted.

We define the Mobility-Based Social Proximity Network (mSPN) as being the network of all distinct contacts between agents. More precisely, the mSPN represents the maximum proximity contact network in which each individual is linked with all other he met during the simulation. Thus, at every instant, the instantaneous graphs of proximity contacts, described on Figure 2(b), are sets of disconnected small graph clusters of mSPN that represent current agents contacts. Obviously, mSPN is much more dense than the instantaneous proximity contact graphs. More formally, let us give $T = <t_0, t_1, ..., t_m>$ as the time sequence over which agents are moving. More formally, let us give $T = <t_0, t_1, ..., t_m>$ as the time sequence over which agents are moving. We denote the instantaneous proximity contact graphs at instant t_j by $G_{t_j} = \left(V, E_{t_j}\right)$, where V is the set of agents and E_{t_j} is the set of contacts occurred at time t_j. Thus, mSPN=(V, E_T) is given by the union of all edges of the instantaneous proximity contact graphs from time 0 to time m.

Figure 2. Example of how ER Model (a) Induces dynamic proximity contacts (b). Gray dots on (a) are agents who come into contact

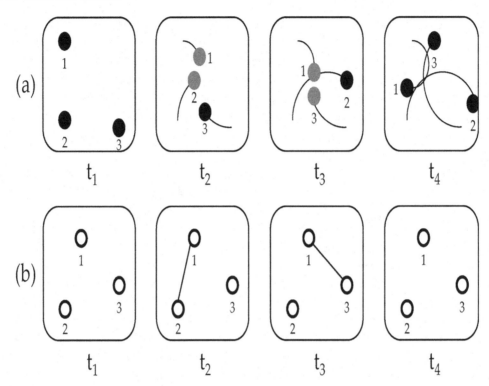

$$E_T = \bigcup_{j=0}^{m} E_{t_j} \tag{3}$$

When the fTL is constant, the periodic movements generated by the ER model ensures that there is convergence of the mSP N towards a steady state, $\overline{G} = (V, \overline{E})$ for which contacts are no longer created. This steady state is reached when all agents are back to their starting point, i.e. when $t_j = $ fTL.

$$\overline{E} = \bigcup_{j=0}^{fTL} E_{t_j} \tag{4}$$

On Figures 3, 4 and 5, three examples of mSPN obtained with density=15% and fTL constant are depicted. All nodes linked by the same color belong to the same component. As expected, we can observe that mobility has a direct impact on the overall number of contacts, since the density of the network increases with fTL. A mSPN is a network that summarizes the dynamics: its properties give insight on the process of information spread. For example, we can observe (see figures 3, 4 and 5) that too low mobility values may not guarantee the network connectivity of a mSPN and indeed we will show that this gives a clue to the inability to percolate. In the following section, we focus on the network degree distribution (number of social contacts per agent).

Figure 3. mSPNs obtained with density = 15% for fTL = 3. All nodes linked by the same color belong to the same component

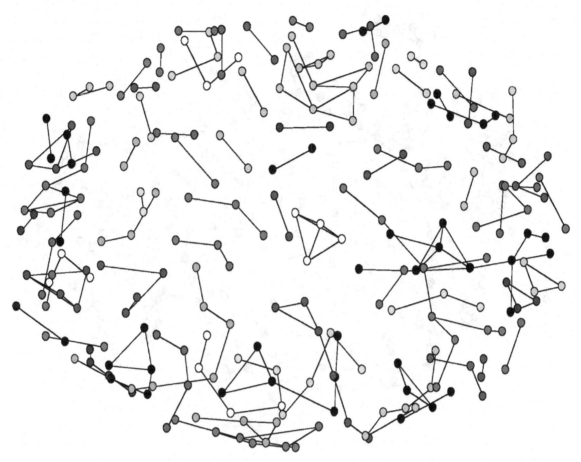

Social-Contacts Per Agent

We consider an agent total number of contacts over time. This number is the degree of the corresponding node in the mSPN. In this section, we study the influence of mobility on the degree distribution. At a given time, one agent a_j is in the vicinity of the agent a_i, if a_j is in the circular disk of radius 1 centered on a_i. In such a case, we assume that there is incidental social contact between the agents a_i and a_j. For each agent a_i, if C_i is the set of all the agents a_j ($i \neq j$) in its vicinity over time: $C_i = \{ a_j^i \}$. Thus the total number of contacts the agent a_i is $\#C_i$. Of course a social contact requires a spatio-temporal coincidence, i.e. two agents must be at the same place at the same time. In the case of no-mobility, the mean number of social-contacts is approximate as in Equation (5): this result is obtained by simulations lead on 1000 agents and is averaged over 100 runs.

$$\text{mean } \#Ci \approx 0.4 \times \delta \tag{5}$$

Figure 4. mSPNs obtained with density = 15% for fTL = 10. All nodes linked by the same color belong to the same component

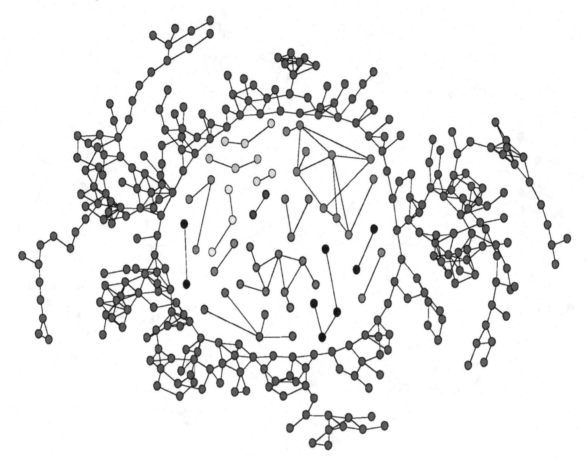

More generally, if agents are moving according to the ER model with a same mobility, the mean number of social-contacts appears to be approximately proportional to the density of agents (see figure 6). Conversely, for a given density, mean $\#C_i$ appears to be approximately proportional to fTL: the more the mobility, the more the number of contacts (see Figure 7). Finally, if mobility is identical for all the agents, data obtained by simulation allow to establish that $\#C_i$ follows a Normal distribution with the same mean and standard-deviation.

MOBILITY AND PERCOLATION PROCESS

Considering the percolation paradigm, we are able to find epidemic thresholds for identifying non-invasive regimes from invasive regimes. In host-parasite systems, thresholds are values beyond which a given vertex belongs to an infinite open cluster. They define transitions towards invasion. The *percolation threshold* δ_c is the critical value beyond which large clusters appear and the system is connected from one side to another. For percolation on a square lattice, this value was shown to be near 0.59. In the context of this study, the mobility of agents brings a new dimension and the dissemination threshold is not

Figure 5. mSPNs obtained with density = 15% for fTL = 20. All nodes linked by the same color belong to the same component

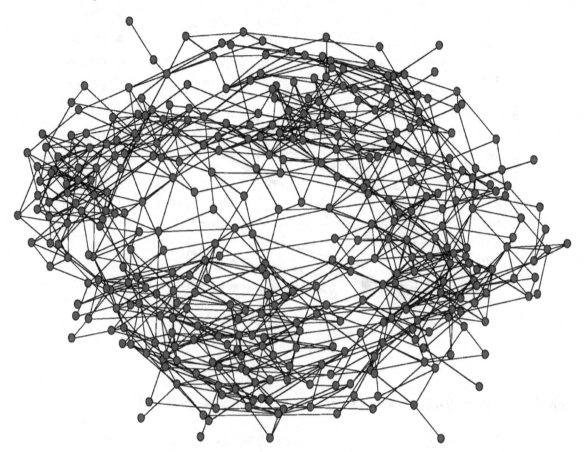

identified. When agents are static, the ability of transmitting the information between neighbors controls the probability of invasion. Thus it depends on the density of agents only. The situation is more complex with the ER mobility model since the critical threshold, if any, depends both on density and mobility.

We assume that each individual can be in two discrete states, either susceptible or infected, or more generally *no-yet-informed* or *informed*: all agents are initially in the susceptible state except one randomly selected agent that is infected. The transmission is being done only by proximity. The infection is spread thanks to proximity: an infected (resp. informed) agent can transmit disease (resp. information, knowledge, rumor) to his nearest neighbors only. When two agents are in the same neigborhood, the probability that the infected one infects the susceptible one is set to one. Thus, considering the *Mobility-Based Social Proximity Network*, we show that the percolation paradigm can be extended to the case of mobile agents. Our results have practical implications for the analysis information dissemination and in particular for the disease control strategies. In this section, we focus on determining the percolation threshold in two situations characterized by homogeneous mobility or mixed mobility in the population.

Figure 6. mean #C vs. density From bottom to top: fTL = 10, 20, 80, 180, 270, 360

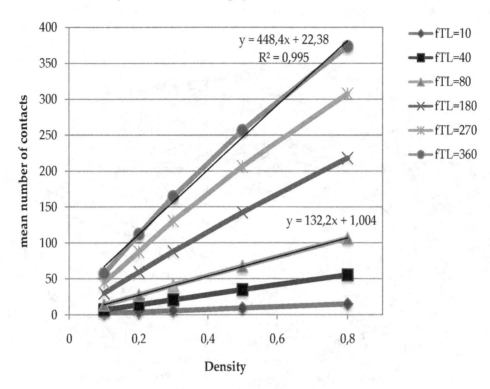

Figure 7. mean #C vs. fTL From bottom to top: δ = 10%, 20%, 30%, 50%, 80%

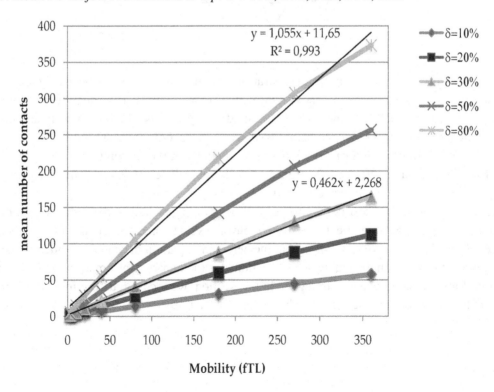

Figure 8. Percolation threshold vs. fullTurnLength

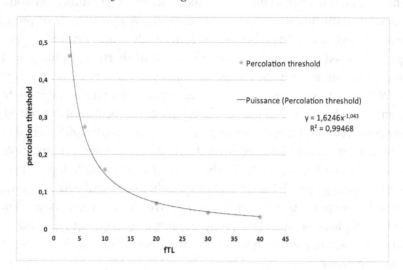

Percolation Threshold With Homogeneous Mobility Population

Assuming that all agents have a same mobility, we have conducted experiments to determine the percolation threshold δ_c according to given values for mobility. The critical threshold value δ_c is calculated on the basis of a proportion of 50% infected agents. As shown on Figure 8, when mobility increases, δ_c monotonously decreases from 60% and asymptomatically reaches zero. δ_c reaches 5% for a rather small mobility fTL equal to 30. This results are much important since they show the strong impact of mobility on the ability to propagate information. Mobility emphasizes the effect of local actions at global level. We can observe too that δ_c follows an approximate power-law decrease according to the mobility. One assumption is that a small quantity of travelers in a mixed population of mobile agents should be enough to ensure percolation.

Percolation Threshold With Mixed-Mobility Population

What proportion of a sedentary individuals need to become travelers in order that a giant connected component emerges in the mSPN? The aim is to show that in a population of sedentary individuals with many small connected components, only few people need to increase their mobility to connect with one another over components.

This model is obtained by starting from a population of sedentary agents (for instance we set fTL equal to 3 for all the individuals). This initial condition induces a proximity network with numerous small connected components. Then we switch at random the mobility of each agent with a probability p. So the parameter p determines the probability that an edge will get rewired in the proximity network. As previously, agents move locally, each edge connects pairs of agents that are relatively close to each other. We refer to this latter property as locality and measure it with the proportion of short links[1]. To fix the new mobility for an agent a_i, we randomly chose a target agent a_j such as a_i and a_j are not yet connected, then we set the mobility of a_i to make a contact with a_j possible: more precisely, we set fTL_i as $\pi \times d(a_i, a_j)$. This "rewiring" process tends to replace short edges by new edges with randomly selected endpoints. To some extent, this method introduces shortcuts in the proximity network which topology can thus be seen as many small clusters connected by shortcuts. When the rewiring probability p is small, only few edges are "rewired" and when p is close to 1, most edges are "rewired".

The natural question to ask at this point is then the effect of shortcuts on the percolation threshold. Figure 9 shows the evolution of the giant-component size according to density for different values of the probability p. Without any shortcut (p = 0) we can observe the phase transition for a density near 0.35. The main point is that low values of p do not really affect the locality of connected agents since the proportion of short edges remains high. However, rewiring even a small number of edges makes the size of the largest component drastically higher compared with the initial value. For example, figure 8 shows that for density=0.3 and a starting fTL of 3, if only 1 percent of the population changes his mobility (p =0.01) then a big component gathers 88 percent of the population while the locality remains high (0.73). These values have to be compared with the case p = 0 for which the largest component gathers 16% of the population with the highest locality (1). In conclusion, we observe that this kind of mixed-mobility proximity networks are much interesting since they both preserves the locality of sedentary population and presents a giant component.

MOBILITY AND INFORMATION DISSEMINATION

The ER model and proximity contacts have been defined and built in order to understand how an information can be broadcast on the grid network when agent-nodes are in motion. In this section, we detail simulations conducted and experimental results we obtained.

In this work, the epidemics context serves as a reference since its models are well defined and much comprehensible and they stay generic enough to be extended to other cases. For experiment relevance, one crucial condition on the grid structure is its ability to allow spreading for which the minimum agent density has to be determined. Thus the density is set to 70% to be greater than the density thresholds highlighted in Section 3 and thus to ensure percolation. In this section epidemic algorithms are used to support propagation of information in the network while minimizing the number of agents, i.e. the resources cost. Regarding diffusion, social links between agents are deterministic and spreading laws are non deterministic. They are defined according to the SIR diffusion model detailed below, they thus depend on probabilities of agent infection and recover. There are two kinds of parameters that control dissemination: probability α of transition *Susceptible* → *Infected* and probability β of transition *Infected* → *Recover*.

S-I-R model of Diffusion

In epidemics modeling, individuals are supposed to be classified into different epidemic states, according to the level of the disease development. Since it is admitted that most common diseases confer long-lasting immunity, it makes sense to divide the population into those who are susceptible to contract the disease (individuals that are not infected and not immune), those who are infected (individuals that can transmit the disease) and those who are recovered (individuals that have been infected and are immune).

Numerous epidemic models have been proposed. The simplest one is the Susceptible-Infected model (SI) that assumes susceptible individuals can become infected with a certain probability. Another standard model is the SIR model that extends SI with a recovered state reached by infected individuals with

Figure 9. Giant-component size versus density for various vs. of rewiring probability

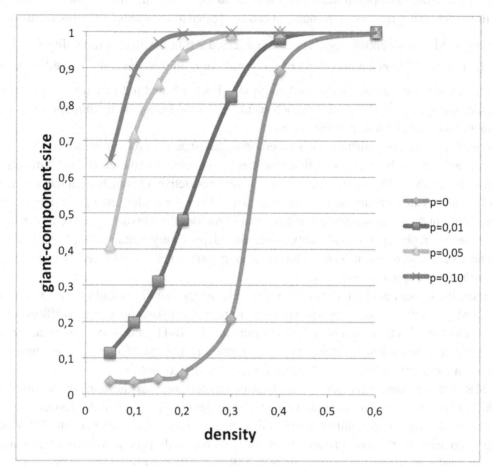

Figure 10. Locality and giant-component size vs. rewiring probability (density =0.3, fTL = 3)

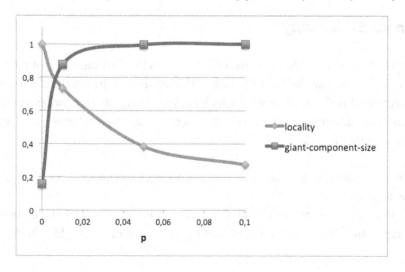

a probability β. On the same principle, we can also found the SIS or the SIRS models. In this work, we use the SIR model, as it is the most common and can be applied to knowledge or rumor diffusion as well.

According to SIR, a susceptible agent i becomes infected at time t_j with the probability $1 - (1 - \alpha)^{\# N^i_{t_j}}$ if $N^i_{t_j}$ is the number of infected neighbors of the agent i at t_j. In this way, the probability of being infected increases with the number of infected neighbors. Each infected individual has a probability β to recover. Once the agent is in R state, it cannot transmit the pathogen again. Its immunity is supposed to be permanent and it cannot return in the S state.

Traditionally, information diffusion is studied on steady state networks in which neither agents nor links among them are evolving. Even in that case it is hard to obtain real datasets and simulations have frequently to be involved. This static point of view is very restrictive. On one hand it lacks realism since real world behaviors are dynamic and on the other hand it may be irrelevant since it does not consider true connectivity in the social network. The ER model provides the missing dynamic dimension with a synthetic pattern of mobility. When mobility is introduced, proximity contacts are permanently creating and deleting social links between agents. The underlying contact network induced evolves and provides dynamic paths for the spread of information.

Obviously, the contact network dynamics induced by agent mobility should have an impact on the spread. Indeed, preliminary works carried out on the impact of network dynamics in diffusion processes have shown positive effects (Read et al., 2008; Stattner et al., 2011). In this section, we address this issue by investigating dependencies between the agent mobility and the diffusion process based on SIR.

ies between the agent mobility and the diffusion process based on SIR.

With SIR, the spreading behavior depends on parameters such as the number of initial infected individuals, the probability of transmission α or the probability of recovery β. Moreover, as our objective is to assess the impact of mobility on spreading, two additional parameters of the ER Model have to be taken into account: the mobility and the density. So our study is twofold. We want to understand both how the different parameters of the models (SIR and ER) modify the propagation and how the propagation behaves according to mobility factors. First, we show that there are SIR model parameters that maximize the diffusion. Afterwards, by setting these parameters, we compare the effects of various mobility values on spreading. Our results provide valuable insights about how and why mobility has an impact on diffusion.

SIR Diffusion vs. ER Mobility

As usual in epidemiology, the incidence curve of infection is the first indicator of the process behavior over time. It gives a true snapshot of the diffusion telling details on the potential occurrence of the epidemics. In this section, it is the main tool on which comparative tests have been conducted in order to highlight the impact of mobility on diffusion. For this purpose, three categories of agents are defined according to their mobility factor:

- *Imm* are immobile agents, simulated by a *fullTurnLenght* equal to 0. Typically, these agents remain at the same location.
- *Sed* are sedentary agents simulated by a *fullTurnLenght* in the range [3,45], i.e. mobility∈[0,0.125]. These are agents that only explore a very small part of their close neighborhood (see Figure 9a).

Figure 11. Agent's trajectory: density = 2%, t = 40 for sedentary agents

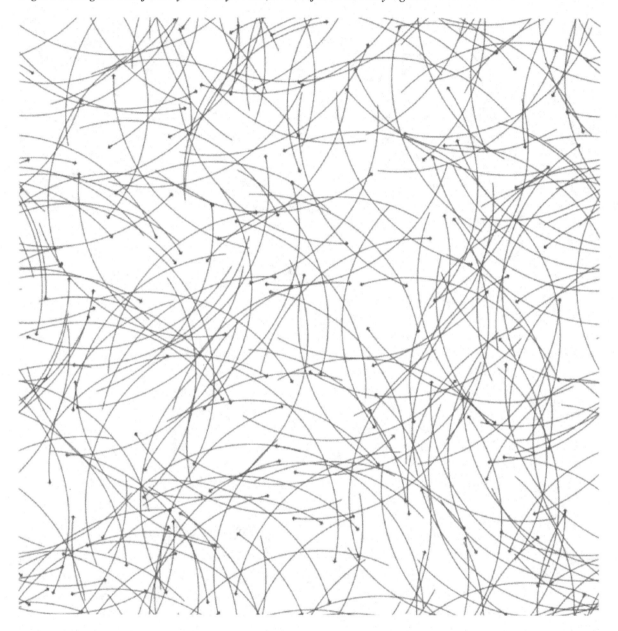

- *Tra* are travelers agents simulated by a *fullTurnLenght* in the range [315,360] i.e. mobility∈[0.875,1]. They represent agents that explore a large part of the space (see Figure 9b).

In our experiments, we assume that initially only one individual is infected. This individual is called the patient-zero and is randomly selected. Each test was solely composed of agents with the same kind of mobility Imm, Sed or Tra and all results are averaged over 100 runs.

It is admitted that when epidemic is possible, the SIR model provides a typical bell-shaped infection curve, for which the peak is easily observable, as shown on Figure 13. According to this model,

Figure 12. Agent's trajectory: density = 2%, t = 40 for travelers

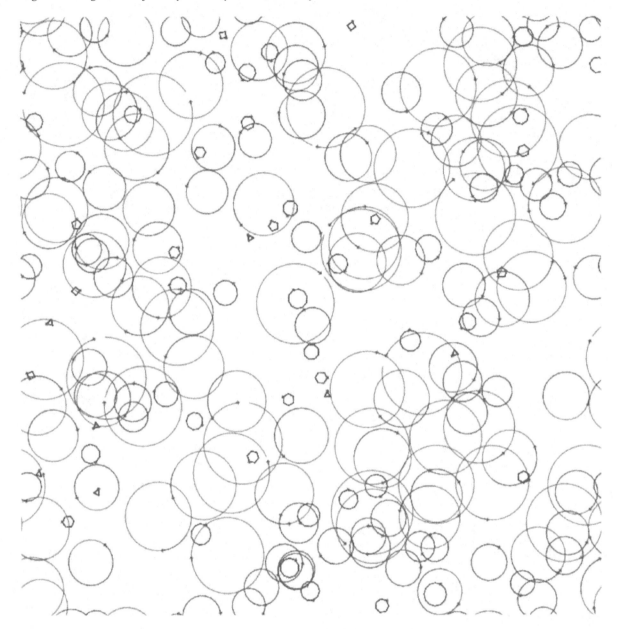

the epidemic is characterized by the time-point where the percentage of infected individuals reaches its maximum before decreasing. In the rest of this section, we refer to this point on the curve as the epidemic peak or the peak. We observe its value and occurrence time that are known to be dependent on the agent density and on probabilities α and β.

Since we aimed at evaluating the impact of mobility solely, we selected two different sets of SIR parameters that generate very different incidence curves in the no-mobility case (*Imm* agents) (a) $\alpha=0.325$ and $\beta=0.2$ without any epidemic peak and (b) $\alpha=0.775$ and $\beta=0.05$ with an epidemic peak as shown by Figure 13. Figure 13 presents also the infection curves obtained on both categories *Sed* and *Tra* agents.

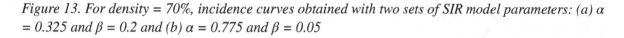

Figure 13. For density = 70%, incidence curves obtained with two sets of SIR model parameters: (a) α = 0.325 and β = 0.2 and (b) α = 0.775 and β = 0.05

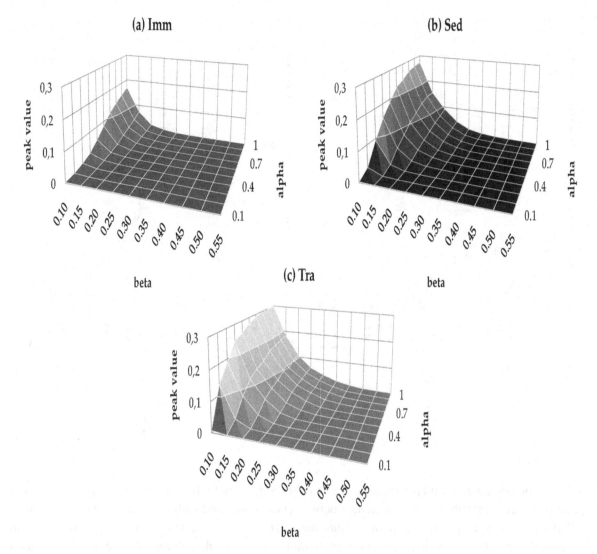

As expected, results demonstrate that even with mobile agents α and β parameters have strong effect on the peak value and on its occurrence in time: (i) either for *Sed* or *Tra* agents, the peak value is much greater and it appears earlier when α increases while β decays. The diffusion process is obviously mobility dependent, since (ii) peak values and occurrence times are varying according to the kind of mobility when α and β are fixed. Moreover, (iii) we observe the same tendency regarding the area under the infection curve (AUC) that is much varying between (a) and (b) and according to the kind of mobility.

To better understand how the peak behaves according to these parameters, it is interesting to draw a 3D Figure showing the evolution of the peak value according to probabilities α and β, as depicted on Figure 14 with the same 70% density. Figure 14 presents the results obtained for (a) stationary agents, (b) sedentary and (c) travelers. On this figure, we observe that whatever is the kind of mobility, peak values

Figure 14. Evolution of the peak value according to the mobility for density 70% (a) stationary, (b) sedentary, (c) travelers

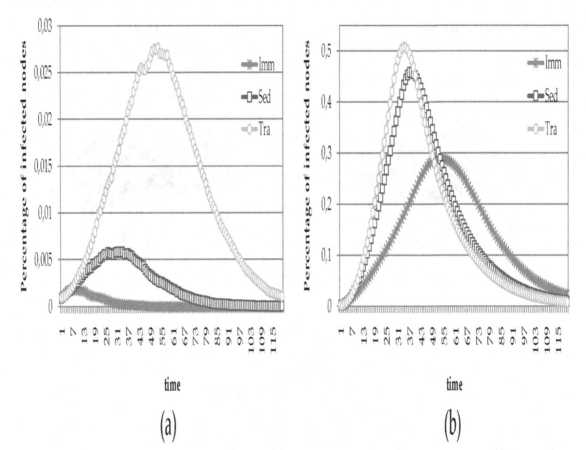

increase when α increases and β decreases. We can also notice that for high values of α and low values of β, there are significant observable differences between peaks obtained with the different mobility values.

Thus, if we consider only α or β values that maximize the peak value (here α=1or β=0.1), we can compare the impact of mobility on: (1) the peak value, (2) the peak occurrence time and (3) the area under the infection curve. On Figure 15, we compare these features for density 70%. The first remark is the way peak values obtained with the three kinds of mobility are sorted:

$$PeakValue_{Imm} \leq PeakValue_{Sed} \leq PeakValue_{Tra} \qquad (6)$$

Indeed, whatever are α or β variations, the diffusion is always the strongest for mobile individuals, since the peak value obtained for Tra and Sed agents is always greater than those obtained for Imm. Similarly, we can also observe that traveler agents systematically allow wider dissemination than sedentary ones. This is consistent with previous results of the 2nd section showing that the average number of contacts is depending on mobility when all agents have the same mobility. The more mobile are agents, the more likely they are to favor the spread among themselves since they have more contacts.

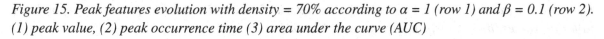

Figure 15. Peak features evolution with density = 70% according to α = 1 (row 1) and β = 0.1 (row 2). (1) peak value, (2) peak occurrence time (3) area under the curve (AUC)

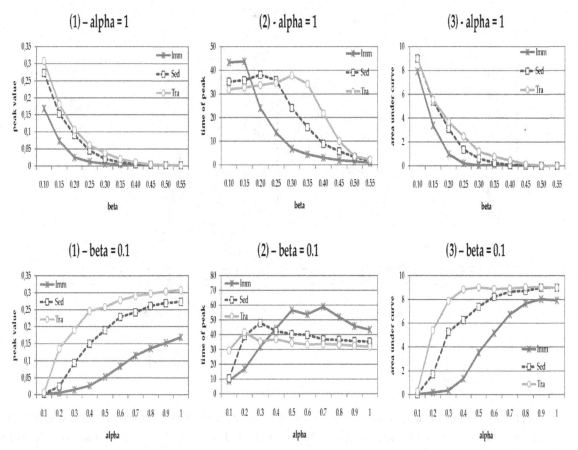

In this section agent mobility values are in *Imm*, *Sed* and *Tra* ranges only. Thus it is worthwhile to know how many contacts each of these kinds of mobility may induce for an agent. Here the number of contacts to consider is of course the aggregated values of all contacts over time that are modeled in the *mSPN* network (see Section 2). Figure 16 shows the distribution of contacts according to mobility. On Figure 16a, we observe that for immobile agents the degree is in the range [1,5]. Similarly, the number of contacts for *Sed* agents are in the range [26, 226] and in the range [376, 476] for *Tra* (see Figure 16b). Results obtained for peak values are thus confirmed: when the agent mobility is increasing, the number of contacts is also increasing, providing more opportunities for spreading.

On Figures 10(a) and (b), we cannot highlight any canonical ranking according to mobility for the peak occurrence time. More generally, we can observe on Figure 12(2) that the peak occurs first for *Tra* then Sed and finally Imm with β=0.1 and α ∈ [0.4, 1]. The peaks are sorted through reverse order for α=1 and β ∈ [0.30, 0.50].

Interesting observations can be made on the evolution of the area under the curve (see Figures 12(3)) too. As for the peak value, whatever are α or β variations, values are sorted in the same way:

$$AUC_{Imm} \leq AUC_{Sed} \leq AUC_{Tra} \tag{7}$$

Figure 16. Degree distribution of the mSPN obtained with 70% density according to the type of mobility (a)for all values (b) with distribution values in [0,0.03]

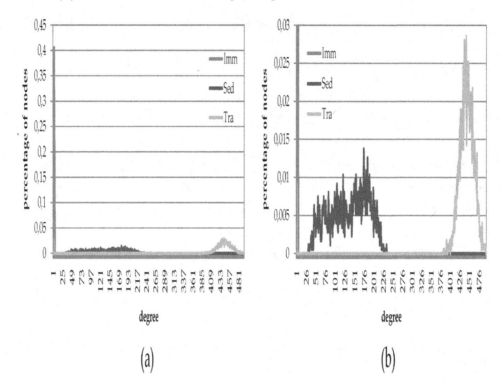

(a) (b)

For high values of α, the area seems to reach a stability state. For example for β=0.1 and α ∈ [0.4, 1], the AUC obtained by traveler agents is in [8.4, 8.9]. With β=0.1, we can also observe a stability level for *Sed* when α ∈ [0.6, 1] and for *Imm* when α ∈ [0.8, 1]. It is important to note that while the area remains stable for these values of α, the peak value increases. This is characteristic of a curve that is tightening, and thus a spreading phenomenon that is becoming more virulent and brief.

All results discussed until now in this section, have been obtained with a constant density = 70%. To complete the study, we look at the three features when density is varying. Indeed, if we consider parameters that maximize the peak value (here α=1 and β=0.1) for the three mobility patterns, we can draw and compare their variations according to density, and thus check if the observed trends are confirmed for all density. Figure 14 presents, according to density, the evolution of the (a) peak value (b) time of occurrence (c) area under the curve. These results show that the propagation is possible with a low density (i.e. density ≥ 20%) when agents are moving. In contrast, spreading occurs for immobile agents when density ≥ 70%. These observations are consistent with the percolation study we lead (Collard et al., 2012). No matter what the density is, if the system percolates, the results confirm the impact of mobility on spreading.

Figure 17. Evolution of the (a) peak value (b) peak occurrence time (c) AUC according to density with α = 1 and β = 0.1

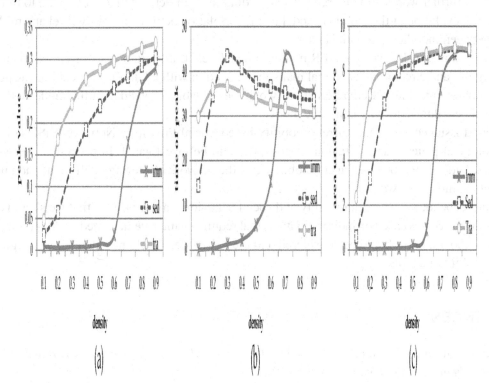

CONCLUSION AND FUTURE WORKS

In this paper, we have presented a framework that provides knowledge for a better comprehension of the phenomenon of information diffusion when spreader mobility plays an important role. We have proposed a network-based approach for modeling the dissemination on a social network where the dynamics is driven by agent mobility. The underlying assumption is on the ternary association Mobility → Proximity → Transmission: mobility induces proximity that in turn creates the condition for transmission.

Considering the Mobility-Based Social Proximity Network, we have shown that the percolation paradigm can be extended to the case of mobile agents. Our results have practical implications for the analysis information dissemination and in particular for the disease control strategies in more realistic systems: we have observed that the impact of mobility on the ability to propagate information is tough and in particular that the percolation threshold follows an approximate power-law decrease according to the mobility. Such a relation allows either to approximate the threshold of percolation when mobility is known or, conversely, for a given density, to compute the required mobility for percolation. We have proposed a simple mixed-mobility model to identify the proportion of sedentary individuals that should become travelers in order that a giant connected component may emerge in the proximity network. We have shown that the network then both preserves the locality of sedentary population and presents a giant component. We have obtained significant results that contribute to a better comprehension of dissemination phenomena. Indeed we have shown that mobility has strong impact on diffusion features, maximum occurrence and amplitude.

The ER model we have proposed raises a variety of new interesting research issues that we plan to address. Our further works will be organized according three directions that correspond to three levels in the model: evolution of the mobility model itself, correlation between mobility level and mSPN, correlation between mobility and social behaviour.

First, we should make evolve the ER model to match real transportation maps either on simulating similar regular and circular paths on real maps in connection with a GIS or on checking ER principles on real human motion data. Both alternatives would be valuable for validating the modelBoth alternatives would be valuable for validating the model

A second issue concerns the current mobility-based Social Proximity Network (mSPN) for which both topological patterns and diffusion processes should be investigated. In particular, we will study the potential correlation between agent mobility and the network clustering coefficient and number of communities into the network.

The interdependence between mobility and social behavior is a third aspect that we should develop: transmission processes based on indirect contacts that require an intermediate media (door knob, e-news, forum, blackboard, etc.) should be considered and the ER model should be extended to integrate more complex mobility patterns.

REFERENCES

Amor, S. B., Bui, M., & Lavallée, I. (2010). *Optimizing mobile networks connectivity and routing using percolation theory and epidemic algorithms.* IICS.

Bai, F., Sadagopan, N., & Helmy, A. (2003). The important framework for analyzing the impact of mobility on performance of routing protocols for adhoc networks. *AdHoc Networks Journal, 1*(4), 383–403. doi:10.1016/S1570-8705(03)00040-4

Belik, V., Geisel, T., & Brockmann, D. (2011). Recurrent host mobility in spatial epidemics: Beyond reaction-diffusion. *European Physical Journal B-Condensed Matter, 84*(4), 579.

Borner, K., Sanyal, S., & Vespignani, A. (2007). Network science. Annual Review of Information Science and Technology, 41, 537-607.

Brockmann, D. (2010). Human mobility and spatial disease dynamics. In Reviews of nonlinear dynamics and complexity (pp. 1–24). Wiley-VCH Verlag GmbH & Co. KGaA.

Camp, T., Boleng, J., & Davies, V. (2002). A survey of mobility models for ad hoc network research. *Wireless Communications and Mobile Computing, 2*(5), 483–502. doi:10.1002/wcm.72

Chaintreau, A., Hui, P., Crowcroft, J., Diot, C., Gass, R., & Scott, J. (2005, February). *Pocket Switched Networks: Real-world mobility and its consequences for opportunistic forwarding* (Tech. Rep.). 2006 Computer Laboratory, University of Cambridge.

Christensen, C., Albert, I., Grenfell, B., & Albert, R. (2010, February 26). Disease dynamics in a dynamic social network. *Physica A: Statistical Mechanics and its Applications*.

Collard, M., Collard, P., & Stattner, E. (2012). Mobility and information flow: Percolation in a multi-agent model. *Procedia CS, 10*, 22–29.

Crooks, A., Hudson-Smith, A., & Dearden, J. (2009). Agent street: An environment for exploring agent-based models in second life. *Journal of Artificial Societies and Social Simulation, 12*(4), 10. Retrieved from http://jasss.soc.surrey.ac.uk/12/4/10.html

Daude, E., & Eliot, E. (2005). Exploration de l'effet des types de mobilites sur la diffusion des epidemies. Proceedings of théo quant'05.

De, P., & Das, S. K. (2008). Epidemic models, algorithms, and protocols in wireless sensor and ad hoc networks. In *Algorithms and protocols for wireless sensor networks* (pp. 51–75). John Wiley and Sons, Inc. doi:10.1002/9780470396360.ch3

Edwards, A. M., Phillips, R. A., Watkins, N. W., Freeman, M. P., Murphy, E. J., Afanasyev, V., & Viswanathan, G. M. et al. (2007). Revisiting levy flight search patterns of wandering albatrosses, bumblebees and deer. *Nature, 449*(7165), 1044–1048. doi:10.1038/nature06199 PMID:17960243

Eubank, S., Anil Kumar, V., & Marathe, M. (2008). Epidemiology and wireless communication: Tight analogy or loose metaphor? In P. Lio, E. Yoneki, J. Crowcroft, & D. Verma (Eds.), *Bioinspired computing and communication* (Vol. 5151, pp. 91–104). Heidelberg, Germany: Springer Berlin. doi:10.1007/978-3-540-92191-2_9

Eveland, J. D., & Bikson, T. K. (1986). Evolving electronic communication networks: an empirical assessment. In *Proceedings of the 1986 ACM conference on computer-supported cooperative work* (pp. 91–101). New York, NY: ACM. doi:10.1145/637069.637080

Gonzalez, M. C., Hidalgo, C. A., & Barabási, A.-L. (2008). Understanding individual human mobility patterns. *Nature, 453*(7196), 779–782. doi:10.1038/nature06958 PMID:18528393

Gross, T., DLima, C. J. D., & Blasius, B. (2006, May). Epidemic dynamics on an adaptive network. *Physical Review Letters, 96*(20), 208701. doi:10.1103/PhysRevLett.96.208701 PMID:16803215

Hall, T. E. (1963). A system for the notation of proxemic behaviour. *American Anthropologist, 65*(5), 1003–1026. doi:10.1525/aa.1963.65.5.02a00020

Huang, Y., Shen, C., Williams, D., & Contractor, N. S. (2009). Virtually there: Exploring proximity and homophily in a virtual world. CSE, 4, 354-359.

Jardosh, A., Belding-Royer, E. M., Almeroth, K. C., & Suri, S. (2003). Towards realistic mobility models for mobile ad hoc networks. In *Proceedings of the 9th annual international conference on mobile computing and networking* (pp. 217–229). New York, NY: ACM. doi:10.1145/938985.939008

Kim, M., & Kotz, D. (2006). Extracting a mobility model from real user traces. Proceedings of IEEE Infocom. doi:10.1109/INFOCOM.2006.173

Read, J. M., Eames, K. T. D., & Edmunds, W. J. (2008). Dynamic social networks and the implications for the spread of infectious disease. *Journal of the Royal Society Interface the Royal Society, 5*(Issue: 26), 1001–1007. doi:10.1098/rsif.2008.0013 PMID:18319209

Rhee, I., Shin, M., Hong, S., Lee, K., Kim, S. J., & Chong, S. (2011). On the levy-walk nature of human mobility. *ACM Transactions on Networking, 19*(3), 630–643. doi:10.1109/TNET.2011.2120618

Song, C., Qu, Z., Blumm, N., & Barabási, A. (2010). Limits of predictability in human mobility. *Science, 327*(5968), 1018–1021. doi:10.1126/science.1177170 PMID:20167789

Stattner, E., Collard, M., & Vidot, N. (2011). Diffusion in dynamic social networks: Application in epidemiology. *22nd International Conference on Database and Expert Systems Applications*. doi:10.1007/978-3-642-23091-2_49

Toroczkai, Z., & Guclu, H. (2007). Proximity networks and epidemics. *Physica, 378*(1), 13.

Wilensky, U. (1999). Center for connected learning and computer-based modeling. Evanston, IL: Northwestern University. Retrieved from http://ccl.northwestern.edu/netlogo/

Yoon, J., Noble, B. D., Liu, M., & Kim, M. (2006). Building realistic mobility models from coarse-grained traces. In *Proceedings of the 4th international conference on mobile systems, applications and services* (pp. 177–190). New York, NY: ACM. doi:10.1145/1134680.1134699

ENDNOTE

[1]   A link is considered as short if its length is lower than the max length of links corresponding to the starting fTL value.

Chapter 16
Towards a Unified Semantic Model for Online Social Networks to Ensure Interoperability and Aggregation for Analysis

Asmae El Kassiri
Mohammed V University, Morocco

Fatima-Zahra Belouadha
Mohammed V University, Morocco

ABSTRACT

The Online Social Networks (OSN) have a positive evolution due to the diversity of social media and the increase in the number of users. The revenue of the social media organizations is generated from the analysis of users' profiles and behaviors, knowing that surfers maintain several accounts on different OSNs. To satisfy its users, the social media organizations have initiated projects for ensuring interoperability to allow for users creating other accounts on other OSN using an initial account, and sharing content from one media to others. Believing that the future generations of Internet will be based on the semantic web technologies, multiple academic and industrial projects have emerged with the objective of modeling semantically the OSNs to ensure interoperability or data aggregation and analysis. In this chapter, we present related works and argue the necessity of a unified semantic model (USM) for OSNs; we introduce a kernel of a USM using standard social ontologies to support the principal social media and it can be extended to support other future social media.

DOI: 10.4018/978-1-5225-2814-2.ch016

INTRODUCTION

In this chapter, we argue the advantages of the OSN semantic modeling, the advantages of Unified Semantic Model, and we investigate related works.

The idea is to use a Unified Semantic Model USM to present different social media for aggregating data from these media. The model reuses the existent social ontologies, more precisely FOAF, SCOT, MOAT, AMO, SKOS and SIOC. To respond to needs not covered by these ontologies, it uses three other ontologies ActOnto, InterestOnto and AclOnto extending the SIOC ontology.

The USM is not only an aggregation model from OSN, it is also an interoperability model supposed allowing to a user migrating from a media to another with his profile, his relations and his posts. It will facilitate comprehension between social media to cooperate for a better management of users' data. It can be used as a storage model for social networks data what allow simplifying the social mining process.

Many factors motivate us to think that the idea of adopting a unified semantic model seems relevant:

- The evolutionary success of OSN;
- The phenomenon of purchasing the small actors of OSN by the giants, such as the purchase of Tumbler by Yahoo in Mai 2013, and Facebook who bought Instagram, Whatsapp and Oculus in 2014. The USM could allow having the same model for these different social medias and simplifying their data aggregation and analysis;
- The academic attempts to federate and unify some existent ontologies like MUTO (Lohmann, 2011) (Kim, Scerri, Passant, Breslin, & Kim, 2011);
- The necessity of ensuring the interoperability between OSN proved by the OGP;
- The adoption of the W3C of the FOAF, SKOS and SIOC as standards;

BACKGROUND

Mika was the first to thought to a semantic model for OSN (Mika, 2005), and then Chen and al. studied a method based on social network ontology to annotate nodes and edges (Chen., Wei., & Qingpu, 2010). Others proposed their proper ontologies; we cite for example the SNO (Social Network Ontology) (Masoumzadeh & Joshi, 2011), the SNS (Social Network Sites) Ontology (Kumar & Kumar, 2013) and the TPO (Tours Plan Ontology) limited to tourism social medias (Luz, 2010). These models are suited to analyze some kinds of OSN and for some cases but not to ensure their interoperability. While the unified semantic model USM must model the pertinent existent OSN and be easily extended to support other OSN.

The social web has raised lot of attention from the semantic community, so several ontologies are used to represent OSN. We class them into four principle categories: User description, online activities, tagging and access management.

User Description

The *FOAF (Friend Of A Friend)* (Brickley & Miller, 2014) is the ontology proposed to describe users' profiles. The FOAF project was launched in 2000 with the objective of creating web documents network. The documents must be understandable by machines and describe persons and their relationships; then

Figure 1. FOAF Concepts (Brickley et Miller 2010)

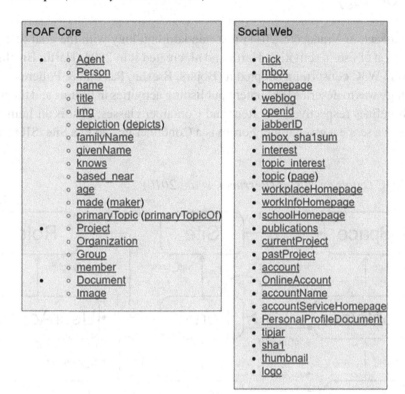

FOAF was considered by the W3C as a good ontology (Golbeck et Rothstein 2008) (Brickley et Miller 2010). The ontology give concepts that can be classed according four axes:

- **The Identity:** Elementary properties are proposed to identify a user like foaf:title, foaf:name, foaf:firstName, foaf:familyName, foaf:nick, foaf:birthday, foaf:depiction, etc.
- **The Contact Information:** Information concerning users' accounts like foaf:account, foaf:mbox, foaf:homepage, foaf:jabbered, etc.
- **The Web Activities:** A reduced number of activities like foaf:publication, foaf:interest, etc.
- **The Relationships:** A specific module (RELATIONSHIP) was conceived to specialize the "knows" property of FOAF, so it characterizes users relationships (rel:friendOf, rel:acquaintanceOf, rel:parentOf, rel:siblingOf, rel:childOf, rel:grandchildOf, rel:spouseOf, rel:enemyOf, rel:antagonistOf, rel:ambivalentOf) (Vitiello, 2002).

Online Activities

SIOC (Semantically-Interlinked Online Communities) is a standard ontology describing user's activities to allow the interoperability between social media activities. However, it constitutes the core ontology for online interaction description, it focuses on the activities forums (Breslin, Passant, & Decker, 2009). So, it was extended to support other OSN.

1. Core SIOC Ontology

SIOC (Breslin, Passant, & Vrandečić, 2011) is a standard ontology with the goal to extend FOAF for a specific description of user's activities. Harth and al. created it in 2004 (Harth, Breslin, I., & Decker, 2004); later in 2007 W3C consortium adopted it (Bojārs, Breslin, Passant, & Polleres, 2007) The initial goal of this ontology was to describe the content publishing activities in forums and the interactions with these contents. It defines respectively the Item and Container classes; Post is an Item that can answer another and have as a scope a given topic; Forum is a Container hosted in a Site. SIOC also defines the

Figure 2. Core SIOC Ontology classes (Berrueta, et al., 2010)

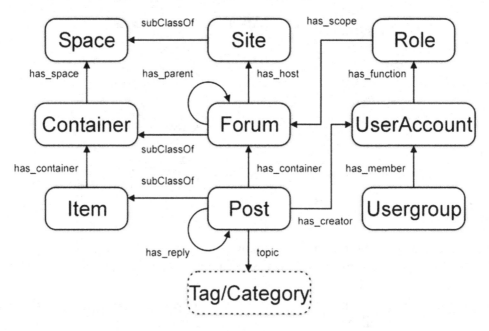

Figure 3. Example of forum activities described using SIOC

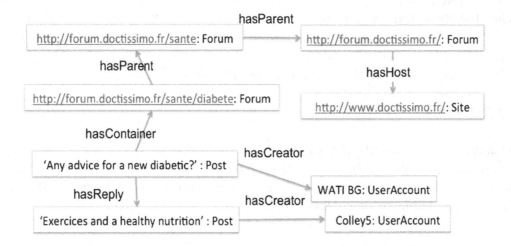

UserGroup, UserAccount and Role classes. A user account represents a member of a UserGroup, which plays a role (e.g. administrator or simple user) in the forum and can create posts.

The SIOC ontology defines respectively the classes Post, Forum, Site as subclasses of Item, Container and Space; and also defines the relationships between these classes. A post can answer another and have as a scope a given topic. It is contained in a forum that can be parent of another forum hosted in a given site. SIOC also defines the UserGroup, UserAccount and Role classes. A user account represents a member of a UserGroup, which plays a role (e.g. administrator or simple user) in the forum and can create posts.

The example shown in Figure 3 illustrates two users in a forum. The User WATI BG created a post on diabetes forum of the Health forum located in the forum of doctissimo Site, and the user Colley5 replied by another post.

The SIOC ontology has been the subject of extensions to meet new needs. So, multiple modules were proposed, some are maintained and other were abandoned like the SIOC Chat Module and the SIOC Mining Module.

Table 1. Examples of sioct sub-classes

SIOC classes	SIOC Types sub-classes
sioc:Container	sioct:AddressBook, sioct:AnnotationSet, sioct:AudioChannel, sioct:BookmarkFolder, sioct:Briefcase, sioct:EventCalendar
sioc:Forum	sioct:ChatChannel, sioct:MessageBoard, sioct:Weblog, sioct:MailingList, sioct:VideoCannel, sioct:ImageGalery
sioc:Post	sioct:InstantMessage, sioct:MailMessage, sioct:WikiArticle, sioct:Comment, sioct:BlogPost, sioct:BoardPost,

Figure 4. Example of mailing activities described by SIOCT

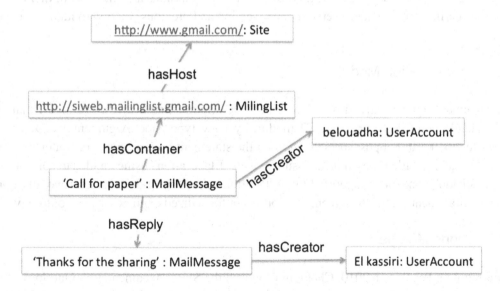

2. SIOC Types Module (SIOCT)

As we mentioned above, the initial SIOC ontology focused on the description of the activities especially in the forums. Many extensions were directed by W3C consortium and academic researchers to make it able to describe other elements and cover new needs.

The SIOC Types module (Passant, 2009) extends the SIOC ontology by subclasses that specify the types of contents and containers (Breslin, Passant, & Vrandečić, 2011). As shown in Table 1, it defines new subclasses of containers and published contents such as Weblogs, chat channels, video channels, galleries, images and blog posts elements. It also introduces new concepts such as sioct:Answer, sioct:BestAnswer and sioct:Question to support sites like Yahoo!Answers.

The Figure 4 illustrates an example of interactions between two persons using SIOCT. The user Belouadha sent a message to the mailling list siweb and the user EL Kassiri replied by another message. In this case, SIOCT allows explicitly expressing the notions of message and mailing list against SIOC that describes them respectively as post and forum.

3. SIOC Services (SIOCS) Module

module allows describing a service available on a given site and binding it to its interface, a service can be in the WSDL format (Web Services Description Language) (Kopecký & Innsbruck, 2007). For this purpose, it defines the siocs:Service class and the siocs:Service_definition property.

4. SIOC Orlandi Module

In 2008, under the supervision of Passant, Orlandi has proposed an extension of SIOC (Orlandi, 2008) to improve the representation of wikis. He proposed to use the class sioct:Category and the property has_discussion to express the type of wiki articles and the discussions associated with them, as well as the properties earlier_version, later_version, next_version and previous_version to identify its different versions.

5. SIOC Argumentation Module

The aim is to model argumentative discussions. The SIOC Argumentation module (Lange, Bojārs, Groza, Breslin, & Handschuh, 2008) enrich SIOCT module by a new type "sioct:ArgumentativeDiscussion" as a sub-class to sioc:Forum, a post specialization by the statement notion "sioc_arg:Statement" that can express an "Issue", an "Idea" based on an issue, or a an "Elaboration" using an idea to solve a problem; and the "Decision" concept is supported by a "Position". The "Position" can approve, disapprove or neutralize a "Statement". The "Argument" notion is not formalized explicitly by the ontology.

6. SIOC Actions Module

Collaborating with Passant, in 2010, Champin proposed the SIOC Argumentation Ontology to present the dynamics of online communities. This module was based on the existent ontology EVENT to present how users interact with the digital artefacts supported by the media (Champin & Passant, 2010).

Figure 5. The SIOC Argumentation module (Lange, Bojārs, Groza, Breslin, & Handschuh, 2008)

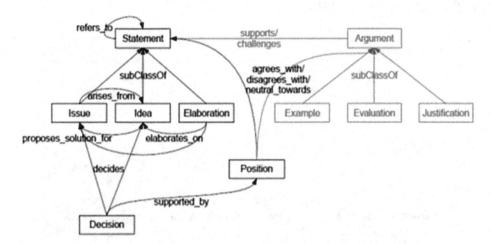

Figure 6. Equivalency between the SIOC Action Module and the EVENT Ontology (Champin & Passant, 2010)

7. SIOC Quotes Module

Passant and al. have collaborated to develop an ontology supporting quoting in online conversations; the objective was modeling conversations permitting identifying posts, its responses and responses concerning a sub-part of a post. It was engineered as a SIOC Module because ontologies are suited to give a common scheme and SIOC is widely used in the Web and gives the basic classes and properties that can be reused by the Quotes ontology (Passant, Zimmermann, Schneider, & Breslin, 2010).

8. SemSNI ontology

Another extension of the SIOC ontology has been proposed as part of a research project (Erétéo, Buffa, Gandon, & Corby, 2009). In this work, Erétéo and al. propose the SemSNI ontology (Semantic Social Network Interaction) that introduces new elements to express interactions such visits and private messages as shown in Figure 8.

The SemSNI ontology also introduces the notion of the user profile page used in social media such as Facebook or Google+, but it considers it as an item and not container. A major advantage of this ontology is that it allows to gather the visits made by a user to a resource and the private messages exchanged between two users in a social media.

Figure 7. The SIOC Quotes Module with an example of Modeling Quotes in a Conversation (Passant, Zimmermann, Schneider, & Breslin, 2010)

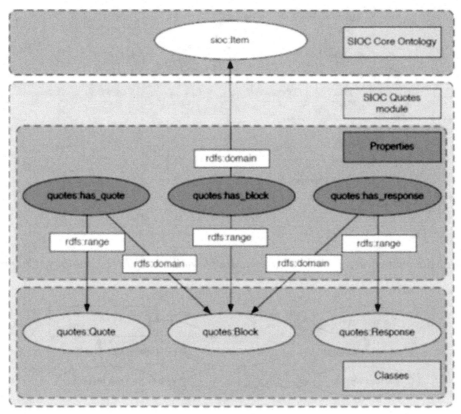

Figure 8. SemSNI Ontology (Erétéo, Buffa, Gandon, & Corby, 2009)

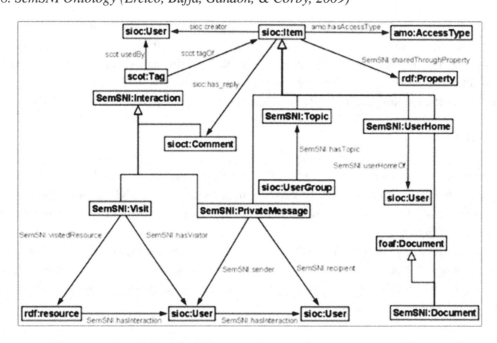

Tagging

There are two main objectives of Tagging Ontologies: the first one is to have a unified representation of tagging activity to facilitate the tags sharing and reuse. The aim is to respond to these questions: which tag used? Which user? Which resource? And when? the second one is to present the semantic of the used tag.

Concerning the first objective, Mika proposed a tripartite graph to model the tagging activity: three kinds of nodes A = {a1,...,ak}, C = {c1,...,cl}, I = {i1,...,im}. A represent Actors, C for tags and I for tagged items (Mika, 2005), then Newman and al. translate it to an ontology named Tag Ontology (Newman, Ayers, & Russell, 2005). And Knerr proposed Tagging Ontology based on tag Ontology by adding the concept of tagging (domain, type and a visibility) (Knerr, 2007). when the Gruber's model (Gruber, 2007) added the source concept; it means the space where the tagging action has been performed (Flickr, Facebook, etc.).

Concerning the formal representation of tags semantics allowing understanding the semantic relations between tags. We cite four pertinent ontologies:

- **The SKOS (Simple Knowledge Organization System):** (Alistair & Sean, 2013) (Brickley & Miller, 2014) describes concepts and their relations (matching, mapping, semantics, transitive, etc.) and their alternatives in different languages. Using SKOS, we can specify the meaning of tags and posts topics.
- **The SCOT (Social Semantic Cloud of Tags):** (Kim, Breslin, Yang, & Kim, 2008) gives a semantic structure of tagging data for a social interoperability among the different social medias. It uses concepts and properties of Tag Ontology, SIOC and SKOS with the main objective to aggregate tags used by the same persons in clouds.

Figure 9. Comparison between tagging ontologies (Lohmann, 2011)

Name	Release	Main purpose	Newly introduced concepts	OWL sublanguage	RDF/XML URI reference
Tag Ontology	23/03/2005	First formal tagging ontology	Fundamental concepts and structure, restricted tagging	OWL Full	http://www.holygoat.co.uk/owl/redwood/0.1/tags/
Tagging Ontology	2006	Comprehensive domain description	Tagging source and note, private and group tagging	OWL Full	http://bubb.ghb.fh-furtwangen.de/TagOnt/tagont.owl
Ontology of Folksonomy	2007	Comprehensive domain description	Aggregated tag, tag position, polarity, and type	OWL DL	http://www.eslomas.com/tagontology-1.owl
Social Semantic Cloud of Tags	23/03/2007	TAGS extension for tag clouds	Tag clouds, frequencies, coccurrences, and spelling variants	OWL Full	http://scot-project.org/scot/ns#
Meaning of a Tag	15/01/2008	TAGS extension for semantic tagging	Tag meaning, automatic tagging	OWL Full	http://moat-project.org/ns#
Upper Tag Ontology	2008	Upper ontology	Voting via tags	OWL Lite	http://info.slis.indiana.edu/~dingying/uto.owl
Common Tag	08/06/2009	Minimal ontology (optimized for RDFa)	Author vs. reader tags	OWL Full	http://commontag.org/ns#
TAGora Tagging Ontology	2009	Automatic tag sense disambiguation	--	OWL Lite	http://tagora.ecs.soton.ac.uk/schemas/tagging
NiceTag Ontology	09/01/2009	Taggings as speech acts (intention of tags)	Named graphs, tag intensions	OWL Full	http://ns.inria.fr/nicetag/2010/09/09/voc
Modular Unified Tagging Ontology	02/09/2011	Unification, modularization	--	OWL Lite	http://purl.org/muto/core#

- **The MOAT (Meaning Of A Tag):** (Passant & Laublet, 2008) describes a tagging by (tag, resource, user, meaning) to specify the local meaning of a tag because there are several terms with a multitude of global meanings. For example, if we use the tag « Washington » it can mean the US city or the American president « George Washington ».
- **The MUTO (Modular Unified Tagging Ontology):** (Lohmann, 2011) is an extensible ontology of tagging and folksonomies unifying existing ontologies. It supports different forms of tagging, such as common, semantic, group, private, and automatic tagging.

Access Management

The access management ontologies aim is giving a semantic description of users' roles and permissions on resources. They are used to manage and protect privacy on OSN by inferring permissions (Carminati, Ferrari, Heatherly, Kantarcioglu, & Thuraisingham, 2009) (Pwint Oo, 2013) (Kumar & Kumar, 2013), and to predict trust propagation (Barbian, 2011).

The issue of defining access control semantically has been addressed by multiples ontologies:

- **The WAC (Web Access Control vocabulary):** (Villata, Delaforge, Gandon, & Gyrard, 2011) made for specifying ACL (Access Control List) concerning the permissions Read, Write, Control and Append;
- **The S4AC (Social Semantic SPARQL Security for Access Control Ontology):** (Villata, Delaforge, Gandon, & Gyrard, 2011) based on WAC, allows expressing the Access Condition concept to have a privilege with a temporal validity;

Figure 10. AMO classes and properties (Buffa & Faron-Zucker, 2012)

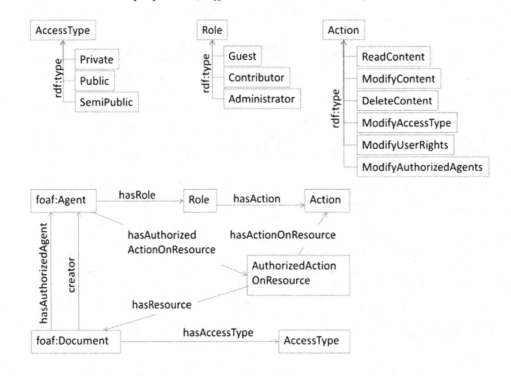

- **The AMO (Access Management Ontology):** (Buffa & Faron-Zucker, 2012) allows annotating the resources and modelling the access control policy.

Besides, the SIOC Access (SIOCA) module is another extension of SIOC ontology (Breslin, Passant, & Vrandečić, 2011) developed to describe access rights for containers and content items and the user role. This module defines the sioca:Status property which can be assigned to content items to indicate their publication status (e.g. public, private, draft, etc.), and the sioca:Permission property to describe the type of action that can be performed on a container such as a forum or a site.

WHY A UNIFIED SEMANTIC MODEL

Social networks enable users to communicate and offer possibilities to share user-generated content like photos and videos and features such as social games. Social advertising and social gaming are two major points of revenue for social networks (Number of social media users worldwide from 2010 to 2020 (in billions), 2017).

The unified model seems benefit to ensure interoperability between social media and to aggregate data from the different OSN for a pertinent analysis.

Aggregation

Recent statistics prove that approximately 74% of adults use OSN, and the average of accounts by user reach 5,54 including 2,82 active accounts (Lim, Lu, Chen, & Kan, 2015), and more than 56% of online adults uses more than one social media platform (Lister, 2017). In parallel, analyzing users' behavior online earns interests of both scientific and industrial communities. Kosinkia and al. have demonstrated that from public behavior like "likes/dislikes" it's possible to predict personal properties like religious, politic and sexual orientations, age, emotions and other personality traits (Kosinskia, Stillwella, & Graepel, 2013).

Otherwise, analyzing users' data from different accounts allows better comprehension of their behavior on the different OSN. In this context, Kong and al. have introduced the Anchor Link notion, that means a link maintained between two users over the different OSN, they use it to predict links for a new user on an OSN using his relations from author OSN (Kong, Zhang, & Yu, 2013). In parallel, Lu and al. use several OSN as sources to calculate topographic properties for a supervised link prediction (Lu, Savas, Tang, & Dhillon, 2010). While Gilbert and Karahalios analyze users' interactions over different OSN to predict the link straight (Gilbert & Karahalios, 2009).

Other researches were oriented to analyze behavioral variation over OSN. Lim and al. have conclued that users describe themselves differenttly according the networking site and reproduct posts from a network source towards destination networks (Lim, Lu, Chen, & Kan, 2015). Zafarani and Liu have demostrated that reputation is influenced and friends' distribution of users change from an OSN to another (Zafarani & Liu, 2016). Even Buccafurri and al. have compared behavior of the same users on Facebook and Twitter, and they have deduced that 87% of users prefer keeping their Facebook accounts private on Twitter, they are rather inactive on Twitter, while users having just a Twitter account are more active, and they led to the same result concerning the difference of friends' distribution on the both OSN (Buccafurri, Lax, Nicolazzo, & Nocera, 2015).

And recently, UnifyID (a Startup company in San Francisco) decided to develop an implicit authentication based on an automatic detection of the user identity by analyzing his behavior and interactions on his proper devices. The idea is based on two modules a users' devices app and a cloud service; the app collect sensor data from users' devices, process it and send features to the cloud server to discover what make a user unique; it generates specific data, send it to the concerned devices that encrypt and anonymize and store in local to be used online and offline (UnifyID's ingenious user authentication platform wins Innovation Sandbox Contest, 2017).

Interoperability

Social media organizations are conscious that surfers maintain multiple accounts on other OSN. And it's evident that social media create business value by analyzing users profile and they try to obtain more information about users from others social media (Looy, 2016), per example Instagram earns $595 million in mobile ad revenue per year, 50 million businesses use Facebook Business Pages whose 2 million use it for advertising (Lister, 2017). So, having at least, a partial interoperability is benefic for social media organizations.

In this context, the social graph API and the open graph protocol were proposed in order to insure this interoperability. In 2007, Facebook has proposed the social graph API and Google initialized the open social API. Both uses the FOAF ontology and XFN micro-formats (XHTML Friends Network) (Breslin, Passant, & Vrandečić, 2011). Those two API were developed to allow a user using its account created in a given networking site, to authenticate in other OSN implementing this API, without having to create a new profile, and to recuperate his data and his old relations. The user can select among his profile data and friendship relations those that he wishes to share.

Then, Facebook decided to pass to the Open Graph (OGP), the OGP is managed by the Open Web Foundation. It allows different sites such as twitter, google+ and Facebook to interact via an interpretable information exchange. It uses in addition to FOAF and XFN, a name space OG that defines a controlled vocabulary based on RDF metadata to describe the web page data. A web page with annotated content by the OGP allows an automatic interpretation of its semantics. Using the open graph protocol, a user can share a content via a site like YouTube on another site like Facebook, and Facebook could identify the elements of the shared content (video title, associated description, etc.).

Based on the use of FOAF and XFN and/or a name space describing the web page content, the social graph API and the open graph protocol allow respectively to social media sharing the users' profiles and their friendship relations, and exchanging objects with normalized representation. Otherwise, they allow interoperability between social media at the level of users' profile and objects composing the web pages' content.

OSN Analysis Challenges

By the analysis of OSN data, the researchers were confronted to three categories of challenges (Gundecha et Liu 2012):

- **Unstructured and Dynamic Data:** Each social platform use its proper structuration method for data storage, and data is permanently updated by users;

- **Large and Distributed Data:** There are multiple social media on line, and each one has a fragment of source data needed to OSN Analysis. Recent statistics estimate that Snapchat hits 10 billion daily video views and its revenue were close to 1 billion dollars in 2016, and Instagram reached 600 Million users (Roberts, 2016); 100 million hours of video content are watched on Facebook daily, and 22% of the world's total population uses Facebook; and LinkedIn boasts more than 450 million user profiles (Lister, 2017); On Facebook, the number of active users has reached 1.871 billion (Chaffey, 2017);
- **Noised Data:** Spammers generate more data than legitim users (Yardi, et al. 2010) (Chu, et al. 2010).

Other issues were raised like the online accounts duplicated, the inactive nodes (unused and undeleted accounts), the malicious users, the diversity of sources, the privacy and the size of the OSN making the identification and analysis of implicit relationships between users more difficult (Bonchi, et al. 2011).

Tang and Liu have studied the OSN characteristics, and they have identified three main properties (Tang et Liu 2010): the *scale-free distributions* reporting an heterogenous distribution of friends proved by an analysis done on YouTube and Flicker (Mislove, et al. 2007); the *small-world effect property* deduced from an applied study on a network with more than 180 million users, it proved that the average path between each pair of users is 6.6 nodes (Leskovec et Horvitz 2008); and the *strong community structure* property raised from the clustering coefficient, it estimate that those networks can be partitioned into communities.

Tang and Liu have identified three other challenges (Tang et Liu 2010):

- **The Dynamic Nature of the OSN:** It's a natural result of the services kind deserved by the social media allowing users changing their relationships and expressing new interests over time;
- **The OSN Size:** It makes unused the traditional algorithms of Social Network Analysis SNA, because those algorithms were adapted to networks of few thousand of nodes;
- **The OSN Heterogeneity:** The type nodes diversity in the OSN is another challenge making the tradition SNA algorithms inadequate for its analysis.

In brief, the OSN analysis challenges are: the modeling, the data cleaning; and the adaptation of SNA algorithms to support the size, the heterogeneity and the dynamism of OSN.

In the present chapter, we are interested in the modeling of OSN data to ensure interoperability and aggregation using existent ontologies cited above.

SOLUTIONS AND RECOMMENDATIONS

Works and efforts cited above prove that interoperability and aggregating data from the different OSN is a serious need and issue, so we thought about a unique model to ensure the both needs. Convinced that semantic web will be a part of the future version of the web, and knowing its benefits for normalizing data presentation, and its capacities for reusing data and inferring latent information, we have opted for a unified model based on ontologies.

Based on the successful attempts of using the well-known ontologies to represent OSN for aggregating users data, EL KASSIRI & BELOUADHA have decided to participate in improving existent ontologies to produce a USM allowing a unique representation for the OSN ensuring their interoperability, a semantic description of users profile (name, city, birth date, etc.) and online activities (posting, sharing, liking, tagging, etc.) allowing inferring behaviors thanks at ontologies (EL KASSIRI & Belouadha, 2015).

Furthermore, the combination between the two good ontologies recommended by the W3C: FOAF and SIOC with the standard SKOS is possible and allow presenting users and most of their behavior. So, EL KASSIRI & BELOUDHA decide to start out with these three ontologies to develop the USM and try covering detected lacks by three other ontologies, with the open possibility to improve it to ensure potential future needs.

The three proposed ontologies are:

- **ActOnto:** Ontology is an extension of SIOC used to describe OSN resources and interactions not supported by SIOC (EL KASSIRI & BELOUADHA, 2014);
- **InterestOnto:** Is an ontology designed to detail the local meaning of a tag for simplifying the SNA and enhance the process inferring of equivalent tags (EL KASSIRI & Belouadha, 2015);
- **AclOnto:** To meet the security and privacy needs in OSN by defining roles and permissions (authorizations and restrictions) concepts (EL KASSIRI & Belouadha, 2015).

ActOnto Ontology

The ActOnto ontology (EL KASSIRI & BELOUADHA, 2014) is another extension of SIOC structured on two modules: the SiocCont module specifying containers (UserHome and SocialPage <page/group>) and the SiocInt module that describing the interactions with posted contents (visits, evaluations <like, dislike, note> and modifications). ActOnto allows presenting the creator of a Social Resource (Item or container) and the date of creation to accompany the OSN evolution over time.

Although the SIOC Types module extended SIOC to support the representation of several types of containers such as wikis, blogs, image galleries and video channels, this ontology doesn't represent

Figure 11. SiocCont module of the ontology ActOnto

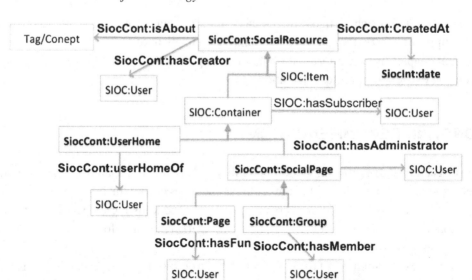

information related to other types of containers used by several social networking sites such as profile pages, pages and groups. As shown in Figure 11, the SiocCont module specializes the SIOC:Container class by two subclasses UserHome describing a profile page and SocialPage generalizing two other subclasses Page and Group. Page and Group have respectively the properties hasFun and hasMember to describe pages and groups created on Facebook or LinkedIn and their funs/members (they have more access privileges compared to simple Subscribers) and administrators. We note that the SIOC:User class is equivalent to the SIOC:UserAccount class.

Given that every container has a creator, creation date and subject, we defined the class SocialResource that generalizes both the Item and Container classes, and we add the properties hasCreator, CreatedAt and isAbout. The page properties hasFun and isAbout can be used to infer the user's interest for a given topic. While the group property hasMember allows us to deduce a possible relationship between two members of a given group. Similarly, the property CreatedAt would permit to deduce, when analyzing social networks, the fact that a user was interested in a topic during a given time period and that it is no longer the case now.

Moreover, the ActOnto permits describing the scenario on Facebook when a user X wants to share a photo P on his friend Y profile page. However, SIOC can describe the fact that the user X published the item P on the container Page_Y found on the Facebook website, without being able to express the fact that Page_Y is the profile page of the user Y. The SemSNI ontology also can't fill this need because it represents a profile page (SemSNI:UserHome) as an Item and not as a container where it is possible to publish items. However, being able to identify the owner of a profile page on which an item has been shared, can guide the social network analysis to deduce that he should be interested in the topic of the shared item.

Besides, as shown in Figure 12, the SiocInt module defines the SiocInt:Interaction class generalizing three subclasses SiocInt:Visit, SiocInt:Evaluation and SiocInt:Modification. We note that we keep the SIOC properties modified_at and has_modifier for specifying the user who modified the Item, a container can also be modified (e.g. it is possible to change the subject of a page). So, we have associated the class SiocInt:Modification with the class SiocInt:Resource. The subclass SiocInt:Evaluation is specialized

Figure 12. SiocInt module of the ontology ActOnto

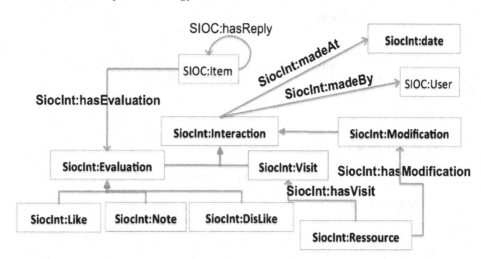

by three subclasses SiocInt:Like, SiocInt:Dislike and SiocInt:Note. These classes allow integrating the concept of content evaluation by users. So, it become possible describing user activities related to the use of "like" and "dislike" buttons in Facebook and Youtube, the "+1" button in Google+ and a numerical value to evaluate an item. The ActOnto ontology defines also the SiocInt:madeBy and SiocInt:madeAt properties to specify the maker and the date of the interaction. The classes and properties defined allow: firstly, gathering the feelings and opinions of users about the published contents, and secondly, detecting or predicting their potential interesting through the resources (containers or content) visits and modifications, per example, regular visits to a given page or a given profile page can be interpreted by a special interest for the page topic or a friend. The property madeAt permits to identify new and old user interactions, and the changes of page topic done by a given user over time, can therefore be used to analyze his trends and predict his interest for some subjects in the future.

The example given in Figure 13, written according to the ontology ActOnto, represents a scenario where a user has shared a video on the Facebook profile page of his friend who liked this publication that another user who commented it by an image.

InetrestOnto Ontology

The tagging ontologies allow specifying tags used by actors for resources. An inferring process based on tags and SKOS can deduce posts with the same topics, or identify users with the same interests. But, the informal language contains multiple homonyms, and only the MOAT allows specifying the meaning of the tag by the user but it doesn't give a precise semantic context, so the user can use other terms more ambiguous. The objective of InetrestOnto is to define specific sub-classes of the Tag class.

The aim of Interest Ontology (InetrestOnto) is to meet the following requirements:

Figure 13. Example of activities described by ActOnto

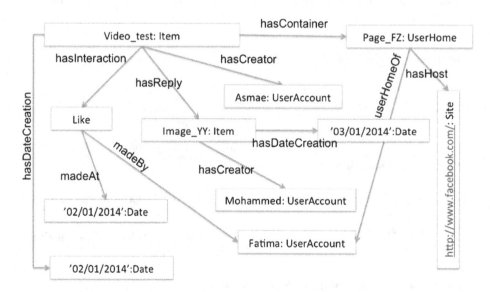

- InterestOnto concepts have to respond to the main SNA (Social Networks Analysis) needs. A tag can reference a person (user, famous person), a subject, a product or a location (city, country, etc.) (See Figure 14);
- InetrestOnto must be extensible and combinable with FOAF, MUTO, SKOS, SIOC and their extension to ensure the interoperability.

Figure 14. InterestOnto Classes

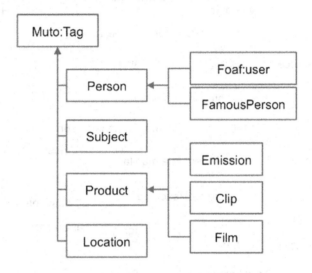

AclOnto Ontology

We note some limits concerning the existent Access Control Ontologies:

- Lack of compatibility with the existent ontologies that we have choice for our unified sematic model;
- SIOC Access allows defining permissions only by users;
- AMO allows authorizing permissions only by roles;
- There is no restriction of permissions.

Our AclOnto ontology is based on AMO. It applies roles and AccessType on SoicalResources (item or container), it defines the Actor concept that can be a role or a user to receive authorizations or restrictions.

The class AclOnto:Role allows to a user to create groups of permissions. The Container Access Type defines the default permissions to applying on all its items, and the different actions (AMO:Action) concerning the container.

Based on this ontology, we can represent the case when, on Facebook for example, a user wants allow to a group of his friends with a specific role to see a post but forbid it to a user having this role. Generally, restriction is higher priority than authorization, and user direct permissions are higher than permissions inherited from roles. For examples:

Figure 15. On the channel Hit Radio on Youtube, the admin has shared a Video about an emission «Test Machmoum », and the subscriber Asmae has tagged it with the 'Momo', a famous person. Another subscriber Amine has published a video about the clip « Inta Maallam » and tagged it with a name of a famous person « Saad Lamjarred ».

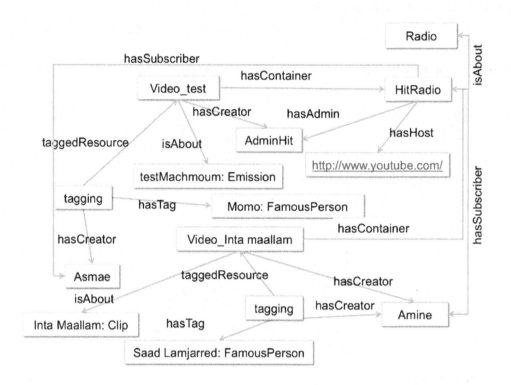

Figure 16. AclOnto Classess and properties

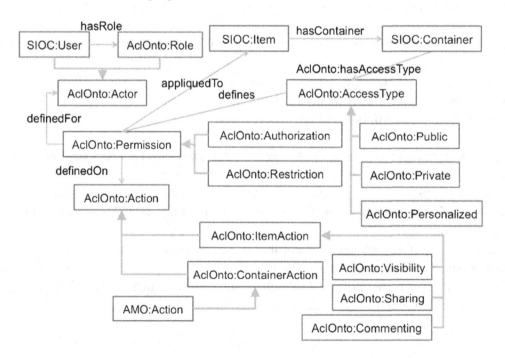

A user on facebook has a default role defined on his profile (ActOnto:UserHome) named "Friends". For a user X having a profile with a private access type (all permissions are granted for friends only ("Friends" role)), has defined the "Family" role. Y is an X's Friend:

- X limits Sharing and Commenting permissions on an Item I to "Family" and revoke it from "Friends". If Y belongs or not to "Friends", he has only the Visibility permission (restriction is high priority). But if X gives the Commenting permission to Y, he will have the Visibility and Commenting permission on I.
- If X changes his profile access type to public; by defaults, all users will have all permissions on all Items to be sharing after.
- A profile with Personalized access type is a home page with different permissions granted to different users and roles.
- For a social page (ActOnto:SocialPage) or group (ActOnto:Group) with private access type, there are two default roles "Administrators" and "Members". The first ones are authorized to modify the page's contents and properties (AMO:Action), to share, comment and see (AclOnto:ItemAction); while the "Members" have only authorization for the AclOnto:ItemAction permissions.

An Example of Implementation and Experimentation

To illustrate the easy possibility to use the ActOnto ontology for aggregating data from social media, EL KASSIRI & BELOUADHA developed in Eclipse environment an application in Java and we tested it through an example collected from Facebook (EL KASSIRI & BELOUADHA, ActOnto: An extension of the SIOC standard for social media analysis and interoperability, 2014). This application allows generating the RDF file that represents, according to ActOnto ontology, data extracted from social media. To first extract the data that form the input of the application, we used the Graph API Explorer tool to extract

Figure 17. X shares an Item I on his profile, so Y has all permissions because he belongs to "Friends"

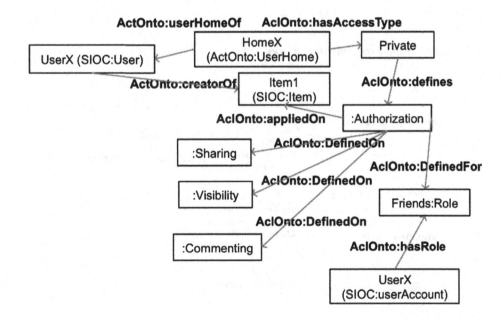

data from Facebook. This tool allows, through a graphical interface, specifying data access permissions that will be granted to the graph explorer by the user. According to these permissions, an access token is provided by Facebook to the social graph explorer that will be able to return relevant data, annotated according to the vocabulary of the open graph protocol, in JSON (JavaScript Object Definition) format. The JSON format is a simple text data format which is generic, derivative from objects notation JavaScript and used to represent structured information in Web applications.

We used Protégé OWL, an open source ontology editor distributed by the University of Stanford Medical Informatics, to create our ActOnto ontology. Protégé is not a tool especially dedicated to OWL, but a highly extensible editor, able to handle a wide variety of formats.

As illustrated in Figure 19, the implemented application allows generating a RDF file from both a JSON file of social media data and ActOnto ontology. It consists of two components: Processing Com-

Figure 18. Graph API Explorer Interface

Figure 19. Architecture of the experimentation tool

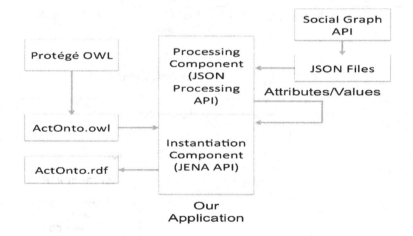

ponent and Instantiation Component. The mission of the Processing Component is to analyze the JSON file in order to identify the different pairs (attribute, value) from the data it contains. For this purpose, it uses JSON Processing API (Java API for JSON Processing (JSON-P)). The Instantiation Component is designed to instantiate the ActOnto ontology. Using the Jena API recommended for semantic applications development, it is able to read and reuse ActOnto pairs (attribute, value) which are obtained through the Processing Component, to instantiate RDF triplets and generate the corresponding RDF file.

For experimenting the developed application, we extracted from Facebook, the data concerning the user El Kassiri (personal data, list of friends, group list, pages and publications she likes). Figure 20 shows a mapping of an extract of the content of the obtained JSON file, and concepts from ActOnto ontology. This extract interprets the fact that the user El Kassiri (id 1451960389) published a post (id 1451960389_10202266540812228) about the topic (161 signatures are still needed!) on its profile page in the date (2013 - 11-13). Figure 20 illustrates, as a graph, a part of the RDF file content, relating to this extract. This part further indicates that the user (id 509268650) evaluated the post published on the profile page (https://www.facebook.com/asmae.kass) using 'LIKE' at the same day of its publication. We can remark that the generated file specifies a profile page as container, dates of activities and an interaction of evaluation type, which are details not provided by SIOC.

FUTURE RESEARCH DIRECTIONS

As cited above, the OSN are business organizations aiming engaging a business value from users data by analyzing their profile and their online behavior for publicity recommendation, product or service

Figure 20. A mapping example from JSON to ActOnto RDF triplets

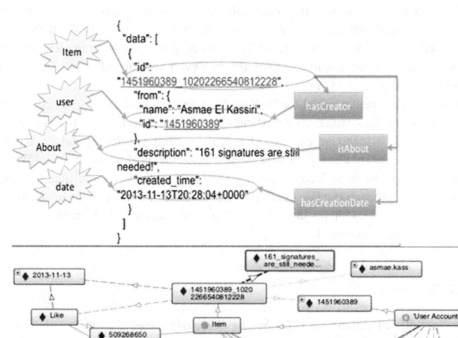

or person reputation analysis, etc., so the USM will offer an interoperability permitting accessing to data from other OSN, and by consequence the leader organizations (Facebook, Google, Twitter, etc.) should refuse sharing its data because it maintain the giant volume of data and the share will increase the concurrency. By the way those organizations can use the USM to aggregate data from all its social media for a complete analysis.

We have demonstrated that is possible to model Facebook data by the proposed model (El Kassiri & Belouadha, 2014), but we let to OSN administrators the choice to implement their own solutions to immigrate their data to the USM and select data to disclose and data to keep in dark according to their business plan and their strategy.

The advantage of using ontologies for representation of OSN data is the *modularity* allowing extending model to support other OSN not supported by the actual model; and the data *reusability* thanks to the standardization ensured by ontologies.

The *USM* must offer *interoperability* to permit, if used as platform of structuring data by the social media, users moving between social media with a unique account; and *aggregation* for a complete and efficient analysis, in next papers, we intend to explain how use it to analyze data from heterogeneous sources and for diverse needs.

Our idea consists on an ontological approach aiming offering a platform for *generic analysis* covering the different aspects of OSN analysis needs (influence propagation, trust analysis, recommendation, privacy and confidence, similarity analysis, expert detection, community detection and link prediction), and supporting the *most popular social media*. The objective of the USM is preparing the platform to support the most popular social media.

CONCLUSION

OSN are a rich source of information that can be exploited in different domains such as marketing and politics, for product recommendation, reputation management, electoral prediction, detecting terrorist communities, protecting privacy, trust mining, etc. The OSN analysis has attracting a lot of interests from business and academic communities, motiving by the web evolution towards a semantic web, several ontologies were proposed to model OSN.

To engineer a unified semantic model for OSN to describe the social medias content, we proposed the ActOnto (El Kassiri & Belouadha, 2014) extending SIOC, and the InterestOnto and the AclOnto (El Kassiri & Belouadha, 2015) to enrich, respectively, the tagging ontologies and the access control ontologies. Those ontologies are aligned with the standard ontologies of semantic social Web.

The unified model will allow collecting and aggregating knowledge from different OSN, to lead to efficient results of social analysis. For example, federating relationships of a user from Facebook, YouTube and Twitter can reveal interesting patterns. But, it remains a basic framework of a semantic analysis approach that can be extended.

REFERENCES

Alistair, M., & Sean, B. (2013, June 4). *SKOS Simple Knowledge Organization System Reference.* Retrieved from W3C Recommendation: http://www.w3.org/TR/skos-reference/

Barbian, G. (2011, 09 12-14). Trust Centrality in Online Social Networks. *Proceedings of Intelligence and Security Informatics Conference (EISIC'11)*, 372 - 377.

Berrueta, D., Brickley, D., Decker, S., Fernández, S., Görn, C., Harth, A., . . . Polo, L. (2010, March 25). *SIOC Core Ontology Specification.* Retrieved from RDFS: http://rdfs.org/sioc/spec/

Bojārs, U., Breslin, J. G., Passant, A., & Polleres, A. (2007, June 12). *SIOC Ontology: Related Ontologies and RDF Vocabularies.* Retrieved from W3C Member Submission.

Bonchi, F., Castillo, C., Gionis, A., & Jaimes, A. (2011). 04). Social Network Analysis and Mining for Business Applications. *ACM Transactions on Intelligent Systems and Technology, 2*(3). doi:10.1145/1961189.1961194

Breslin, J., Passant, A., & Decker, S. (2009). *The Social Semantic Web.* Springer-Verlag Berlin Heidelberg. doi:10.1007/978-3-642-01172-6

Breslin, J., Passant, A., & Vrandečić, D. (2011). Social Semantic Web. In J. Domingue, & D. Fensel (Eds.), Handbook of Semantic Web Technologies (pp. 467-506). Springer Berlin Heidelberg. doi:10.1007/978-3-540-92913-0_12

Brickley, D., & Miller, L. (2010, Août 9). *FOAF Vocabulary Specification 0.98.* Retrieved June 4, 2013, from http://xmlns.com/foaf/spec/

Brickley, D., & Miller, L. (2014, Janvier 14). *FOAF Vocabulary Specification 0.99. Namespace Document.* Retrieved from xmlns.com: http://xmlns.com/foaf/spec/

Buccafurri, F., Lax, G., Nicolazzo, S., & Nocera, A. (2015). 11). Comparing Twitter and Facebook user behavior. *Journal Computers in Human Behavior, 52*(C), 87–95. doi:10.1016/j.chb.2015.05.045

Buffa, M., & Faron-Zucker, C. (2012). Ontology-Based Access Rights Management. In F. Guillet, G. Ritschard, & D. A. Zighed (Eds.), Advances in Knowledge Discovery and Management (pp. 49-61). Springer Berlin Heidelberg. doi:10.1007/978-3-642-25838-1_3

Carminati, B., Ferrari, E., Heatherly, R., Kantarcioglu, M., & Thuraisingham, B. (2009). A semantic web based framework for social network access control. *Proceedings of the 14th ACM symposium on Access control models and technologies SACMAT'09*, 177-186. doi:10.1145/1542207.1542237

Chaffey, D. (2017, February 27). *Global social media research summary 2017.* Retrieved from Smart Insights: http://www.smartinsights.com/social-media-marketing/social-media-strategy/new-global-social-media-research/

Champin, P. A., & Passant, A. (2010). SIOC in Action – Representing the Dynamics of Online Communities. *Proceedings the 6th International Conference on Semantic Systems, I-SEMANTICS 2010* (pp. 12:1-12.7). Graz, Austria: ACM.

Chen, L., Wei, S., & Qingpu, Z. (2010). Semantic Description of Social Network Based on Ontology. *International Conference on E-Business and E-Government* (pp. 1936 - 1939). IEEE. doi:10.1109/ICEE.2010.489

Chu, Z., Gianvecchio, S., Wang, H., & Jajodia, S. (2010). Who is tweeting on Twitter: Human, bot, or cyborg? *Computer Security Applications Conference ACSAC, 10*(26), 21–30.

El Kassiri, A., & Belouadha, F.-Z. (2014). ActOnto: An extension of the SIOC standard for social media analysis and interoperability. *Third IEEE International Colloquium in Information Science and Technology (CIST'14)*, 62-67.

El Kassiri, A., & Belouadha, F.-Z. (2015). Towards a Unified Semantic Model for Online Social Networks Analysis and Interoperability. *10th International Conference on Intelligent Systems: Theories and Applications (SITA)*, 62-67.

Erétéo, G., Buffa, M., Gandon, F., & Corby, O. (2009). Analysis of a Real Online Social Network Using Semantic Web Frameworks. *8th International Semantic Web Conference, ISWC 2009* (pp. 180-195). Chantilly, VA: Springer Berlin Heidelberg. doi:10.1007/978-3-642-04930-9_12

Gilbert, E., & Karahalios, K. (2009). Predicting tie strength with social media. *Proceedings of the SIGCHI Conference on Human Factors in Computing Systems CHI '09*, 211-220.

Golbeck, J., & Rothstein, M. M. (2008). Linking social networks on the web with FOAF: a semantic web case study. *Proceeding AAAI'08 Proceedings of the 23rd national conference on Artificial intelligence, 2*, 1138-1143.

Gruber, T. (2007). Ontology of folksonomy: A mashup of apples and oranges. *International Journal on Semantic Web and Information Systems, 3*(2).

Gundecha, P., & Liu, H. (2012). *Mining Social Media: A Brief Introduction.* The Institute for Operations Research and the Management Sciences (INFORMS), TutORials in Operations Research. Retrieved from http://www.public.asu.edu/~pgundech/book_chapter/smm.pdf

Harth, A., Breslin, J. G., & Decker, S. (2004). Linking Semantically Enabled Online Community Sites. *1st Workshop on Friend of a Friend, Social Networking and the Semantic Web.* W3C.

Java API for JSON Processing (JSON-P). (n.d.). Retrieved April 03, 2017, from Java.net: https://json-processing-spec.java.net/

Kim, H.-L., Breslin, J., Yang, S.-K., & Kim, H.-G. (2008). *Social Semantic Cloud of Tag: Semantic Model for Social Tagging. In Agent and Multi-Agent Systems: Technologies and Applications.* Springer Berlin Heidelberg.

Kim, H.-L., Scerri, S., Passant, A., Breslin, J. G., & Kim, H.-G. (2011). Integrating Tagging into the Web of Data: Overview and Combination of Existing Tag Ontologies. *Journal of Internet Technology, 12*(4), 561–572.

Knerr, T. (2007, Jan 15). *tagont.* Retrieved from code.google.com/archive: https://code.google.com/archive/p/tagont/downloads

Kong, X., Zhang, J., & Yu, P. S. (2013). Inferring anchor links across multiple heterogeneous social networks. *Proceedings of the 22nd ACM international conference on Conference on information & knowledge management*, 179-188. doi:10.1145/2505515.2505531

Kopecký, J., & Innsbruck, D. (2007, June 26). *Web Services Description Language (WSDL) Version 2.0: RDF Mapping*. Retrieved from WSDL: http://www.w3.org/TR/wsdl20-rdf/

Kosinskia, M., Stillwella, D., & Graepel, T. (2013). Private traits and attributes are predictable from digital records of human behavior. *Proceedings of the National Academy of Sciences of the United States of America, 110*(15), 5802–5805. doi:10.1073/pnas.1218772110 PMID:23479631

Kumar, V., & Kumar, S. (2013). Access Control Framework for Social Network System using Ontology. *International Journal of Computers and Applications, 79*(4), 10–18. doi:10.5120/13728-1524

Kumar, V., & Kumar, S. (2013). Access Control Framework for Social Network System using Ontology. *International Journal of Computer Applications, 7*(4).

Lange, C., Bojārs, U., Groza, T., Breslin, J., & Handschuh, S. (2008). Expressing Argumentative Discussions in Social Media Sites. *First Workshop on Social Data on the Web (SDoW2008)*.

Leskovec, J., & Horvitz, E. (2008). Planetary-scale views on a large instant-messaging network. *WWW '08: Proceeding of the 17th international conference on World Wide Web*, 915–924. doi:10.1145/1367497.1367620

Lim, B. H., Lu, D., Chen, T., & Kan, M.-Y. (2015, 08 25-28). #mytweet via Instagram: Exploring User Behaviour across Multiple Social Networks. *Proceedings of the 2015 IEEE/ACM International Conference on Advances in Social Networks Analysis and Mining ASONAM '15*, 113-120. doi:10.1145/2808797.2808820

Lister, M. (2017, Jan 20). *40 Essential Social Media Marketing Statistics for 2017*. Retrieved from Word Stream: http://www.wordstream.com/blog/ws/2017/01/05/social-media-marketing-statistics

Lohmann, S. (2011, November 16). *Modular Unified Tagging Ontology (MUTO)*. Retrieved from muto socialtagging: http://muto.socialtagging.org/core/v1.html

Looy, A. V. (2016). *Social Media Management*. Springer International Publishing. doi:10.1007/978-3-319-21990-5

Lu, Z., Savas, B., Tang, W., & Dhillon, I. S. (2010). Supervised Link Prediction Using Multiple Sources. *Proceedings of the 2010 IEEE International Conference on Data Mining ICDM '10*, 923-928. doi:10.1109/ICDM.2010.112

Luz, N. (2010). *Semantic Social Network Analysis* (PhD Thesis). Instituto Politécnico do Porto, Instituto Superior de Engenharia do Porto.

Masoumzadeh, A., & Joshi, J. (2011). Ontology-based access control for social network systems. *International Journal of Information Privacy, Security and Integrity*, 59 - 78.

Mika, P. (2005). Ontologies are us: A unified model of social networks and semantics. *International Semantic Web Conference LNCS* (pp. 522–536). Springer. doi:10.1007/11574620_38

Mislove, A., Marcon, M., Gummadi, K. P., Druschel, P., & Bhattacharjee, B. (2007). Measurement and analysis of online social networks. *IMC '07: Proceedings of the 7th ACM SIGCOMM conference on Internet measurement*, 7, 29–42. doi:10.1145/1298306.1298311

Newman, R., Ayers, D., & Russell, S. (2005, December 21). *Tag ontology design*. Retrieved from holygoat. co.uk: http://www.holygoat.co.uk/projects/tags/

Number of social media users worldwide from 2010 to 2020 (in billions). (2017, April 3). Retrieved from The Statistics Portal: http://www.statista.com/statistics/278414/number-of-worldwide-social-network-users/

Orlandi, F. (2008). *Using and extending the sioc ontology for a fine-grained wiki modeling* (Master's Thesis). Università degli Studi di Modena e Reggio Emilia.

Passant, A. (2009, Octobre 20). *SIOC Types and Health Care and Life Sciences*. Retrieved from W3C Submission: http://www.w3.org/TR/hcls-sioc/

Passant, A., & Laublet, P. (2008). Meaning of a tag: A collaborative approach to bridge the gap between tagging and linked data. *Proceedings of the WWW 2008 Workshop Linked Data on the Web (LDOW2008)*.

Passant, A., Zimmermann, A., Schneider, J., & Breslin, J. G. (2010). A semantic framework for modelling quotes in email conversations. *Proceedings of the 1st International Conference on Intelligent Semantic Web-Services and Applications (ISWSA '10)* (pp. 11:1-11:8). Amman, Jordan: ACM. doi:10.1145/1874590.1874601

Pwint Oo, S. H. (2013). Intelligent access control policies for social network site. *International Journal of Computer Science & Information Technology*, 183-190.

Roberts, P. (2016). *Social Media Statistics for 2017*. Retrieved from Our Social Times: http://oursocial-times.com/7-social-media-statistics-for-2017/

Tang, L., & Liu, H. (2010). *Community Detection and Mining in Social Media* (Vol. 1). Morgan & Claypool.

UnifyID's ingenious user authentication platform wins Innovation Sandbox Contest. (2017, Febrary 15). Retrieved from Help Net Security: https://www.helpnetsecurity.com/2017/02/15/unifyid-user-authentication-platform/

Villata, S., Delaforge, N., Gandon, F., & Gyrard, A. (2011). An Access Control Model for Linked Data. On the Move to Meaningful Internet Systems: OTM 2011 Workshops, 454-463.

Vitiello, E. J. (2002, July 19). *Relationship: A module for defining relationships in FOAF*. Retrieved April 03, 2017, from http://www.perceive.net: http://www.perceive.net/schemas/20021119/relationship/

Yardi, S., Romero, D., Schoenebeck, G., & boyd, d. (2010, Janvier 4). Detecting spam in a Twitter network. *First Monday, 15*(1).

Zafarani, R., & Liu, H. (2016). Users joining multiple sites: Friendship and popularity variations across sites. *Journal Information Fusion, 28*(C), 83–89. doi:10.1016/j.inffus.2015.07.002

Chapter 17
Can We Trust the Health Information We Find Online?
Identification of Influential Nodes

Leila Weitzel
Universidade Federal Fluminense, Brazil

Jose Palazzo Moreira de Oliveira
Universidade Federal do Rio Grande do Sul, Brazil

Paulo Quaresma
Universidade de Evora, Brazil

Danilo Artigas
Universidade Federal Fluminense, Brazil

ABSTRACT

The Internet is becoming increasingly an important source of information for people who are seeking healthcare information. Users do so without professional guidance and may lack sufficient knowledge and training to evaluate the validity and quality of health web content. This is particularly problematic in the era of Web 2.0. Hence, the main goal of this research is to propose an approach to infer user reputation based on social interactions. Reputation is a social evaluation towards a person or a group of people. The results show that our rank methodology and the network topology succeeded in achieving user reputation. The results also show that centrality measures associated with the weighted ties approach suitably controls suitably the ranking of nodes.

1. INTRODUCTION

The Internet has revolutionized communications, to the extent that it is now our preferred medium of everyday communication. It consolidated itself as a very powerful platform that has changed forever the way we do business. As such, it has become the Universal source of information for millions of people, on the go, at home, at school, and at work ("Internet usage and World population statistics," 2016). Internet is also becoming increasingly important source of information for people who are seeking healthcare information (de Boer, Versteegen, & van Wijhe, 2007).

DOI: 10.4018/978-1-5225-2814-2.ch017

Many, if not most, users proactively seek information on their own to obtain answers instead of waiting for their next appointment with the doctor. Since, users do so without professional guidance, they may lack sufficient knowledge and training to evaluate the validity and quality of health web content (Eysenbach, 2002). Indeed, people increasingly go online to share their own health and illness experiences and to access information that others have posted. Internet is used as a serious and often the first source of information about health.

Looking on the bright side, the acquired information is intended to elicit discussion and communication between patient and the primary care physician. Looking at the negative side, incorrect information could be life-threatening (Anderson, 2004). Given that, the internet sites contain information of different quality levels, thus it makes it difficult for users to determine the quality of the information and the reputation of its providers (Agichtein, Castillo, Donato, Gionis, & Mishne, 2008).

Considering that not every article shared on Web is true, the concept of trust becomes imperative. How can we really trust the health information that we find online? We have to ask themselves, for example, is there any evidence that the author has some authority in health domain? What are the author's qualifications, credentials and connections to the subject? Are there clues that the authors are biased? How shall we know what our sources are worth? How shall we be able to separate the bad sources from the good ones?

According to Bhattacharya et al (2014) Federal Government Agencies are increasingly interested in using social media to distribute information at the national, state and local levels. While it is a good news, this is not enough on its own to solve all the problems, it is very easy for outsiders to spread misinformation. For instance, anti-vaccination posts may sway parents into refusing to vaccinate their children, which can increase disease risk.

Despite all information acquired, using searching tools offers an unprecedented opportunity for applications to monitor and improve the quality of life of people. However, less than half of the medical information available online has been reviewed by medical experts and only 20% of Internet users verify the information by visiting authoritative websites such as CDC and FDA (Chomphoosang, 2012).

Many concerns have arisen about the quality in health domain, and the possibility that poor information has detrimental effects on health (Stvilia, Mon, & Yi, 2009; L. Weitzel, Quaresma, & de Oliveira, 2012). Indeed, health information is critical to health-related decisions, mostly because, health information acquired from Internet have the potential to both improve health and do harm. This is particularly problematic in era of Web 2.0. The Web 2.0 is a second generation of World Wide Web. It is the ultimate manifestation of User-Generated Content (UGC), and as such, holds more potential for growth than any other form of content on the Web today.

The explosion of UGC in health care is, in part, the result of broader internet trends: more and more people have broadband access and the tools for creating content are getting easier to use (Hughes, Joshi, Lemonde, & Wareham, 2009; Stvilia et al., 2009). Popular UGC systems domains include blogs and web forums, social bookmarking sites, photo and video sharing communities, as well as social networking platforms such as Twitter, Facebook and MySpace. Given the widespread use of Twitter, people are increasingly using it to share their experiences with illness and treatments as well as other health concerns.

Due to the global nature of the Web 2.0, anyone can post anything on the web, regardless of his or her background or medical qualifications. Everyone is, or could be an authority or expert. In this sense, from the information consumer's perspective, a very reasonable reversal of the real life process is taking place. In real world, we cannot assume that all anonymous users would behave honestly or would have correct health information to share. The suggestion is that we do not necessarily trust a source of information (e.g. a "John Doe Expert Blog") just because it exists. We should increase our level of trust as we realize that a consistent quality of information is being delivered. One systematic review assessing the quality of consumer health information on the Internet concluded that "health quality" was a problem (Eysenbach, 2002). Freedom of information on the internet dictates that anyone can publish anything. On the internet, as the old saying goes, "nobody knows you are a dog" (Stvilia et al., 2009).

This book chapter will be of interest to methodologically minded social and computer scientists. It is also relevant for anyone who are searching for medical information on the web. We are aware that the issues (mostly about trust or reputation) outlined in this chapter do not provide a complete picture. Some of them are discussed elsewhere e.g. (Gudes, 2015; Sabater & Sierra, 2005; Shergill & Kaur, 2015; Hughes et al., 2009; Stvilia et al., 2009; Agarwal, Liu, Tang, & Yu, 2008; Eisenegger, 2009; Agichtein, Castillo, Donato, Gionis, & Mishne, 2008; Golbeck, 2005). In this chapter we address only a certain aspects of one particular way of solving the searching for reliable health information. We also stressed that this chapter does not intend to fulfill the problem solving. The chapter can be used by the future researchers as a roadmap to explore new trust and reputation models.

2. MOTIVATION AND GOAL

According to Gudes et al (Gudes, 2015; Sabater & Sierra, 2005; Shergill & Kaur, 2015) trust is a belief an agent has that the other individual will do what it says. Trust involves willingness that is not based on having control or power over the other party. Trust is based on direct experiences, witness information; whose opinion we value (also called word-of-mouth). The more we have learned to trust an agent (for example, a company), the more comfortable we are likely to be relying on that agent in the long term. Nevertheless, it is only in rare cases that we can base our trust in those with whom we interact on our own experience. Thus, when no such direct or indirect experience is available this is where reputation comes in (Eisenegger, 2009). In this sense, trusting beliefs and intentions reflect the idea of reputation.

Reputation is the method by which you are viewed by the group of people or society and the way these people think of you. It is also the quality of being a "trusted source" or more simply, "credibility". Reputation plays also an important role in the internet society and enables us to establish trust, which is essential for interaction in the real world. Social network creates trust; and consequently reputation; between agents because they allow their members to learn about each other through repeated interactions.

Trust and reputation is a concept that we use in many aspects of our social life (off line world) and as part of our decision making process. In the offline world, general trust occurs, e.g., when one trust doctors, as a group, to have the medical skills and abilities necessary to treat physical ailments (Sabater & Sierra, 2005). On the other hand, on-line trust can emerge in numerous trustor/trustee relationships. Latterly, there is a tendency to use Social Network Analysis (SNA) in order to evaluate trust and reputation. The underlying idea behind the strategy is that individuals trust the recommendations of their friends thus; the technique is an effective way to convince users to buy a product or accept a message or creating ties over time. In this sense, SNA is used by industry and the academy, to explore links between individuals, behavior and artifacts to find patterns, such as the flows of information and influence. The fact is that, in an online social network, when two actors are directly connected, they may have a certain degree of confidence, however, for actors that are not directly connected there does not exist trust information by default.

Based on the context described herein, the main goal of this research is to propose an approach to infer user reputation based on social interactions. Since reputation is a social evaluation toward a person or a group of people, thus it was selected Social Network Analysis - SNA to evaluate reputation. The concept reputation is used interchangeable with the meaning of the influences or importance that a user comprises, considering that the content of the information disseminated within her/his social network is thought to be credible and worthy of belief. The authors take into account that, discussion of reputation is usually not meaningful without a specific purpose and context. In this regard, the authors considered reputation as a quality of being a "trusted source". It must be stressed that, reputation concept in this work is not addressed in the context of commercial reputation systems, i.e., between buyers and sellers. Since these systems determine reputation by a rating "score", which is calculated based on cumulative rating by its members.

This research is structured as follows: In the next section, it is discussed difficulties in finding high quality resources, including some studies about criteria and tools. The section four outlines the literature review, highlighting in particular those that refer to the quality of online medical information. The section five includes the social network analysis, and its main features. The Section six outlines our main methodology, the reputation factors and network topology. The following section shows the results and lastly the findings are discussed.

3. MEASURING ONLINE INFORMATION QUALITY

In this section it is discussed how the disseminating health and medical information on the Internet can improve knowledge transfer from health professionals to the population, and help individuals to maintain and improve their health. A large body of research exists analyzing the quality of this medical information, but it is unclear how effective these quality evaluation tools are.

3.1 Conduct Code Initiative

Health web portals are sources that provide health information developed to educate patients. The content can be developed by medical experts or by Federal Government Agencies. In this case, the trust of information is based on the trust of the portal itself. Unfortunately, for each Governmental site, there is a variety of other informal sites. Scoring systems have been developed based on indicators of quality to standardize evaluation. These scoring systems – or quality evaluation tools – are essentially a set of indicators of quality applied to a website in order to derive a quality score.

The oldest quality evaluation tool is the HONcode .The Health On the Net Foundation (HON) ("Health On the Net Code of Conduct," 2016). The HON has elaborated the Code of Conduct – named Health On the Net Code of Conduct (HONcode). The HONcode is an instrument to address one of Internet's main healthcare issues, which allows approved websites to display an award-like badge. The HONcode is a kind of a certification based on a standard conduct code called Net Code of Conduct. The code has the intent to allow websites to publish more transparent information. Some principles of HONcode are: Authoritative: indicate the qualifications of the authors; Complementarity: information should support, not replace, the doctor-patient relationship; and many others. It must be stressed that the HON Foundation does not guarantee the complete accuracy of the medical information provided and cannot be held responsible for any adverse effects that may arise from the use of the content of the sites. Thus, codes such as these do not claim to be able to evaluate accuracy of medical information, but instead relate to ethics of the information presented.

Another quality-rating instrument based on technical criteria was proposed by the Agency for Health Care Policy and Research – AHCPR ("Code Ethics," 2016), the agency aims to produce evidence to make health care safer, higher quality, more accessible, equitable, and affordable, and to work within the U.S. Department of Health and Human Service. The Agency proposed a "Code Ethics". The Code sets out ethical concepts that inform the processes of self-assessment and compliance based on interpretation and specification. For instance, Credibility: includes the source, currency, relevance/utility, and editorial review process for the information; Content: must be accurate and complete, and an appropriate disclaimer provided etc. The Code Ethics is just a guide that should be follow. The user by itself should analyze and verify manually if the set of ethical concept is present on the website.

The Information Access Project ("Information Access Project," 2016) proposed a set of technical parameters. They identified six properties or types of metadata that are essential for carrying out a quality evaluation of a health web site. For example, it should indicate the author of the page (known as authority) or the identification of the sponsors. Thus, to make sure that a website delivers reliable and trustful information, it is necessary simply to verify that it has a code of conduct. The task seems to be simple and easy to do, but that is not what happens in reality, only a very few sites have the conduct (or ethics) code. When the sites do not have the code, the users do this by yourself; this can be very confusing, annoying and time consuming. Indeed, evaluating sources when doing research can be a complex task. There are many questions about credibility that users have to ask and search, for example: Is there any evidence that the author of the Web information has some authority in the field about which she or he is providing information? Or what are the author's qualifications, credentials and connections to the subject?

Many other studies investigated quality of health information based on conduct codes for instance: Bernstam, Sagaram, Walji, Johnson, & Meric-Bernstam (2005); Boberg et al. (2003); Breckons, Jones, Morris, & Richardson (2008); Griffiths et al. (2005); Hirst (2003); Houston & Allison (2002); Khazaal, Chatton, Cochand & Zullino (2008); Kronstadt, Moiduddin, & Sellheim (2009); Kumar (2011); Scanfeld, Scanfeld, & Larson (2010); Stvilia et al. (2009) and Wang & Liu (2007). Wang and Liu (Wang & Liu, 2007) proposed an automated method for detecting indicators to identify author name, references, that could be used for evaluating reputation or authority. Indeed, it is a method for detecting indicators and selecting detectable indicators, it is not a quality tool. Griffiths, Tang, Hawking, and Christensen (Griffiths, Tang, Hawking, & Christensen, 2005) described the development of an automated quality assessment procedure designed to automatically rank depression websites according to their evidence-based quality (content similarity). Shon and Musen (Shon & Musen, 1999) conducted a study to determine what information was available in Web pages. The study revealed that basic publishing elements (metadata).

4. RELATED WORKS: MEASURING INFLUENCE ON TWITTER

This section outline an overview of searching and evaluating the literature. It discusses some seminal and relevant texts about user-reputation and trust-management. The most of research about trust and reputation address in the context of commercial reputation (or trust) systems, i.e., between buyers and sellers (electronic markets - E-bay, AliExpress, etc.) or endorsements in social networks such as LinkedIn, Research Gate (RG score, H-index) etc. These systems use reputation through user feedback, by a rating "score" which is calculated based on cumulative by its members. In our point of view, these systems are not suitable to tackle the Trustee's reputation problem.

Social Networking Services have started to appear on the World Wide Web as early as the year 2000, with sites such as Friendster and Myspace. Since then, they have multiplied and taken over the Internet, with hundreds of different services used by more than one billion people. Among them, Twitter is one of the most popular. It is used to report live events, share viewpoints regarding a variety of topics, monitor public opinion, track e-reputation, etc. The service consequently dragged the attention of politicians, firms, celebrities and marketing specialists. Which now largely base their communication on Twitter, trying to become as visible and influential as possible. With the rapidly development of microblogging, the information diffusion in microblogging has received a considerable attentions from academic researchers. Microblogging such as Twitter and Sina Weibo (Chinese microblogging website) has rapidly developed as a recently emerging service because of its timeliness, convenience and it is a lightweight easy form of communication and share information.

Twitter was created in 2006, and since 2010 is being studied extensively in the contexts of social network analysis, computer science, and sociology. Posts or updates are made by succinctly describing one's current status within a limit of 140 characters, known as "Tweets". These posts are of research interest because they are where the social interactions are often played out. It must be stressed that there is strong evidence that people use them to find information (Kwak, Lee, Park, & Moon, 2010). The Twitters' ties are asymmetric, they are formed when a user follow someone, mostly because they are interested in topics that user publishes. Twitter allows a user to "follow" updates from other members who are added as "follower". The "follower" concept, in Twitter perspective, represents the user who is following you. The "following" or "followee" concept represents the user who you follow. Twitter follower/following relationships resemble subscriptions to the RSS feeds of Websites more than friendship ties in Facebook. Twitter, therefore, constitutes a very open social network space, whose lack of barriers to access, e.g., even non-registered users are able to use Twitter to track breaking news on their chosen topics, from "World Economic Crisis" to "European Football Championship".

Twitter social networkers communicate with each other by posting tweets allowing for public interactive dialogue, if other users like or find its content truly interesting, they repost it or "Retweet" it. "Retweeting" is a key mechanism for information diffusion in microblogging. By allowing "Twitterers" to pass on information that they deem interesting, important or entertaining. The retweeting process behaves just like an informal recommendation system. Furthermore, when someone "retweet" you, they are giving you a kind of reputation by sharing your post with their own followers or contacts. Users are more discerning when choosing what or who to retweet whereas not all tweets are reposted (Kwak et al., 2010).

Due to its diversity, Twitter users play an important role. There are numerous reasons why one would want to categorize its users, e.g., market segmentation and marketing target identification, detection of opinion trends, quality of service improvement (e.g. by blocking spammers), sociological studies, and others. Word-of-mouth diffusion has long been regarded as an important mechanism by which information can reach large populations. It is believed that electronic word-of-mouth has greater influence than traditional marketing tools. Influential members can be helpful in giving recommendations, providing customer support and troubleshooting since their solutions are trustworthy because of the sense of authority these members possess (Agarwal, Liu, Tang, & Yu, 2008).

Many works have been dedicated to the characterization of Twitter profiles. These researches attempt to quantify e identify importance in terms of who and what is influential. There is a great variation in the way in which influence has been defined across literature.

Kwak and colleagues (Kwak et al., 2010) rank Twitter users' by popularity. The popularity was estimated by followers count, PageRank and retweet count. All results shown that celebrities (actors, musicians, politicians, sports stars, etc.) or news media were ranked on the top of the list. The PageRank and follower count metrics rank mostly celebrities on the top. The retweet count metrics ranked not only celebrities but also news and media on the top of the list.

Cha et al (Cha, Haddadi, Benevenuto, & Gummadi, 2010) presented an empirical analysis of influence patterns in Twitter. Influential members and opinion leaders are usually well connected in large communities; consequently, they play a special role in multiple ways. They compared three different measures of influence: Indegree, retweets, and mentions. The authors founded that, the most influential users were: news sources (CNN, New York Times), politicians (Barack Obama), athletes (Shaquille O'Neal), as well as celebrities (Ashton Kutcher, Britney Spears). The most retweeted users were content aggregation services (Mashable, TwitterTips, TweetMeme), businessmen (Guy Kawasaki), and news sites (The New York Times, The Onion). Finally, the most mentioned users were mostly celebrities.

Jianwei et al (Jianwei, Lili, & Tianzhu, 2008) proposed a new measure for characterizing nodes importance with tunable parameters based on Degree centrality, Betweenness centrality and Closeness centrality. They used a sexy relation network of the AIDS (SRNA) as a case of study, where a node is a person with the AIDS, and edges if sexy relation exists. The authors argued that their measure can give a distinctly different ranking of nodes, has a stronger adaptability and are more discriminative compared to other several centrality measures.

Weitzel et al (2012) proposed a methodology based on credible and worthy of belief source. The hypothesis was that Trust can be modeled by a pair reputation factor and a set of quality indicators. They utilized the SNA to figure out user's reputation. The authors measure the user´s importance using a new topological structure based on RT weighted ties. They also proposed a set of technical indicators for evaluate the health quality content. The major contribution of the work was providing a framework to evaluate health web page in particular for ordinary users.

There is a still considerable amount of researches that evaluate node importance (or influence), such as co-follower rate (ratio between follower and following), frequency of tweets (updates), who your followers follow, and many others (Bongwon, Lichan, Pirolli, & Chi, 2010; Boyd, Golder, & Lotan, 2010; Hong, Dan, & Davison, 2011; Weng, Lim, Jiang, & He, 2010; Yamaguchi, Takahashi, Amagasa, & Kitagawa, 2010).

5. SOCIAL NETWORK ANALYSIS

The SNA has its origins in the fields of social science as well as graph theory. Its structure is usually expressed through graphs. SNA is the mapping and measuring of relationships and flows between people, groups, organizations, computers, URLs, and other connected information/knowledge entities (Wasserman, 1999). A social network is a social structure between actors, mostly individuals or organizations. The recent proliferation of web applications and mobile devices has made online social network more accessible than ever before. People connect with each other beyond geographical and timeline barriers, diminishing the constraints of physical boundaries in creating new ties. These ties can characterize any type of relationship, friendship, authorship, etc. (Bisgin, Agarwal, & Xiaowei, 2010).

Participating users join a network, publish their profile, express their interests and any content, and create links to any other users with whom they associate. Online Social Network (OSN) provides a basis for maintaining social relationships, for finding users with similar interests, and for locating content and knowledge. Numerous OSNs have emerged, including networks of professionals (e.g., LinkedIn), networks of friends (e.g., MySpace, Facebook, Orkut), and networks for sharing specific types of content such as short messages (e.g., Twitter), diaries and journals (e.g., LiveJournal), photos (e.g., Flickr), and videos (e.g., YouTube). SNA focuses on understanding the nature and consequences of ties between individuals or groups. It is used widely in the social and behavioral sciences, as well as in political science, economics, organizational science, and industrial engineering (Borgatti, Mehra, Brass, & Labianca, 2009; Bruns, 2009; Crandall et al., 2010; Wasserman, 1999). The main goal is to identify strong and weak ties within a network or within a sub-network. One could achieve this by adding specific weight to each edge. There is a variety of weights and as a result, they could take several forms according to the situation on which they are applied. For example, we could put weights that represent the frequency of interactions that are performed.

The ties (or edges) analysis is the one of several focus of SNA, depending on the topic of interest: Psychologists and sociologists have studied friendship ties, such as, (Balkundi & Kilduff, 2005; Granovetter, 1973 McPherson, Smith-Lovin, & Cook, 2001). Other studies attempt to identify communities of users with similar interests, and within such communities, they try to identify of the most "influential" users for general purposess (Balkundi & Kilduff, 2005; Cai, Shao, He, Yan, & Han, 2005; Cha et al., 2010; Cosley, Huttenlocher, Kleinberg, Lan, & Suri, 2010; Jianwei et al., 2008; Page, Brin, Motwani, & Winograd, 1999; Pal & Counts, 2011; Romero, Galuba, Asur, & Huberman, 2011; Sakaki & Matsuo, 2010; Yamaguchi et al., 2010; Yu & Singh, 2000).

5.1 Network Models

In addition to the characterization of networks in terms of informative sets of measurements, it is important to construct models capable of reproducing the evolution and function of real systems or some of their main features. The random graph of Erdos and Rényi (ER) uses what is possibly the simplest way to construct a complex graph: starting with a set of N disconnected vertices, edges are added for each pair of vertices with probability p (Erdõs & Rényi, 1960). Consequently, the degree distribution follows a Poisson distribution for large N with average degree $<k> = p\ (N - 1)$ and average clustering coefficient $<c> = p$. Random graphs are simple but unsuitable to model real networks because the latter are characterized by heterogeneous connections and an abundance of cycles of order three. The model developed by Watts and Strogatz (1998), referred to as small-world networks. It overcomes the lack of cycles of order three in random graphs, but does not provide non-uniform distribution of connectivity. To construct a small-word network, one starts with a regular lattice of N vertices in which each vertex is connected to k nearest neighbors. Next, each edge is randomly rewired with probability p. When $p = 0$ there is an ordered lattice with high number of cycles of order three but large average shortest path length, and when $p \to 1$ the network becomes a random network.

In order to explain the uneven distribution of connectivity present in several real networks, Barabási and Albert (2000) developed the so-called scale-free network model, henceforth abbreviated as BA model, which is based on two rules: growth and preferential attachment. The process starts with a set of m vertices and, at each subsequent step, the network grows with the addition of new vertices. For each new vertex, m new edges connecting it to previous vertices are inserted. The vertices receiving the new edges are chosen according to a linear preferential attachment rule, i.e. the probability of the new vertex i to connect to an existing vertex j is proportional to the degree of j, i.e., this evolution is related to the

"the rich get richer" paradigm. The most connected vertices have greater probability to receive new vertices. Network models have been increasingly considered to investigate different types of dynamics. Indeed, the relation between the function and structure of networks may help understand many real-world phenomena, such as the association between biological networks and the products of such interaction or between society and epidemic spreading. A good review on dynamical processes in complex networks appeared in (Boccaletti, Latora, Moreno, Chavez, & Hwang, 2006 and M. E. J. Newman, 2003).

5.2 Measures Frequently Used to Rank Influential Users

One common type of social analysis is the identification of communities of users with similar interests, and within such communities the identification of the most "influential" users. In this sense, measuring the node (user) importance or influence has become a worth studying issue in Twitter sphere (Gruzd, Wellman, & Takhteyev, 2011). Within graph theory and network analysis, various measures of the centrality of a node have been proposed to determine the relative importance of a vertex. A metric is a simple mathematical equation that helps us to provide information about network (Newman, 2003). The centrality analysis in social network analysis is mainly used to analyze the central position that an individual or organization is in its social network. Perhaps the most frequently used centrality measures are Degree, Closeness, Betweenness, and Eigenvector (Dorogovtsev & Mendes, 2002). These metrics provide the means for identifying key players according to what we are researching and it can be combined to define a criterion to rank each user of a network.

- **Betweenness Centrality:** (BC) It is based on the shortest paths between nodes, focuses on the number of visits through the shortest path. Reflects the number of members to whom a member is indirectly connecting through their direct links, taking into account the connectivity of the node's neighbors and giving a higher value for nodes, which bridge clusters. It is considered as a Bridge, i.e., it is an edge that, if deleted, would cause its endpoints to lie in different components of a graph. If a member is in the shortest path between many other actors, this actor is in an important position (Freeman, L. 1979).
- **Closeness Centrality:** (CC) It reflects the ability of a node to access information through the other network members. An actor is considered central if he can reach all the other nodes in the fewest possible steps. It measures the visibility or accessibility of each node with respect to the entire network. This means that the amount of social distance a node would travel to get to anyone else in the network using both direct and indirect links (Dorogovtsev & Mendes, 2002; M. E. Newman, 2003).
- **Degree Centrality:** (DC) It is a measure of direct connections. Generally speaking, if a member has direct association with many other members, then the member is in central position. Under the guidance of this kind of thinking, the calculation of one point's degree centrality can use the number of points which have a direct relationship with the point (Dorogovtsev & Mendes, 2002; Newman, 2003). In a directed graph, for a vertex v, we denote the In-Degree $d_{in}(v)$ as the number of arcs to v and the Out-degree $d_{out}(v)$ as the number of arcs from it, thus Dc is equal to $d_{in} + d_{out}$
- **Weighted Degree:** (Dcw) The weighted degree of a node is the same as degree. It is based on the number of edge for a node. It is doing the sum of the weight of the edges. For example, a node with 4 edges that weight 1 (1+1+1+1=4) is equivalent to: a node with 2 edges that weight 2 (2+2=4)

or a node with 2 edges that weight 1 and 1 edge that weight 2 (1+1+2=4) or a node with 1 edge that weight 4.

- **Eigen Vector Centrality:** (EVC) It takes into account the importance of a node in a network, assigning relative scores/weights to all nodes. Assumes "that connections to high-scoring nodes contribute more to the score of the node in question than equal connections to low-scoring nodes". Eigen Centrality are linked to well-connected nodes and so may influence many others in the network either directly or indirectly through their connections (Bonacich, 1972).
- **PageRank:** It is another common measure, it is generally used to rank Webpages and ultimately to rank "popularity". PageRank is defined formally as the stationary distribution of a stochastic process whose states are the nodes of the web graph; it computes the rank of websites by the number and quality of incoming links (Page et al., 1999).

In Twitter sphere, there is an infinity of other measure proposed to rank node importance. For instance, follower count (just count the follow-up relationships between users). Indeed, it represents the In-degree centrality. There are variations of this measure, as the co-follower rate (ratio between follower and following) (Bongwon et al., 2010; Boyd et al., 2010; Hong et al., 2011; Weng et al., 2010; Yamaguchi et al., 2010) . Frequently these measures are used to handle with a class of issue.

6. METHODOLOGY

In this section, it is presented the topological structure of social network based on retweet ties. Latest studies show that not only the network structural characteristics underlying a user's importance, but also the user's communication activity, i.e. the exchange of information for instance via messages or wall posts (Bakshy, Rosenn, Marlow, & Adamic, 2012; Cha, Mislove, & Gummadi, 2009 and Shen, Syu, Nguyen, & Thai, 2012).

Twitter users post tweets and if other users like or find its content truly interesting, they repost it or "retweet it". Thus, users retweet (RT) to forward a message from another source to their own followers. The retweeting process is a key mechanism for information diffusion in microblogging (Weitzel L., Palazzo J. M., & Quaresma, P. 2013). By allowing "Twitterers" to forward information that they estimate interesting or important the retweeting process behaves just like an informal recommendation system. One can believes that, when a user "retweet" your post, he/she gives you a kind of reputation by sharing your post with their own followers or contacts. Kwak et al (2010) argue that users are more discerning when choosing what or who to retweet whereas not all tweets are reposted and this retweeting is independent of a reciprocal relationship. Starbird, Palen, Hughes and Viewg (2010) discuss that people spread information that they feel or know to be credible. Members of online communities use source credibility as a reputation to validate information. Some researchers argue that not only the network structural characteristics identify the user's importance and also the user's communication activity as the exchange of information via messages, posts, comments (Bakshy et al., 2012; Cha et al., 2009; Shen et al., 2012; Weitzel L., Quaresma, P. & Palazzo, J.M. 2012). It is consider that the retweet function is likely to be interpreted as a form of endorsement for both the message and the originating user. The content of the information disseminated is thought to be worthy of belief due to its quality. Retweet function represents the degree or level of interactions between users, forging trust-based relations. The

"Retweeting" function is likely to be interpreted as a form of endorsement for both the message and the originating user (Weitzel, L. et al., 2012).

Weitzel et al (2012) proposed a network structure based on retweet weighted ties named Retweet-Network or simply RT-network. The RT-network was modeled as a direct graph G_{RT} where each node $u \in V$ represents the users and each edge $a_k = (u_i, u_j) \in A$ represents RT relationship, i.e., an edge a_k from u_i to u_j stands that user u_i retweets user u_j. These edges w_{a_k} between nodes are weighted according the equation 1.

$$w_{a_k} = \frac{\sum RT}{RT_{max}} + \alpha \qquad (1)$$

Where $\sum RT$ is the retweet count for u_j, and RT_{max} is the maximum number of retweet that user j obtained. The parameter α is a sort of discount rate representing. They argue that the parameter α intends to discount the weight of the follow phenomenon, since many celebrities and mass media have hundreds of thousands of followers. In our work it was used a slight variation of this Equation 1. In this case, we found that there was no statistical difference at 95% level between the results for both equation (1 and 2, thus the α parameter was not used. Here we present only the results of equation 2.

The *RT-network* was modeled as a direct graph $G_{RT} = \left(\mathcal{V}, \mathcal{E}, \mathcal{W} \right)$ where node $\mathcal{V} = \left\{ v_k \right\}$ is a set of nodes (or user), $\mathcal{E} = \left\{ e_k \right\}$ is a set of edges and $W_{i \rightarrow j} = \left\{ w_k \right\}$ set of weights. Thus, an edge e_k from v_i to v_j stands that user v_i "retweet" user v_j and these edges $e_i \in G_{RT}$ have an associated weight $w_{i \rightarrow j}$ defined by:

$$W_{i \rightarrow j} = \frac{\sum RT_{v_j}}{RT_{total}} \qquad (2)$$

Where the parameter $\sum RT_{v_j}$ is the sum of retweets for v_j (target user) from a specific source user v_i, and RT_{total} is the total number of retweet in order to normalize the weight. According to Weitzel, L. et al., 2012, the equation 2 is based on weak ties theory (Granovetter, 1973). Granovetter (1973) discuss the differences between strong and weak ties in social networks. He argue that weak ties can bind groups of strong ties together, how they create connections between networks. Weak ties bring circles of networks into contact with each other, strengthening relationships and forming new bonds between existing relationship circles. Thus, these ties encourage sharing of information across different groups.

We also modeled a binary network, named *RT-Binary* to evaluate the quality of proposed approach. The RT-Binary network was modeled also as a directed graph $G_{RT} = \left(\mathcal{V}, \mathcal{E}, \mathcal{W} \right)$, with the following properties:

1. The set of nodes (denoting the set of users) $\mathcal{V} = \left\{ v_1, v_{2,...} \right\}$
2. The set of edges (representing retweet function) $\mathcal{E} = \left\{ e_1, e_2, ... \right\}$

The set of weights $\mathcal{W} = \{ w_1, w_2, ... \} = 1$ if $\exists$ edge $e_k = \left(v_i, v_j \right) \in \mathcal{E}$, i.e., from v_i to v_j and zero otherwise.

6.1 Methodology to Rank Reputation

In order to address the goal of this work, it is defined a rank approach combining weighted centralities measures (Equation 3) that best fit node importance. It is a hybrid centrality measure, by developing hybrid centrality measures, which it is expected to have a better understanding of importance of actors (nodes) in a network that can assist in exploring different characteristics and role of the actors in the network. Let $\mathcal{M} = \{ m_1, .., m_n \}$ denote a set of centrality measures such as, $\{ \mathcal{D}c, \mathcal{B}c, \mathcal{C}c, \mathcal{E}vc, \textbf{\textit{PRank}}, \textbf{\textit{Din}}, \textbf{\textit{Dout}}, \textbf{\textit{Dcweighted}} \}$. Where: Bc - Betweenness, Dc - Degree, Cc Closeness, Prank - PageRank, Evc - EigenVector, Din - InDegree, Dout - OutDegree and Dcw Weighted Degree. Let $\mathcal{W} = \{ w_1, ..., w_n \}$ denote a set of non-negative weights, w_i. Thus, the Rank Reputation - $\mathcal{R}a\mathcal{R}$ of a user v_j is defined as:

$$\mathcal{R}a\mathcal{R}_{v_i} = \frac{\sum_{i=1}^{n} (m_i * w_i)}{\text{Max}\{ (m_i * w_i), .., (m_n * w_n) \}} \tag{3}$$

$\mathcal{R}a\mathcal{R}_{v_i}$ Measure varies between $\{0,..,1\}$

$$0 < \mathcal{R}a\mathcal{R}_{v_i} < 1, \sum_{i=1}^{n} w_i = 1, j = 1,..,\textbf{m}$$

The following steps summarize the reputation algorithm:

Step 1: Initialize set an arbitrary weight $\forall w_i \in \mathbb{W}, \sum_{i=1}^{n} w_i = 1$

Step 2: for each node v_i compute $\sum_{i=1}^{n}(m_i * w_i)$

Step 3: Compute $\mathcal{R}a\mathcal{R}_{v_j}$

Step 4: Assigning a label to $\mathcal{R}a\mathcal{R}_{v_j}$ and Compute Precision at n ($P_@k$)

Step 5: If $\text{P}@\text{k}\left(\mathcal{R}a\mathcal{R}_{v_j}^{\text{Æ}}\right) \geq \text{P}@\text{k}\left(\mathcal{R}a\mathcal{R}_{v_j}^{\varphi+1}\right)$ Then keep $\mathcal{R}a\mathcal{R}_{v_j}^{\varphi}$

Go to step 1 until no additional gain (which means, the p@N value is the highest achieved)

In first step, it is set out arbitrarily the weights $w_i \in \mathcal{W}$, these weights $\mathcal{W}$ are tunable parameter, which can be changed while the simulation is running. Iteratively, the algorithm tunes these weights during the simulation loop in order to achieve the best performance based on p@N measure (see step two). These arbitrary weights are initialized with values equal to zero and then increased by 0.1 step. It must be stressed that these weights should comply with the condition $\forall w_i \in, \sum_{i=1}^{n} w_i \mathcal{W} = 1$ and can $\exists w_k = 0 \mid m_k * w_k = 0$ at each iteration. In the second step, for each node $v_j \in \mathcal{V}$, it is computed $\sum_{i=1}^{n}(m_i * w_i)$, then in the third step is calculated the $\mathcal{R}a\mathcal{R}_{v_j}$, and it is assigning a label to this measure as follows $\mathcal{R}a\mathcal{R}_{v_j}^{\mathscr{A}}$ in step 4. This process is repeated until there are no more changes in the reputation rank (p@N improvement) and then algorithm reached its goal.

6.2 Performance Measurement

Retrieval systems are typically evaluated by some combination of precision, the proportion of retrieved documents that are relevant, and recall, the proportion of relevant documents that were retrieved. When "retrieved" is defined in terms of whether a document is ranked before some cutoff N, precision and recall can be calculated at any rank k. In optimal ranked retrieval system, a set of relevant retrieved documents are given by the top N retrieved documents. It was computed recall and average precision (P@N). Average precision represents the proportion of retrieved top-N documents that are relevant, i.e., set a rank threshold N, then it computes the percentage of relevant in top N and it ignores documents ranked lower than N (Baeza-Yates & Ribeiro-Neto, 1999). It was considered relevant documents, in our case, relevant users, those that are public healthcare, physician sites, government agency and medical association. The authors select this alternative mostly because, if the site receives funding from commercial firms or private foundations, then the financial dependence has the potential to bias the information presented. For instance, if the purpose of the information is primarily to sell a product, there may be a conflict of interest since the manufacturer may not want to present findings that would discourage you from purchasing the product (Kumar, 2011).

In order to gain insight about our rank and weighted approach, the findings of (Jianwei, Lili, & Tianzhu, 2008), (Cha et al., 2009) and (L. Weitzel et al., 2012) were applied as a baseline. Except the last work, that used retweet network, the first two used a follow/follwee network.

7. MAIN RESULTS

The retweets were acquired during 2015/2016. The network has 46164 users (nodes) and 55954 edges. From the total of users, it was selected 43 users related to health, such as, public health care (CDCgov, CDCFlu, HealthCareGov, etc), Government Agency (White House and United States Department of Agriculture) and physician site (Dr Oz, Dr Weil, Dr Wayne Dyer, etc). The Table 1 shows some features of retweet network. In spite of high number of community, the network behaves as scale-free network whose degree distribution follows a power-law. The nodes of a scale-free network are not randomly or evenly connected. A process called "preferential attachment" generated this model of network. The process assumes a linear relationship between the numbers of neighbors of a node in a network and the probability of attachment. In contrast, the small-world network such as an online social network has normal distribution, i.e., the degree distribution converges to a Poisson distribution.

Table 1. RT network feature

Average path length	3.807
Diameter	9
Number of community	217
Strongly connected component	46140
Weakly connected component	189
Average Weighted degree	0.011

The Table 2 shows the Pearson correlation at 99% significant level, 2-tail for RT-Network, and Table 3 shows the correlation of RT-Binary. It is highlighted the strong positive correlation between Prank, Evc and DC. The high correlation between Degree and Prank mostly because Prank grow with the degree grow, both follow an almost identical pattern, i.e., a curve ending with a broad tail that follows a power law with exponent. Likewise, the high correlation achieved between Evc and Dc and between Evc and Prank. Thus, the three measures provide very similar information, especially for the most influential user. The remaining correlations were low, at significant level at $p < 0.01$ and $p < 0.05$. It is interesting to note that the correlation keeps almost the same on both network topology.

The proposed algorithm was run searching for the best result at level of 100 (Precision at level 100), i.e., it was considered only the first 100 position. We also compute recall at level 100 and 43. The strategy adopted was aims to check the sensitivity of the proposed methodology, i.e., we aims to find out if

Table 2. Pearson Correlation between measures – RT-Network

	Dc	Cc	Bc	Prank	Evc
Dc	1	-,039**	,432**	**,826****	**,999****
Cc	-,039**	1	-,011*	-,032**	-,036**
Bc	,432**	-,011*	1	,619**	,447**
Prank	,826**	-,032**	,619**	1	**,843****
Evc	,999**	-,036**	,447**	,843**	1

**. Correlation is significant at the 0.01 level (2-tailed).
*. Correlation is significant at the 0.05 level (2-tailed).

Table 3. Pearson Correlation between measures – RT-Binary

	Dc	Cc	Bc	Prank	Evc
Dc	1	-,039**	,432**	**,898****	**,999****
Cc	-,039**	1	-,011*	-,036**	-,036**
Bc	,432**	-,011*	1	,564**	,447**
Prank	,898**	-,036**	,564**	1	**,914****
Evc	,999**	-,036**	,447**	,914**	1

**. Correlation is significant at the 0.01 level (2-tailed).
*. Correlation is significant at the 0.05 level (2-tailed).

the size of the rank affects the performance. The Table 4 and Table 5 show the representatives results achieved by two network, it was shown the best and worst-case planning equation (CT).

The majority of CT retrieved relevant user, except Dout and a surprising Cc measure. The Closeness measure indicates a user influence on transmitting and controlling information but also efficiency for

Table 4. Representatives outcomes achieved RT-network: precision at level 100 (P at 100), Recall at level (R at N) 100 and 43.

CT	Equations	P at 100	R at 100	R at 43	Reference
CT1	(0,7*Cc)+(0,2*Din)+(0,1*Dout)	89%	100%	81%	Weitzel et al (2012)
CT2	(0,6*Dc)+(0,3*Cc)+(0,1*Bc)	89%	100%	81%	JianWei et al. (2008)
CT3	(0,5*Dc)+(0,3*Cc)+(0,2*Bc)	89%	100%	81%	JianWei et al. (2008)
CT4	Din	89%	100%	81%	Cha et al (2009)
CT8	(0,1*Bc)+(0,7*Cc)+(0,1*EVc)+(0,1*prank)	37%	100%	27%	
CT9	(0,1*Bc)+(0,1*Evc)+(0,8*prank)	89%	100%	81%	
CT12	Dout	4%	6%	4%	
CT13	Dc	87%	97%	81%	
CT14	Cc	2%	6%	6%	
CT15	Bc	37%	53%	53%	
CT16	Prank	86%	100%	79%	
CT17	Evc	89%	100%	81%	
CT18	Dc weighted	81%	90%	79%	

Table 5. Representatives Outcomes achieved RT-binary

CT	Equations	Precision at 100	Recall at 100	Recall 43	Reference
CT1	(0,7*Cc)+(0,2*Din)+(0,1*Dout)	87%	97%	81%	Weitzel et al (2012)
CT2	(0,6*Dc)+(0,3*Cc)+(0,1*Bc)	87%	97%	81%	JianWei et al. (2008)
CT3	(0,5*Dc)+(0,3*Cc)+(0,2*Bc)	87%	97%	81%	JianWei et al. (2008)
CT4	Din	89%	100%	81%	Cha et al (2009)
CT8	(0,1*Bc)+(0,7*Cc)+(0,1*Evc)+(0,1*prank)	3%	6%	6%	
CT10	(0,1*Bc)+(0,2*Evc)+(0,7*prank)	89%	100%	81%	
CT12	Dout	1%	6%	4%	
CT13	Dc	87%	97%	81%	
CT14	Cc	3%	6%	6%	
CT15	Bc	43%	53%	53%	
CT16	Prank	87%	100%	81%	
CT17	Evc	89%	100%	81%	
CT18	DCw	87%	97%	81%	

communication with others or efficiency in spreading information within the network. This result shows that these two measures were not a proper alternative to identify relevant users. As regards to Dout measure, it achieved a low performance, since the network was modeled as a direct graph.

The CT15 (or Bc) was not suited at detecting the relevant user in both networks. The CT8 showed an interesting outcome in RT-binary, the extreme variation in recall at level 100 and level 43, mostly because the algorithm ordered the relevant user at the end of the rank. As one can be seen, the results achieved by RT-binary were little worse than RT-network. We also compute the Kendall Tau rank correlation. This correlation is a rank-based statistical methods called "non-parametric". The values range between 70% and 100% in most case test and in both network. All correlations were significant at the 0.01 level (2-tailed).

The correlation between CT12, CT14, CT15 and the remaining of cases were very low, ranging between -3% and 42%; and between them including in RT-Binary network. This is justified since these three case tests reached the lowest measures. The Tau correlation of RT-network was very low between CT4 (30%) and the remaining, except between CT4 and CT16 and CT17, and between them, which it was high (100%). This is explainable on the basis that the measures Evc and Prank take into account the In-Degree.

8. CONCLUSION

The main goal of this work was to provide an approach that models the reputation of a user inserted in a network built with information based on health information extracted from twitter. For this purpose, the authors considered reputation as a measure of quality of a supposed "reliable source". In our study, reputation has the same meaning of credible source information in medical domain.

The process of retweeting creates strong and significant ties between users, based on trust relationship. Then reputation can be modeled as direct graph of retweet network. Since reputation is a social evaluation toward a person or a group of people. The authors consider that, Twitter's communicative structure is determined by two overlapping and interdependent networks – one based on follower-following relationships, the most obviously; and other relatively short-term and emergent, based on shared interest in a topic or event, often coordinated by a retweet function. Therefore, retweet network must be understood as separate from follower/following Network. It was used and adapted the available methods, by combining some well-known metrics. These metrics are frequently used in Social Network Analysis to evaluate popularity or reputation in other contexts. The study gives us a clear understanding of the how measure selection can affect the reputation rank (especially in medical domain).

Choose the most appropriate measure depends on what we want to represent. The best results achieved take into account in particular, a set of weighted metrics, such as, Eigen vector and Page Rank. The worst result is related to Closeness centrality and Out-Degree. The Closeness centrality considers that the more central a node is, the closer it is to all other nodes, representing the user has better access to information, and that it was not what we were looking for. In spite of Out-Degree represents the number of that the node directs to others (outgoing edges), the metric failed to detect relevant user. The contributions of this work were mostly providing a methodology to rank medical trustworthy source using a new network structure based on retweet ties. The results shown that the rank methodology and the network topology have succeeded in achieving user reputation. Additionally, it was verified that in Twitter community, trust plays an important role in spreading information; the culture of "retweeting" demonstrates the potential to reach trust.

In addition, the experimental results offer an important insight of the relationships among Twitter users. The findings suggest that relations of "friendship" or follows are important but not enough to find out how important nodes are. In future work we plan to perform a more depth study testing in other application such as disease propagation.

REFERENCES

Agarwal, N., Liu, H., Tang, L., & Yu, P. S. (2008). Identifying the influential bloggers in a community. *Proceedings of the 2008 International Conference on Web Search and Data Mining*. doi:10.1145/1341531.1341559

Agichtein, E., Castillo, C., Donato, D., Gionis, A., & Mishne, G. (2008). *Finding high-quality content in social media*. doi:10.1145/1341531.1341557

Anderson, J. G. (2004). Consumers of e-Health: Patterns of Use and Barriers. *Social Science Computer Review*, *22*(2), 242–248. doi:10.1177/0894439303262671

Baeza-Yates, R. A., & Ribeiro-Neto, B. (1999). Modern Information Retrieval. Addison-Wesley Longman Publishing Co., Inc.

Bakshy, E., Rosenn, I., Marlow, C., & Adamic, L. (2012). *The role of social networks in information diffusion*. Academic Press.

Balkundi, P., & Kilduff, M. (2005). The ties that lead: A social network approach to leadership. *The Leadership Quarterly*, *16*(6), 941–961. doi:10.1016/j.leaqua.2005.09.004

Barabási, A.-L., Albert, R., & Jeong, H. (2000). Scale-free characteristics of random networks: the topology of the world-wide web. *Physica A: Statistical Mechanics and Its Applications, 281*(1), 69-77.

Barber, K. S., & Kim, J. (2001). Belief Revision Process Based on Trust: Agents Evaluating Reputation of Information Sources. In R. Falcone, M. Singh, & Y.-H. Tan (Eds.), *Trust in Cyber-societies* (Vol. 2246, pp. 73–82). Berlin: Springer Berlin Heidelberg. doi:10.1007/3-540-45547-7_5

Bernstam, E. V., Sagaram, S., Walji, M., Johnson, C. W., & Meric-Bernstam, F. (2005). Usability of quality measures for online health information: Can commonly used technical quality criteria be reliably assessed? *International Journal of Medical Informatics*, *74*(7–8), 675–683. doi:10.1016/j.ijmedinf.2005.02.002 PMID:16043090

Bhattacharya, S., Srinivasan, P., & Polgreen, P. (2014). Engagement with Health Agencies on Twitter. *PLoS ONE*, *9*(11), e112235. doi:10.1371/journal.pone.0112235 PMID:25379727

Bisgin, H., Agarwal, N., & Xiaowei, X. (2010). *Investigating Homophily in Online Social Networks*. Academic Press.

Boberg, E. W., Gustafson, D. H., Hawkins, R. P., Offord, K. P., Koch, C., Wen, K.-Y., & Salner, A. et al. (2003). Assessing the unmet information, support and care delivery needs of men with prostate cancer. *Patient Education and Counseling, 49*(3), 233–242. doi:10.1016/S0738-3991(02)00183-0 PMID:12642195

Boccaletti, S., Latora, V., Moreno, Y., Chavez, M., & Hwang, D. U. (2006). Complex networks: Structure and dynamics. *Physics Reports, 424*(4–5), 175–308. doi:10.1016/j.physrep.2005.10.009

Bonacich, P. (1972). Technique for analyzing overlapping memberships. *Sociological Methodology, 4*, 176–185. doi:10.2307/270732

Bongwon, S., Lichan, H., Pirolli, P., & Chi, E. H. (2010). *Want to be Retweeted?* Large Scale Analytics on Factors Impacting Retweet in Twitter Network.

Borgatti, S. P., Mehra, A., Brass, D. J., & Labianca, G. (2009). Network Analysis in the Social Sciences. *Science, 323*(5916), 892–895. doi:10.1126/science.1165821 PMID:19213908

Boyd, D., Golder, S., & Lotan, G. (2010). Tweet, Tweet, Retweet: Conversational Aspects of Retweeting on Twitter. Academic Press.

Breckons, M., Jones, R., Morris, J., & Richardson, J. (2008). What Do Evaluation Instruments Tell Us About the Quality of Complementary Medicine Information on the Internet? *Journal of Medical Internet Research, 10*(1), e3. doi:10.2196/jmir.961 PMID:18244894

Bruns, A. (2009). *Social Media: Tools for User-Generated Content Social Drivers behind Growing Consumer Participation in User-Led Content Generationts only* (Vol. 2). Smart Services CRC Pty Ltd.

Cai, D., Shao, Z., He, X., Yan, X., & Han, J. (2005). Community mining from multi-relational networks. *Knowledge Discovery in Databases: PKDD, 2005*, 445–452.

Cha, M., Haddadi, H., Benevenuto, F., & Gummadi, K. (2010). Measuring User Influence in Twitter: The Million Follower Fallacy. *Proceedings of the 4th International AAAI Conference on Weblogs and Social Media (ICWSM-2010)*.

Cha, M., Mislove, A., & Gummadi, K. P. (2009). A measurement-driven analysis of information propagation in the flickr social network. *Proceedings of the 18th international conference on World wide web*. doi:10.1145/1526709.1526806

Chomphoosang, P., Durresi, A., Durresi, M., & Barolli, L. (2012). *Trust Management of Social Networks in Health Care*. Paper presented at the 2012 15th International Conference on Network-Based Information Systems.

Code Ethics. (2016). *Agency for Health Care Policy and Research*. Available at http://www.aaai.org/ocs/index.php/ICWSM/ICWSM10/

Crandall, D. J., Backstrom, L., Cosley, D., Suri, S., Huttenlocher, D., & Kleinberg, J. (2010). Inferring social ties from geographic coincidences. *Proceedings of the National Academy of Sciences of the United States of America, 107*(52), 22436–22441. doi:10.1073/pnas.1006155107 PMID:21148099 de Boer, M. J., Versteegen, G. J., & van Wijhe, M. (2007). Patients use of the Internet for pain-related medical information. *Patient Education and Counseling*, *68*(1), 86–97. doi:10.1016/j.pec.2007.05.012 PMID:17590563

Dorogovtsev, S. N., & Mendes, J. F. F. (2002). Evolution of networks. *Advances in Physics*, *51*(4), 1079–1187. doi:10.1080/00018730110112519

Eisenegger, M. (2009). Trust and reputation in the age of globalisation. In J. Klewes & R. Wreschniok (Eds.), *Reputation Capital* (pp. 11–22). Berlin: Springer Berlin Heidelberg. doi:10.1007/978-3-642-01630-1_2

Erdõs, P., & Rényi, A. (1960). On the evolution of random graphs. *Publications of the Mathematical Institute of the Hungarian Academy of Sciences*, *5*, 17–61.

Eysenbach, G., Powell, J., Kuss, O., & Sa, E.-R. (2002). Empirical Studies Assessing the Quality of Health Information for Consumers on the World Wide Web: A Systematic Review. *Journal of the American Medical Association*, *287*(20), 2691–2700. doi:10.1001/jama.287.20.2691 PMID:12020305

Freeman, L. (1979). Centrality in social networks: Conceptual clarification. *Social Networks*, *1*(3), 215–239. doi:10.1016/0378-8733(78)90021-7

Golbeck, J. (2005). *Computing and Applying Trust in Web-Based Social Networks* (PhD thesis). Univ. Maryland, College Park, MD.

Granovetter, M. S. (1973). The Strength of Weak Ties. *American Journal of Sociology*, *78*(6), 1360–1380. doi:10.1086/225469

Griffiths, M. K., Tang, T. T., Hawking, D., & Christensen, H. (2005). Automated Assessment of the Quality of Depression Websites. *Journal of Medical Internet Research*, *7*(5), e59. doi:10.2196/jmir.7.5.e59 PMID:16403723

Gruzd, A., Wellman, B., & Takhteyev, Y. (2011). Imagining Twitter as an Imagined Community. *The American Behavioral Scientist*, *55*(10), 1294–1318. doi:10.1177/0002764211409378

Gudes, E. (2015). Reputation - from Social Perception to Internet Security. In C. Damsgaard Jensen, S. Marsh, T. Dimitrakos, & Y. Murayama (Eds.), *Trust Management IX: 9th IFIP WG 11.11 International Conference* (pp. 3-10). Cham: Springer International Publishing.

Health on the Net Code of Conduct. (2016). Health on the Net Foundation.

Hirst, J. (2003). Charities and patient groups should declare interests. *BMJ (Clinical Research Ed.)*, *326*(7400), 1211–1211. doi:10.1136/bmj.326.7400.1211-a PMID:12775630

Hong, L., Dan, O., & Davison, B. D. (2011). *Predicting popular messages in Twitter*. Academic Press. doi:10.1145/1963192.1963222

Houston, T. K., & Allison, J. J. (2002). Users of Internet health information: Differences by health status. *Journal of Medical Internet Research*, *4*(2), E7. doi:10.2196/jmir.4.2.e7 PMID:12554554

Hughes, B., Joshi, I., Lemonde, H., & Wareham, J. (2009). Junior physicians use of Web 2.0 for information seeking and medical education: A qualitative study. *International Journal of Medical Informatics*, *78*(10), 645–655. doi:10.1016/j.ijmedinf.2009.04.008 PMID:19501017

Information Access Project. (2016). *Healthy People*. Retrieved from https://phpartners.org/hp/

Internet World Stats. (n.d.). *Internet usage and World population statistics*. Retrieved 2016/08/21, from http://www.internetworldstats.com/emarketing.htm

Jianwei, W., Lili, R., & Tianzhu, G. (2008). *A New Measure of Node Importance in Complex Networks with Tunable Parameters*. Academic Press.

Khazaal, Y., Chatton, A., Cochand, S., & Zullino, D. (2008). Quality of web-based information on cocaine addiction. *Patient Education and Counseling*, *72*(2), 336–341. doi:10.1016/j.pec.2008.03.002 PMID:18423952

Kronstadt, J., Moiduddin, A., & Sellheim, W. (2009). *Consumer Use of Computerized Applications to Address Health and Health Care Needs*. Retrieved from U.S. Department of Health and Human Services - Office of the Secretary Assistant Secretary for Planning and Evaluation: http://aspe.hhs.gov/sp/reports/2009/consumerhit/report.shtml

Kumar, V. (2011). Impact of Health Information Systems on Organizational Health Communication and Behavior. *The Internet Journal of Allied Health Sciences and Practice*, *9*(2).

Kwak, H., Lee, C., Park, H., & Moon, S. (2010). *What is Twitter, a social network or a news media?* doi:10.1145/1772690.1772751

Manning, C. D., Raghavan, P., & Schütze, H. (2008). *Introduction to information retrieval*. New York: Cambridge University Press. doi:10.1017/CBO9780511809071

McPherson, M., Smith-Lovin, L., & Cook, J. M. (2001). Birds of a feather: Homophily in social networks. *Annual Review of Sociology*, *27*(1), 415–444. doi:10.1146/annurev.soc.27.1.415

Newman, M. E. (2003). The structure and function of complex networks. *SIAM Review*, *45*(2), 167–256. doi:10.1137/S003614450342480

Page, L., Brin, S., Motwani, R., & Winograd, T. (1999). *The PageRank Citation Ranking: Bringing Order to the Web*. Stanford InfoLab.

Pal, A., & Counts, S. (2011). *Identifying topical authorities in microblogs*. doi:10.1145/1935826.1935843

Romero, D. M., Galuba, W., Asur, S., & Huberman, B. A. (2011). *Influence and passivity in social media*. doi:10.1145/1963192.1963250

Sabater, J., & Sierra, C. (2005). Review on Computational Trust and Reputation Models. *Artificial Intelligence Review*, *24*(1), 33–60. doi:10.1007/s10462-004-0041-5

Scanfeld, D., Scanfeld, V., & Larson, E. L. (2010). Dissemination of health information through social networks: Twitter and antibiotics. *American Journal of Infection Control*, *38*(3), 182–188. doi:10.1016/j.ajic.2009.11.004 PMID:20347636

Shen, Y., Syu, Y. S., Nguyen, D. T., & Thai, M. T. (2012). *Maximizing circle of trust in online social networks*. Academic Press.

Shergill, M. K., & Kaur, H. (2015). *Survey of Computational Trust and Reputation Models in Virtual Societies*. Academic Press.

Shon, J., & Musen, M. A. (1999). The low availability of metadata elements for evaluating the quality of medical information on the World Wide Web. *AMIA Symposium*, 945-949.

Starbird, K., Palen, L., Hughes, A. L., & Vieweg, S. (2010). Chatter on the red: what hazards threat reveals about the social life of microblogged information. *Proceedings of the 2010 ACM conference on Computer supported cooperative work*. doi:10.1145/1718918.1718965

Stvilia, B., Mon, L., & Yi, Y. J. (2009). A model for online consumer health information quality. *Journal of the American Society for Information Science and Technology, 60*(9), 1781–1791. doi:10.1002/asi.21115

Wang, Y., & Liu, Z. (2007). Automatic detecting indicators for quality of health information on the Web. *International Journal of Medical Informatics, 76*(8), 575–582. doi:10.1016/j.ijmedinf.2006.04.001 PMID:16750417

Wasserman, S. (1999). *Social network analysis: methods and applications*. Cambridge, UK: Cambridge University Press.

Watts, D. J., & Strogatz, S. H. (1998). Collective dynamics of small-world networks. *Nature, 393*(6684), 440–442. doi:10.1038/30918 PMID:9623998

Weitzel, L., Palazzo, J. O., & Quaresma, P. (2013). *Exploring Trust to Rank Reputation in Microblogging*. Paper presented at the Database and Expert Systems Applications. doi:10.1007/978-3-642-40173-2_36

Weitzel, L., Quaresma, P., & de Oliveira, J. P. M. (2012). *Evaluating Quality of Health Information Sources*. Paper presented at the Advanced Information Networking and Applications (AINA), 26th International Conference on. doi:10.1109/AINA.2012.41

Weng, J., Lim, E.-P., Jiang, J., & He, Q. (2010). *TwitterRank: finding topic-sensitive influential twitterers*. doi:10.1145/1718487.1718520

Yamaguchi, Y., Takahashi, T., Amagasa, T., & Kitagawa, H. (2010). TURank: Twitter User Ranking Based on User-Tweet Graph Analysis. In L. Chen, P. Triantafillou, & T. Suel (Eds.), Web Information Systems Engineering – WISE 2010 (Vol. 6488, pp. 240-253): Springer Berlin / Heidelberg.

Yu, B., & Singh, M. P. (2000). A Social Mechanism of Reputation Management in Electronic Communities. In M. Klusch & L. Kerschberg (Eds.), Cooperative Information Agents IV - The Future of Information Agents in Cyberspace (Vol. 1860, pp. 355-393). Springer Berlin / Heidelberg. doi:10.1007/978-3-540-45012-2_15

Zhou, W.-X., Jiang, Z.-Q., & Sornette, D. (2007). Exploring self-similarity of complex cellular networks: The edge-covering method with simulated annealing and log-periodic sampling. *Physica A: Statistical Mechanics and Its Applications, 375*(2), 741-752.

Compilation of References

Abowd, G. D., Dey, A. K., Brown, P. J., Davies, N., Smith, M., & Steggles, P. (1999, September). Towards a better understanding of context and context-awareness. In *International Symposium on Handheld and Ubiquitous Computing* (pp. 304-307). Springer Berlin Heidelberg. doi:10.1007/3-540-48157-5_29

Abu-Doleh, A., & Çatalyürek, Ü. V. (2015, October). Spaler: Spark and GraphX based de novo genome assembler. In *Big Data (Big Data), 2015 IEEE International Conference on* (pp. 1013-1018). IEEE.

Aceto, S., Borotis, S., Devine, J., & Fischer, T. (2014). *Mapping and Analysing Prospective Technologies for Learning* (P. Kampylis & Y. Punie, Eds.). Seville, Spain: Joint Research Centre, Institute for Prospective Technological Studies.

Acquisti, A., & Gross, R. (2005). Information Revelation and Privacy in Online Social Networks. *Proceedings of the 2005 ACM workshop on Privacy in the electronic society (WPES)*.

Adamic, L. A. (1999). The Small World Web. *Proceedings of the Third European Conference,* 443.

Agarwal, N., Liu, H., Tang, L., & Yu, P. S. (2008). Identifying the influential bloggers in a community. *Proceedings of the 2008 International Conference on Web Search and Data Mining.* doi:10.1145/1341531.1341559

Aggarwal, C. C. (2011). An introduction to social network data analytics. In Social network data analytics (pp. 1-15). Springer US. doi:10.1007/978-1-4419-8462-3_1

Aggarwal, C., Lin, S., & Yu, P. S. (2014). On influential node discovery in dynamic social networks. *SDM,* 636-647.

Aggarwal, C. C. (2014). *Data Mining: The Textbook.* Springer International Publishing.

Agichtein, E., Castillo, C., Donato, D., Gionis, A., & Mishne, G. (2008). *Finding high-quality content in social media.* doi:10.1145/1341531.1341557

Ahmed, N. K., Duffield, N., Neville, J., & Kompella, R. (2014). Graph Sample and Hold: A Framework for Big-graph Analytics. In *Proceedings of the 20th ACM SIGKDD International Conference on Knowledge Discovery and Data Mining* (pp. 1446–1455). New York, NY: ACM. doi:10.1145/2623330.2623757

Ahmed, N. M., & Chen, L. (2016). An efficient algorithm for link prediction in temporal uncertain social networks. *Information Sciences, 331,* 120–136. doi:10.1016/j.ins.2015.10.036

Ahn, S., & Kim, D. (2006, February). Proactive context-aware sensor networks. In *European Workshop on Wireless Sensor Networks* (pp. 38-53). Springer Berlin Heidelberg.

Aiello, W., Chung, F., & Lu, L. (2000). A Random Graph Model for Massive Graphs. *Proceedings of the 32nd ACM Symposium on the Theory of Computing,* 171. doi:10.1145/335305.335326

Akhtar, Javed, & Sengar. (2013). Analysis of High Degree Nodes in a Social Network. *International Journal of Electronics, Communication and Computer Engineering, 4*(3).

Akhtar, N., Javed, H., & Sengar, G. (2013). Analysis of Facebook Social Network. *IEEE International Conference on Computational Intelligence and Computer Networks (CICN).*

Aksu, H., Canim, M., Chang, Y.-C., Korpeoglu, I., & Ulusoy, O. (2013). Multi-Resolution Social Network Community Identification and Maintenance on Big Data Platform. *Proceedings of the IEEE Conference on BigData*, 102-109. doi:10.1109/BigData.Congress.2013.23

Albert, R., & Barabasi, A. L. (2002). Statistical mechanics of complex networks. *Reviews of Modern Physics, 74*(1), 47–97. doi:10.1103/RevModPhys.74.47

Alistair, M., & Sean, B. (2013, June 4). *SKOS Simple Knowledge Organization System Reference*. Retrieved from W3C Recommendation: http://www.w3.org/TR/skos-reference/

Almansoori, W., Zarour, O., Jarada, T. N., Karampales, P., Rokne, J., & Alhajj, R. (2011). Applications of Social Network Construction and Analysis in the Medical Referral Process. *Proceedings of IEEE Ninth International Conference on Dependable, Autonomic and Secure Computing (DASC)*, 816-823. doi:10.1109/DASC.2011.140

Anagnostopoulos, A., Becchetti, L., Bordino, I., Leonardi, S., Mele, I., & Sankowski, P. (2015). Stochastic query covering for fast approximate document retrieval. *ACM Transactions on Information Systems, 33*(3), 11. doi:10.1145/2699671

Anderson, J. (1983). A Spreading Activation Theory of Memory. *Journal of Verbal Learning and Verbal Behavior, 22*(3), 261–295. doi:10.1016/S0022-5371(83)90201-3

Anderson, J. G. (2004). Consumers of e-Health: Patterns of Use and Barriers. *Social Science Computer Review, 22*(2), 242–248. doi:10.1177/0894439303262671

Anderson, T., & McGreal, R. (2012). Disruptive Pedagogies and Technologies in Universities. *Journal of Educational Technology & Society, 15*(4), 380–389.

Anderson, T., Upton, L., Dron, J., Malone, J., & Poelhuber, B. (2015). Social Interaction in Self-paced Distance Education. *Open Praxis, 7*(1), 7–23. doi:10.5944/openpraxis.7.1.164

Ariza, E. N., & Hancock, S. (2003). Second Language Acquisition Theories as a Framework for Creating Distance Learning Courses. *The International Review of Research in Open and Distributed Learning, 4*(2). doi:10.19173/irrodl.v4i2.142

Arrow, K. J. (1971). *The theory of discrimination* (Working Paper No. No. 30A). Princeton, NJ: Princeton University.

Asavathiratham, C., Roy, S., Lesieutre, B., & Verghese, G. (2001). The influence model. *IEEE Control Systems, 21*(6), 52–64. doi:10.1109/37.969135

Automatic Summarization. (n.d.). In *Wikipedia*. Retrieved from https://en.wikipedia.org/wiki/Automatic_summarization

Axelrod, R. (Ed.). (2015). *Structure of decision: The cognitive maps of political elites*. Princeton university press.

Baeza-Yates, R. A., & Ribeiro-Neto, B. (1999). Modern Information Retrieval. Addison-Wesley Longman Publishing Co., Inc.

Bagci, H., & Karagoz, P. (2016). Context-Aware Friend Recommendation for Location Based Social Networks using Random Walk. In *Proceedings of the 25th International Conference Companion on World Wide Web* (pp. 531-536). International World Wide Web Conferences Steering Committee. doi:10.1145/2872518.2890466

Baker, R. S. J. D., & Yacef, K. (2009). The State of Educational Data Mining in 2009: A Review and Future Visions. *Journal of Educational Data Mining, 1*(1), 3–17.

Baker, R. S., & Inventado, P. S. (2014). Educational Data Mining and Learning Analytics. In J. A. Larusson & B. White (Eds.), *Learning Analytics: from research to practice* (pp. 61–75). New York: Springer New York. doi:10.1007/978-1-4614-3305-7_4

Bakshy, E., Rosenn, I., Marlow, C., & Adamic, L. (2012). *The role of social networks in information diffusion*. Academic Press.

Balkundi, P., & Kilduff, M. (2005). The ties that lead: A social network approach to leadership. *The Leadership Quarterly, 16*(6), 941–961. doi:10.1016/j.leaqua.2005.09.004

Barabási, A.-L., Albert, R., & Jeong, H. (2000). Scale-free characteristics of random networks: the topology of the world-wide web. *Physica A: Statistical Mechanics and Its Applications, 281*(1), 69-77.

Barabasi, A. L., Jeong, H., Neda, Z., Ravasz, E., Schubert, A., & Vicsek, T. (2002). Evolution of the Social Network of Scientific Collaborations. *Physica A, 331*(3-4), 590–614. doi:10.1016/S0378-4371(02)00736-7

Barber, K. S., & Kim, J. (2001). Belief Revision Process Based on Trust: Agents Evaluating Reputation of Information Sources. In R. Falcone, M. Singh, & Y.-H. Tan (Eds.), *Trust in Cyber-societies* (Vol. 2246, pp. 73–82). Berlin: Springer Berlin Heidelberg. doi:10.1007/3-540-45547-7_5

Barber, M. J. (2007). Modularity and community detection in bipartite networks. *Physical Review E: Statistical, Nonlinear, and Soft Matter Physics, 76*(6), 11. doi:10.1103/PhysRevE.76.066102 PMID:18233893

Barbian, G. (2011, 09 12-14). Trust Centrality in Online Social Networks. *Proceedings of Intelligence and Security Informatics Conference (EISIC'11)*, 372 - 377.

Barbosa, E. M., Moro, M. M., Lopes, G. R., & de Oliveira, J. P. M. (2012). VRRC: web based tool for visualization and recommendation on co-authorship network. In *Proceedings of the 2012 ACM SIGMOD International Conference on Management of Data* (pp. 865-865). ACM. doi:10.1145/2213836.2213975

Barjis, J., Gupta, A., & Sharda, R. (2011). Knowledge work and communication challenges in networked enterprises. *Information Systems Frontiers, 13*(5), 615–619. doi:10.1007/s10796-010-9240-6

Basaras, P., Katsaros, D., & Tassiulas, L. (2013). Detecting Influential Spreaders in Complex, Dynamic Networks. *IEEE Computer Magazine, 46*(4), 26-31.

Bastian, M., Heymann, S., & Jacomy, M. (2009). Gephi: An Open Source Software for Exploring and Manipulating Networks. In *Third International AAAI Conference on Weblogs and Social Media* (p. 9). San José, CA: The AAAI Press.

Bastian, M., Heymann, S., & Jacomy, M. (2009). *Gephi: An Open Source Software for Exploring and Manipulating Networks*. Association for the Advancement of Artificial Intelligence.

Batagelj, V., & Zaversnik, M. (2002). *An O(m) Algorithm for Cores Decomposition of Networks*. University of Ljubljana, Department of Theoretical Computer Science. http://arxiv.org/abs/cs.DS/0310049

Batarfi, O., Shawi, R. E., Fayoumi, A. G., Nouri, R., Beheshti, S.-M.-R., Barnawi, A., & Sakr, S. (2015). Large scale graph processing systems: Survey and an experimental evaluation. *Cluster Computing, 18*(3), 1189–1213. doi:10.1007/s10586-015-0472-6

Battiti, R., & Protasi, M. (2001). Reactive Local Search for the Maximum Clique Problem. *Algorithmica, 29*(4), 610–637. doi:10.1007/s004530010074

Becker, G.-S. (1993). *Human capital: a theoretical and empirical analysis, with special reference to education* (3rd ed.). New York: National Bureau of Economic Research: Distributed by Columbia University Press. doi:10.7208/chicago/9780226041223.001.0001

Benevenuto, F., Rodrigues, F., & Cha, M. (2009). Characterizing User Behavior in Online Social Networks. *Proc. of ACM IMC.* doi:10.1145/1644893.1644900

Berland, M., Baker, R. S., & Blikstein, P. (2014). Educational Data Mining and Learning Analytics: Applications to Constructionist Research. *Technology. Knowledge and Learning, 19*(1–2), 205–220. doi:10.1007/s10758-014-9223-7

Bernstam, E. V., Sagaram, S., Walji, M., Johnson, C. W., & Meric-Bernstam, F. (2005). Usability of quality measures for online health information: Can commonly used technical quality criteria be reliably assessed? *International Journal of Medical Informatics, 74*(7–8), 675–683. doi:10.1016/j.ijmedinf.2005.02.002 PMID:16043090

Berrueta, D., Brickley, D., Decker, S., Fernández, S., Görn, C., Harth, A., . . . Polo, L. (2010, March 25). *SIOC Core Ontology Specification.* Retrieved from RDFS: http://rdfs.org/sioc/spec/

Bhattacharya, S., Srinivasan, P., & Polgreen, P. (2014). Engagement with Health Agencies on Twitter. *PLoS ONE, 9*(11), e112235. doi:10.1371/journal.pone.0112235 PMID:25379727

Bisgin, H., Agarwal, N., & Xiaowei, X. (2010). *Investigating Homophily in Online Social Networks.* Academic Press.

Blondel, V. D., Guillaume, J.-L., Lambiotte, R., & Lefebvre, E. (2008). Fast unfolding of communities in large networks. *Journal of Statistical Mechanics, 2008*(10), P10008. doi:10.1088/1742-5468/2008/10/P10008

Boberg, E. W., Gustafson, D. H., Hawkins, R. P., Offord, K. P., Koch, C., Wen, K.-Y., & Salner, A. et al. (2003). Assessing the unmet information, support and care delivery needs of men with prostate cancer. *Patient Education and Counseling, 49*(3), 233–242. doi:10.1016/S0738-3991(02)00183-0 PMID:12642195

Boccaletti, S., Latora, V., Moreno, Y., Chávez, M., & Hwang, D.-U. (2006). Complex networks: Structure and dynamics. *Physics Reports, 424*(4–5), 175–308. doi:10.1016/j.physrep.2005.10.009

Bojārs, U., Breslin, J. G., Passant, A., & Polleres, A. (2007, June 12). *SIOC Ontology: Related Ontologies and RDF Vocabularies.* Retrieved from W3C Member Submission.

Bonacich, P. (1972). Technique for analyzing overlapping memberships. *Sociological Methodology, 4,* 176–185. doi:10.2307/270732

Bonato, A. (2005). A survey of models of the web graph,Combinatorial and algorithmic aspects of networking. Lecture Notes in Computer Science, 3405, 159-172.

Bonchi, F., Castillo, C., Gionis, A., & Jaimes, A. (2011). 04). Social Network Analysis and Mining for Business Applications. *ACM Transactions on Intelligent Systems and Technology, 2*(3). doi:10.1145/1961189.1961194

Bonchi, F., Gullo, F., Kaltenbrunner, A., & Volkovich, Y. (2014). Core Decomposition of Uncertain Graphs. *Proceedings of the ACM Conference on Knowledge Discovery and Data Mining,* 1316-1325.

Bongwon, S., Lichan, H., Pirolli, P., & Chi, E. H. (2010). *Want to be Retweeted?* Large Scale Analytics on Factors Impacting Retweet in Twitter Network.

Borgatti, S. (2005). Centrality and network flow. *Social Networks, 27*(1), 55–71. doi:10.1016/j.socnet.2004.11.008

Borgatti, S. P., Mehra, A., Brass, D. J., & Labianca, G. (2009). Network Analysis in the Social Sciences. *Science, 323*(5916), 892–895. doi:10.1126/science.1165821 PMID:19213908

Borgatti, S., & Everett, M. (2006). A graph-theoretic perspective on centrality. *Social Networks*, *28*(4), 466–484. doi:10.1016/j.socnet.2005.11.005

Bornmann, L., & Daniel, H. D. (2007). What do we know about the h index? *Journal of the American Society for Information Science and Technology*, *58*(9), 1381–1385. doi:10.1002/asi.20609

Bottazzi, D., Montanari, R., & Toninelli, A. (2007). Context-aware middleware for anytime, anywhere social networks. *IEEE Intelligent Systems*, *22*(5), 23–32. doi:10.1109/MIS.2007.4338491

Bourse, F., Lelarge, M., & Vojnovic, M. (2014, August). Balanced graph edge partition. In *Proceedings of the 20th ACM SIGKDD international conference on Knowledge discovery and data mining* (pp. 1456-1465). ACM.

Boyd, D., Golder, S., & Lotan, G. (2010). Tweet, Tweet, Retweet: Conversational Aspects of Retweeting on Twitter. Academic Press.

Boyd, D. M., & Ellison, N. B. (2007, October). Social Network Sites: Definition, History, and Scholarship. *J. Comp.-Mediated Comm.*, *13*(1), 210–230. doi:10.1111/j.1083-6101.2007.00393.x

Brandão, M. A., & Moro, M. M. (2017). Social professional networks: A survey and taxonomy. *Computer Communications*, *100*, 20–31. doi:10.1016/j.comcom.2016.12.011

Brandão, M. A., Moro, M. M., Lopes, G. R., & Oliveira, J. P. (2013). Using link semantics to recommend collaborations in academic social networks. In *Proceedings of the 22nd International Conference on World Wide Web* (pp. 833-840). ACM. doi:10.1145/2487788.2488058

Brandes, U., Delling, D., Gaertler, M., Gorke, R., Hoefer, M., Nikoloski, Z., & Wagner, D. (2008). On modularity clustering. *IEEE Transactions on Knowledge and Data Engineering*, *20*(2), 172–188. doi:10.1109/TKDE.2007.190689

Brandes, U., Indlekofer, N., & Mader, M. (2012). Visualization methods for longitudinal social networks and stochastic actor-oriented modeling. *Social Networks*, *34*(3), 291–308. doi:10.1016/j.socnet.2011.06.002

Brandes, U., Kenis, P., & Raab, J. (2006). Explanation through network visualization. *Methodology: European Journal of Research Methods for the Behavioral and Social Sciences*, *2*(1), 16–23. doi:10.1027/1614-2241.2.1.16

Brans, J., & Vincke, P. (1985). A preference ranking organisation method: The PROMETHEE method for MCDM. *Management Science*, *31*(6), 647–656. doi:10.1287/mnsc.31.6.647

Breckons, M., Jones, R., Morris, J., & Richardson, J. (2008). What Do Evaluation Instruments Tell Us About the Quality of Complementary Medicine Information on the Internet? *Journal of Medical Internet Research*, *10*(1), e3. doi:10.2196/jmir.961 PMID:18244894

Breslin, J., Passant, A., & Vrandečić, D. (2011). Social Semantic Web. In J. Domingue, & D. Fensel (Eds.), Handbook of Semantic Web Technologies (pp. 467-506). Springer Berlin Heidelberg. doi:10.1007/978-3-540-92913-0_12

Breslin, J., Passant, A., & Decker, S. (2009). *The Social Semantic Web*. Springer-Verlag Berlin Heidelberg. doi:10.1007/978-3-642-01172-6

Breunig, M., Kriegel, H., Ng, R., & Sander, J. Identifying Density-Based Local Outliers. *Proceedings of the 2000 ACM SIGMOD International Conference on Management of Data,* 93–104. doi:10.1145/342009.335388

Brickley, D., & Miller, L. (2010, Août 9). *FOAF Vocabulary Specification 0.98*. Retrieved June 4, 2013, from http://xmlns.com/foaf/spec/

Brickley, D., & Miller, L. (2014, Janvier 14). *FOAF Vocabulary Specification 0.99. Namespace Document*. Retrieved from xmlns.com: http://xmlns.com/foaf/spec/

Brin, S., & Page, L. (1998). The anatomy of a large-scale hypertextual web search engine. *Proceedings of the 7th World-Wide-Web Conference (WWW7)*. doi:10.1016/S0169-7552(98)00110-X

Broder, A., Kumar, R., Maghoul, F., Raghavan, P., Rajagopalan, S., Stata, R., & Wiener, J. et al. (2002). Graph Structure in the Web. *Computer Networks*, *33*(1-6), 309–320. doi:10.1016/S1389-1286(00)00083-9

Brown, P. J., Bovey, J. D., & Chen, X. (1997). Context-awareness applications: From the laboratory to the marketplace. *IEEE Pers. Commun.*, *4*(5), 58–64. doi:10.1109/98.626984

Bruns, A. (2009). *Social Media: Tools for User-Generated Content Social Drivers behind Growing Consumer Participation in User-Led Content Generationts only* (Vol. 2). Smart Services CRC Pty Ltd.

Buccafurri, F., Lax, G., Nicolazzo, S., & Nocera, A. (2015). 11). Comparing Twitter and Facebook user behavior. *Journal Computers in Human Behavior*, *52*(C), 87–95. doi:10.1016/j.chb.2015.05.045

Buffa, M., & Faron-Zucker, C. (2012). Ontology-Based Access Rights Management. In F. Guillet, G. Ritschard, & D. A. Zighed (Eds.), Advances in Knowledge Discovery and Management (pp. 49-61). Springer Berlin Heidelberg. doi:10.1007/978-3-642-25838-1_3

Bukowitz, W. R., & Williams, R. L. (2000). *The knowledge management fieldbook*. Financial Times/Prentice Hall.

Business Application of Social Network Analysis (BASNA). (2013). Retrieved from www.basna.in

Cacioppo, J. T., Fowler, J. H., & Christakis, N. A. (2009). Alone in the crowd: The structure and spread of loneliness in a large social network. *Journal of Personality and Social Psychology*, *97*(6), 977–991. doi:10.1037/a0016076 PMID:19968414

Cai, D., Shao, Z., He, X., Yan, X., & Han, J. (2005). Community mining from multi-relational networks. *Knowledge Discovery in Databases: PKDD*, *2005*, 445–452.

Calvet Liñán, L., & Juan Pérez, Á. A. (2015). Educational Data Mining and Learning Analytics: Differences, similarities, and time evolution. *RUSC Universities and Knowledge Society Journal*, *12*(3), 98. doi:10.7238/rusc.v12i3.2515

Campbell, A. P. (2004). Using LiveJournal for Authentic Communication in EFL Classes. The Internet TESL Journal, 5(9).

Cancho, R. F., & Sole, R. V. (2001). *The Small-World of Human Language*. Santa Fe Institute Working Paper 01-03-016.

Carminati, B., Ferrari, E., Heatherly, R., Kantarcioglu, M., & Thuraisingham, B. (2009). A semantic web based framework for social network access control. *Proceedings of the 14th ACM symposium on Access control models and technologies SACMAT'09*, 177-186. doi:10.1145/1542207.1542237

Carmi, S., Havlin, S., Kirkpatrick, S., Shavitt, Y., & Shir, E. (2007). A Model of Internet Topology Using k-Shell Decomposition. *Proceedings of the National Academy of Sciences of the United States of America*, *104*(27), 11150–11154. doi:10.1073/pnas.0701175104 PMID:17586683

Carrington, P. J., & Scott, J. (2011). Introduction. In *The Sage Handbook of Social Network Analysis*. SAGE. Retrieved from http://www.facebook.com/notes/facebook/500millionstories/409753352130

Carrington, P. J., Scott, J., & Wasserman, S. (2005). *Models and Methods in Social Network Analysis*. Cambridge University Press. doi:10.1017/CBO9780511811395

Cazals, F., & Karande, C. (2008). *A note on the problem of reporting maximal cliques*. Academic Press.

Cha, Y., & Cho, J. (2012). Social-Network Analysis Using Topic Models. *SIGIR'12*. doi:10.1145/2348283.2348360

Chaffey, D. (2017, February 27). *Global social media research summary 2017*. Retrieved from Smart Insights: http://www.smartinsights.com/social-media-marketing/social-media-strategy/new-global-social-media-research/

Chakraborty, T. (2015). Liveraging disjoint communities for detecting overlapping community structure. *Journal of Statistical Mechanics, 2015*(5), P05017. doi:10.1088/1742-5468/2015/05/P05017

Cha, M., Haddadi, H., Benevenuto, F., & Gummadi, K. (2010). Measuring User Influence in Twitter: The Million Follower Fallacy. *Proceedings of the 4th International AAAI Conference on Weblogs and Social Media (ICWSM-2010).*

Cha, M., Mislove, A., & Gummadi, K. P. (2009). A measurement-driven analysis of information propagation in the flickr social network. *Proceedings of the 18th international conference on World wide web.* doi:10.1145/1526709.1526806

Champin, P. A., & Passant, A. (2010). SIOC in Action – Representing the Dynamics of Online Communities. *Proceedings the 6th International Conference on Semantic Systems, I-SEMANTICS 2010* (pp. 12:1-12.7). Graz, Austria: ACM.

Chang, C. C., & Chin, Y. C. (2011). Predicting the usage intention of social network games: An intrinsic-extrinsic motivation theory perspective. *International Journal of Online Marketing, 1*(3), 29–37. doi:10.4018/ijom.2011070103

Cheathan, M., & Cleereman, K. (2006). Application of Social Network Analysis to Collaborative Team Formation. *International Symposium on Collaborative Technologies and Systems*, 306-311. doi:10.1109/CTS.2006.18

Chen, Ororbia II, & Giles. (2015). *ExpertSeer: a Keyphrase Based Expert Recommender for Digital Libraries.* arXiv preprint.

Chen, C. H. (Ed.). (1996). *Fuzzy Logic and Neural Network Handbook.* McGraw-Hill, Inc.

Cheng, J., Ke, Y., Chu, S., & Ozsu, M. T. (2011). Efficient Core Decomposition in Massive Networks. *Proceedings of the IEEE International Conference on Data Engineering*, 51-62.

Chen, H. H., Gou, L., Zhang, X., & Giles, C. L. (2011). Collabseer: a search engine for collaboration discovery. In *Proceedings of the 11th annual international ACM/IEEE joint conference on Digital libraries* (pp. 231-240). ACM. doi:10.1145/1998076.1998121

Chen, L., Wei, S., & Qingpu, Z. (2010). Semantic Description of Social Network Based on Ontology. *International Conference on E-Business and E-Government* (pp. 1936 - 1939). IEEE. doi:10.1109/ICEE.2010.489

Chen, P. (1976). The Entity-Relationship Model - Toward a Unified View of Data. *ACM Transactions on Database Systems, 1*(1), 9–36. doi:10.1145/320434.320440

Chomphoosang, P., Durresi, A., Durresi, M., & Barolli, L. (2012). *Trust Management of Social Networks in Health Care.* Paper presented at the 2012 15th International Conference on Network-Based Information Systems.

Christakis, N. A., & Fowler, J. H. (2007). The spread of obesity in a large social network over 32 years. *The New England Journal of Medicine, 357*(4), 370–379. doi:10.1056/NEJMsa066082 PMID:17652652

Christakis, N. A., & Fowler, J. H. (2013). Social contagion theory: Examining dynamic social networks and human behavior. *Statistics in Medicine, 32*(4), 556–577. doi:10.1002/sim.5408 PMID:22711416

Chu, Z., Gianvecchio, S., Wang, H., & Jajodia, S. (2010). Who is tweeting on Twitter: Human, bot, or cyborg? *Computer Security Applications Conference ACSAC, 10*(26), 21–30.

Cioffi-Revilla, C. (2014). Computation and Social Science. In *Introduction to Computational Social Science* (pp. 23–66). Springer London. doi:10.1007/978-1-4471-5661-1_2

Clauset, A., Newman, M. E. J., & Moore, C. (2004). Finding community structure in very large networks. *Physical Review E: Statistical, Nonlinear, and Soft Matter Physics, 70*(6), 066111. doi:10.1103/PhysRevE.70.066111 PMID:15697438

Code Ethics. (2016). *Agency for Health Care Policy and Research*. Available at http://www.aaai.org/ocs/index.php/ICWSM/ICWSM10/

Coffrin, C., Corrin, L., de Barba, P., & Kennedy, G. (2014). Visualizing Patterns of Student Engagement and Performance in MOOCs. In *Proceedings of the Fourth International Conference on Learning Analytics And Knowledge* (pp. 83–92). New York, NY: ACM. doi:10.1145/2567574.2567586

Collins, A. M., & Loftus, E. F. (1975, November). A spreading-activation theory of semantic processing. *Psychological Review, 82*(6), 407–428. doi:10.1037/0033-295X.82.6.407

Combe, D., Largeron, C., Egyed-Zsigmond, E., & Géry, M. (2010). A comparative study of social network analysis tools. *International Workshop on Web Intelligence and Virtual Enterprises, 2.*

Cook, D. J., & Holder, L. B. (2007). *Mining Graph Data, Electrical Engineering and Computer Science, Washington State University*. Pullman, WA: John Wiley & Sons, Inc.

Crandall, D. J., Backstrom, L., Cosley, D., Suri, S., Huttenlocher, D., & Kleinberg, J. (2010). Inferring social ties from geographic coincidences. *Proceedings of the National Academy of Sciences of the United States of America, 107*(52), 22436–22441. doi:10.1073/pnas.1006155107 PMID:21148099

Crandall, D., Cosley, D., Huttenlocher, D., Kleinberg, J., & Suri, S. (2008, August). Feedback effects between similarity and social influence in online communities. In *Proceedings of the 14th ACM SIGKDD international conference on Knowledge discovery and data mining* (pp. 160-168). ACM. doi:10.1145/1401890.1401914

Crestani, F. (1997). Application of Spreading Activation Techniques in Information Retrieval. *Artificial Intelligence Review, 11*(6), 453–482. doi:10.1023/A:1006569829653

Cummings, J. N. (2004). Work groups, structural diversity, and knowledge sharing in a global organization. *Management Science, 50*(3), 352–364. doi:10.1287/mnsc.1030.0134

da F. Costa, L., Rodrigues, F. A., Travieso, G., & Boas, P. R. V. (2007). Characterization of complex networks: A survey of measurements. *Advances in Physics, 56*(1), 167 – 242.

Daelemans, W., & Bosch, A. (2005). *Memory-Based Language Processing*. Cambridge University Press. doi:10.1017/CBO9780511486579

Dawson, S. (2008). A Study of the Relationship between Student Social Networks and Sense of Community. *Journal of Educational Technology & Society, 11*(3), 224–238.

Dawson, S., & Siemens, G. (2014). Analytics to literacies: The development of a learning analytics framework for multiliteracies assessment. *International Review of Research in Open and Distance Learning, 15*(4). doi:10.19173/irrodl.v15i4.1878

de Boer, M. J., Versteegen, G. J., & van Wijhe, M. (2007). Patients use of the Internet for pain-related medical information. *Patient Education and Counseling, 68*(1), 86–97. doi:10.1016/j.pec.2007.05.012 PMID:17590563

de Laat, M., & Schreurs, B. (2013). Visualizing Informal Professional Development Networks Building a Case for Learning Analytics in the Workplace. *The American Behavioral Scientist, 57*(10), 1421–1438. doi:10.1177/0002764213479364

de Sousa, G. A., Diniz, M. A., Brandão, M. A., & Moro, M. M. (2015). CNARe: Co-authorship Networks Analysis and Recommendations. In *Proceedings of the 9th ACM Conference on Recommender Systems* (pp. 329-330). ACM.

Dean, J., & Ghemawat, S. (2004). MapReduce: Simplified Data Processing on Large Clusters. *Proceedings of USENIX Conference on Operating System Design and Implementation*, 137-150.

Debatin, B., Lovejoy, J. P., Horn, A.-K., & Hughes, B. N. (2009). Facebook and Online Privacy: Attitudes, Behaviors, and Unintended Consequences. *Journal of Computer-Mediated Communication, 15*(1), 83–108. doi:10.1111/j.1083-6101.2009.01494.x

Deconta, M. C., Obrst, L. J., & Smith, K. T. (2003). *The Semantic Web: A guide to future of XML, Web Services and Knowledge Management.* Wiley Publishing Inc.

Dehaene, S. (2003). The neural basis of the Weber–Fechner law: A logarithmic mental number line. *Trends in Cognitive Sciences, 7*(4), 145–147. doi:10.1016/S1364-6613(03)00055-X PMID:12691758

Delors, J., Mufti, I. A., Amagi, I., Carneiro, R., Chung, F., & Geremek, B. (1996). International Commission on Education for the Twenty-First Century. Learning, the treasure within: Report to UNESCO of the International Commission on Education for the Twenty-first Century. Paris: UNESCO.

Di Stefano, A., La Corte, A., Leotta, M., Lió, P., & Scatá, M. (2013). It measures like me: An IoTs algorithm in WSNs based on heuristics behavior and clustering methods. *Ad Hoc Networks, 11*(8), 2637–2647. doi:10.1016/j.adhoc.2013.04.011

Di Stefano, A., Scatà, M., La Corte, A., Liò, P., Catania, E., Guardo, E., & Pagano, S. (2015). Quantifying the role of homophily in human cooperation using multiplex evolutionary game theory. *PLoS ONE, 10*(10), e0140646. doi:10.1371/journal.pone.0140646 PMID:26496351

Ding, L., Zhou, L., & Finin, T. (2003). Trust based knowledge outsourcing for semantic web agents. *Proceedings of IEEE/WIC International Conference on Web Intelligence.* doi:10.1109/WI.2003.1241219

Doerr, B., Fouz, M., & Friedrich, T. (2012). Why rumors spread fast in social networks. *Communications of the ACM, 55*(6), 70–75. doi:10.1145/2184319.2184338

Dorogovtsev, S. N., & Mendes, J. F. F. (2002). Evolution of networks. *Advances in Physics, 51*(4), 1079–1187. doi:10.1080/00018730110112519

Du, D. Z., & Pardalos, P. M. (1991). *The Maximum Clique Problem. In Handbook of Combinatorial Optimization: Supplement* (Vol. A, pp. 1–74). Springer.

Dyckhoff, A. L., Zielke, D., Bültmann, M., Chatti, M. A., & Schroeder, U. (2012). Design and Implementation of a Learning Analytics Toolkit for Teachers. *Journal of Educational Technology & Society, 15*(3), 58–76.

Easley, D., & Kleinberg, J. (2010). *Networks, crowds, and markets: Reasoning about a highly connected world.* Cambridge University Press. doi:10.1017/CBO9780511761942

Easley, D., & Kleinberg, J. (2012). Networks, crowds, and markets: Reasoning about a highly connected world. *Significance, 9*, 43–44.

Eidsaa, M., & Almaas, E. (2013). s-Core Network Decomposition: A Generalization of k-Core Analysis to Weighted Networks. *Physical Review E: Statistical, Nonlinear, and Soft Matter Physics, 88*(062819). PMID:24483523

Eisenegger, M. (2009). Trust and reputation in the age of globalisation. In J. Klewes & R. Wreschniok (Eds.), *Reputation Capital* (pp. 11–22). Berlin: Springer Berlin Heidelberg. doi:10.1007/978-3-642-01630-1_2

El Kassiri, A., & Belouadha, F.-Z. (2014). ActOnto: An extension of the SIOC standard for social media analysis and interoperability. *Third IEEE International Colloquium in Information Science and Technology (CIST'14),* 62-67.

El Kassiri, A., & Belouadha, F.-Z. (2015). Towards a Unified Semantic Model for Online Social Networks Analysis and Interoperability. *10th International Conference on Intelligent Systems: Theories and Applications (SITA),* 62-67.

Elias, T. (2011). *Learning Analytics: The Definitions, the Processes, and the Potential.* Retrieved from http://learninga-nalytics.net/LearningAnalyticsDefinitionsProcessesPotential.pdf

Engeström, Y. (1987). *Learning by Expanding: An Activity-theoretical Approach to Developmental Research.* Helsinki: Orienta-Konsultit.

Epskamp, S., Cramer, A. O. J., Waldorp, L. J., Schmittmann, V. D., & Borsboom, D. (2012). qgraph: Network visualizations of relationships in psychometric data. *Journal of Statistical Software, 48*(4), 1–18. doi:10.18637/jss.v048.i04

Erdõs, P., & Rényi, A. (1960). On the evolution of random graphs. *Publications of the Mathematical Institute of the Hungarian Academy of Sciences, 5,* 17–61.

Erétéo, G., Buffa, M., Gandon, F., & Corby, O. (2009). Analysis of a Real Online Social Network Using Semantic Web Frameworks. *8th International Semantic Web Conference, ISWC 2009* (pp. 180-195). Chantilly, VA: Springer Berlin Heidelberg. doi:10.1007/978-3-642-04930-9_12

Everett, M. G., & Borgatti, S. P. (2005). Extending centrality. In P. J. Carrington, J. Scott, & S. Wasserman (Eds.), *Models and Methods in Social Network Analysis* (pp. 181–201). Cambridge University Press. doi:10.1017/CBO9780511811395.004

Eysenbach, G., Powell, J., Kuss, O., & Sa, E.-R. (2002). Empirical Studies Assessing the Quality of Health Information for Consumers on the World Wide Web: A Systematic Review. *Journal of the American Medical Association, 287*(20), 2691–2700. doi:10.1001/jama.287.20.2691 PMID:12020305

Ferguson, R. (2012). Learning Analytics: Drivers, Developments and Challenges. *International Journal of Technology Enhanced Learning, 4*(5/6), 304–317. doi:10.1504/IJTEL.2012.051816

Figueira, J. R., Greco, S., Roy, B., & Słowiński, R. (2013). An overview of ELECTRE methods and their recent extensions. *Journal of Multi-Criteria Decision Analysis, 20*(1-2), 61–85. doi:10.1002/mcda.1482

Fildes, J. (2010). *Google admits Buzz testing flaws.* BBC News.

Fong, P. W. L., Anwar, M., & Zhao, Z. (2009). A Privacy Preservation Model for Facebook-Style Social Network Systems. *Proceedings of the 14th European Symposium on Research in Computer Security (ESORICS).* doi:10.1007/978-3-642-04444-1_19

Fortunato, S. (2010). *Community detection in graphs.* Complex Networks and Systems Lagrange Laboratory ISI Foundation.

Fortunato, S. (2010). Community detection in graphs. *Physics Reports, 486*(3), 75–174. doi:10.1016/j.physrep.2009.11.002

Foster, I., Ghani, R., Jarmin, R. S., Kreuter, F., & Lane, J. (2016). *Big Data and Social Science. A Practical Guide to Methods and Tools.* Boca Raton, FL: CRC Press.

Fournier, H., Kop, R., & Sitlia, H. (2011). The Value of Learning Analytics to Networked Learning on a Personal Learning Environment. In *Proceedings of the 1st International Conference on Learning Analytics and Knowledge* (pp. 104–109). New York, NY: ACM. doi:10.1145/2090116.2090131

Freeman, L. C. (2000). Visualizing social networks. *Journal of Social Structure, 1*(1), 4.

Freeman, L. C. (2002). *The Study of Social Networks.* Available: http://www.insna.org/INSNA/na_inf.html

Freeman, L. C. (1978). Centrality in social networks: Conceptual clarification. *Social Networks, 1*(3), 215–239. doi:10.1016/0378-8733(78)90021-7

Freeman, L. C. (2004). *The Development of Social Network Analysis. A Study in the Sociology of Science.* Vancouver: Empirical Press.

Fruchterman, T. M. J., & Reingold, E. M. (1991). Graph drawing by force-directed placement. *Software, Practice & Experience*, *21*(11), 1129–1164. doi:10.1002/spe.4380211102

Garas, A., Schweitzer, F., & Havlin, S. (2012). A k-Shell Decomposition Method for Weighted Networks. *New Journal of Physics*, 14.

Gephi. (n.d.). Retrieved from https://gephi.org

Giacchi, E., Di Stefano, A., La Corte, A., & Scatà, M. (2014, November). A dynamic context-aware multiple criteria decision making model in social networks. In *Information Society (i-Society), 2014 International Conference on* (pp. 157-162). IEEE. doi:10.1109/i-Society.2014.7009032

Gigerenzer, G., & Goldstein, D. G. (1996). Reasoning the fast and frugal way: Models of bounded rationality. *Psychological Review*, *103*(4), 650–669. doi:10.1037/0033-295X.103.4.650 PMID:8888650

Gilbert, E., & Karahalios, K. (2009). Predicting tie strength with social media. *Proceedings of the SIGCHI Conference on Human Factors in Computing Systems CHI '09*, 211-220.

Girvan, M., & Newman, M. E. J. (2002). Community structure in social and bi-ological networks. *Proceedings of the National Academy of Sciences of the United States of America*, *99*(12), 7821–7826. doi:10.1073/pnas.122653799 PMID:12060727

Gjoka, M., Kurant, M., Butts, C. T., & Markopoulou, A. (2010). A walk in Facebook: Uniform sampling of users in online social networks. *Proceedings - IEEE INFOCOM*.

Golbeck, J. (2005). *Computing and Applying Trust in Web-Based Social Networks* (PhD thesis). Univ. Maryland, College Park, MD.

Golbeck, J., & Rothstein, M. M. (2008). Linking social networks on the web with FOAF: a semantic web case study. *Proceeding AAAI'08 Proceedings of the 23rd national conference on Artificial intelligence, 2*, 1138-1143.

Golbeck, L., Parsia, B., & Hendler, J. (2003). Trust network on the semantic web. Proceedings of Cooperative Intelligent Agents. doi:10.1007/978-3-540-45217-1_18

Goldstein, M., & Uchida, S. (2016). A Comparative Evaluation of Unsupervised Anomaly Detection Algorithms for Multivariate Data. *PLoS ONE*, *11*(4). doi:10.1371/journal.pone.0152173 PMID:27093601

Gonzalez, J. E., Xin, R. S., Dave, A., Crankshaw, D., Franklin, M. J., & Stoica, I. (2014). GraphX: Graph Processing in a Distributed Dataflow Framework. In *Proceedings of the 11th USENIX Symposium on Operating Systems Design and Implementation* (pp. 599–613). Broomfield, CO: USENIX.

Goodman, L. A. (1961). Snowball sampling. *Annals of Mathematical Statistics*, *32*(1), 148–170. doi:10.1214/aoms/1177705148

Grabisch, M., & Rusinowska, A. (2010). A model of influence in a social network. *Theory and Decision*, *69*(1), 69–96. doi:10.1007/s11238-008-9109-z

Graham, I. D., Logan, J., Harrison, M. B., Straus, S. E., Tetroe, J., Caswell, W., & Robinson, N. (2006). Lost in knowledge translation: Time for a map? *The Journal of Continuing Education in the Health Professions*, *26*(1), 13–24. doi:10.1002/chp.47 PMID:16557505

Granovetter, M. S. (1973). The Strength of Weak Ties. *American Journal of Sociology*, *78*(6), 1360–1380. doi:10.1086/225469

Greco, S., Figueira, J., & Ehrgott, M. (2005). *Multiple criteria decision analysis.* Springer's International Series.

Gregory, S. (2007). An algorithm to find overlapping community structure in networks. In J. N. Kok, J. Koronacki, R. Lopez de Mantras, S. Matwin, D. Mladenic, & A. Skowron (Eds.), *PKDD 2007. LNCS (LNAI)* (Vol. 4702, pp. 91–102). Heidelberg: Springer. doi:10.1007/978-3-540-74976-9_12

Gregory, S. (2008). A fast algorithm to find overlapping communities in networks. In W. Daelemans (Ed.), *ECML PKDD 2008, LNAI* (Vol. 5212, pp. 408–423). Berlin: Springer. doi:10.1007/978-3-540-87479-9_45

Gregory, S. (2010). Finding overlapping communities in networks by label propagation. *New Journal of Physics, 12*(10), 10301. doi:10.1088/1367-2630/12/10/103018

Griffiths, M. K., Tang, T. T., Hawking, D., & Christensen, H. (2005). Automated Assessment of the Quality of Depression Websites. *Journal of Medical Internet Research, 7*(5), e59. doi:10.2196/jmir.7.5.e59 PMID:16403723

Gruber, T. (2007). Ontology of folksonomy: A mashup of apples and oranges. *International Journal on Semantic Web and Information Systems, 3*(2).

Gruzd, A., Wellman, B., & Takhteyev, Y. (2011). Imagining Twitter as an Imagined Community. *The American Behavioral Scientist, 55*(10), 1294–1318. doi:10.1177/0002764211409378

Gudes, E. (2015). Reputation - from Social Perception to Internet Security. In C. Damsgaard Jensen, S. Marsh, T. Dimitrakos, & Y. Murayama (Eds.), *Trust Management IX: 9th IFIP WG 11.11 International Conference* (pp. 3-10). Cham: Springer International Publishing.

Guermah, H., Fissaa, T., Hafiddi, H., Nassar, M., & Kriouile, A. (2013, May). Context modeling and reasoning for building context aware services. In *Computer Systems and Applications (AICCSA), 2013 ACS International Conference on* (pp. 1-7). IEEE. doi:10.1109/AICCSA.2013.6616439

Guerra-Gomez, J. A., Wilson, A., Liu, J., Davies, D., Jarvis, P., & Bier, E. (2016). Network Explorer: Design, Implementation, and Real World Deployment of a Large Network Visualization Tool. In *Proceedings of the International Working Conference on Advanced Visual Interfaces* (pp. 108-111). ACM. doi:10.1145/2909132.2909281

Gui, N., De Florio, V., Sun, H., & Blondia, C. (2011). Toward architecture-based context-aware deployment and adaptation. *Journal of Systems and Software, 84*(2), 185–197. doi:10.1016/j.jss.2010.09.017

Gundecha, P., & Liu, H. (2012). *Mining Social Media: A Brief Introduction.* The Institute for Operations Research and the Management Sciences (INFORMS), TutORials in Operations Research. Retrieved from http://www.public.asu.edu/~pgundech/book_chapter/smm.pdf

Gundecha, P., & Liu, H. (2012). *Mining Social Media: A Brief Introduction. In Tutorials in Operations Research.* INFORMS.

Gupta, Goel, Lin, Sharma, Wang, & Zadeh. (n.d.). WTF: The who-to-follow system at Twitter. *Proceedings of the 22nd international conference on World Wide Web.*

Hage, P., & Harary, F. (1983). *Structural Models in Anthropology.* Cambridge, UK: Cambridge University Press.

Han, J., & Kamber, M. (2006). Data Mining: Concepts and Techniques (2nd ed.). Academic Press.

Han, J., Kamber, M., & Pei, J. (2012). *Data Mining. Concepts and Techniques.* Amsterdam: Morgan Kaufmann.

Hanneman, R. A., & Riddle, M. (2005). *Introduction to social network methods.* Riverside, CA: University of California, Riverside. Retrieved from http://faculty.ucr.edu/~hanneman/

Hanneman, R., & Riddle, M. (2005). *Introduction to Social Network Methods.* Available: http://www.faculty.ucr.edu/~hanneman/nettext/

Hanneman, R. A., & Riddle, M. (2005). *Introduction to social network methods*. Riverside, CA: University of California.

Harenberg, S., Bello, G., Gjeltema, L., Ranshous, S., Jitendra, H., Ramona, S., … Samatova, N. (2014). Community detection in large-scale networks: a survey and empirical evaluation. *WIREs Comput Stat, 6*, 426-439.

Harth, A., Breslin, J. G., & Decker, S. (2004). Linking Semantically Enabled Online Community Sites. *1st Workshop on Friend of a Friend, Social Networking and the Semantic Web*. W3C.

Hatak, I. R., & Roessl, D. (2015). Relational Competence-Based Knowledge Transfer Within Intrafamily Succession An Experimental Study. *Family Business Review, 28*(1), 10–25. doi:10.1177/0894486513480386

hcyu. (2015). *GraphX triangle counting*. Retrieved October 13, 2015 From http://note.yuhc.me/2015/03/graphx-triangle-count-label-propagation/

Health on the Net Code of Conduct. (2016). Health on the Net Foundation.

Hearst, M. A. (1999). Untangling text data mining. *Proc. of 37th ACL*, 3- 10.

He, J., & Chu, W. W. (2010). *A social network-based recommender system*. Springer.

Hinge, A., & Auber, D. (2015, July). Distributed Graph Layout with Spark. In *2015 19th International Conference on Information Visualisation* (pp. 271-276). IEEE. doi:10.1109/iV.2015.56

Hirst, J. (2003). Charities and patient groups should declare interests. *BMJ (Clinical Research Ed.), 326*(7400), 1211–1211. doi:10.1136/bmj.326.7400.1211-a PMID:12775630

Ho, A. D., Reich, J., Nesterko, S. O., Seaton, D. T., Mullaney, T., Waldo, J., & Chuang, I. (2014). *HarvardX and MITx: The First Year of Open Online Courses, Fall 2012-Summer 2013 (SSRN Scholarly Paper No. No. 1)*. Rochester, NY: Social Science Research Network. doi:10.2139/ssrn.2381263

Hoede, C., & Bakker, R. R. (1982). A theory of decisional power. *The Journal of Mathematical Sociology, 8*(2), 309–322. doi:10.1080/0022250X.1982.9989927

Höfler, M., Brückl, T., Bittner, A., & Lieb, R. (2007). Visualizing multivariate dependencies with association chain graphs. *Methodology: European Journal of Research Methods for the Behavioral and Social Sciences, 3*(1), 24–34. doi:10.1027/1614-2241.3.1.24

Holland, J. H. (2006). Studying Complex Adaptive Systems. *Journal of Systems Science and Complexity, 19*(1), 1–8. doi:10.1007/s11424-006-0001-z

Holme, P., & Saramäki, J. (2012). Temporal networks. *Physics Reports, 519*(3), 97–125. doi:10.1016/j.physrep.2012.03.001

Holten, D., & Van Wijk, J. J. (2009). Force-Directed Edge Bundling for Graph Visualization. *Computer Graphics Forum, 28*(3), 983–990. doi:10.1111/j.1467-8659.2009.01450.x

Hong, L., Dan, O., & Davison, B. D. (2011). *Predicting popular messages in Twitter*. Academic Press. doi:10.1145/1963192.1963222

Horowitz, Sahani, & Mehta. (2008). *Fundamentals of Data Structures in C++* (2nd ed.). Universities Press (India) Private Limited.

Houston, T. K., & Allison, J. J. (2002). Users of Internet health information: Differences by health status. *Journal of Medical Internet Research, 4*(2), E7. doi:10.2196/jmir.4.2.e7 PMID:12554554

Hughes, B., Joshi, I., Lemonde, H., & Wareham, J. (2009). Junior physicians use of Web 2.0 for information seeking and medical education: A qualitative study. *International Journal of Medical Informatics*, *78*(10), 645–655. doi:10.1016/j.ijmedinf.2009.04.008 PMID:19501017

Huisman & van duijn. (2011). *Software for social network analysis*. 2004 Graph and Network Analysis Dr. Derek Greene Clique Research Cluster. University College Dublin.

ibm01. (2011). *About MapReduce*. Retrieved June 13, 2011 From https://www-01.ibm.com/software/data/infosphere/hadoop/mapreduce/

Ibrahim, S. Z., Blandford, A., & Bianchi-Berthouze, N. (2012). Privacy Settings on Facebook: Their Roles and Importance. *Proceedings of the 2012 IEEE International Conference on Green Computing and Communications (GreenCom)*. doi:10.1109/GreenCom.2012.67

IGraph. (n.d.). Retrieved from IGraph.sourceforge.net

Inayat, I., Amin, R., Inayat, Z., & Salim, S. S. (2013). Effects of Collaborative Web Based Vocational Education and Training (VET) on Learning Outcomes. *Computers & Education*, *68*, 153–166. doi:10.1016/j.compedu.2013.04.027

Information Access Project. (2016). *Healthy People*. Retrieved from https://phpartners.org/hp/

International Network of Social Network Analysis (INSNA). (n.d.). Retrieved from www.insna.org

Internet World Stats. (n.d.). *Internet usage and World population statistics*. Retrieved 2016/08/21, from http://www.internetworldstats.com/emarketing.htm

J. Scott. (1994). *Social Network Analysis: A handbook*. Newbury Park, CA: Sage Publications.

Jacobson, M. J., & Wilensky, U. (2006). Complex Systems in Education: Scientific and Educational Importance and Implications for the Learning Sciences. *Journal of the Learning Sciences*, *15*(1), 11–34. doi:10.1207/s15327809jls1501_4

Jacomy, M., Heymann, S., Venturini, T., & Bastian, M. (2010). ForceAtlas2, A Continuous Graph Layout Algorithm for Handy Network Visualization. *PLoS ONE*, *9*(6). PMID:24914678

Jacomy, M., Venturini, T., Heymann, S., & Bastian, M. (2014). ForceAtlas2, a Continuous Graph Layout Algorithm for Handy Network Visualization Designed for the Gephi Software. *PLoS ONE*, *9*(6), e98679. doi:10.1371/journal.pone.0098679 PMID:24914678

Jacquet-Lagreze, E., & Siskos, Y. (2001). Preference disaggregation: 20 years of MCDA experience. *European Journal of Operational Research*, *130*(2), 233–245. doi:10.1016/S0377-2217(00)00035-7

Jain & Srivastava. (2013). Data Mining. *International Journal of Research in Engineering and Technology, 2*(11).

Jamali, M., & Abolhassani, H. (2006). Different Aspects of Social Network Analysis. *IEEE/WIC/ACM International Conference on Web Intelligence*, 66-72.

Java API for JSON Processing (JSON-P). (n.d.). Retrieved April 03, 2017, from Java.net: https://json-processing-spec.java.net/

Jeh, G., & Widom, J. (2000). SimRank: A Measure of Structural Context Similarity. *The ACM SIGKDD International Conference on Knowledge Discovery and Data Mining*, 538-543.

Jiang, S., Ferreira, J., & González, M. C. (2012). Clustering daily patterns of human activities in the city. *Data Mining and Knowledge Discovery*, *25*(3), 478–510. doi:10.1007/s10618-012-0264-z

Jianwei, W., Lili, R., & Tianzhu, G. (2008). *A New Measure of Node Importance in Complex Networks with Tunable Parameters*. Academic Press.

Johnson, M., Engelman, S., & Bellovin, S. M. (2012). Facebook and Privacy: It's Complicated. *Proceedings of the Eighth Symposium on Usable Privacy and Security (SOUPS)*. doi:10.1145/2335356.2335369

Jones, C. (2004). Networks and learning: Communities, practices and the metaphor of networks. *Research in Learning Technology, 12*(1). doi:10.3402/rlt.v12i1.11227

Ju, C., Cao, J., Zhang, W., & Ji, M. (2013). Influential node control strategy for opinion evolution on social networks. Academic Press.

Judge, J., Sogrin, M., & Troussov, A. (2007). Galaxy: IBM Ontological Network Miner. *Proceedings of the 1st Conference on Social Semantic Web (CSSW)*.

Kadushin, C. (2012). *Understanding Social Networks. Theories, Concepts and Findings*. Oxford, UK: Oxford University Press.

Kate, E., & Inga, C. (2005). *Inside Social Network Analysis*. IBM Technical Report.

Keeney, R. L., & Raiffa, H. (1993). *Decisions with multiple objectives: preferences and value trade-offs*. Cambridge University Press. doi:10.1017/CBO9781139174084

Keller, G., Nüttgens, M., & Scheer, A. W. (1992). Semantische Prozeßmodellierung auf der Grundlage "Ereignisgesteuerter Prozeßketten (EPK)". Institute of Business Informatics, University of Saarland.

Kempe, D., Kleinberg, J., & Tardos, É. (2003, August). Maximizing the spread of influence through a social network. In *Proceedings of the ninth ACM SIGKDD international conference on Knowledge discovery and data mining* (pp. 137-146). ACM. doi:10.1145/956750.956769

Kempe, D., Kleinbergy, J., & Tardosz, E. (2005). Influential nodes in a diffusion model for social networks. *LNCS, 3580*, 1127–1138.

Khaouid, W., Barsky, M., Srinivasan, V., & Thomo, A. (2015). k-Core Decomposition of Large Networks on a Single PC. *Proceedings of the VLDB Endowment, 9*(1), 13–23. doi:10.14778/2850469.2850471

Khazaal, Y., Chatton, A., Cochand, S., & Zullino, D. (2008). Quality of web-based information on cocaine addiction. *Patient Education and Counseling, 72*(2), 336–341. doi:10.1016/j.pec.2008.03.002 PMID:18423952

Kim, H.-L., Breslin, J., Yang, S.-K., & Kim, H.-G. (2008). *Social Semantic Cloud of Tag: Semantic Model for Social Tagging. In Agent and Multi-Agent Systems: Technologies and Applications*. Springer Berlin Heidelberg.

Kim, H.-L., Scerri, S., Passant, A., Breslin, J. G., & Kim, H.-G. (2011). Integrating Tagging into the Web of Data: Overview and Combination of Existing Tag Ontologies. *Journal of Internet Technology, 12*(4), 561–572.

Kinsella, S., Harth, A., Troussov, A., Sogrin, M., Judge, J., Hayes, C., & Breslin, J. G. (2008). Navigating and Annotating Semantically-Enabled Networks of People and Associated Objects. In T. Friemel (Ed.), *Why Context Matters: Applications of Social Network Analysis* (pp. 79–96). VS Verlag. doi:10.1007/978-3-531-91184-7_5

Kinshuk, Hui-Wen, H., Sampson, D., & Chen, N.-S. (2013). Trends in Educational Technology through the Lens of the Highly Cited Articles Published in the Journal of Educational Technology and Society. *Journal of Educational Technology & Society, 16*(2), 3–20.

Kleinberg, J. (1998). Authoritative sources in a hyperlinked environment. *Proc. 9th ACM-SIAM Symposium on Discrete Algorithms*.

Klienburg. (1998). Authoritative sources in a hyperlinked environment. *Proceedings of Ninth Annual ACM-SIAM Symposium on Discrete Algorithms.*

Knerr, T. (2007, Jan 15). *tagont.* Retrieved from code.google.com/archive: https://code.google.com/archive/p/tagont/downloads

Kolountzakis, M. N., Miller, G. L., Peng, R., & Tsourakakis, C. E. (2012). Efficient triangle counting in large graphs via degree-based vertex partitioning. *Internet Mathematics, 8*(1-2), 161–185. doi:10.1080/15427951.2012.625260

Kong, X., Zhang, J., & Yu, P. S. (2013). Inferring anchor links across multiple heterogeneous social networks. *Proceedings of the 22nd ACM international conference on Conference on information & knowledge management,* 179-188. doi:10.1145/2505515.2505531

Kopecký, J., & Innsbruck, D. (2007, June 26). *Web Services Description Language (WSDL) Version 2.0: RDF Mapping.* Retrieved from WSDL: http://www.w3.org/TR/wsdl20-rdf/

Kop, R. (2011). The challenges to connectivist learning on open online networks: Learning experiences during a massive open online course. *The International Review of Research in Open and Distributed Learning, 12*(3), 19–38. doi:10.19173/irrodl.v12i3.882

Korhonen, P., & Wallenius, J. (1997). Behavioral issues in MCDM: Neglected research questions. In *Multicriteria analysis* (pp. 412–422). Springer Berlin Heidelberg. doi:10.1007/978-3-642-60667-0_39

Kosinskia, M., Stillwella, D., & Graepel, T. (2013). Private traits and attributes are predictable from digital records of human behavior. *Proceedings of the National Academy of Sciences of the United States of America, 110*(15), 5802–5805. doi:10.1073/pnas.1218772110 PMID:23479631

Kossinets, G. (2006). Effects of missing data in social Networks. *Social Networks, 28*(3), 247–268. doi:10.1016/j.socnet.2005.07.002

Krashen, S. D. (1982). *Principles and practice in second language acquisition.* Oxford, UK: Pergamon.

Krashen, S. D. (1985). *The input hypothesis: issues and implications.* London: Longman.

Krasnova, H., Günther, O., Spiekermann, S., & Koroleva, K. (2009). Privacy concerns and identity in online social networks. *Identity in the Information Society, 2*(1), 39–63. doi:10.1007/s12394-009-0019-1

Krebs, V. (2006). *How to do Social Network Analysis.* Available: http://www.orgnet.com/sna.html

Kronstadt, J., Moiduddin, A., & Sellheim, W. (2009). *Consumer Use of Computerized Applications to Address Health and Health Care Needs.* Retrieved from U.S. Department of Health and Human Services - Office of the Secretary Assistant Secretary for Planning and Evaluation: http://aspe.hhs.gov/sp/reports/2009/consumerhit/report.shtml

Kumar, V., & Kumar, S. (2013). Access Control Framework for Social Network System using Ontology. *International Journal of Computer Applications, 7*(4).

Kumar, V. (2011). Impact of Health Information Systems on Organizational Health Communication and Behavior. *The Internet Journal of Allied Health Sciences and Practice, 9*(2).

Kumar, V., & Kumar, S. (2013). Access Control Framework for Social Network System using Ontology. *International Journal of Computers and Applications, 79*(4), 10–18. doi:10.5120/13728-1524

Kuramochi, M., & Karypis, G. (2001). Frequent subgraph discovery. *Proceedings of the 2001 International Conference on Data Mining,* 313–320. doi:10.1109/ICDM.2001.989534

Kwak, H., Lee, C., Park, H., & Moon, S. (2010). *What is Twitter, a social network or a news media?* doi:10.1145/1772690.1772751

Lada, A., & Adar, E. (2003). Predicting missing links via local information. *Social Networks, 25*(3), 211–230.

Lambiotte, R., Delvenne, J.-C., & Barahona, M. (2009). *Laplacian dynamics and multiscale modular structure in networks.* arXiv:0812.1770

Lambiotte, R., & Panzarasa, P. (2009). Communities, knowledge creation, and information diffusion. *Journal of Informetrics, 3*(3), 180–190. doi:10.1016/j.joi.2009.03.007

Lancichinetti, A., Fortunato, S., & Kertesz, J. (2009). Detecting the overlapping and hierarchical community structure of complex networks. *New Journal of Physics, 11*(3), 033015. doi:10.1088/1367-2630/11/3/033015

Lancichinetti, A., Radicchi, F., Ramasco, J. J., & Fortunato, S. (2011). Finding statistically significant communities in networks. *PLoS ONE, 6*(4), e18961. doi:10.1371/journal.pone.0018961 PMID:21559480

Lange, C., Bojārs, U., Groza, T., Breslin, J., & Handschuh, S. (2008). Expressing Argumentative Discussions in Social Media Sites. *First Workshop on Social Data on the Web (SDoW2008).*

Latapy, M. (2008). Main-memory triangle computations for very large (sparse (power-law)) graphs. *Theoretical Computer Science, 407*(1-3), 458–473. doi:10.1016/j.tcs.2008.07.017

Latora, V., & Marchiori, M. (2007). A measure of centrality based on network efficiency. *New Journal of Physics, 9*(6), 188. doi:10.1088/1367-2630/9/6/188

Lave, J., & Wenger, E. (1998). *Communities of practice: Learning, meaning, and identity.* Academic Press.

Lee, B.-C., Yoon, J.-O., & Lee, I. (2009). Learners acceptance of e-learning in South Korea: Theories and results. *Computers & Education, 53*(4), 1320–1329. doi:10.1016/j.compedu.2009.06.014

Leicht, Holme, & Newman. (2006). Vertex similarity in networks. *Phys. Rev. E., 73*, 26-120.

Leontiev, A. N. (1974). The Problem of Activity in Psychology. *Social Psychology, 13*(2), 4–33. doi:10.2753/RPO1061-040513024

Leontiev, A. N. (1978). *Activity, consciousness, and personality.* Englewood Cliffs, NJ: Prentice-Hall.

Leskovec, J., & Krevl, A. (2015). *SNAP Datasets: Stanford Large Network Dataset Collection.* Retrieved November 12, 2015 from http://snap.stanford.edu/data

Leskovec, J., & Horvitz, E. (2008). Planetary-scale views on a large instant-messaging network. *WWW '08: Proceeding of the 17th international conference on World Wide Web*, 915–924. doi:10.1145/1367497.1367620

Leskovec, J., Lang, K. J., Dasgupta, A., & Mahoney, M. W. (2009). Community structure in large networks: Natural cluster sizes and the absence of large well-defined clusters. *Internet Mathematics, 6*(1), 29–123. doi:10.1080/15427951.2009.10129177

Leskovee, J., & Faloutsos, C. (2006). Sampling from Large Graphs. *KDD'06 Proceedings of the 12th ACM SIGKDD International Conference on Knowledge Discovery & Datamining*, 631-636.

Lewis, K., Gonzalez, M., & Kaufman, J. (2012). Social selection and peer influence in an online social network. *Proceedings of the National Academy of Sciences of the United States of America, 109*(1), 68–72. doi:10.1073/pnas.1109739109 PMID:22184242

Li, J., Chen, Y., & Lin, Y. (2010). Research on traffic layout based on social network analysis. *Education Technology and Computer (ICETC), 2010 2nd International Conference on*. IEEE.

Liljeros, F., Edling, C. R., Amaral, L A N., Stanley, H. E., & Aberg, Y. (2001). The Web of Human Sexual Contacts. *Nature, 411*(6840), 907–908. doi:10.1038/35082140 PMID:11418846

Lim, B. H., Lu, D., Chen, T., & Kan, M.-Y. (2015, 08 25-28). #mytweet via Instagram: Exploring User Behaviour across Multiple Social Networks. *Proceedings of the 2015 IEEE/ACM International Conference on Advances in Social Networks Analysis and Mining ASONAM '15*, 113-120. doi:10.1145/2808797.2808820

Lin, N. (1975). Analysis of Communication Relations. In G. J. Hanneman & W. J. McElwen (Eds.), *Communication and Behavior*. Reading, MA: Addison-Wesley.

Linnert, P. (1975). Handbuch Organisation. Gernsbach: Deutscher Betriebswirte-Verlag GmbH.

Lippe, W.-M. (2006). *Softcomputing mit Neuronalen Netzen, Fuzzy-Logic und Evolutionären Algorithmen*. Berlin: Springer-Verlag.

Lippe, W.-M. (2009). *Funktionale und Applikative Programmierung*. Berlin: Springer-Verlag.

Lipschutz, S. (2004). Schaum's outline of Data Structures. Tata McGraw-Hill Publishing Company Limited.

Lister, M. (2017, Jan 20). *40 Essential Social Media Marketing Statistics for 2017*. Retrieved from Word Stream: http://www.wordstream.com/blog/ws/2017/01/05/social-media-marketing-statistics

Liu, H., Macintyre, R., & Ferguson, R. (2012). Exploring Qualitative Analytics for e-Mentoring Relationships Building in an Online Social Learning Environment. In *Proceedings of the 2Nd International Conference on Learning Analytics and Knowledge* (pp. 179–183). New York, NY: ACM. doi:10.1145/2330601.2330646

Liu, W., Li, X., & Huang, D. (2011, June). A survey on context awareness. In *Computer Science and Service System (CSSS), 2011 International Conference on* (pp. 144-147). IEEE.

Liu, Z., Navathe, S. B., & Stasko, J. T. (2011). Network-based Visual Analysis of Tabular Data. In *Visual Analytics Science and Technology (VAST), 2011 IEEE Conference on* (pp. 41–50). Providence, RI: IEEE. doi:10.1109/VAST.2011.6102440

Liu, W., & Lu, L. (2010). Link prediction based on local random walk. *Europhysics Letters Association., 89*(5), 1–12.

Liu, Y., Gummadi, K. P., Krishnamurthy, B., & Mislove, A. (2011). Analyzing Facebook Privacy Settings: User Expectations vs. Reality. *Proceedings of the 2011 ACM SIGCOMM conference on Internet measurement conference*. doi:10.1145/2068816.2068823

Liu, Z., Navathe, S. B., & Stasko, J. T. (2014). Ploceus: Modeling, visualizing, and analyzing tabular data as networks. *Information Visualization, 13*(1), 59–89. doi:10.1177/1473871613488591

Lohmann, S. (2011, November 16). *Modular Unified Tagging Ontology (MUTO)*. Retrieved from muto socialtagging: http://muto.socialtagging.org/core/v1.html

Looy, A. V. (2016). *Social Media Management*. Springer International Publishing. doi:10.1007/978-3-319-21990-5

Lopes, G. R., Moro, M. M., Wives, L. K., & De Oliveira, J. P. M. (2010). Collaboration recommendation on academic social networks. In *International Conference on Conceptual Modeling* (pp. 190-199). Springer Berlin Heidelberg.

López-Pintado, D. (2008). Diffusion in complex social networks. *Games and Economic Behavior, 62*(2), 573–590. doi:10.1016/j.geb.2007.08.001

Luhmann, N. (1987). *Soziale Systeme. Grundriß einer allgemeinen Theorie*. Frankfurt: Suhrkamp Verlag.

Luo, S., Du, Y., Liu, P., Xuan, Z., & Wang, Y. (2015). A study on coevolutionary dynamics of knowledge diffusion and social network structure. *Expert Systems with Applications*, *42*(7), 3619–3633. doi:10.1016/j.eswa.2014.12.038

Luz, N. (2010). *Semantic Social Network Analysis* (PhD Thesis). Instituto Politécnico do Porto, Instituto Superior de Engenharia do Porto.

Lu, Z., Savas, B., Tang, W., & Dhillon, I. S. (2010). Supervised Link Prediction Using Multiple Sources. *Proceedings of the 2010 IEEE International Conference on Data Mining ICDM '10*, 923-928. doi:10.1109/ICDM.2010.112

Malak, M. S., & East, R. (2016). *Spark GraphX in action*. Academic Press.

Manning, C. D., Raghavan, P., & Schütze, H. (2008). *Introduction to information retrieval*. New York: Cambridge University Press. doi:10.1017/CBO9780511809071

Martínez-Cerdá, J.-F., & Torrent-Sellens, J. (2015). Graph analysis to survey data: A first approximation. *International Journal of Complex Systems in Science*, *5*(1), 29–36.

Maruev, S., Stefanovsky, D., Frolov, A., Troussov, A., & Curry, J. (2014a). Deep Mining of Custom Declarations for Commercial Goods. *Procedia Economics and Finance, 12*, 397–402.

Maruev, S., Stefanovskyi, D., & Troussov, A. (2015). "Semantics of Techno-Social Spaces", in the. In J. Zizka & F. Darena (Eds.), *Modern Computational Models of Semantic Discovery in Natural Language*. IGI Global. doi:10.4018/978-1-4666-8690-8.ch008

Masoumzadeh, A., & Joshi, J. (2011). Ontology-based access control for social network systems. *International Journal of Information Privacy, Security and Integrity*, 59 - 78.

Mazzola, L., & Mazza, R. (2011). Visualizing learner models through data aggregation: a test case. *Proceedings of the red-conference, rethinking education in the knowledge society*, 372–380.

McDaid, A. F., Greene, D., & Hurley, N. (2013). *Normalized Mutual Information to evaluate overlapping community finding algorithms*. CORRabs/1110.2515

McIntosh, N. E. (1979). Barriers to implementing research in higher education. *Studies in Higher Education*, *4*(1), 77–86. doi:10.1080/03075077912331377121

McPherson, M., Smith-Lovin, L., & Cook, J. M. (2001). Birds of a feather: Homophily in social networks. *Annual Review of Sociology*, *27*(1), 415–444. doi:10.1146/annurev.soc.27.1.415

Measurement and Analysis of Online Social Networks by Alan Mislove. (2007). Max Planck Institute for Software Systems.

Meng, X., Bradley, J., Yuvaz, B., Sparks, E., Venkataraman, S., Liu, D., & Xin, D. et al. (2016). Mllib: Machine learning in apache spark. *JMLR*, *17*(34), 1–7.

Mika, P. (2005). Ontologies are us: A unified model of social networks and semantics. *International Semantic Web Conference LNCS* (pp. 522–536). Springer. doi:10.1007/11574620_38

Miorandi, D., & de Pellegrini, F. (2010). k-Shell Decomposition for Dynamic Complex Networks. *Proceedings of the IEEE Conference on Modeling and Optimization in Mobile, Ad Hoc, and Wireless Networks*, 488-496.

Mirkin, B. (2016). Clustering: A Data Recovery Approach (2nd ed.). Chapman & Hall/CRC Computer Science & Data Analysis.

Mislove, A., Marcon, M., Gummadi, K. P., Druschel, P., & Bhattacharjee, B. (2007). Measurement and analysis of online social networks. *IMC '07: Proceedings of the 7th ACM SIGCOMM conference on Internet measurement*, 7, 29–42. doi:10.1145/1298306.1298311

Monclar, R. S. (2011). Using social networks analysis for collaboration and team formation identification. *Computer Supported Cooperative Work in Design (CSCWD), 2011 15th International Conference on*. IEEE. doi:10.1109/CSCWD.2011.5960128

Montesor, A., de Pellegrini, F., & Miorandi, D. (2012). Distributed k-Core Decomposition. *IEEE Transactions on Parallel and Distributed Systems*, 24(2), 288–300. doi:10.1109/TPDS.2012.124

Moore, M. G. (1989). Editorial: Three types of interaction. *American Journal of Distance Education*, 3(2), 1–7. doi:10.1080/08923648909526659

Moore, M. G., & Kearsley, G. (2011). *Distance education: A systems view of online learning*. Belmont, CA: Wadsworth Cengage Learning.

Morton, K. W., & Mayers, D. F. (2005). *Numerical Solution of Partial Differential Equations, An Introduction*. Cambridge University Press. doi:10.1017/CBO9780511812248

Mrvar, A., & Batagelj, V. (2016). Analysis and visualization of large networks with program package Pajek. *Complex Adaptive Systems Modeling*, 4(1), 1–8. doi:10.1186/s40294-016-0017-8

Nardi, B. A. (1996). Studying context: A comparison of activity theory, situated action models and distributed cognition. In B. A. Nardi (Ed.), *Context and consciousness: Activity theory and human-computer interaction* (pp. 69–102). Cambridge, MA: MIT Press.

NetMiner. (n.d.). Retrieved from http://www.netminer.com/

Networkx. (n.d.). Retrieved from http://Networkx.lanl.gov/index.html

Nevidomsky, A., & Troussov, A. (2010). Structure and Dynamics of Enterprise 2.0 Communities. *Web Science Conference 2010 (WebSci10)*.

Newman, M. (2012). Retrieved from http://www-personal.umich.edu/ mejn/netdata/

Newman, M. E. J. (2001). The Structure of Scientific Collaboration Networks. *Proceedings of the National Academy of Sciences of the United States of America*, 98, 404.

Newman, M. E. J. (2015). *Real world network datasets*. Retrieved October 10, 2015, from http://www-personal.umich.edu/~mejn/netdata/

Newman, R., Ayers, D., & Russell, S. (2005, December 21). *Tag ontology design*. Retrieved from holygoat.co.uk: http://www.holygoat.co.uk/projects/tags/

Newman, M. E. J. (2001). Clustering & preferential attachment in growing networks. *Physical Review Letters E. Physical Review E: Statistical, Nonlinear, and Soft Matter Physics*, 64(2), 1–13. doi:10.1103/PhysRevE.64.025102

Newman, M. E. J. (2001). The structure of scientific collaboration networks. *Proceedings of the National Academy of Sciences of the United States of America*, 98(2), 404–409. doi:10.1073/pnas.98.2.404 PMID:11149952

Newman, M. E. J. (2003). The Structure and Function of Complex Networks. *SIAM Review*, 45(2), 167–256. doi:10.1137/S003614450342480

Newman, M. E. J. (2006). Finding community structure in networks using the eigenvectors of matrices. *Physical Review E: Statistical, Nonlinear, and Soft Matter Physics*, *74*(3), 036104. doi:10.1103/PhysRevE.74.036104 PMID:17025705

Newman, M. E. J. (2006). Modularity and community structure in networks. *Proceedings of the National Academy of Sciences of the United States of America*, *103*(23), 8577–8582. doi:10.1073/pnas.0601602103 PMID:16723398

Nicosia, V., Mangioni, G., Carchiolo, V., & Malgeri, M. (2009). Extending the definition of modularity to directed graphs with overlapping communities. *Journal of Statistical Mechanics*, *2009*(03), 03024. doi:10.1088/1742-5468/2009/03/P03024

Nicosia, V., Tang, J., Mascolo, C., Musolesi, M., Russo, G., & Latora, V. (2013). Graph metrics for temporal networks. In *Temporal Networks* (pp. 15–40). Springer Berlin Heidelberg. doi:10.1007/978-3-642-36461-7_2

Nisar, M. U., Fard, A., & Miller, J. A. (2013). Techniques for Graph Analytics on Big Data. In *2013 IEEE International Congress on Big Data* (pp. 255–262). Santa Clara, CA: IEEE. doi:10.1109/BigData.Congress.2013.78

Nooy, W., Mrvar, A., & Batagelj, V. (2005). *Exploratory Social Network Analysis with Pajek*. Cambridge University Press. doi:10.1017/CBO9780511806452

Norwich, K. H. (1993). *Information, sensation, and perception*. San Diego, CA: Academic Press.

Nowell, D. L., & Kleinberg, J. (2007). The link-prediction problem for social networking. *Journal of the American Society for Information Science and Technology*, *58*(7), 1019–1031. doi:10.1002/asi.20591

Number of social media users worldwide from 2010 to 2020 (in billions). (2017, April 3). Retrieved from The Statistics Portal: http://www.statista.com/statistics/278414/number-of-worldwide-social-network-users/

Orlandi, F. (2008). *Using and extending the sioc ontology for a fine-grained wiki modeling* (Master's Thesis). Università degli Studi di Modena e Reggio Emilia.

Pachidi, S., Spruit, M., & Van De Weerd, I. (2014). Understanding users behavior with software operation data mining. *Computers in Human Behavior*, *30*, 583–594. doi:10.1016/j.chb.2013.07.049

Page, L., Brin, S., Motwani, R., & Winograd, T. (1999). *The PageRank Citation Ranking: Bringing Order to the Web*. Stanford InfoLab.

Pahl, C. (2004). Data Mining Technology for the Evaluation of Learning Content Interaction. *International Journal on E-Learning*, *3*(4), 47–55.

Pajek. (n.d.). Retrieved from vlado.fmf.uni-lj.si/pub/networks/pajek

Pal, A., & Counts, S. (2011). *Identifying topical authorities in microblogs*. doi:10.1145/1935826.1935843

Palla, G., Derenyi, I., Farkas, I., & Vicsek, T. (2005). Uncovering the overlapping community structure of complex networks in nature and society. *Nature*, *435*(7043), 814–818. doi:10.1038/nature03607 PMID:15944704

Panchenko, A. (2014). *Working with FB and VK Data*. Academic Press.

Paraschiv, I. C., Dascalu, M., Dessus, P., Trausan-Matu, S., & McNamara, D. S. (2016). A Paper Recommendation System with ReaderBench: The Graphical Visualization of Semantically Related Papers and Concepts. In *State-of-the-Art and Future Directions of Smart Learning* (pp. 445–451). Springer Singapore. doi:10.1007/978-981-287-868-7_53

Passant, A. (2009, Octobre 20). *SIOC Types and Health Care and Life Sciences*. Retrieved from W3C Submission: http://www.w3.org/TR/hcls-sioc/

Passant, A., & Laublet, P. (2008). Meaning of a tag: A collaborative approach to bridge the gap between tagging and linked data. *Proceedings of the WWW 2008 Workshop Linked Data on the Web (LDOW2008)*.

Passant, A., Zimmermann, A., Schneider, J., & Breslin, J. G. (2010). A semantic framework for modelling quotes in email conversations. *Proceedings of the 1st International Conference on Intelligent Semantic Web-Services and Applications (ISWSA '10)* (pp. 11:1-11:8). Amman, Jordan: ACM. doi:10.1145/1874590.1874601

Patel, H. J., Prajapati, R., Panchal, M., & Patel, M. J. (2013). A survey of graph pattern mining algorithm and techniques. *International Journal of Application or Innovation in Engineering & Management, 2*(1), 125–129.

Pelillo, M., & Torsello, A. (2006). Payoffmonotonic game dynamics and the maximum clique problem. *Neural Computation, 18*(5), 1215–1258. doi:10.1162/neco.2006.18.5.1215 PMID:16595063

Pentland, A. (2014). *Social physics: How good ideas spread-the lessons from a new science.* Penguin.

Perer, S. (2006). Balancing systematic and flexible exploration of social networks. Visualization and Computer Graphics. *IEEE Transactions, 12*(5), 693–700.

Persico, D., Pozzi, F., & Sarti, L. (2010). Monitoring collaborative activities in computer supported collaborative learning. *Distance Education, 31*(1), 5–22. doi:10.1080/01587911003724603

Pettenati, M. C., & Cigognini, M. E. (2007). Social networking theories and tools to support connectivist learning activities. *International Journal of Web-Based Learning and Teaching Technologies, 2*(3), 42–60. doi:10.4018/jwltt.2007070103

Pons, P., & Latapy, M. (2005). *Computing communities in large networks using random walks.* arXiv:physics/0512106

Pons, P., & Latapy, M. (2005). Computing communities in large networks using random walks. *Computer and Information Sciences-ISCIS 2005*, 284-293.

Porta, S., Crucitti, P., & Latora, V. (2008). Multiple centrality assessment in Parma: a network analysis of paths and open spaces. *Urban Design International, 13*(1), 41-50.

Prior, A. N. (1957). *Time and Modality.* Oxford, UK: Oxford University Press.

Protasiewicz, J., Pedrycz, W., Kozłowski, M., Dadas, S., Stanisławek, T., Kopacz, A., & Gałężewska, M. (2016). A recommender system of reviewers and experts in reviewing problems. *Knowledge-Based Systems, 106*, 164–178. doi:10.1016/j.knosys.2016.05.041

Pwint Oo, S. H. (2013). Intelligent access control policies for social network site. *International Journal of Computer Science & Information Technology*, 183-190.

Qi, M., & Edgar-Nevill, D. (2011). Social networking searching and privacy issues. *Information Security Technical Report, 16*(2), 74–78.

Raghavan, U. N., Albert, R., & Kumara, S. (2007). Near linear time algorithm to detect community structures in large-scale networks. *Physical Review E: Statistical, Nonlinear, and Soft Matter Physics, 76*(3), 036106. doi:10.1103/PhysRevE.76.036106 PMID:17930305

Rahman, M., & Karim, R. (2016). Comparative study of different methods of social network analysis and visualization. In *2016 International Conference on Networking Systems and Security (NSysS)* (pp. 1-7). IEEE. doi:10.1109/NSysS.2016.7400702

Rao, B., & Mitra, A. (2014). A New Approach for Detection of Common Communities in a Social Network using Graph Mining Techniques. *Proceedings of the International Conference on High Performance Computing & Application* (pp. 1-6). Bhubaneswar, India: IEEEXplore.

Rao, B., & Mitra, A. (2014). An approach to Merging of two community sub-graphs to form a community graph using Graph Mining Techniques. *Proceedings of the International Conference on Computational Intelligence and Computing Research* (pp. 1-7). Coimbatore, India: IEEEXplore.

Rao, B., & Mitra, A. (2015). A Proposed Algorithm for Partitioning Community Graph into Sub-Community Graphs using Graph Mining Techniques. *Proceedings of 3rd International Conference on Advanced Computing, Networking and Informatics* (pp. 3-15). KIIT University.

Rao, B., Mitra, A., & Narayana, U. (2014). An approach to study properties and behavior of Social Network using Graph Mining Techniques. *Proceedings of DIGNATE 2014:ETEECT 2014*, 13-17.

Rao, Mitra, & Mondal. (2015). Algorithm for Retrieval of Sub-Community Graph from a Compressed Community Graph using Graph Mining Technique. Procedia Computer Science, 57(2015), 678-685.

Rao, S. C., & Krishna Prasad, M. (2015). A survey on community detection algorithms in large scale real world networks. In *Proceedings of 2nd international conference on computing for sustainable global development (IndiaCom 2015)* (pp 1323-1327). New Delhi: IEEE.

Redecker, C., Punie, Y., & Ferrari, A. (2012). eAssessment for 21st Century Learning and Skills. In A. Ravenscroft, S. Lindstaedt, C. D. Kloos, & D. Hernández-Leo (Eds.), 21st Century Learning for 21st Century Skills (pp. 292–305). Saarbrücken, Germany: Springer Berlin Heidelberg.

Redner, S. (1998). How Popular is Your Paper? An Empirical Study of the Citation Distribution. *The European Physical Journal B, 4*(2), 131–134. doi:10.1007/s100510050359

Ressler, S. (2006). Social Network Analysis as an Approach to Combat Terrorism: Past, Present, and Future Research. *Homeland Security Affairs, 2*(2).

Reza, Z., Abbasi, M. A., & Liu, H. (2014). *Social Media Mining: An Introduction*. Cambridge University Press.

Ricci, F., Rokach, L., & Shapira, B. (2011). *Introduction. In Recommender Systems Handbook* (pp. 1–35). Springer.

Rieder, B. (2013). *Studying Facebook via Data Extraction: The Netvizz Application. In WebSci'13* (pp. 2–4). Paris, France: ACM. doi:10.1145/2464464.2464475

Roberts, P. (2016). *Social Media Statistics for 2017*. Retrieved from Our Social Times: http://oursocialtimes.com/7-social-media-statistics-for-2017/

Rodriguez, J. A., & Yebra, J. L. A. (1999). Bounding the diameter and the mean distance of a graph from its eigenvalues: Laplacian versus adjacency matrix methods. *Discrete Mathematics, 196*(1-3), 267–275. doi:10.1016/S0012-365X(98)00206-4

Roger, E. M., & Agarwala-Rogers, R. (1976). *Communication in Organizations*. New York: The Free Press.

Romero, C., & Ventura, S. (2007). Educational data mining: A survey from 1995 to 2005. *Expert Systems with Applications, 33*(1), 135–146. doi:10.1016/j.eswa.2006.04.005

Romero, D. M., Galuba, W., Asur, S., & Huberman, B. A. (2011). *Influence and passivity in social media*. doi:10.1145/1963192.1963250

Ronald, S. B. (1987). Social contagion and innovation: Cohesion versus structural equivalence. *American Journal of Sociology, 92*(6), 1287–1335. doi:10.1086/228667

Rossi, R., & Ahmed, N. (2015). The Network Data Repository with Interactive Graph Analytics and Visualization. In *AAAI 2015 Proceeding* (pp. 4292–4293). Austin, TX: The AAAI Press.

Rosvall, M., & Carl, T. B. (2008). Maps of random walks on complex networks reveal community structure. *Proceedings of the National Academy of Sciences of the United States of America*, *105*(4), 1118–1123. doi:10.1073/pnas.0706851105 PMID:18216267

Roy, B. (2005). Paradigms and challenges. In *Multiple criteria decision analysis: state of the art surveys* (pp. 3–24). Springer New York. doi:10.1007/0-387-23081-5_1

Roy, B. (2013). *Multicriteria methodology for decision aiding* (Vol. 12). Springer Science & Business Media.

Rübenkönig, O. (2006). *The Finite Difference Method (FDM) - An introduction*. Albert Ludwigs University of Freiburg.

Rusinowska, A., & de Swart, H. (2006). Generalizing and modifying the Hoede-Bakker index. In *Theory and Applications of Relational Structures as Knowledge Instruments II* (pp. 60–88). Springer Berlin Heidelberg. doi:10.1007/11964810_4

Russell, M. A. (2014). *Mining the Social Web. Data Mining Facebook, Twitter, Linkedin, Google+, Github,and more*. Sebastopol, CA: O'Reilly Media Inc.

Sabater, J., & Sierra, C. (2005). Review on Computational Trust and Reputation Models. *Artificial Intelligence Review*, *24*(1), 33–60. doi:10.1007/s10462-004-0041-5

Salton, G., & McGill, M. J. (1983). *Introduction to Modern Information Retrieval*. Auckland, New Zealand: MaGraw-Hill.

Samanta, S., & Pal, M. (2013). Telecommunication System Based on Fuzzy Graphs. *Journal of Telecommunications System & Management*, *3*(1), 1–6.

Samanta, S., & Pal, M. (2014). A New Approach to Social Networks Based on Fuzzy Graphs. *Turkish Journal of Fuzzy Systems*, *5*(2), 78–99.

Sao Pedro, M. A., Baker, R. S. J. D., & Gobert, J. D. (2013). What Different Kinds of Stratification Can Reveal About the Generalizability of Data-mined Skill Assessment Models. In *Proceedings of the Third International Conference on Learning Analytics and Knowledge* (pp. 190–194). New York, NY: ACM. doi:10.1145/2460296.2460334

Sariyuce, A. E., Gedik, B., Jacques-Silva, G., Wu, K.-L., & Catalyurek, U. V. (2013). Streaming Algorithms for k-Core Decomposition. *Proceedings of the VLDB Endowment*, *6*(6), 433–444. doi:10.14778/2536336.2536344

Sariyuce, A. E., Gedik, B., Jacques-Silva, G., Wu, K.-L., & Catalyurek, U. V. (2016). Incremental k-Core Decomposition: Algorithms and Evaluation. *The VLDB Journal*, *25*(3), 425–447. doi:10.1007/s00778-016-0423-8

Saroop, A., & Karnik, A. (2011). Crawlers for social networks & structural analysis of Twitter. *Proceedings of IEEE 5th International Conference on Internet Multimedia Systems Architecture and Application (IMSAA)*, 1-8. doi:10.1109/IMSAA.2011.6156368

Satish, N., Sundaram, N., Patwary, M. M. A., Seo, J., Park, J., & Hassaan, M. A., … Dubey, P. (2014). Navigating the Maze of Graph Analytics Frameworks Using Massive Graph Datasets. In *Proceedings of the 2014 ACM SIGMOD International Conference on Management of Data* (pp. 979–990). New York, NY: ACM. doi:10.1145/2588555.2610518

Scanfeld, D., Scanfeld, V., & Larson, E. L. (2010). Dissemination of health information through social networks: Twitter and antibiotics. *American Journal of Infection Control*, *38*(3), 182–188. doi:10.1016/j.ajic.2009.11.004 PMID:20347636

Scatà, M., Di Stefano, A., Giacchi, E., La Corte, A., & Liò, P. (2014, August). The bio-inspired and social evolution of node and data in a multilayer network. In *Data Communication Networking (DCNET), 2014 5th International Conference on* (pp. 1-6). SCITEPRESS. doi:10.5220/0005119600410046

Scatà, M., Di Stefano, A., La Corte, A., Liò, P., Catania, E., Guardo, E., & Pagano, S. (2016). Combining evolutionary game theory and network theory to analyze human cooperation patterns. *Chaos, Solitons, and Fractals*, *91*, 17–24. doi:10.1016/j.chaos.2016.04.018

Schick, J., Kuboschek, M., & Lippe, W. M. (2014). Context Specific Entity based Modeling of Organizational Structures. *Proceedings of the 2014 IEEE International Conference on Behavioral, Economic, Socio-Cultural Computing (BESC 2014)*. doi:10.1109/BESC.2014.7059513

Schilit, B., Adams, N., & Want, R. (1994, December). Context-aware computing applications. In *Mobile Computing Systems and Applications, 1994. WMCSA 1994. First Workshop on* (pp. 85-90). IEEE. doi:10.1109/WMCSA.1994.16

Schilit, B. N., & Theimer, M. M. (1994). Disseminating active map information to mobile hosts. *IEEE Network*, *8*(5), 22–32. doi:10.1109/65.313011

Schultz, T.-W. (1961). Investment in Human Capital. *The American Economic Review*, *51*(1), 1–17.

Scott, J. (1988). Social Network Analysis. *Sociology*, *22*(1), 109–127. doi:10.1177/0038038588022001007

Scott, J. (1992). *Social Network Analysis*. Newbury Park, CA: Sage.

Seidman, S. B. (1983). Network structure and minimum degree. *Social Networks*, *5*(3), 269–287. doi:10.1016/0378-8733(83)90028-X

Sentiment Analysis. (n.d.). In *Wikipedia*. Retrieved from https://en.wikipedia.org/wiki/Sentiment_analysis

Seung-Hee, B., Daniel, H., Jevin, W., Rosvall, M., & Howe, B. (2013). Scalable Flow-Based Community Detection for Large-Scale Network Analysis. In *Proceedings of IEEE International Conference on Data Mining Workshops (ICDMW 2013)* (pp. 303-310). Dallas, TX: IEEE.

Shannon, C. E. (1948). A Mathematical Theory of Communication. *The Bell System Technical Journal*, *27*(3), 379–423. doi:10.1002/j.1538-7305.1948.tb01338.x

Sharma, D., Sharma, U., & Khatri, S. K. (2014). An experimental comparison of the link prediction techniques in social networks. *International Journal of Modelling and Optimization*, *4*(1), 21–24. doi:10.7763/IJMO.2014.V4.341

Shen, Y., Syu, Y. S., Nguyen, D. T., & Thai, M. T. (2012). *Maximizing circle of trust in online social networks*. Academic Press.

Shergill, M. K., & Kaur, H. (2015). *Survey of Computational Trust and Reputation Models in Virtual Societies*. Academic Press.

Shin, K., Eliassi-Rad, T., & Faloutsos, C. (2016). CoreScope: Graph Mining using k-Core Analysis - Patterns, Anomalies and Algorithms. *Proceedings of the IEEE Conference on Data Mining*, 469-478. doi:10.1109/ICDM.2016.0058

Shlaer, S., & Mellor, S. J. (1988). *Object-oriented Systems Analysis. Modeling the World in Data*. Englewood Cliffs, NJ: Prentice Hall PTR.

Shon, J., & Musen, M. A. (1999). The low availability of metadata elements for evaluating the quality of medical information on the World Wide Web. *AMIA Symposium*, 945-949.

Siemens, G., & Baker, R. S. J. d. (2012). Learning Analytics and Educational Data Mining: Towards Communication and Collaboration. In *Proceedings of the 2Nd International Conference on Learning Analytics and Knowledge* (pp. 252–254). New York, NY: ACM. doi:10.1145/2330601.2330661

Slade, S., & Prinsloo, P. (2013). Learning Analytics Ethical Issues and Dilemmas. *The American Behavioral Scientist, 57*(10), 1510–1529. doi:10.1177/0002764213479366

Snijders, C., Matzat, U., & Reips, U.-D. (2012). 'Big Data': Big gaps of knowledge in the field of Internet. *International Journal of Internet Science, 7*, 1–5.

Stanford University. (2012). Retrieved from http://snap.stanford.edu/data/

Starbird, K., Palen, L., Hughes, A. L., & Vieweg, S. (2010). Chatter on the red: what hazards threat reveals about the social life of microblogged information. *Proceedings of the 2010 ACM conference on Computer supported cooperative work.* doi:10.1145/1718918.1718965

Stavrianou, Andritsos, & Nicoloyannis. (2007). Overview and Semantic Issues of Text Mining. *SIGMOD Record, 36*(3).

Stein, B., & Nigemman, O. (1999). On the nature of structure and its identification. Lecture Notes in Computer Science, 1665, 122–134.

Stutzman, F., & Kramer-Duffield, J. (2010). Friends Only: Examining a Privacy-Enhancing Behavior in Facebook. *Proceedings of the SIGCHI Conference on Human Factors in Computing Systems.* doi:10.1145/1753326.1753559

Stvilia, B., Mon, L., & Yi, Y. J. (2009). A model for online consumer health information quality. *Journal of the American Society for Information Science and Technology, 60*(9), 1781–1791. doi:10.1002/asi.21115

Surian, D., Liu, N., Lo, D., Tong, H., Lim, E. P., & Faloutsos, C. (2011). Recommending people in developers' collaboration network. In *18th Working Conference on Reverse Engineering* (pp. 379-388). IEEE.

Swartz, A., & Hedler, J. (2001). The Semantic Web: A network of content for the digital city. *Proceedings of Second Annual Digital Cities Workshop.*

Tang, J., Hu, X., & Liu, H. (2013). Social recommendation: A review. *Social Network Analysis and Mining, 3*(4), 1113–1133. doi:10.1007/s13278-013-0141-9

Tang, L., & Liu, H. (2010). *Community Detection and Mining in Social Media* (Vol. 1). Morgan & Claypool.

Tasselli, S. (2015). Social networks and inter-professional knowledge transfer: The case of healthcare professionals. *Organization Studies.*

Topic Model. (n.d.). In *Wikipedia.* Retrieved from https://en.wikipedia.org/wiki/Topic_model

Troussov, A., Darena, F., Zizka, J., Parra, D., & Brusilovsky, P. (2011). Vectorised Spreading Activation Algorithm for Centrality Measurement. *Acta Universitatis Agriculturae et Silviculturae Mendelianae Brunensis, 59*(7), 469-476.

Troussov, A., Levner, E., Bogdan, C., Judge, J., & Botvich, D. (2009). Spreading Activation Methods. In A. Shawkat & Y. Xiang (Eds.), *Dynamic and Advanced Data Mining for Progressing Technological Development.* IGI Global.

Troussov, A., Parra, D., & Brusilovsky, P. (2009b). Spreading Activation Approach to Tag-aware Recommenders: Modelling Similarity on Multidimensional Networks. *Proceedings of Workshop on Recommender Systems and the Social Web at the 2009 ACM conference on Recommender systems, RecSys '09.*

UnifyID's ingenious user authentication platform wins Innovation Sandbox Contest. (2017, Febrary 15). Retrieved from Help Net Security: https://www.helpnetsecurity.com/2017/02/15/unifyid-user-authentication-platform/

Upadhyaya, K. T., & Mallik, D. (2013). E-Learning as a Socio-Technical System: An Insight into Factors Influencing its Effectiveness. *Business Perspectives & Research, 2*(1), 1–12. doi:10.1177/2278533720130101 van Borkulo, C. D., Borsboom, D., Epskamp, S., Blanken, T. F., Boschloo, L., Schoevers, R. A., & Waldorp, L. J. (2014). A new method for constructing networks from binary data. *Scientific Reports*, *4*, 10. doi:10.1038/srep05918 PMID:25082149

van Dongen, S. M. (2000). *Graph clustering by flow simulation* (PhD thesis). Universiteit Utrecht.

Varis, T., & Puukko, M. (Eds.). (2010). *Challenges of Global eLearning*. Tampere: Tampere University, Research Centre for Vocational Education.

Vavilapalli, V. K., Murthy, A. C., Douglas, C., Agarwal, S., Konar, M., Evans, R., & Saha, B. et al. (2013, October). Apache hadoop yarn: Yet another resource negotiator. In *Proceedings of the 4th annual Symposium on Cloud Computing* (p. 5). ACM. doi:10.1145/2523616.2523633

Vaz de Melo, P. O., Viana, A. C., Fiore, M., Jaffrès-Runser, K., Le Mouël, F., Loureiro, A. A., & Guangshuo, C. (2015). Recast: Telling apart social and random relationships in dynamic networks. *Performance Evaluation*, *87*, 19–36. doi:10.1016/j.peva.2015.01.005

Vespignani, A. (2009). Predicting the behavior of techno-social systems. *Science*, *325*(5939), 425–428. doi:10.1126/science.1171990 PMID:19628859

Viégas, F. B., & Donath, J. (2004). Social network visualization: Can we go beyond the graph. *Workshop on social networks, CSCW*, *4*, 6-10.

Villata, S., Delaforge, N., Gandon, F., & Gyrard, A. (2011). An Access Control Model for Linked Data. On the Move to Meaningful Internet Systems: OTM 2011 Workshops, 454-463.

Virtanen, A., Tynjälä, P., & Eteläpelto, A. (2014). Factors promoting vocational students learning at work: Study on student experiences. *Journal of Education and Work*, *27*(1), 43–70. doi:10.1080/13639080.2012.718748

Vitiello, E. J. (2002, July 19). *Relationship: A module for defining relationships in FOAF*. Retrieved April 03, 2017, from http://www.perceive.net: http://www.perceive.net/schemas/20021119/relationship/

VK. (2016). Retrieved from https://en.wikipedia.org/wiki/VK_(social_networking)

Wagner, E. D. (1997). Interactivity: From Agents to Outcomes. *New Directions for Teaching and Learning*, *1997*(71), 19–26. doi:10.1002/tl.7103

Walker, R., Arima, E., Messina, J., Soares-Filho, B., Perz, S., Vergara, D., & Castro, W. et al. (2013). Modeling spatial decisions with graph theory: Logging roads and forest fragmentation in the Brazilian Amazon. *Ecological Applications*, *23*(1), 239–254. doi:10.1890/11-1800.1 PMID:23495649

Wang, T. Chen, Y., Zhang, Xu, T., Jin, L., Hui, P., ... Li, x. (2011). Understanding Graph Sampling Algorithms for Social Network Analysis, Simplex'11. IEEE ICDCS, 123-128.

Wang, S., & Noe, R. A. (2010). Knowledge sharing: A review and directions for future research. *Human Resource Management Review*, *20*(2), 115–131. doi:10.1016/j.hrmr.2009.10.001

Wang, W., Wu, B., & Zhang, Z. (2010). Website clustering from query graph using social network analysis. *Proceedings of IEEE International Conference on Emergency Management and Management Sciences (ICEMMS)*, 439-442.

Wang, Y., & Liu, Z. (2007). Automatic detecting indicators for quality of health information on the Web. *International Journal of Medical Informatics*, *76*(8), 575–582. doi:10.1016/j.ijmedinf.2006.04.001 PMID:16750417

Wang, Y., & Ruhe, G. (2007). The Cognitive Process of Decision Making. *International Journal of Cognitive Informatics and Natural Intelligence*, *1*(2), 73–85. doi:10.4018/jcini.2007040105

Wasserman, S., & Faust, K. (1994). Social Network Analysis: Methods and Applications. Cambridge, UK: Cambridge University Press.

Wasserman, S. (1999). *Social network analysis: methods and applications*. Cambridge, UK: Cambridge University Press.

Wasserman, S., & Faust, K. (1994). *Social Network Analysis, Methods and Applications*. Cambridge University Press. doi:10.1017/CBO9780511815478

Waters, S., & Ackerman, J. (2011). Exploring Privacy Management on Facebook: Motivations and Perceived Consequences of Voluntary Disclosure. *Journal of Computer-Mediated Communication*, *17*(1), 101–115. doi:10.1111/j.1083-6101.2011.01559.x

Watt, D. A. (1990). Programming Language Concepts and Paradigms. Hertfordshire, UK: Prentice Hall International (UK) Ltd.

Watts, D. J., & Strogatz, S. H. (1998). Collective Dynamics of 'Small-World Networks. *Nature*, *393*(6684), 440–442. doi:10.1038/30918 PMID:9623998

Wayne, G., & Ortrud, R. O. (2011). Distance in Graphs, structural Analysis of Complex Networks. Springer.

Wei, , Wen, & Lin. (2011). Research on emergency information management based on the social network analysis — A case analysis of panic buying of salt. *Proceedings of International Conference on Management Science and Engineering (ICMSE)*, 1302-1310.

Weitzel, L., Palazzo, J. O., & Quaresma, P. (2013). *Exploring Trust to Rank Reputation in Microblogging*. Paper presented at the Database and Expert Systems Applications. doi:10.1007/978-3-642-40173-2_36

Weitzel, L., Quaresma, P., & de Oliveira, J. P. M. (2012). *Evaluating Quality of Health Information Sources*. Paper presented at the Advanced Information Networking and Applications (AINA), 26th International Conference on. doi:10.1109/AINA.2012.41

Wen, D., Qin, L., Zhang, Y., Lin, X., & Yu, J. X. (2016). I/O Efficient Core Graph Decomposition at Web Scale. *Proceedings of the IEEE International Conference on Data Engineering*, 133-144. doi:10.1109/ICDE.2016.7498235

Weng, J., Lim, E.-P., Jiang, J., & He, Q. (2010). *TwitterRank: finding topic-sensitive influential twitterers*. doi:10.1145/1718487.1718520

Wilson, R. E., Gosling, S. D., & Graham, L. T. (2012). A Review of Facebook Research in the Social Sciences Perspectives. *Psychological Science*, *7*(3), 203–220.

Wojtasiewicz, M., & Ciesielski, K. (2014). Identifying bridges for information spread control in social networks. In *Lecture Notes in Computer Science: Vol. 8852. Workshop on Social Influence* (pp. 390–401). Berlin: Springer.

Wu, H., Cheng, J., Lu, Y., Ke, Y., Huang, Y., Yan, D., & Wu, H. (2015). Core Decomposition in Large Temporal Graphs. *Proceedings of the IEEE International Conference on Big Data*, 649-658.

Xia, F., Chen, Z., Wang, W., Li, J., & Yang, L. T. (2014). MVCWalker: Random Walk-Based Most Valuable Collaborators Recommendation Exploiting Academic Factors. *IEEE Transactions on Emerging Topics in Computing*, *2*(3), 364–375. doi:10.1109/TETC.2014.2356505

Xiang, R., Neville, J., & Rogati, M. (2010). Modeling Relationship Strength in Online Social Networks. *Proceedings of the 19th International Conference on World Wide Web*. doi:10.1145/1772690.1772790

Xie, J. R., Kelley, S., & Szymanski, B. K. (2013). Overlapping community detection in networks: The state of the art and comparative study. *ACM Computing Surveys*, *45*(4), 1–43. doi:10.1145/2501654.2501657

Xie, J., & Szymanski, B. K. (2012). Towards linear time overlapping community detection in social networks. In *Proceedings of PAKDD Conf.* (pp. 25-36) Kuala Lumpur, Malaysia: ACM doi:10.1007/978-3-642-30220-6_3

Xie, J., Szymanski, B. K., & Liu, X. (2011). SLPA: Uncovering Overlapping communities in Social Networks via A Speaker-listener Interaction Dynamic Process. In *Proceedings of 11th IEEE International Conference on Data Mining Workshops (ICDM)* (pp. 344-349). Vancouver, BC: IEEE. doi:10.1109/ICDMW.2011.154

Xin, R. S., Gonzalez, J. E., Franklin, M. J., & Stoica, I. (2013, June). Graphx: A resilient distributed graph system on spark. In *First International Workshop on Graph Data Management Experiences and Systems* (p. 2). ACM. doi:10.1145/2484425.2484427

Xin, R., Deyhim, P., Ghodsi, A., Meng, X., & Zaharia, M. (2014). *GraySort on Apache Spark by Databricks*. GraySort Competition.

Yager, R. R. (2004). Modeling prioritized multicriteria decision making. *IEEE Transactions on Systems, Man, and Cybernetics. Part B, Cybernetics*, *34*(6), 2396–2404. doi:10.1109/TSMCB.2004.837348 PMID:15619938

Yamaguchi, Y., Takahashi, T., Amagasa, T., & Kitagawa, H. (2010). TURank: Twitter User Ranking Based on User-Tweet Graph Analysis. In L. Chen, P. Triantafillou, & T. Suel (Eds.), Web Information Systems Engineering – WISE 2010 (Vol. 6488, pp. 240-253): Springer Berlin / Heidelberg.

Yang, J., & Leskovec, J. (2013). Overlapping Community Detection at Scale: A Nonnegative Matrix Factorization Approach. In *Proceedings of WSDM*, (pp. 587-596). Rome, Italy: ACM. doi:10.1145/2433396.2433471

Yardi, S., Romero, D., Schoenebeck, G., & boyd, d. (2010, Janvier 4). Detecting spam in a Twitter network. *First Monday, 15*(1).

Ye, S., Lang, J., & Wu, F. (2010). Crawling online social graphs. *Proceedings of International Asia-Pacific Web Conference*, 236–242.

Yu, B., & Singh, M. P. (2000). A Social Mechanism of Reputation Management in Electronic Communities. In M. Klusch & L. Kerschberg (Eds.), Cooperative Information Agents IV - The Future of Information Agents in Cyberspace (Vol. 1860, pp. 355-393). Springer Berlin / Heidelberg. doi:10.1007/978-3-540-45012-2_15

Yu, X., Xu, Z., & Liu, S. (2013). Prioritized multi-criteria decision making based on preference relations. *Computers & Industrial Engineering*, *66*(1), 104–115. doi:10.1016/j.cie.2013.06.007

Zafarani, R., & Liu, H. (2016). Users joining multiple sites: Friendship and popularity variations across sites. *Journal Information Fusion*, *28*(C), 83–89. doi:10.1016/j.inffus.2015.07.002

Zaharia, M., Chowdhury, M., Das, T., Dave, A., Ma, J., McCauley, M., & Stoica, I. et al. (2012, April). Resilient distributed datasets: A fault-tolerant abstraction for in-memory cluster computing. In *Proceedings of the 9th USENIX conference on Networked Systems Design and Implementation* (pp. 2-2). USENIX Association.

Zelenkauskaite, A., Bessis, N., Sotiriadis, S., & Asimakopoulou, E. (2012). Interconnectedness of Complex Systems of Internet of Things through Social Network Analysis for Disaster Management. *Proceedings of 4th International Conference on Intelligent Networking and Collaborative Systems (INCoS)*, 503-508. doi:10.1109/iNCoS.2012.25

Zernik, J. (2010). Data Mining as a Civic Duty–Online Public Prisoners Registration Systems. *International Journal on Social Media: Monitoring, Measurement Mining*, *1*(1), 84–96.

Zhang, A. X., Bhardwaj, A., & Karger, D. (2016). Confer: A Conference Recommendation and Meetup Tool. In *Proceedings of the 19th ACM Conference on Computer Supported Cooperative Work and Social Computing Companion* (pp. 118-121). ACM.

Zhefeng, X., Bo, L., Huaping, H., & Tian, Z. (2012). Design and Implementation of Facebook Crawler Based on Interaction Simulation. *Proceedings of IEEE 11th International Conference on Trust, Security and Privacy in Computing and Communications (TrustCom)*, 1109-1112.

Zhou, W.-X., Jiang, Z.-Q., & Sornette, D. (2007). Exploring self-similarity of complex cellular networks: The edge-covering method with simulated annealing and log-periodic sampling. *Physica A: Statistical Mechanics and Its Applications, 375*(2), 741-752.

Zhu, X., & Davidson, I. (2007). Knowledge Discovery and Data Mining: Challenges and Realities. Academic Press.

Zimmerman, T. D. (2012). Exploring learner to content interaction as a success factor in online courses. *The International Review of Research in Open and Distributed Learning, 13*(4), 152–165. doi:10.19173/irrodl.v13i4.1302

Zwillinger, D., & Kokoska, S. (1999). *CRC standard probability and statistics tables and formulae*. Crc Press. doi:10.1201/9781420050264

About the Contributors

Natarajan Meghanathan is a tenured Full Professor of Computer Science at Jackson State University, Jackson, MS. He graduated with a Ph.D. in Computer Science from The University of Texas at Dallas in May 2005. Dr. Meghanathan has published more than 150 peer-reviewed articles (more than half of them being journal publications). He has also received federal education and research grants from the U. S. National Science Foundation, Army Research Lab and Air Force Research Lab. Dr. Meghanathan has been serving in the editorial board of several international journals and in the Technical Program Committees and Organization Committees of several international conferences. His research interests are Wireless Ad hoc Networks and Sensor Networks, Graph Theory and Network Science, Cyber Security, Machine Learning, Bioinformatics and Computational Biology. For more information, visit http://www.jsums.edu/nmeghanathan.

* * *

Mohd Vasim Ahamad has completed his M.Tech in Computer Science and Engineering (Software Engineering) from Department of Computer Engineering, Zakir husain College of Engineering and Technology, AMU Aligarh in 2015. He has professional experience of 1.5 years as a Software Engineer. Currently, He is serving as a Guest Teacher in Computer Engineering Section, University Women's Polytechnic, AMU Aligarh. His current area of interest is Data Mining, Big Data Analytics and Machine Learning.

Nadeem Akhtar received his B.Tech. and M.Tech. in Computer Engineering at Aligarh Muslim University, Aligarh, India. He has been working as Assistant Professor in the Department of Computer Engineering, AMU for the last 13 years. His research interests include soft computing, data science and text mining.

Danilo Artigas is a professor at Computer Science Departament at Universidade Federal Fluminense in Rio das Ostras, Brazil.

Ahmad Askarian received the Bachelor degree in electrical engineering from the Shahed University, Tehran, Iran, in 2008 and the M.E. degree from the Isfahan University of Technology (IUT), Isfahan, Iran, in 2010. He is currently pursuing the doctoral degree at the University of Texas at Dallas (UTD). Since 2012, he is a research assistant in the Scalable Network Engineering Techniques Laboratory, UTD, Dallas, US. His research interest includes network optimization, graph theory and distributed processing systems.

Fatima-Zahra Belouadha received a PhD in Computer Science from the engineering school Ecole Mohammadia d'Ingénieurs (EMI) in Rabat, Morocco. She is Professor at the Computer Science Department of EMI since 1996. She is currently member of EMI and Mohammed V University in Rabat Councils. Active in research area, she has published many papers on semantic Web service composition and composability. Her current research interests are focused on Business Process Management, Semantic data mining and Big Data.

Michele Brandão received her PhD and Masters in Computer Science from Universidade Federal de Minas Gerais, Brazil, and Bachelor in Computer Science from Universidade Estadual de Santa Cruz, Brazil. Her research interests include data mining and analysis, recommendation and social networks.

S Rao Chintalapudi received both Bachelor of Technology and Master of Technology from Bonam Venkata Chalamayya Engineering College, Odalarevu, affiliated to JNTU Kakinada. Currently, he is working as a full-time research scholar in the department of computer science and engineering, University College of Engineering Kakinada (Autonomous), Jawaharlal Nehru Technological University Kakinada, Andhra Pradesh, India. He worked as assistant professor in Bharat Institute of Engineering and Technology and CMR Technical Campus in Hyderabad. He is a member of CSI, IEEE and ACM. He has ten research papers published in international conferences and peer reviewed journals. He is a member of the board of reviewers in International journal of Rough Sets and Data Analysis (IJRSDA). His research interests are Social Network Analysis, Graph Mining, High Performance Computing, Big Data Analytics and Data Mining.

Martine Collard has been full professor in computer science at the University of the French West Indies in Guadeloupe, France from 2009. Her research interests are about knowledge engineering and knowledge extraction from data with a particular emphasis on applications in environment and in social computing. She is a member of the laboratory of Mathematics and Computer Science at her university, where she is the head of the Knowledge and Data Engineering team. Martine Collard has carried out several projects applying knowledge extraction from data analysis for studying and modeling local natural phenomena in the Caribbean area in such domains as flood prediction or smart agriculture for instance. Martine Collard was previously member of the University of Nice-Sophia Antipolis, France from which she received her PhD thesis in computer science. Martine is IEEE member and she has a nice record of publications to her credit and is regularly appearing as a speaker at international conferences and workshops.

Guilherme de Sousa is an undergraduate student in Information System at Universidade Federal de Minas Gerais.

Paramita Dey is presently working as assistant professor in Information Technology department in Government College of Engineering & Ceramic Technology. She has teaching experiences more than 14 years. She authored several international publications and one book chapter. Her research interest includes social network analysis, big data analysis, cloud computing.

Alessandro Di Stefano received his B.S. and M.S. degrees in Telecommunications Engineering from the Dipartimento di Ingegneria Elettrica, Elettronica e Informatica (DIEEI) at University of Catania, Italy, in 2009 and 2012, respectively. He holds a Ph. D. in Systems Engineering at DIEEI under the guidance of Prof. Aurelio La Corte from January 2013 to December 2015, with a thesis entitled: "Evolutionary Dynamics of Social Behaviors on Multilayer Networks". During the Ph. D., he attended severe schools and conferences on complex systems and he made various internships at Computer Laboratory, Department of Computer Science, University of Cambridge (UK), under the supervision of Prof. Pietro Liò, both in 2014 and 2015, with whom he has been collaborating since 2012. Currently, he works as a post-doctoral researcher at DIEEI, University of Catania and, moreover, he collaborates also with other Universities in Europe. He works as a post-doctoral researcher at DIEEI, University of Catania. He has an interdisciplinary approach to research and his current research interests include evolutionary game theory, multilayer networks, human cooperation, social behaviors, homophily, complex systems, healthcare, epidemics, Big Data, ICT and bio-inspired algorithms.

Matheus Diniz is an undergraduate student in Computer Science at Universidade Federal de Minas Gerais.

Krishnendu Dutta is an Assistant Professor of Mathematics and former Head of Dept. of Computer Science and Engg. in Govt. College of Engineering & Ceramic Technology. He has held position at Krishnagar Govt. College and Future Institute of Engg. & Management. He has a teaching experience of more than 15 years both at under graduate and post graduate levels. He has a good number of research publications in International Journals and authored book on Functional Analysis. His research interest includes Topology, Functional Analysis, Measure Theory, Automata Theory, Discrete Structure and Graph Analysis.

Asmae El Kassiri is a Computer Sciences Engineer from ENSIAS School (Mohammed V. University) Rabat, Morocco, and a Ph.D thesis Student at EMI School (Mohammed V. University) Rabat, Morocco. Thesis title: "A Semantic Approach for Online Social Networks Analysis."

Andras Farago received the B.Sc., M.Sc. and Ph.D. degrees in Electrical Engineering from the Technical University of Budapest, Budapest, Hungary. Between 1977-1997, he was faculty member at the Department of Telecommunications and Telematics, Technical University of Budapest. He also worked as a visiting Senior Research Fellow at the University of Massachusetts at Amherst in 1991/92, and spent a sabbatical year at Boston University in 1996. In 1996 he obtained the distinguished title "Doctor of Sciences" from the Hungarian Academy of Sciences. In 1998 Dr. Farago moved to the USA, and since then he is Professor of Computer Science at the University of Texas at Dallas. He is a Senior Member of IEEE, member of ACM, and of the IFIP Working Group "Performance of Communication Systems." He serves as editor for the journal Wireless Networks. Dr. Farago's research focuses on modeling, design and analysis methods of communication networks, as well as on algorithms and complexity.

Evelina Giacchi was born in Ragusa, Italy, in 1986. She received her B.S. and M.S. degrees in Telecommunications Engineering from the Department of Electric, Electronic and Computer Engineering (DIEEI), Catania, Italy. Currently, she is a Ph.D Student at DIEEI, University of Catania, Catania, Italy, under the guidance of Prof. Aurelio La Corte. Her current research interests include Decision Theory, Security and Risk Analysis, Bio-Inspired and Internet of Things.

Dimple Juneja is working as Faculty at Department of Computer Applications at NIt Kurukshetra.

Dimitrios Katsaros was born in 1974. He spent a year (July 1997-June 1998) as a visiting researcher at the Department of Pure and Applied Mathematics at the University of L'Aquila, Italy. After receiving his PhD, he earned a "PYTHAGORAS" research grant (2005-2007) at the Aristotle university for conducting postdoctoral research in the synergy between social network analysis and wireless ad hoc networks. During the spring semester of 2015, he was a visiting fellow in the Department of Electrical Engineering at the Yale university. He is Associate Editor for IEEE Access, Area Editor for EAI Endorsed Transactions on Security and Safety (for "Security in Ad hoc Networks"); he co-guest edited special issues on "Cloud Computing" in IEEE Internet Computing and IEEE Network magazines, and served as publication advisor in the translation for the greek language of the book "Google's PageRank and Beyond: The Science of Search Engine Rankings". He co-developed the popular scientometric index called contemporary h-index. His research interests are in the area of distributed systems.

Mieczysław Kłopotek obtained his M.Sc. Eng. and Dr. Eng. degrees from the Dresden University of Technology (Germany) and Habilitation from Institute of Computer Science of Polish Academy of Sciences. He was honoured with the professor title by the President of Poland. He started his career in industrial domain at the Semiconductor Scientific Research and Production Center (CEMI) Warsaw, working later among others for Netezza Corporation and IBM Poland. He pursued his scientific career mainly at Polish Academy of Science. Fields of interest include artificial intelligence, reasoning, decision-making theory, machine learning, data and web mining, network mining, managing uncertainty in knowledge-based systems, Bayesian networks, Dempster- Shafer's theory of evidence, programming on the Internet, computer vision, construction of semantic search engines.

Martin Kuboschek received his diploma in Electrical Engineering in 1989 from the Leibniz Universität Hannover in Germany. After that, he had several publications in the areas of large area microchip design, redundancy and fault tolerance during his work for the Institute of Electromagnetic Theory at the Leibniz Universität. Since 2006, he works for the German government in several IT projects as computer scientist and official. Currently, he is responsible for some information management topics at the Informationstechnikzentrum Bund (ITZBund).

Aurelio La Corte received the degree in electrical engineering from the University of Catania in 1988, and the Ph. D. in Electronic Engineering and Computer Science in 1994. From 1994 he is at the University of Catania. He is an associate professor in Telecommunication Engineering. His scientific interests include digital signal processing, distributed systems, network and QoS management techniques, risk analysis of ICT systems, bio-inspired models for information security, protocols and architecture for integrated communications, social networks, multilayer networks and game theory. He has authored or co-authored about one hundred research papers, published in international journals and conference proceedings.

Wolfram M. Lippe is professor emeritus at the Westfälische Wilhelms-Universität Münster. His research interests include softcomputing, functional programming and process management. He got his diploma at the Universität des Saarlandes in 1971. After he received his Ph.D. degree, he was scientific assistant, private lecturer and professor at the Universität Kiel and the Technische Universität München. In 1984, he was appointed to the Westfälische Wilhelms-Universität Münster to establish the institute of computer science. He was director of the institute of applied computer science and acting director of the institute of information systems.

H. M. Krishna Prasad M. is currently Full Professor, Department of Computer Science and Engineering, University College of Engineering Kakinada (Autonomous), JNTUK, Andhra Pradesh. He did his B.E. from Osmania University, Hyderabad, M.Tech and Ph.D. in data mining from JNTU, Hyderabad. Dr. Munaga successfully completed a two year MIUR fellowship (Jan 2007 – Dec 08) at University of Udine, Udine, Italy. He has about 50+ research papers in various International Journals and Conferences, and attended many national and international conferences in India and abroad. He is a member of Association for Computing Machinery (ACM), ISTE and IAENG (Germany). He is an active member of the board of reviewers in various International Journals and Conferences. His research interests include Data mining, BigData Analytics and High Performance Computing.

Juan-Francisco Martínez-Cerdá is a PhD Candidate Researcher at the Universitat Oberta de Catalunya (UOC) in Barcelona. He worked as a postgraduate researcher at the Autonomous University of Barcelona (UAB) for more than four years. Previously, he worked as a Head of Studies at the Catalan Observatory on Information Society for nearly two years, after more than ten years as an expert consultant on Information Society in several companies related to ICT industrial sector. His main research interests are linked to e-learning, employability skills, networks and complexity, co-innovative sources, and socio-technical systems.

Sergey Maruev is deputy dean of the Faculty of Economics of The Russian Presidential Academy of National Economy and Public Administration (RANEPA), head of the chair of system analysis and computer science of RANEPA, professor of the chair System analysis in economy of The Moscow Institute of Physics and Technology (State University). He has more than 20 years of research and development experience and teaching at universities. His research interests include: mathematical modeling, economics of education, machine learning and network analysis.

Saroja Nanda Mishra is currently working as Professor and Head of the Department of Computer Science, Engg. & Applications at Indira Gandhi Institute of Technology (IGIT), Sarang, Dhenkanal, Odisha, India. He has published more than 70 papers in International Journals and National Journals of repute. His research area focuses on fractal graphics, fractal geometry and internet data analysis. He has more than 25 years of teaching and research experiences. Many students obtained PhD degree and are continuing their PhD and M. Tech research work under his guidance.

Sasmita Mishra is currently working as Associate Professor in the Department of Computer Science, Engg. & Applications at Indira Gandhi Institute of Technology, Sarang, Dhenkanal, Odisha, India. She has published more than 80 papers in International Journals and National Journals of repute. Her research area focuses on multidimensional database, spatial data analysis and fractal & its applications. She has more than 25 years of teaching and research experiences. She is guiding many PhD and MTech scholars for their research work.

Mirella M. Moro is associate professor at Department of Computer Science, Universidade Federal de Minas Gerais – UFMG, Brazil. She holds a PhD in Computer Science from University of California in Riverside (2007). She is a former Education Director of the Brazilian Computer Society (SBC, 2009-2015), and is member of the ACM Education Board. Her research area is Databases, with current interests in social networks data processing and recommendation.

José Palazzo Moreira de Oliveira is full professor of Computer Science at Federal University of Rio Grande do Sul – UFRGS. He as a doctor degree in Computer Science from Institut National Politechnique de Grenoble, France IMAG (1984), a M.Sc. degree in Computer Science from PPGC-UFRGS (1976) and has graduated in Electronic Engineering (1968). His research interests include information systems, e-learning, database systems and applications, conceptual modeling and ontologies, applications of database technology and distributed systems. He has published about 320 papers, has being advisor of 79 graduate students (19 Ph.D. and 60 M.Sc.). The official full CV for the Brazilian National Research Council – CNPq is available at CV Lattes. The most comprehensive site content is available in Portuguese.

Madhumangal Pal is a professor in Department of Mathematics in Vidyasagar University. He has guided more than 26 research scholarsmore than 250 research articles in international and national journals. His specializations include computational and fuzzy graph theory, genetic algorithms and parallel algorithms, fuzzy matrices and fuzzy algebra. He is the author of eight books published from India and UK and these are written for undergraduate and postgraduate students and other professionals. He is the Editor-in-Chief of the Journal of Physical Sciences and Annals of Pure and Applied Mathematics. Dr. Pal is the member of the editorial board of several reputed journals. He has visited China, London, Greece, Hong Kong, Thailand, Malaysia, UAE, Bangladesh for academic purpose.

Katerina Pechlivanidou, MSc, (female) is a Software Engineer and a Research Scientist. Her main research interests lie in the areas of Cloud Computing, Big Data, IoT Systems and Data Mining. Her research work aims to process huge volumes of data and to discover hidden patterns in clustered systems. In order to retrieve meaningful information from structured or semi-structured data and create clustered systems, state-of-the-art, Java-based algorithms and tools are used. She has participated in numerous national and EU-funded projects. Her research resulted in scientific publications at international conferences. Katerina received her BSc in Computer, Telecommunications and Network Engineering from University of Thessaly, Greece in 2013 and her MSc degree in Electrical and Computer Engineering, University of Thessaly, Greece in 2014. She has been a teaching assistant in the area of Computer Algebra at University of Thessaly (2013-2015), a researcher studies at Center for Research and Technology, Hellas and a Research Scientist at Athens Information Technology. She is currently participating in research projects in collaboration with INTRASOFT International S.A.

Anuradha Pillai has received her M. Tech and PhD in Computer Engineering from MD University Rohtak, in the years 2004 and 2011 respectively. She has published 30 research papers in various International journals and conferences. She has more than 13 years of teaching experience. Presently she is serving as Assistant Professor at YMCA University of Science & Technology, A State Govt. University, Faridabad Haryana. Her research interests include Web Mining, Data Structures and Algorithms, Databases. Research Papers listed in database: 30.

Paulo Quaresma is a professor at the Computer Science Department of the University of Evora, Portugal. Research field: natural language processing, information retrieval and machine learning.

Bapuji Rao is currently pursuing PhD (CSE) from Biju Patnaik University of Technology (BPUT), Rourkela, Odisha, India. He received M.Tech (Computer Science) from Berhampur University, Berhampur, Odisha, India. He has published 15 papers in International and National Conferences which includes IEEE-5, Springer-3, Elsevier-1, and McGraw-Hill-1. He has authored two book chapters titled "Graph Mining and Its Applications in Studying Community Based Graph under the Preview of Social Network" in Product Innovation through Knowledge Management and Social Media Strategies, IGI Global, USA and titled "Some Other Applications in Community Graph Under the Preview of Social Graph Using Graph Mining Techniques" in "Web Data Mining and the Development of Knowledge-Based Decision Support Systems", IGI Global, USA. His Current research area focuses on Graph Mining, Social Network, Data Mining, Opinion Mining, Attributed Graph, and Multi-Layer Graph.

Sovan Samanta is an Assistant Professor in Tamralipta Mahavidyalaya (Vidyasagar University). He was involved in teaching in Indian Institute of Information Technology, Nagpur from July 2016 to March, 2017. Before that he has completed his post doc from Hanyang University, South Korea. He has published more than 35 research articles in reputed journals (including 15 SCI/SCIE journals) within last five years.

Marialisa Scatà received her B.S. and M.S. degrees in Telecommunication Engineering, from Dipartimento di Ingegneria Elettrica, Elettronica e Informatica (DIEEI), University of Catania, Italy. She holds a Ph. D. in Computer Science and Telecommunication Engineering at the same department, under the guidance of Prof. Aurelio La Corte, in 2012. During the Ph.D. she attended severe schools and conferences. She made an internship at Computer Laboratory, Department of Computer Science, University of Cambridge (UK), under the supervision of Prof. Pietro Liò, with whom she has been collaborating since 2011. Currently, she works as postdoctoral researcher at DIEEI, University of Catania. Continuing to collaborate with the University of Cambridge and other Universities, her scientific outputs falls on my research topics. She has an interdisciplinary approach to research and my interests include bio-inspired models, social networks, multilayer networks, epidemic models, human behaviors, game theory, complex systems, data mining, ICT.

Johannes Schick received his diploma in Geoinformatics from the Westfälische Wilhelms-Universität Münster in 2004. Since 2004 he works for the German government in several IT security projects as computer scientist and official. In 2012 he started doctoral studies in computer sciences and had several presentations and publications with IT security background and social media. He is currently responsible for quality assurance of the identity management system of the German National Meteorological Service.

Atul Srivastava was born in Unnao, India, in 1989. He received the B. Tech. degree in Information Technology from the UP Technical University, Lucknow, India, in 2008, and the M.Tech. degree in Information Technology from YMCA University of Science and Technology, Faridabad, India in 2012. In 2012, he joined the Department of Computer Engineering, YMCA University of Science and Technology, Faridabad, India, as a Ph. D. scholar. He has been imparting his knowledge in the field of Computer Science through research and teaching since 2012. His research areas are Social Network Analysis, Big Data and distributed computing.

Erick Stattner is assistant professor in Computer Science at the University of the French West Indies. He is member of the laboratory of Mathematics and Computer Science and he has published more than 30 articles on the areas of Social Network Analysis and Mining, the study of diffusion phenomena and the social data collection.

Leandros Tassiulas is the John C. Malone Professor of Electrical Engineering at Yale University. His research interests are in the field of networking with emphasis on mathematical models and algorithms of complex networks, architectures and protocols of wireless systems, sensor networks, mobile services, novel internet architectures and experimental platforms for network research. His most notable contributions include the max-weight scheduling algorithm and the back-pressure network control policy, opportunistic scheduling in wireless, the maximum lifetime approach for wireless network energy management, and the consideration of joint access control and antenna transmission management in multiple antenna wireless systems. Dr. Tassiulas is a Fellow of IEEE (2007). His research has been recognized by several awards including the IEEE Koji Kobayashi computer and communications award in 2016, the inaugural INFOCOM 2007 Achievement Award "for fundamental contributions to resource allocation in communication networks," the INFOCOM 1994 best paper award, a National Science Foundation (NSF) Research Initiation Award (1992), an NSF CAREER Award (1995), an Office of Naval Research Young Investigator Award (1997) and a Bodossaki Foundation award (1999). He holds a Ph.D. in Electrical Engineering from the University of Maryland, College Park (1991). He has held faculty positions at Polytechnic University, New York, University of Maryland, College Park, and University of Thessaly, Greece.

Joan Torrent-Sellens works as a Senior Lecturer and Research Director at the Universitat Oberta de Catalunya (UOC) in Barcelona. His teaching areas on Economics and Business Studies are related to Economic and Knowledge Society (economic growth, productivity, competitiveness, labour markets and network firm). He is the director of the Interdisciplinary Research Group on ICTs (i2TIC). His research field is concerned with the labour, economic, social and policy issues associated with information and communication technologies and knowledge economy and society. Specially focused on productivity and economic growth, competitiveness and development, human capital and labour markets, innovation and network firms, welfare and well-being.

Alexander Troussov is Director of the International Research Laboratory for Mathematical Methods for Social Network Mining at the Russian Presidential Academy of National Economy and Public Administration. Former Chief Scientist of IBM Dublin Center for Advanced Studies (2000-2013), one of the creators of the major IBM linguistic technology LanguageWare, and leader of IBM team participation in the three-year integrated 6th framework EU project NEPOMUK, he has published more than 40 peer reviewed journal and conference papers and has six patents.

Sergey Vinogradov received his MSc. in computer sciences from the Far Eastern Federal University, Vladivostok, Russia, 2000. At SberTech he is the head of development computer systems to identify internal and external banking fraud; he is conducting research on Big Data at the Russian Presidential Academy of National Economy and Public Administration. Research interests include image processing using neural networks, cyber-crime investigation (including study of cyber criminal ecosystem on Social Networks), study of transaction patterns.

Index

A

Academic Attainment 75-76
AclOnto 268, 283-284, 288
ActOnto 268, 280-282, 285-288
Adjacency Matrix 3, 36, 44-45, 47-49, 61, 63, 65, 67, 198
algorithms 6, 12, 14, 22-24, 28, 30-31, 54-55, 102, 122, 125-126, 128, 135, 144, 146, 148-149, 151-153, 162, 168, 173-175, 178-180, 185, 189-193, 196-198, 200-204, 211-213, 221, 226, 229-230, 235, 254, 279
Apache Spark 148, 153, 156, 158, 160, 162

B

Behavior 1, 7, 15, 18, 20, 34, 54, 59, 69, 75-77, 86, 96, 100, 110-111, 117, 122, 144, 196, 216, 221-222, 230, 242-243, 245, 256, 264, 277-278, 280, 287, 295
big data 54, 76, 88, 96, 147-148, 160, 207-208, 210, 216
bridges 174, 182-185, 220-221, 223-224, 226-229, 236, 238-239

C

closeness centrality 105, 299, 308
cluster analysis 220-221, 239
clustering 1, 6, 11-12, 28-31, 35, 55, 96, 98-99, 102, 105, 107, 166, 181-182, 189-190, 192-194, 197, 207-213, 215-217, 220-226, 228-230, 239, 264, 279, 300
clustering coefficient 11-12, 31, 35, 96, 99, 102, 105, 107, 181-182, 197, 264, 279, 300
Community Detection 35, 55, 80, 98-99, 102, 144, 189-194, 196-198, 200-204, 209, 221, 288
community distribution 106
Context-Awareness 53, 55-57, 59-60, 69

D

Disjoint Communities 190-191, 196, 203
distributed 1, 6, 110, 125-130, 134-135, 138, 143-144, 146-149, 151, 153, 155, 162, 246, 286

E

eigen vector centrality 12, 105
Entity 53-56, 59-60, 97, 112, 115
Environment 60, 66, 110, 122, 127, 147-148, 155, 162, 175, 242, 246, 285
evaluation 55, 57-59, 62, 67-69, 127, 135, 143, 190, 198, 228, 281-282, 287, 293, 296-297, 308

F

Facebook 3, 5, 7, 13-14, 18-19, 24, 29, 95-96, 101-103, 109-110, 114-118, 121, 125-126, 128, 144, 190, 273, 275, 277-278, 281-283, 285-288, 294, 298, 300
FOAF 269-270, 278, 280
Formalization 109-110

G

Gephi 18, 20-21, 23-24, 30-31, 80, 95-96, 101-103, 135
Graph Analytics 76-77, 86, 88-89
Graph Theory 19, 34, 50, 53, 55, 57-59, 77, 97, 126, 165, 209, 299, 301
graphs 2, 7, 14, 19, 22-23, 35, 55, 59, 95-97, 99-102, 125-128, 135, 137, 143, 146, 153, 166, 175, 189, 193, 196, 209, 220-221, 223-224, 226, 228-230, 235, 242, 247, 299-300
Graphx 88, 146-147, 152-153, 155-157, 162

H

Hadoop 127-131, 133, 135-139, 143-144, 146-149, 151-152, 160, 162

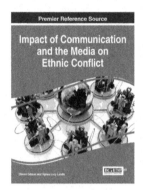

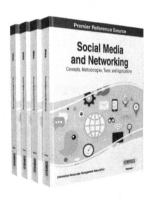

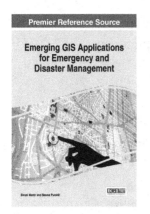
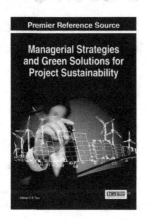

Printed in the United States
By Bookmasters